THE INSTITUTE OF ECONOMICS

The Carnegie Corporation of New York in establishing the Institute of Economics declared:

"The Carnegie Corporation, in committing to the Trustees the administration of the endowment, over which the Corporation will have no control whatsoever, has in mind a single purpose—namely, that the Institute shall be conducted with the sole object of ascertaining the facts about current economic problems and of interpreting these facts for the people of the United States in the most simple and understandable form. The Institute shall be administered by its Trustees without regard to the special interests of any group in the body politic, whether political, social, or economic."

THE BROOKINGS INSTITUTION

The Brookings Institution—Devoted to Public Service Through Research and Training in the Humanistic Sciences—was incorporated on December 8, 1927. Broadly stated, the Institution has two primary purposes: The first is to aid constructively in the development of sound national policies; and the second is to offer training of a super-graduate character to students of the social sciences. The Institution will maintain a series of co-operating institutes, equipped to carry out comprehensive and inter-related research projects.

Final responsibility for the final determination of the Institution's policies and its program of work and for the administration of its endowment is vested in a self-perpetuating Board of Trustees. The Trustees have, however, defined their position with reference to the investigations conducted by the Institution in a by-law provision reading as follows: "The primary function of the Trustees is not to express their views upon the scientific investigations conducted by any division of the Institution, but only to make it possible for such scientific work to be done under the most favorable auspices." Major responsibility for "formulating general policies and co-ordinating the activities of the various divisions of the Institution" is vested in the President. The by-laws provide also that "there shall be an Advisory Council selected by the President from among the scientific staff of the Institution and representing the different divisions of the Institution."

"Perhaps the best symbol of the new Mexico is Diego Rivera's powerful fresco in which, while the armed revolutionist on horseback stops to rest, the rural school teacher is surrounded by a few children and adults, as poorly clad as herself, but eager with the hope of new things." Pedro Henriquez Ureña, "The Revolution in Intellectual Life," *Survey Graphic*, May, 1924, p. 166.

THE MEXICAN AGRARIAN
REVOLUTION

BY

FRANK TANNENBAUM

New York
THE MACMILLAN COMPANY
1929

Each investigation conducted under the auspices of The Brookings Institution is in a very real sense an institutional product. Before a suggested project is undertaken it is given thorough consideration, not only by the Director and the staff members of the Institute in whose field it lies, but also by the Advisory Council of The Brookings Institution. As soon as the project is approved, the investigation is placed under the supervision of a special Committee consisting of the Director of the Institute and two or more selected staff members.

It is the function of this supervising Committee to advise and counsel with the author in planning the analysis and to give such aid as may be possible in rendering the study worthy of publication. The Committee may refuse to recommend its publication by the Institution, if the study turns out to be defective in literary form or if the analysis in general is not of a scholarly character. If, however, the work is admittedly of a scholarly character and yet members of the Committee, after full discussion, cannot agree with the author on all phases of the analysis, the book will be published in the form desired by the author, with the disagreeing Committee member or members writing a criticism of the points in issue for publication as an appendix.

After the book is approved by the Institute for publication a digest of it is placed before the Advisory Council of The Brookings Institution. The Advisory Council does not undertake to revise or edit the manuscript, but each member is afforded an opportunity to criticize the analysis and, if so disposed, to prepare a dissenting opinion.

DIRECTOR'S PREFACE

It was inevitable that the Mexican revolution of 1910 should arouse the deepest interest and cause no little concern to both statesmen and commercial interests within the United States. This concern was probably heightened rather than diminished as it became apparent that the struggle involved not merely the dispossession of one political group by a rival faction, but represented a rather sweeping and fundamental attempt to reconstitute the economic structure of the country.

Perception that a whole socio-economic philosophy was at issue did not come as a result of lucid explanation by the proponents of the revolution itself or the analytical treatises of outside students of the movement. It came rather from the hard impact of events, particularly as the new system of property rights challenged the economic position or ambitions of our commercial interests in Mexico. As the "land claims" of the nationals of the United States and other foreign countries passed to the state of acute controversy, it became apparent that we had only very inadequate understanding of the Mexican side of the situation in its historic, ethnological, and social setting. Without such a view, sound diplomatic policy and sane public opinion are difficult, if not impossible.

In the present volume Mr. Tannenbaum has given a broad and detailed view of Mexican land institutions based securely on the historical developments of the revolution and a survey of pre-revolutionary conditions and practices. To secure the material necessary for such an account of the matter, he spent fourteen months in Mexico, where he had the benefit of the most cordial co-operation of government agencies and made extensive travels into remote and unfrequented parts of the country. With tireless energy and much ingenuity he brought together the factual material necessary to the construction of a more detailed and authentic account of the actual status of land ownership or control in Mexico than has ever before been available to readers of either English or Spanish.

An outstanding characteristic of the book is that it reveals the difference of approach which peoples of different nationality and institutional history may make to so basic a question as that of landholding. Without indulging in invidious comparison of either scheme of ideas, he has brought out the organic relationship between Mexican life and the Mexican land system and shown the inherent difficulties of reconciling such an economic philosophy with the commercial ambitions and sense of international property right of persons reared in the British or American tradition. Finally, the book answers the question of the actual amount of foreign landholding in Mexico, and the percentage held by citizens of the United States much more accurately and authoritatively than has ever been done in the past.

Thus to bring the whole issue out of the realm of uncertainty, opinion, and prejudice and into the light of definite and accurate knowledge should go far toward promoting a better understanding and the reduction of friction in the relations of the United States and European countries with Mexico.

The Supervisory Committee in charge of the preparation of this volume was composed of Edwin G. Nourse, Charles O. Hardy, and Cleona Lewis of the staff of the Institute.

HAROLD G. MOULTON,

Director.

Institute of Economics,
October, 1928.

AUTHOR'S ACKNOWLEDGMENTS

Had it not been for the genuine interest of my many friends in Mexico, it would have been impossible to gather the material that has gone into the preparation of this book. The mere task of getting the basic facts together involved the official co-operation of each state and county government in the Republic of Mexico. The tapping of these sources of information was made possible for different purposes and at different times by friends occupying high positions in the Department of Agriculture, the Department of Industry, Commerce, and Labor, the Department of Education, and the Department of Statistics, who gave generously of their time and influence. It was also through them that the information available in the archives of the different offices was placed at the disposal of the author. It is only because a full list of those who helped in the gathering of the material would be too long to permit that we omit specific mention of any.

Just as the gathering of the material depended to so large an extent upon the co-operation of friends in Mexico, so the organization, presentation, and interpretation of the data was made possible by the unstinted and continuous aid given the author by the staff of the Institute of Economics.

FRANK TANNENBAUM.

Washington, D. C.,
October, 1928.

CONTENTS

CONTENTS

APPENDIX C

THE MEXICAN AGRARIAN
REVOLUTION

THE MEXICAN AGRARIAN REVOLUTION

CHAPTER I

THE DEVELOPMENT OF THE MEXICAN LAND SYSTEM *

The turbulent four hundred years of Mexican history since the Spanish Conquest of 1519 may, for

* This chapter is to be considered as merely an introductory note to Mexican agrarian history. The reader desiring a more extensive treatment may turn to the excellent study by George McCutchen McBride, *The Land Systems of Mexico,* American Geographical Society Research Series No. 12, 1923; or to L. Mendieta y Nuñéz, *"El Problema Agrario de Mexico,"* La *Población del Valle de Teotihuacán,* by Manuel Gamio, *Secretaría de Agricultura y Fomento, Dirección de Antropología,* Mexico, 1922, Vol. II, pp. 475-573.. Further material on the history of Mexican landholding may be found in Bandelier, A. F., "Distribution and Tenure of Lands and the Customs with Respect to Inheritance among the Ancient Mexicans," in the *Reports* of the Peabody Museum of American Archæology and Ethnology, Harvard University, Vol. II, pp. 76-79, pp. 385-448; Waterman, T. T., "Bandelier's Contribution to the Study of Ancient Mexican Social Organization," *University of California Publications in American Archæology and Ethnology,* Berkeley, 1917, Vol. 12, pp. 249-282; Orozco, Don Wistano Luis, *Legislación y Jurisprudencia Sobre Torrenos Baldíos,* Mexico, 1894; F. de la Maza, Francisco, *Codigo de Colonización y Terrenos Baldíos de la República Mexicana,* 1451 to 1892, Mexico, 1893; Enríquez, Andrés Molina, *Los Grandes Problemas Nacionales,* Mexico, 1909, especially pp. 49-61, 79-123; Roa, Fernando González, *Las Cuestiónes Fundamentales de Actualidad en México,* 1927; Roa, Fernando González and Covarrubias, José, *El Problema Rural de México,* 1917.

1

the purpose of a summary view, be divided into five periods: (1) the conquests; (2) the three hundred years of colonial administration; (3) the struggle for independence, beginning in 1810, and the internal strife that succeeded it, including the war with the United States, the conflict with the church, the Constitution of 1857, and the Maximilian adventure; (4) the consolidation under Diaz from 1870 to 1910; and finally (5) the agrarian revolution from 1910 to the present. Closely intertwined with the developments of these five epochs has been a succession of basic changes in land distribution and land tenure. Indeed, so fundamental has been their importance that one can scarcely hope to understand the political and social history of Mexico without considerable familiarity with these changes in its agrarian structure. This book is largely concerned with the results of the last phase of Mexican agrarian history. This introductory chapter will briefly characterize the earlier developments in landholding and land tenure.

There was, first, the expropriation of the natives resulting from the sudden and violent intrusion of the Spaniards, followed by the slow process of stratification during the long colonial period. The early nineteenth century witnessed the disentailment of the large estates arising from the changes that followed the War of Independence and the subsequent confiscation of the church lands. With the coming of the Diaz régime there ensued a rapid alienation of the national lands and a destruction of village communal ownership. The last phase of the agrarian revolution is still being wrought out under influences of the revolution which began in 1910.

The Spaniards found the Mexican Indians living under a well-defined system of land tenure. The conquest took place in a deeply rooted and organized community and not within a social structure where the population was foot-loose and wandering. The natives had a stable land system with rights, privileges, and obligations that were well defined and well enforced.[1]

This indigenous land system was closely interrelated with the social organization of the Indians. They were found organized as tribes and divided into kinship groups known as *calpulli*. Several of these groups united to form villages. Within the lands surrounding the village, each of the kinship groups (*calpulli*) administered its own section. In each kinship group plots were held by the heads of families with permanent tenure and inheritance. These plots were inalienable and transferred only for non-tillage or in case of the disappearance of the family. In addition to the parcels held by the family, there were lands specifically set aside for other purposes: for the maintenance of the local officials, the payment of tribute to the Aztec overlords, for religious purposes, and for the prosecution

[1] It is true, of course, that the Spaniards at the time they came to Mexico found migratory Indian tribes, especially in the northern parts of the country, but the conquest of these proceeded later.

of wars. These were tilled in common by the people of the villages. Besides this widely-spread system of ownership and tenure, there was an incipient feudalism with bound serfs and fairly large estates belonging to the nobility.[2] Both of these pre-colonial land systems have made their contributions to the character of contemporary landholding in Mexico—the hacienda and the village. In spite of the fact that numerous villages were absorbed into the large estates which the Spaniards carved out for themselves,[3] many communities retained their essential structure as well as some of their lands till well towards the end of the nineteenth century, when their position became increasingly difficult because of the land policy of the Diaz government. Both the present-day village and the hacienda may be said to have more or less perpetuated types of land tenure that existed before the conquest. What is clear is that the area embraced in the haciendas, as well as the number of people subjected to their control, was greatly increased by the conquest.

The three hundred years of Spanish dominion were characterized by a persistent trend in the direction of land concentration. Against this background of

[2] Gamio, Vol. II, pp. 478-485.

There is a dispute as to the character of the pre-Spanish land system of Mexico, especially in the proportionate importance of the communal village and the type of landholding comparable to the European feudal system. It seems clear, however, that a large proportion of the population lived in communal villages. See McBride, pp. 121-122, note 30.

[3] Roa and Covarrubias, pp. 23-25; McBride, pp. 111-116.

land ownership as it existed before the conquest must now be set the results of the reduction of the Indians to the political and economic dominion of their European master. The Spanish conquest was carried out by a very small number of soldiers, adventurers, proselyters, and gold-seekers who took possession of the country in the name of the King and in return were compensated by him for their labor and sacrifice. The compensation took the form of distributing the lands of the conquered Indians, and subjecting the native population to the personal service of the conquerors. That is, the Spaniards had allotted to them the Indian villages and the lands that these Indian villages possessed. The tribute to the chieftains that characterized the pre-colonial system of land tenure was merely transferred to the conquerors. These allotments were known as *repartimientos* or *encomiendas*.

The evil effects of the early allotments of Indians to the Spaniards led to repeated attempts by the Crown to protect the natives by curbing the prerogatives of the colonists. Generally speaking, the power of the local colony was so great that most of these attempts bore little fruit. The Indians in ever-increasing number became bound serfs upon the lands of their white masters. The *encomiendas,* which were originally meant to last only for one generation, were gradually extended from one generation to another, and were not finally abolished till the eighteenth century. These *encomiendas* were of great size, covering in some instances as many as 25,000 square miles, and 115,000 people.[4] As the years passed, the land in the *encomiendas* became family possessions, and some of them persisted as family estates into the nineteenth century in more or less their original form.

In addition to the *encomiendas,* other forms of land ownership were established by gift from the King, by purchase of Crown lands, by rewards for colonization. This process of concentration was greatly aided by the fact that the *encomiendas* could not be subdivided, and that the lands held by the nobility were entailed. The large landowner generally managed by some meritorious service to acquire a patent of nobility, thus placing his possession beyond the danger of division.

Moreover, the church, from the conquest to the end of the colonial regime, gradually acquired very large holdings. The amount of land held by the church is not known. Estimates have varied from one-half to three-fourths of the total area of the Republic. The colonial period was therefore essentially a period of land concentration. Every force seemed to be working in the direction of increasing the area held by a few individuals and decreasing the number of actual owners.

Those older Indian villages not included in *encomiendas,* or established in the mountains by Indians fleeing from the conquerors, or created by

[4] McBride, p. 47.

the Spaniards themselves, carried on a perpetual struggle with the large landowners. This struggle frequently took the form of litigation against the larger estates—a litigation that in some cases seems to have lasted indefinitely.[5] The Spanish colonial legislation,[6] as we have already said, attempted to protect the Indians, and as a result of these efforts some of the Indian groups especially in the more mountainous sections of Mexico succeeded in preserving their freedom. The best lands, the lands in the plains, passed into large estates [7] and the people upon them became bound serfs of the conquerors and their descendants. This general trend of colonial history has been well characterized by McBride in the following words: "Up to the middle of the eighteenth century everything had favored the accumulation of land in a few hands. *Encomiendas* which could not be divided, *mayorazgos* which preserved intact the holdings of the aristocracy, the concentration of property in the hands of the clergy, all had contributed to the maintenance of large holdings." [8]

The end of the eighteenth century and the beginning of the nineteenth saw the first break in the tendency of land concentration in Mexico. The first

[5] Pimentel, Francisco, *Obras Completas,* 1866, Vol. III, pp. 187-188.

[6] Gamio, Vol. II, pp. 500-501.

[7] Pimentel, Francisco, *La Situación Actual de la Raza Indígena,* 1864, p. 167.

[8] McBride, p. 60.

step in the process came with the confiscation of the lands of the Jesuits in 1767. After that date a variety of forces contributed to the attempt to break the hold of the Mexican haciendas upon the rural community. The influence of the American and French Revolutions, especially the Napoleonic influences in Spain, the Spanish liberal Constitution of 1812, the confiscation of the lands of the Inquisition in that country, all combined to stir an internal movement in Mexico that was both agrarian and national.

It is perfectly clear that the War for Independence was largely motivated at least in its early stages by agrarian ambitions on the part of the Indians. It is true that the ultimate achievement of Independence in 1821 was under conservative auspices and that one of the promises of the successful revolution was the maintenance of the *status quo* in land. The struggle for independence did, however, lay the foundation for three policies that contributed to the attempted break-up of the large estates. It led to the abolition of the legal inferiority of the Indian,[9] a gesture, it is true,[10] but yet a change in the relative position of the races in the direction of greater social,

[9] Alexander Humboldt quotes the Bishop of Michoacán, urging upon the Spanish Court: "Let the odious personal impost of the *tribute* be abolished; and let the infamy which unjust laws have attempted to stamp on the people of colour be at an end." Humboldt, Alexander, *Political Essay on the Kingdom of New Spain,* New York, 1811, Vol. I, p. 148, translated from the original French by John Black.

[10] Poinsett, Joel Roberts, *Notes on Mexico,* London, 1822, p. 162.

and ultimately, of political and economic, equality. It led also to an abolition of entailment of large holdings which, in spite of little immediate effect, must be considered as a contribution towards destroying land feudalism in Mexico. Finally, the internal conflicts to which independence gave rise led to the ultimate confiscation of the church lands.

The first attack against the lands of the church took place, as noted above, in 1767, while Mexico was still a colony of Spain. Soon after independence, other attempts [11] to curtail the lands of the church developed. These varied efforts took effective shape in the so-called "ley Lerdo" of June 25, 1856, which ordered the transfer of the church lands to the renters then occupying them at a capitalization which at 6 per cent would yield the church the actual rental then being paid. The lands held by the church but not rented were to be sold at public auction. The opposition to this program led to the so-called Three Years War and the complete confiscation of the church lands on July 12, 1859.[12]

This policy at one blow transferred a great body of land from the hands of the church to laymen. But in the confusion and stress of civil conflict the records were lost, titles to the properties were obscured, land ownership was made more confused

[11] Romero, Matías, *Mexico and the United States*, New York, 1898, Vol. I, pp. 351-357; Gamio, Vol. II, pp. 519-524.

[12] McBride, pp. 67-70.

than ever, and what is still more important, the transfer of the church lands did not change the fundamental character of the land system. The lands of the church seem to have gone either to enlarge existing estates or more generally to create new haciendas of a type already dominant in the country. The purpose of the reform,. therefore, in so far as it was aimed at the creation of small sized holdings was in a general way defeated, though it is probably true that a considerable number of comparatively small properties that did not exist before were carved out of the church lands. But as a whole it is perfectly clear that these lands merely went into the formation of new haciendas.

An important by-product of this conflict between the church and the state was the attack upon the communal village land that, protected by the Spanish Crown, had persisted throughout the colonial period.[13] Soon after independence various attempts were made to distribute these lands individually among their actual owners.[14] But no consistent attack upon them was carried through. It was not till the law of 1856 and the constitution of 1857 that a general prohibition against civil or ecclesiastical [15] corporations owning land was enacted. This legal prohibition against communal ownership was

[13] José Covarrubias, *La Trascendencia Política de la Reforma Agraria,* Mexico, pp. 134-135.

[14] Indalecio A. Dávila, *Trabajos Presentados en la Cuarta Semana Social Mexicana,* Zacatecas, Sept. 23-28, 1912, pp. 99-100.

[15] Gamio, Vol. II, p. 525.

later put into effect under the Diaz administration with resulting consequences which are still being felt in contemporary Mexico.

These attempts to destroy the feudal character of the Mexican land system were defeated by the policy of the Diaz regime. This influence lasted till 1910, or some 35 years. It was during that period that Mexico developed its greatest stride as a unified nation. The Diaz policy seemed to center about the rapid industrialization of the country. The development of railroads, mining, and public utilities was pressed with great speed and with these changes came an increasing flow of foreign investments into Mexico. The results taken together in so far as they influenced the agrarian problem of the country led to a rapid rise in land values and to speculation in land. Under this stimulus and under the assumption that Mexico would be best served by the rapid investment of foreign capital and colonization the Mexican government developed a land policy that proved disastrous to the country.

This whole policy of the Diaz government must be viewed in the light of Mexican agrarian history. The very nature of the colonial land distribution made land titles imperfect, led to abuse on the part of landowners and made it difficult to develop any system of colonization because the government never knew which lands belonged to it or to private owners. This lack of definite boundaries is given as one of the causes for the persistent failure of all attempts at colonization in Mexico.[16] In part the land policy of Diaz must be looked upon as an attempt to straighten out the tangle of land titles. Under the law of 1883 contracts were given to private companies to survey the lands in specified regions embracing areas greater than some of the states. These surveys were for the purpose of discovering the *baldíos*, that is, the lands belonging to the nation. The companies were allowed to retain one-third of all the lands they surveyed. Later, in 1894 a colonization law further extended the range of surveys. Every property owner became subject to the manipulation of the surveying companies, the *companias deslindadores* as these surveying companies were known, for the purpose of correcting and revising their titles. The smaller the land-owner, the more likely was his title to be defective.[17] This was particularly true of the Indian villages. The law made it possible to "denounce" occupied lands that had no registered titles, a specific short-coming of innumerable small villages.

[16] Memoria, A. S. M. El Emperador, Por el Ministro de Fomento, Luis Robles Pezuela, 1865, p. 99; C. Manuel Siliceo, *Memoria del Ministero de Fomento, Colonización, Industria y Commercio de la República Mexicana,* Mexico, 1857, pp. 37-38.

[17] José Covarrubias, *La Trascendencia Política de la Reforma Agraria,* Mexico, 1922, pp. 78-79; *Debates del Congreso Constituyente,* Vol. II, p. 808.

"The Indians here are very numerous and they are still struggling to resist the encroachments of the whites upon their land, though the ultimate result is in all cases the same." Lumholtz, Carl, *Unknown Mexico,* New York, 1902, Vol. I, p. 135.

Under this legislation Mexican land monopolization increased by leaps and bounds. Villages found themselves driven from their holdings or incorporated into large estates. The national lands were appropriated by these companies, mainly foreign, at a rate that led to the absorption of nearly one-fourth [18] of the total area of the Republic in a very few years.[19] The general character of the movement has been described as even more disastrous than the Spanish conquest, because the conquerors were in part compelled to respect the lands of the Indians, while under the Diaz régime these were completely at the mercy of their new masters, not even having the protection of the Spanish colonial legislation.[20] It should, however, be noted that most of the very largest land monopolies created under the Diaz legis-

[18] See below Chapter XV, p. 368.

[19] "Between 1881 and 1888 the government disposed of 25,119,266 hectares." *Boletín de la Estadística de la República Mexicana*, 1892, No. 2, p. 191; *Monopolio y Fraccionamiento de la Propiedad Rústica*, José L. Cossío, Mexico, 1914, p. 12.

[20] "Independent Mexico destroyed all the communal property of the Indians, abolished all the laws for their protection and aggravated large landholding up to a point of inequality which cannot be found in any other part of the world." Roa and Covarrubias, *El Problema Rural de Mexico*, p. 80. Typical of the grants that were made is the one which gave to one company, "*la Compañia Colonizadora, Agrícola e Industrial del Colorado*," 59 titles of 25,000 hectares each. *Ministerio de Fomento, Memoria*, Dec., 1876, Nov., 1877, p. 444: The greatest land grants under this legislation took place in Chihuahua, Sonora, Durango, Chiapas, Tabasco, Campeche, Yucatán, Nayarit, and Lower California, as well as considerable ares in the states of Nuevo León, Coahuila, Tamaulipas, and San Luis Potosí. José Covarrubias, *La Trascendencia Política de la Reforma Agraria*, Mexico, 1922, pp. 80-81.

lation were in the sparsely settled states where land has but little value.[21] What the new land policy did do was to confirm an already existing land system and spread it all over the Republic. It also increased the difficulty of the Indian villages by laying them open to attack through their lack of title, or by compelling them to break up their communal holdings and distribute the parcels among the individual members, a policy which proved disastrous to the villages. In fact, the survival of the villages up to the Diaz régime was due to their communal character. The individual Indian proved himself a helpless child and transferred his title to his little plot of land for a good drink of *aguardiente*, not knowing the import of the transaction. As the Diaz régime came to its close, Mexican lands were apparently held by proportionately fewer people than at any time in its history. The movement to destroy land feudalism had failed. In part this was due to the fact that the racial composition in Mexico lent itself to a type of political and social policy that would have been more difficult to carry through if the population had been homogeneous. The Diaz régime was consistent with a general attitude of contempt towards the Indians and their institutions and with a belief that the only hope of Mexico was in a destruction of the Indian communal organization, a reduction of the Indian population,

[21] Indalecio A. Dávila, *Trabajo Presentado en la Cuarta Semana Social Mexicana*, Zacatecas, Sept. 23-28, 1912, pp. 101-102.

and a replacement by foreign immigration." This perhaps explains the racial nationalism which has accompanied the agrarian revolution that ended the Diaz régime and which we shall detail in the chapters that follow.

[22] *"El Problema de la Colonización Nacional,"* Andrés Molina Enriquez, *Boletín de la Dirección, General de Agricultura, Parte II, Revista de Economía Rural y Sociología,* Mexico, 1911, p. 37. Also see Chapter VI, p. 152.

CHAPTER II

GROUPING AND CHARACTER OF RURAL POPULATION

The distinctive character of the country as well as its history have gone far towards shaping the Mexican agrarian problem. The distribution of the population has been materially influenced by the peculiar character of the Mexican topography. It is essentially a country of widely different geographic regions, and the geography has modified social and economic structure. Looked at from either the Pacific or Atlantic Ocean, Mexico rises steeply from coastal plain to high mountain peaks; from tropical heat to snow-capped mountains; from sea level to an altitude of 18,076 feet,[1] accompanied by rapid changes in temperature, rainfall, flora and fauna. Excepting the low lands of Tabasco, Campeche, and Yucatan, any approach to the interior from the coast involves the ascent of steep mountains, that tend to increase in height as we go south from the United States. Looking north from the mountain peaks that dominate central Mexico, the country takes the form of a V, embraced on each side by the Sierras

[1] The peak of Orizaba. *Geografía de la República Mexicana,* Jesús Galindo y Villa, Mexico, 1925, Vol. I.

that separate the interior from the sea. This interior angle-shaped plain stretches from Mexico City to the American border, declining in altitude and increasing in width as it rolls north. It extends from Texas to the very heart of Mexico and occupies 66,600,000 hectares, or nearly 33.9 of the total area of the Republic, rising slowly from 5,576 feet to 11,906 feet at its upper regions.[2]

Looking south, the ranges that tower over Mexico City and encase all of the numerous villages that crowd the mountain side decline sharply to what is nearly sea level at the Isthmus of Tehuantepec, a narrow tropical neck that ties northern Mexico with its southern end, Chiapas on the west and Tabasco, Campeche, and Yucatan on the east. Beyond the narrow and low neck made by the Isthmus of Tehuantepec the mountains rise rapidly once more, though not to such towering heights as in Central Mexico, and the upper plains of the State of Chiapas, although they are at the southernmost part of Mexico, have a climate comparable to that of Central Mexico. Going up from the coast one goes from the hot tropical country to the cooler, healthier, more populated plains of Mexico, and as one climbs from the *Mesa Central* to the mountain peaks one goes from the warm mild climate to the colder regions that lie hidden in snow the year round. And, so broken are the mountains, so great the variety of interior and coastal pockets, that one can in most

[2] *ibid.*, p. 22.

TOPOGRAPHY OF THE CENTRAL PLATEAU

I. Cross Section of Mexico at Four Given Parallels *

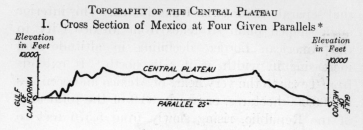

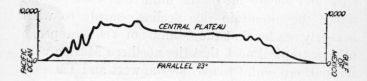

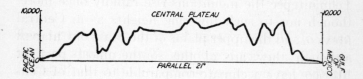

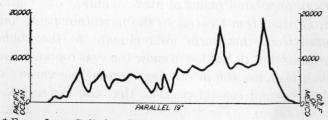

* From Jesus Galinds y Villa, *Geografia de la Republica Mexicana*, Vol. I, p. 24.

II. Location of Given Parallels*

* From Secretaria de Agricultura y Fomento, Direccion de Estudios Geograficos y Climatologicos, *Atlas Geografico de la Republica Mexicana.*

parts of Mexico change his climate almost at will and within a very few hours. These regions, so close together, so much one above the other, so different in temperature, rainfall, climate, flora, fauna, differ correspondingly in the population that has found location within their mountain valleys.

The combination of altitude, temperature, and rainfall has made the central part of Mexico the great abode of Mexican population. The population distribution has followed the mountains because the mountains have determined the rainfall and the temperature. The tropical coastal plains, with the

exception of Yucatan and Tabasco, are thinly populated. That is also true of the desert-like north,
with the exception of an occasional river valley, a
mining region, or a grazing section. It has been
within the compass of the highest mountains and the
most elevated plains that Mexico's population has
found a natural resting place, built its greatest cities,

POPULATION DENSITY, BY STATES, 1921

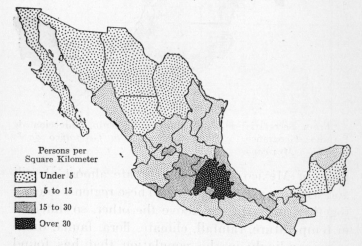

Persons per
Square Kilometer

Under 5

5 to 15

15 to 30

Over 30

and developed its best agriculture. The upper valleys and the surrounding mountains have from time
immemorial dominated the whole of Mexican life.[3]

As one goes from Central Mexico either east or
west, north or south, one goes to lower altitudes, to

[3] Molina Enríquez, *Los Grandes Problemas Nacionales,* Mexico,
1909, p. 12.

POPULATION DENSITY AND LAND ELEVATION BY STATE GROUPS *

Population of State per Square Kilometer	Number of States in Group	Density and Altitude Comparisons by State Groups				Percentual Distribution of Area and Population by State Groups		
		Average Population per Square Kilometer	Average Population per Inhabited Place	Average Altitude of State Capitals[a] (Feet)	Average Temperature at State Capitals[b] (Fahr.)	Area as a percentage of total Mexico	Population as a percentage of total Mexico	Number of inhabited places as a percentage of all in Mexico
30 or more...	5	44.3	504[c] 392	7,713	58.7	4.2	25.4	11.7
15 to 30.....	8	17.2	242	5,246	66.3	13.8	32.7	31.4
5 to 15......	10	7.1	195	3,055	71.8	29.7	29.0	34.6
Less than 5..	8	1.8	134	2,234	69.9	52.3	12.9	22.3

* Compiled from *Anuario Estadístico, 1923–1924*, Vol. II, p. 3.
a The state capitals, generally speaking, represent the altitude at which the mass of population tends to concentrate.
b From "The Temperature of Mexico," by Jesús Hernández, B.C.E., *Monthly Weather Review*, 1923, Supplement No. 23, and records of the United States Weather Bureau.
c Including Distrito Federal.
d Excluding Distrito Federal.

warmer temperature, to lesser population density, to smaller sized communities. This is clearly shown by the table on page 21 and the map on page 20.

This table also shows that the five states whose capitals had the highest mean altitude comprise only 4 per cent of the total area of the Republic, and that this 4 per cent of the area has the greatest population density, containing one-fourth of the total population of Mexico, while 52 per cent of the area, composed of nine states with capitals having the lowest mean altitude has a density of less than 2 per square kilometer and contains only 12 per cent of the total population. So closely interrelated do the factors of rain, temperature, and altitude seem to be that the average size of the Mexican community located at over 7,000 feet is at least three times as large as the one located above 2,000 feet. Mexico can thus be looked upon as a huge mountain rising out of the sea with the best conditions for man centered between 7,000 and 8,000 feet above sea level and almost that much below the upper mountain ranges. About half-way up to the peak, man has found the most suitable climate, settled in closest proximity, and built the largest communities.[4]

[4] As compared with the United States the population growth of Mexico has been very slow. For 1794 their estimates were almost the same, nearly four and a half million. By 1810, however, the United States had far outstripped and by 1840 had more than doubled the population of the neighboring Republic. The Mexican population has kept lagging behind the American at an

The greater part of the Mexican people are either Indian or Mestizo. The most recent figures for the racial distribution of the Mexican population give the *mestizo* 8,504,561, or more than half, and the Indian, 4,179,449, or less than a third of the total

ever lengthening distance and in 1921 [a] had reached only a little above one-ninth of the United States figure, viz.: 14,344,700, a size attained by the United States in 1834.[b]

This slow growth of the Mexican when compared to the American population is in itself a very revealing and striking fact. It can be explained, in part at least, by the restrictive policy of the colonial and Mexican governments against foreigners, the early disappearance of free land, the continuance of serfdom into the first decade of the twentieth century, the low standards of living among the working population that discouraged European immigration, the internal strife and constant turmoil, the poor internal communication,[c] the lack of sufficient and readily tillable soil not requiring heavy expenditure for irrigation, the tropical heat and unhealthy coasts,[d] the lack of sanitation, the inadequate nourishment, poor food habits and terrific death rate, especially among the rural population,[e] the excessive humidity in some parts of Mexico, and great rarity of air in others.[f] Taken together, these make a formidable array of reasons for the slow growth of Mexican population. Whether they fully explain the fact or not, it remains that Mexico has grown at a snail's pace in comparison with the rapid expansion of the American population.

[a] *Estadística Nacional,* April 15, 1927, p. 4.

[b] Computed from figures in *Statistical Abstract,* 1922 and 1925.

[c] *"Informe sobre el Censo General de la República, dado por Don Manuel Orozco y Berra al Ministro de Fomento, Don Manuel Siliceo, el primero de Agosto de 1857,"* quoted by *Estadística Nacional,* April 15, 1927, p. 5.

[d] *Hygiene in Mexico:* A Study of Sanitary and Educational Problems, Alberto J. Pani, Nov. 7, 1917.

[e] Manuel Gamio, *La Población Del Valle de Teotihuacán,* Mexico, 1922, Vol. II, p. 139.

[f] "The Relation of Health to Racial Capacity: The Example of Mexico," Ellsworth Huntington, *The Geographical Review,* Vol. II, 1921, pp. 243-264.

population. The percentage distribution given in the census of 1921 is as follows:

RACIAL DISTRIBUTION OF THE MEXICAN POPULATION *

Race	Percentage of Total
Mestizo (White and Indian)........................	59.33
Pure Indian.......................................	29.16
White...	9.80
Others and unknown..............................	1.00
Foreigners..	0.71

* *Estadística Nacional,* April 15, 1927.

These figures for race must be taken with caution. There is every reason to believe that the Indian percentage is considerably greater than here given. Professor Frederic Starr, who has spent many years studying the Mexican Indian, estimates that there are six million pure blooded Indians.[5] Manual Gamio points out that an "enormous error" has resulted from the fact that the Mexican census has counted as white those who speak Spanish, whereas a matter of fact these "whites" are really Indians by "race and culture." [6]

The Indian population tends to be more predominant in Southern than in Northern Mexico, in the districts where the haciendas embrace smaller rather than larger portions of the area of the states.

[5] *The Mexican People in Mexico and the Caribbean,* edited by Blakeslee, 1900, p. 14.

[6] Manuel Gamio and José Vasconcelos, *Some Aspects of Mexican Civilization,* 1927, p. 118.

It is in Oaxaca, Puebla, Guerrero, Veracruz, Tlaxcala, and Mexico, in the coastal mountain regions of
Michoacán, in the upper ranges of the mountains in
Sonora, Sinaloa, and Nayarit that the Indian has best
preserved himself. He can also be seen in the mountains or deep in the tropical forests of Chiapas,
where the *Lacandones,* for instance, have kept themselves aloof from too much contact with the white
man.[7] As a general statement it may be said that
the Indians have kept purest where they have
escaped from the haciendas and preserved their own
village life in the mountain ranges. As one goes
from the mountain heights to the haciendas located
in the valleys one goes from the pure Indian to the

[7] The *Estadística Nacional* lists 45 indigenous languages and
dialects (Nov. 30, 1926, p. 6). That is probably an understatement. The Racial and Language groups have been variously estimated. There is great diversity between the different racial
groups. "Those between Tarahumaras of Chihuahua, the Huicholes
of Jalisco, the Huaxtecas of San Luís Potosí, the Zapotecas of
Oaxaca, the Lacandones of Chiapas . . . could not be more nota-
ble." A Molina Énríquez, *El Problema de la Colonizacion
Nacional, Boletín de la Direccion General de Agricultura, Part II
Revista de Economía Rural y Sociología,* Mexico, 1911, p. 35.

"I was talking once with the archbishop of Oaxaca. He said,
'In my diocese we have Indians as yellow as lemons and as black
as coal; we have them so short that you could call them pigmies,
and we have them taller than the ordinary white man; we have
Indians who are good, and Indians who are bad.'

"There are then many different tribes of Mexican Indians.
There were a hundred and fifty different languages spoken in that
country at the time of the Conquest. More than fifteen languages
are spoken in the State of Oaxaca today, and more than 90 per
cent of its population are pure blood Indian." Starr in *Mexico
and the Caribbean,* pp. 16-17.

mestizo and as one goes from the hacienda to the urban community one goes from the Mestizo to the white population. That is, there are more whites to the population in the cities, fewer in small county seats, still fewer in the haciendas, and very few in the mountain villages. But so incomplete and inadequate is our knowledge of the Indian population of Mexico, that it seems useless to attempt here to summarize the racial distribution for each state of the Republic.

The Mexican population is predominantly rural. In 1921, if we consider the Federal District, which is dominated by Mexico City with its 906,063 inhabitants, as urban, the rural population was 73.8 of the total. Excluding the Federal District and Quintana Roo we get nearly eighty (78.2) per cent,[8] as rural. That means under the Mexican census classification[9] that approximately 80 per cent of the population lived in occupied places of less than 4,000 inhabitants.[10] Of the 62,272 inhabited places in Mexico in 1921, only 266 contain more than 4,000 inhabitants, and there seems to be little correlation between total density and percentage of rural population. The relative importance of the rural population in the several states of Mexico is shown by the

[8] See Appendix B for detailed tables.
[9] *Tercer Censo de Población de los Estados Unidos Mexicanos,* Vol. I, p. 32. Note that the rural population for 1910 is calculated on the basis of all inhabitants of communities of less than 4,000.
[10] See Appendix B for detailed tables.

following classification in which the Federal District
and Quintana Roo are not included.

Rural population as percentage of total	Number of states
90 to 100	2
80 to 90	11
70 to 80	7
60 to 70	5
50 to 60	4

In 20 out of 29 states, therefore, more than 70 per
cent of the people are located in communities of
under 4,000. We can now turn to an examination
of the occupational distribution of the Mexican
population in 1910.[11]

*In 1910 the large majority of the Mexican popula-
tion were classed as peons.* The rural population of
1910 as grouped by José Covarrubiás,[12] and based
upon the population census of 1910 [13] is summarized as follows:

[11] We give here the occupational distribution in 1910, and in a
later chapter note the changes that the revolution has made in
the occupational distribution. This seems to be the best arrangement for the purpose of both describing the character of the rural
community before the revolution and later pointing out the
major changes that have resulted from it. In the section, therefore, describing the occupational distribution and the residential
distribution between the villages and haciendas, the figures are
drawn from the census of the Mexican population for 1910, while
all other population figures in this chapter are derived from the
population census of 1921.

[12] *La Trascedencia Política de la Reforma Agraria,* México,
1922, pp. 17-23.

[13] *Tercer Censo de Población, 1910, de los Estados Unidos
Mexicanos.*

Hacendados	836
Owners of medium-sized properties (*ranchos*) ..	136,855
Administrators, little landowners and renters..	278,474
Small rural industries and indigenous trades...	104,260
Peones de campo (agricultural laborers)	3,130,402
Semi-rural population	116,513
Total.......................................	3,767,340

The rural population classified by occupation represented in 1910 some 69.3 [14] per cent of the total. Grouped differently and including members of families these population figures appear as follows:

Free rural population	479,074
In servitude (peonage)	9,591,752
Semi-rural	430,896
Total	10,501,722

We therefore get more than nine and one-half million people who are described as *peones de campo*.[15] This heavy percentage of the rural population classified as peons is undoubtedly due to the fact that the Census of 1910 made no distribution of the population between those residing upon the haciendas (the so-called *acasillados*) and those who lived in free villages.

It is a recognized fact that the resident population upon the haciendas had a very different status from

[14] The discrepancy in the figures as given for occupation and population in communities of 4,000 is due to different basis of classification. We are accepting the figures for employment as summarized while the residence figures were grouped by us.

[15] Covarrubias notes that of the total population of Mexico in 1910, 7,345,114 or 50.8 per cent could neither read nor write. This seems to be a considerable underestimate.

that part of the population in the rural community that lived in free villages. It is true of course that the position of the Mexican rural peasant and worker was not the same in all villages. Villages completely surrounded by large haciendas having insufficient lands of their own and dependent upon the surrounding estates for access to tillable soil, occupied a position sharply different from the villages located in the mountains of Oaxaca, Puebla, or Veracruz, away from all embracing haciendas and possessed of lands enough for their needs.

This differentiation between the free village and the hacienda village is important if we are to get a correct picture of the Mexican rural community. It is misleading to classify all of the rural population that was employed in tilling the soil, excepting the owners and larger renters, as *peones de campo*.[16] The rural population in Mexico both before 1910 and at present was and is located in two distinct types of communities, one a free or comparatively free village, with some lands of its own, and the second, a resident hacienda community located upon a large estate and acquiring right of tillage through some form of labor contract. It was the rural population located upon the hacienda that was tied to the soil; the other part of the population lived in free villages. The debt bondage of the Mexican rural worker was therefore generally effec-

[16] This error of the 1910 census is generally followed by students of Mexico.

tive and applied only to the resident hacienda population. In analyzing the population distribution
between hacienda and village we therefore secure an
additional insight into the organization of the
Mexican rural community and later can better
understand the different rôles played by these
different classes of the rural population in the
revolution of 1910 and in noting the different
effects of the revolution upon these two major
groups of the rural population.

In 1910 nearly one-half of the total rural popula-
tion was located (acasillado) upon haciendas and
ranchos.[17] Of the total rural population in com-

[17] These figures were compiled from the *Secretaría de Fomento,*
Colonización e Industria: División Territorial de los Estados
Unidos Mexicanos, 31 Vols., giving separate volume to each state
and based upon the census of 1910. These volumes appeared
irregularly and with slightly differing titles between 1910-1918.
Our figures include only those communities and their inhabitants that have a population of 4,000 or less.

For method employed in organizing the population distribution
here presented see Appendix B. It should be noted that the 1910
and 1921 Censuses have some 100 classifications, while only a few,
like *rancherías, congregaciónes, pueblos, villas, comunidades, haciendas, ranchos,* etc., contain any considerable number of inhabitants, these present no standard classification. They differ widely
between themselves in each state and in the different states.
This resulting confusion has been made worse since 1910 by the
continuous changes in the agrarian legislation (see Chapter X,
p. 248). It has, therefore, seemed best to disregard all the classifications including those between haciendas and ranchos and
classify the population communities by type and size rather than
by names given in the Census of 1910 and 1921 (*Censo General
de Habitantes,* 30 November, 1921). There still remain unpublished the census records of 1921 for the States of San Luís Potosí,
Tamaulipas, Veracruz, Yucatán, and Zacatecas. The census figures
for these as well as nine other states were compiled from the

munities of under 4,000, approximately 47 per cent were resident upon haciendas and ranchos, and 51 per cent in free agricultural villages, while all other rural communities accounted for only 2.2 of the rural population. The 2.2 per cent of the rural population located in non-agricultural villages were chiefly found in the three Northern states: Chihuahua, Coahuila and Sonora,[18] and largely made up of small mining towns.

If we turn to examine the distribution of the rural population between those located on haciendas and those in free villages, we find sharp contrasts between states and between different regions of Mexico. Eight of the eleven states where the greater part of the rural population lives in free agricultural villages, are grouped about Mexico City. It is clear from this that the Mexican rural population has best preserved its independent communities in the mountains that dominate central Mexico. This is indicated by the following figures showing the

original sheets before publication. As it may prove impossible to check our compiled figures with the ultimately published records, discrepancies may occur between our figures for these states and those in the official publication. All of this work was done by the Institute of Economics, using the Censuses of 1910 and 1921 as source material. Copies of the basic tables compiled may be consulted in the Library of the Institute of Economics.

[18] These non-agricultural communities accounted for the following percentages of the rural population in three states: Chihuahua 8.8, Coahuila 11.8, and Sonora 12.5. In not one of the other states does the population living in such communities reach 5 per cent of the total and in ten of the states, less than 1 per cent of the rural population is located in other than agricultural communities.

percentage of the rural population that is located in free villages in eight central states:

Federal District	93
Oaxaca	85
Mexico	82
Hidalgo	78
Puebla	77
Veracruz	76
Morelos	74
Tlaxcala	65

The other three states are Tabasco 67.7, Quintana Roo 88.9, and Sonora 54.4. A glance at this list of states makes it clear that the center of the Mexican revolution during the last 18 years has been in those states where the Indian population has continued residing in villages. We may in fact say that the mountain region surrounding Mexico City is a section apart and one that has best escaped the reduction of the population to peonage upon haciendas. A glance at the map on page 33 will clearly show the concentrated character of the states that have to this date best preserved the free village communities. Beyond these states the large mass of the population tends to live upon haciendas and ranchos. In the agricultural states just north of Mexico City, in the best part of the *Mesa Central*, the percentage of population concentrated upon haciendas is heaviest, while further north and in the extreme south the proportions occupying free villages are somewhat greater, predominantly, however, located upon haciendas and ranchos as wage laborers, and

PROPORTION OF RURAL POPULATION LIVING ON HACIENDAS *
I. In 1910

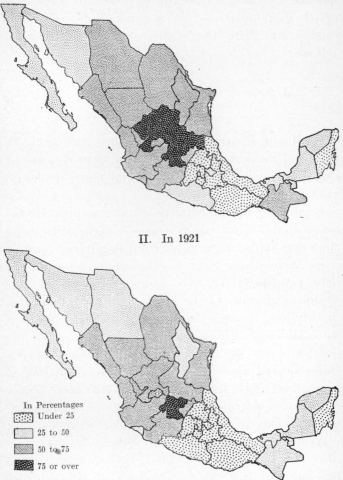

II. In 1921

In Percentages
Under 25
25 to 50
50 to 75
75 or over

* For detailed data see p. 32.

not upon their own land as members of free communities. Classified on the basis of the percentage of their population living upon haciendas and ranchos in 1910, the states of Mexico divide as follows:

Percentage	Number of states
10 to 35	11
35 to 60	8
60 to 85	12

For all states nearly one-half—46.8 per cent—of the total rural population were in 1910 resident in communities located upon privately-owned plantations.

By making a somewhat different grouping we discover that 17 out of 31 states had in 1910 more than one-half of their total rural population located upon haciendas as wage workers under conditions of debt peonage. We can, however, secure a more significant picture of the meaning of this population distribution between haciendas and free villages if we examine not the population distribution but the distribution of the communities themselves between those located upon haciendas and those existing as free villages. By making this distribution we secure a picture of the relative importance of the two types of villages in different sections of Mexico.

Nearly 82 per cent of all inhabited places in Mexico were in 1910 located upon haciendas and ranchos. In 1910 Mexico had 69,549 communities of under 4,000. Of these, 56,825, or 81.70 per cent, were located upon haciendas and ranchos, and 11,117, or 15.98 per cent, were free villages. All other rural communities accounted for only 2.32 per cent of the total.

In this table the ratio of rural communities located on haciendas and ranchos to all rural communities is the basis upon which the states are classified.

Classification	Number of states
90 to 100 ..:................	11
80 to 90	9
70 to 80	2
60 to 70	1
50 to 60	3
40 to 50	3
30 to 40	2

In twenty states more than 80, and in five more than 95 per cent of all inhabited places were located upon private estates. The nine states in which less than 70 per cent of the inhabited places are found upon haciendas are the states where the larger part of the population lives in free villages. In other words, the states having a large proportion of rural communities located upon haciendas also have a heavy percentage of the total rural population living upon haciendas. Before summarizing this general discussion, we must note that the nearly 82 per cent of the communities located on haciendas and ranchos had less than half, and that the 16 per cent of free villages had more than half of the rural population. That is, the free village was considerably larger than the resident hacienda village. If we take all

communities in Mexico we find that the average
for the hacienda and rancho in 1910 is less than 100
and that the average for the free village is more
than 500. The following table summarizes the
whole discussion.

COMMUNITIES OF LESS THAN 4,000, 1910

Type of Community	Population		Communities		Average Size of Community
	In Thousands	As Percentage of Total	Number	As Percentage of Total	
Haciendas[a] and ranchos.	5,511	46.8	56,825	81.70	97
Agricultural villages...	6,011	51.0	11,117	15.98	541
All other....	257	2.2	1,607	2.32	160
All rural communities	11,779	100.0	69,549	100.00	169

[a] Includes all of the rural population except that located in rural villages.
See Appendix B.

We have now described the distribution of the
rural population between haciendas and free villages, and have also seen that 81.70 per cent of all
inhabited places in 1910 were located upon haciendas
and that on the average the resident hacienda
villages were one-fifth as large as the free villages.
We have now to note the size distribution of Mexican rural communities. For this purpose we take
the population census of 1921 rather than 1910. It
was found inconvenient to arrange the Mexican
community by size from the 1910 census. There

have been a number of changes in the total as well as in the rural population since 1910, and there are at present fewer rural communities. In a later chapter we shall discuss in detail the population and community changes in the years 1910-1921. Here we are concerned with presenting a picture of the type of rural community by size that exists in Mexico at present and with comparatively minor changes existed in Mexico up to 1910.

The majority of the Mexican rural population live in communities of over 100 inhabitants. If we take all the rural communities and distribute them by size we get the result shown in the table on this page.

DISTRIBUTION OF RURAL POPULATION IN COMMUNITIES OF
SPECIFIED SIZE, 1921

Population of Community	Communities		Aggregate Population	
	Number	*As Percentage of All Rural Communities*	In Thousands	*As Percentage of All Rural Population*
Under 10.........	7,976	*13.0*	46	*0.4*
10 to 100.........	30,813	*50.3*	1,225	*11.6*
100 to 1,000.......	20,557	*33.6*	6,041	*57.2*
1,000 or over......	1,894	*3.1*	3,251	*30.8*
Total........	61,240	*100.0*	10,563	*100.0*

The small rural community, that of under 100, accounts for more than 60 per cent of the total but contains only 12 per cent of the rural population, while the communities of over 1,000 inhabitants, which represent less than 5 per cent of the total, account for more than 30 per cent of the rural population. What is clear from this table is that the rural population tends to live in the larger communities rather than in the smaller ones. That makes it important to know whether the free villages or the hacienda villages represent the larger or the smaller population unit.

The hacienda village is predominantly smaller than the free village. The table on page 39 brings this point out clearly.

We may summarize this table in various ways and always get the same story. The hacienda villages are smaller in size, more numerous, and have a lesser proportion of the total rural population than the free villages. One way of telling this general and basic fact about Mexico is to point out that 94 per cent of all resident hacienda villages have less than 300 inhabitants each, while 42 per cent of all free villages have more than 300. If we group the different sized communities according to the proportion living in haciendas and in free villages we get the result shown in the table on page 40.

That is, of the 42,973 people living in communities of under ten, 92 per cent are upon haciendas. This percentage keeps decreasing as the communities increase in size, until the population living upon haciendas falls to 57 per cent, when the size of the communities rises to 300. So we can say as the rural community increases in size the proportion living

RURAL POPULATION GROUPED ACCORDING TO TYPE AND SIZE OF COMMUNITY, 1921 *

Population of Community	Ranchos and Haciendas [a]				All Other Villages				Percentage Ratio of Haciendas to Free Villages	
	Number	Percentage of all hacienda communities	Population (In thousands)	Percentage of all hacienda population	Number	Percentage of all free villages	Population (In thousands)	Percentage of all free village population	Communities	Population
Under 10	7,338	16.0	43.0	1.1	638	4.1	3.6	.1	11.5	12.0
10-19	7,704	16.8	107.8	2.8	631	4.1	8.7	.1	12.2	12.5
20-29	4,903	10.8	120.2	3.2	536	3.4	12.6	.2	9.1	9.6
30-39	3,487	7.6	118.2	3.1	448	2.9	15.4	.2	7.8	7.7
40-49	2,770	6.1	122.7	3.2	424	2.7	17.6	.3	6.5	7.0
50-74	4,917	10.8	299.4	7.8	913	5.9	54.9	.8	5.4	5.5
75-99	3,255	7.1	278.0	7.3	825	5.3	69.7	1.1	3.9	4.0
100-199	6,373	14.0	890.9	23.2	2,716	17.5	426.3	6.3	2.3	2.1
200-299	2,460	5.4	595.6	15.5	1,834	11.8	445.6	6.6	1.3	1.3
300-399	1,113	2.4	381.1	9.9	1,338	8.6	451.5	6.7	.8	.8
400-499	562	1.2	249.8	6.5	964	6.2	424.1	6.3	.6	.6
500-1,000	732	1.6	473.1	12.3	2,465	15.9	1,702.6	25.3	.3	.3
1,001-2,000	105	.2	138.8	3.6	1,277	8.3	1,737.4	25.8	.1	.1
2,001-3,000	8	....	19.2	.5	368	2.4	894.5	13.3	.02	.02
3,001-4,000	....	....	....	....	136	.9	461.1	6.9	....	....
Total	45,727	100.0	3,837.8	100.0	15,513	100.0	6,725.6	100.0	....	....

* For detailed tables see Appendix B.

a Only includes rural population classified by census under these two headings. See Appendix B.

upon haciendas decreases in number. Upon passing
to 300 inhabitants, the population upon haciendas
declines sharply, falling to 22 per cent at 1,000 and
to 2 per cent at 3,000, while the population of the
free villages increases correspondingly. Put in general terms the hacienda population goes from 92.3
per cent to 2.1 per cent of the total in any one group
as the size of the rural community goes from under
10 to 3,000, while the free village population at
the same time goes from 7.7 in the first group to 97.9
in the last.

RURAL POPULATION ON HACIENDAS AND IN FREE VILLAGES, CLASSI-
FIED BY SIZE OF COMMUNITIES, CENSUS OF 1921

Population of Community	Total Population (in thousands)	On Ranchos and haciendas [a]		In all other villages	
		Population In Thousands	Percentage of Total	Population In Thousands	Percentage of Total
Under 10	46.5	43.0	92.3	3.5	7.7
10–19	116.4	107.8	92.6	8.6	7.4
20–29	132.8	120.2	90.5	12.6	9.5
30–39	133.6	118.2	88.5	15.4	11.5
40–49	140.3	122.7	87.5	17.6	12.5
50–74	354.3	299.4	84.5	54.9	15.5
75–99	347.7	278.0	79.9	69.7	20.1
100–199	1,317.1	890.9	67.6	426.2	32.4
200–299	1,041.3	595.6	57.2	445.7	42.8
300–399	832.6	381.1	45.8	451.5	54.2
400–499	673.9	249.8	37.1	424.1	62.9
500–1,000	2,175.7	473.1	21.7	1,702.6	78.3
1,001–2,000	1,876.3	138.8	7.4	1,737.5	92.6
2,001–3,000	913.8	19.2	2.1	894.6	97.9
3,001–4,000	461.1	....	...	461.1	100.0
	10,563.4	3,837.8	36.3	6,725.6	63.7

[a] See note on p. 473.

We have, therefore, a rural organization which fundamentally differs from the one we know in the United States. Instead of the individual family Mexico has a small group predominating as the rural population unit. But this community is not large enough in the majority of cases to provide the basis for effective social or co-operative action. It is composed of groups of inhabitants that in the majority of cases consist of from 10, 20, 30, 40 up to 100 people, including men, women and children. These communities are isolated, scattered, far apart, hidden in gulleys set against mountain sides, or located upon semi-desert plains near springs or streams and secluded from the rest of the world. The inter-connecting roads are mainly mule paths that wind their broken way over mountain and valley and are impassable in the rainy season. This isolation of the rural community, made more effective by sharp differences in climate and temperature, and complicated by the racial, cultural, and linguistic barriers, has made it possible for the Mexican rural community to remain almost completely indifferent to changes in other parts of the world. We can now turn to a discussion of the economic basis of these two types of rural communities in Mexico—the village and the hacienda.

CHAPTER III

THE ORGANIZATION OF THE FREE VILLAGE

Having presented a statistical picture of the two great groups of the Mexican rural population, those found in free rural villages and those located on the haciendas, we may now proceed to a more intimate examination of their economic and social organization. The present chapter will deal with the free rural villages, and the one which follows will discuss the organization of the hacienda. Racial and cultural variations are so wide [1] that we must content ourselves with a general outline presenting those outstanding features which are more or less common even in a country made up of "a series of layers composed of materials that do not mix, a compound of races that have not yet been thoroughly combined." [2]

[1] Anyone who wishes to see the number of factors shaping the destinies and structure of the Mexican rural community may turn to Manuel Gamio's *La Problación del Valle de Teotihuacán*, Mexico, 1922. This monumental work is the most comprehensive study of any one region in Mexico that is available in print, and is invaluable as a basis for understanding the population in Central Mexico. For a picture of the more primitive tribes, a good book to turn to is Lumholtz, *Unknown Mexico*, 1910, 2 vols.

[2] *Aspects of Mexican Civilization*, 1927, pp. 3-5.

"The indigenous race of Veracruz is represented by 259,085

Every village has its own traditional forms of internal administration, its own customs as to rights to land, to tillage, to pasture. The means of livelihood and the importance of certain crops vary from village to village, depending upon the climate, the altitude, the soil, habits of migration, distribution of the work between the sexes, and the availability of other means of subsistence, such as commercial or industrial facilities, nearby haciendas, or exceptional raw materials. A thousand different cultural and economic threads weave a varying pattern for the economic and social life for each community. We must content ourselves with noting certain leading types, giving examples of those which seem to be more dominant, sketching the picture in outline and leaving out the details, because of the unavailability of statistical material. Where we do have some figures, these are but samples, partial and incomplete, gathered under diverse conditions for varying purposes. But we use them because no others are available, and because they do seem to illuminate the discussion.

inhabitants. They belong to the following races: Mexican, Totonaca, Huasteca, Otomi, Popoloca, Tepehuana, Zapoteca, Maya, Chinanteca, Tarasco, Mazateca, and Mixteca." *Comercio Interior y Exterior Agricultura e Industrias,* Mexico, April, 1888, No. 34, p. 53.

The present estimate is that in 1921 there were 47 different languages still spoken in Mexico by 1,968,357, or 13.8 per cent, of the total population. (*Some Mexican Problems,* 1927, Map, p. 55.) Professor Starr notes that there were 150 languages in Mexico at the time of the conquest. *The Mexican People in Mexico and the Caribbean,* edited by Blakeslee, 1920, pp. 17-18.

The free Mexican population inhabits two distinct types of community—the scattered and the congregated. In origin these types go back to the Spanish conquest and to the problems which the conquerors had to meet.[3] The Spaniards, broadly speaking, found two distinct population groupings in Mexico —the sedentary agricultural populations located upon the upper plateau, organized into definite villages with an age-old agricultural system, and migratory Indian tribes. The first were comparatively easily conquered, and when beaten in battle accepted the new masters, continuing their stagnant agricultural life with such changes in land holding, crops, tools, and methods of cultivation as were introduced by the Spaniards. They are still largely to be found where the Spaniards first came upon them, and are still following the ancient agricultural technique. The other part of the Indian population could not be so easily conquered; some, like the Apaches and Pimas, have practically disappeared,[4] others have never been conquered. They escaped their early Spanish pursuers by receding [5] into the

[3] Andrés Molina Enríquez, *Los Grandes Problemas Nacionales,* Mexico, 1909, p. 29.

[4] "There are probably not more than sixty Pima families within the state of Chihuahua, unless there are more than I think near Dolores." Lumholtz, *Unknown Mexico,* 1902, Vol. I, p. 128.

[5] "The indigenous tribes are scattered over the Sierra Madre Occidental . . . all of these tribes inhabited the lower plateaus before the Spanish conquests. . . . Because of the invasion they withdrew to the crags of the Sierra, where to this date they live a life of deplorable misery and backwardness . . . some of these Indians proved rebellious and hostile for 300 years, committing

mountain fastness where they still carry on their old organization with such slight modification as four hundred years of persistent border contacts with the whites have brought about.[6] With the increase of stability and the spread of white influences some of these Indian groups have gone farther and farther up into the almost inaccessible mountains, occasionally to descend from their native haunts to work or trade or fight and again retreat.[7]

cruelties in all the villages of Chihuahua, until the Government succeeded in exterminating the greater part of them." *Descripción de la Sierra Madre Occidental que en Chihuaha se encuentra habitada por la raza indigena y Algunos Datos con relación a la civilización de la misma.* (Manuscript.)

[6] An educational missionary speaking of the Kikapus in Nacimiento, Coahuila, says: "It is pre-Cortizan America. They are a proud race and have conserved 95 per cent of their costumes, ideas, religion, government, hatred of the white man and spirit of warfare which they now take out in hunting. They feel that their race is being daily more reduced—they use bows and arrows —look upon schooling as a means to learn evil." *Edu. Pub. Exp.* No. 12-3-4-61. (Manuscript.)

[7] Sonora. "From Dumuripa towards the south there are lands well adapted for the cultivation of cotton, sugar cane and other useful plants, but these lands are in the territory occupied by the Yaqui Indians who denying obedience to the Government maintain a state of affairs which is painful to anyone who sees it at close range. Not only have they this great extent of land unproductive but they carry themselves towards the rest of the inhabitants of the state as a conquering nation imposing conditions on the conquered ones. They pass the Yaqui River to sell their sparse products in the markets of the civilized villages, but the punishment for being found on their side of the river is generally death, or at least, which is rare, being compelled to leave all one's possessions." *Ministerio de Fomento, Memoria,* Mexico, 1883-1885, pp. 416-17.

Nayarit. "The Huichol's self-esteem is equal to anyone's. Never for a moment will a Huichol allow that any other race may be superior to his. Even when far away from home, among

To these two original types of communities the Spaniards added others. In their attempts to convert and to control the Indian population they succeeded in bringing some of the more tractable migratory Indians into villages and definitely congregating them under immediate control of the Spanish soldiers and within the sphere of the church.[8] Still another source for the congregated community has been the development of population centers within the radius of mines where the Indians were originally forced to work and where they have gradually acquired the position and character of free workers, making mining and commercial communities either about the mines or on the roads leading to them. We thus have free communities that lie scattered in the mountains or deep in the tropical forests as far removed from white control as the conditions still permit, and congregated communities that had their origin previous to the Spanish conquest or arose from the political and economic activity of the conquerors. These communities, it must be repeated, differ widely amongst themselves, and we can only in broad outline suggest their different types.

the whites, the Huichols bear themselves as if they had never known masters." Lumholtz, *Unknown Mexico*, 1902, Vol. II, p. 24.

Guerrero. "To the north of the village of El Pueblo de Acapetlahuaya there is an intricate sierra of native villages alien to civilization that reach to the limits of the states of Guerrero and Mexico. This zone reaches up to Tlatlaya, Zacualpán, Anahuistlán and in times of revolution they are fearful bandits." *Edu. Pub. Exp.* 1925, 12-3-7-6. (Manuscript.)

[8] *Aspects of Mexican Civilization*, p. 116.

The scattered Indian community is found mainly in the highest mountain ranges of Mexico or in the very deepest tropical forests. One can begin with the Northern states of Sonora or Chihuahua and follow the upper mountain crests from the United States to the border of Guatemala and almost always keep in touch with an Indian community. One can find these Indian communities scattered in the mountain peaks of Central Mexico: Hidalgo, Puebla, Mexico; in the state of Veracruz, in the forests of Tabasco and Chiapas and in practically the whole of the territory of Quintana Roo.[9] They differ in language, in culture, in race, in methods of making their living from the soil; they may be hunters or agriculturists,[10] or fishermen,[11] or combine

[9] "The governor of the Territory of Quintana Roo is only so in name. The Maya Indians possess the region and only obey their *caciques.* We are concerned with an important part of Mexico which it is necessary to reconquer (such is the word). . . ." Editorial, *Excelsior,* May 17, 1927; *ibid.,* May 26, 1927.

[10] "The general custom among the Tarahumaras in Chihuahua living near to a *barranca* is to plant two crops of corn; one in early March on the crest, and the other one in June, at the beginning of the rainy season, down in the *barranca,* and after having harvested at both places they retire to their winter quarters to enjoy themselves." Lumholtz, *Unknown Mexico,* Vol. I, pp. 162-163.

"The wealth of the Tarahumare consists in his cattle. He is well off when he has three or four head of cattle and a dozen sheep and goats. There is one instance where a man had as many as forty head of cattle, but this was a rare exception. They rarely keep horses, and never pigs, which destroy their corn-fields; and are believed, besides, to be Spaniards (*Gachupines*)." *ibid.,* p. 186.

[11] "They (the Cora Indians) plant maize just once a year, following the rude system which notoriously prejudices the vegetation. They cut down the mountain forest during the

all three pursuits. They come down from their
mountain peaks and go to work on the haciendas
for short periods,[12] or they come upon occasion to
the regular markets in the larger villages located
on the plateaus; they may weave blankets, or make
mats; they may, as the Tharsumaris do, go to work
in the mountain forests as woodcutters.[13]   They

winter and in the spring burn the wood, sowing with the first
rains what they call *cohamiles*. They do not occupy themselves with work after that but pass their time in celebrating
feasts and in banquets and orgies and have for their main object
and distraction dancing with their idols." *Edu. Púb*. Nayarit,
1922, *Exp*. 601, pp. 3-7. (Manuscript.)

[12] "In the Sierra de Alica of Nayarit there are found Huicholes
who to the number of about 5,000 form a nomadic tribe that live
in scattered and most difficult places to reach. Frequently they
are encountered practically naked and feed themselves by hunting
and fishing." *Edu. Pub. Exp*. 601, Nayarit, 1922, pp. 3-7.
(Manuscript.)

"The Chamula Indians of Chiapas are essentially hard workers
and devoted to agriculture, having little pieces of land upon
which they plant maize and a few vegetables. Their instruments are the pick and a pointed stick which they use in depositing their few grains. There are Chamulas that have two or three
beasts of burden which they esteem greatly. These beasts help
them carry the burdens because they make a portion of their
income by serving as the *cargadores* for many of the large cities
of Chiapas." *Edu. Pub. Exp*. 146, Class. 21, 1-7-126. (Manuscript.) This observation can be testified to by the author as he
visited the Chamula Indians in 1926.

"These five villages are composed in a great majority of
instances of Indians who speak their native tongue and who can
neither read nor write. They live scattered in the most broken
parts of the Sierra of Zacualtipense, cultivating tiny pieces of
land. They are both uncultivated and apathetic." *Edu. Pub*.
Hidalgo, 1922, Exp. 330, p. 1. (Manuscript.)

[13] In 1922 the author saw practically naked Tarahumaras wielding axes as woodcutters for an American concern in the mountains to the northwest of Parral, Chihuahua.

may, as do the Yaquis in Sonora, go into the mines,[14] but they always return to the mountains where they carry on their native life. They shun a white man,[15] and even a mestizo.[16] They speak their own language,[17] sing their own songs, and preserve their own religion which is but a very poor mixture of Catholicism and native idolatry, or sometimes, as among the Kikapus in Coahuila,[18] the Lacandones in Chiapas,[19] no mixture at all.

[14] "The Yaqui and Maya Indians are depended upon mostly for labor all through the state. They possess remarkable natural abilities, learn the trades of blacksmithing, carpentering, etc. They are known to manufacture fireworks, are skillful players on the harp and violin. Their character is resolute and very jealous of their lands. . . . They have been known to revolt . . . and commit great atrocities . . . and to fight steadily for hours against the government troops. They shun the society of the whites, and only live near them for the sake of employment." Hamilton, Leonidas, *Border States of Mexico*, 1882, 3rd edition, p. 44.

[15] Chiapas. "No *ladinos* (their name for a white man) has been permitted to acquire a plot among them, not even to travel and visit to any extent." *Edu. Pub. Exp.* Class. 12-1-7-126. (Manuscript.)

[16] "The Huicholes in Nayarit and Jalisco have a profound hatred of the mestizo." *Edu. Pub. Exp.* No. 12-3-8-41. (Manuscript.)

[17] "Not 2 per cent of the 15,000 Indians more or less who inhabit the Sierra of the State of Nayarit speak Spanish." *Edu. Pub. Exp.* 601, Nayarit, 1922, pp. 3-7. (Manuscript.)

[18] "The Catholic Church has for a long time undertaken to convert them to Christianity without succeeding because they believe in their own gods and have their own rites directed by their own priests." *Edu. Pub. Exp.* No. 12-3-4-61. (Manuscript.)

[19] "These have never been reduced or tamed, live scattered in the tropical forests of Chiapas near the Usumacinta River." *Edu. Pub. Exp.* 1469, Class. 12-1-7-126. The author visited the Lacandones in the forests of Chiapas in 1926 and found them quite untouched by Christian influence.

Their exact number is not known,[20] they pay little or no taxes, have their own holidays, their own justice and their own codes.[21] The government has little and sometimes no control over them and in many of these Indian communities the white man has never been allowed to acquire a definite place. The Yaquis of Sonora, the Indians of the upper regions of Puebla, of Oaxaco, Guerrero, of the Sierra of Nayarit, the Chamulas in Chiapas, have succeeded in keeping themselves isolated from too much scrutiny by the white man. Even the present government with its attempts to build schools among the native population has found great difficulty in over-

[20] "After about ten days' work at counting, the Mexicans went away, and the commotion subsided. The officials averred that a record had been made of all the inhabitants, with the exception of about 200, whom neither persuasion nor threat could induce to report at San Andrés." Lumholtz, *Unknown Mexico,* 1902, Vol. II, p. 100.

"It has never been possible to find the exact number of Chamulas because it is difficult to make an exact counting of them. A white secretary of an Indian village presented a list of 400. He was told that for so small a number it would be impossible to establish a school. A few days later he presented a list of 4,000. The difficulty with the Chamulas is that they live scattered in all the mountains. The villages are only the places where there is a church and the office of the political administration with two or three more houses. These are surrounded by innumerable Indian communities but always scattered over a great area, and he who wants to make a census of them has to travel the whole mountainside and to do that he would have to be accompanied by some native authority so as not to be attacked because the Indians know that when they are counted it is for the purpose of molesting them and they manage to hide." *Edu. Pub. Exp.*, 1469, Class. 12-1-7-126. (Manuscript.)

[21] Lumholtz, Vol. I, pp. 139-140.

coming the suspicion and the hostility of the Indians.[22] The Indians of these communities are generally scattered on little individual plots, living on little ranchos,[23] sometimes of just a few hectares, sometimes of great area [24] because of the sparsity of

[22] "It has been a real problem to undertake the education of the Indian races because they have always been recalcitrant towards civilization, fearing to lose their traditions and customs. The great majority repudiate all that which' they derive from the white race." *Descripcion de la Sierra Madre Occidental.* (Manuscript.)

[23] "Only during feast days were they seen to occupy the houses which they possess in the principal towns founded by them, such as Jesús Maria, Mesa del Mayar, Dolores, Santa Teresa and San Francisco. After the days of festivity they leave and remount the most inaccessible peaks, leaving the villages uninhabited." *Educ. Pub. Exp.* 601, pp. 3 and 7. (Manuscript.)

"In some of the towns the families live from January to May and only inhabit their ranchos from June to December and also at times of public occasion when the native authority calls them to deliberate upon some problem of government. Then they gather to resolve by unanimous assent, what seems best for the community." *Edu. Pub. Exp.* 581, pp. 162 and 164. (Manuscript.)

[24] "The Indians of the coast that live in the villages under the jurisdiction of the Municipios of Purificación and Cihuatlán are the owners in common of large extensions of land fit for cultivation but due to the low culture of these Indians all of these large extensions of land remain uncultivated. If they do cultivate the land it is in the form of little parcels called *caumiles* where they plant some maize. In some places as in Jirosto these *cuamiles* are in the folds of the mountains and have the form of a square having a parcel some 25 meters each. As they do not work the greater part of the year for them most of the time is one of 'sweet idleness.' They travel about half naked with their hair long and the skin very dark due to the absolute lack of cleanliness. The men, just as the women, from their waist up do not wear anything to cover their nakedness. The children are completely naked." *Edu. Pub.,* 1922, Jalisco, *Exp.* 369, pp. 76-78. (Manuscript.)

the population and the inaccessibility of the region, but they almost never congregate in large communities.[25]

The different tribal groups have, as a rule, a specific place of meeting, where the Indians gather during the year for some religious holiday or for political purposes. It is there that one will find a few houses, a church if they are "Christians," and today perhaps a school, and occasionally a white secretary, who by speaking both languages acts as a link with the larger government. But the place is, properly speaking, not a community at all. It is merely the center of government where the elected officials live for the brief period of their tenure and give way to the new officials who may be elected and who in turn occupy the houses and till the soil that has been set aside for those occupying the position of governors during the year. The Indians live scattered in the mountains for many miles around. They live upon their little patches of ground, and go off to work to help eke out the yearly income. If their land will support them they will descend into the lower regions so as to earn some cash to be spent for the holidays, —mainly for *aguardiente*—for sugar, for salt, for an occasional dress, if they do not make these them-

[25] "Indian pueblos throughout Mexico are almost abandoned for the greater part of the year. I refer, of course, only to those which have not yet become Mexican settlements. . . . Only the native-chosen authorities, who are obliged to reside there during their term of office, form something like a permanent population in the pueblos. The natives come together only on the occasion of feasts, and on Sundays, to worship in the way they understand it." Lumholtz, *Unknown Mexico*, Vol. I, pp. 136-138.

selves. These Indians, making up what we have
called the "scattered communities," are not only the
most primitive of the Mexican people but also the
least numerous. While their exact number is not
known, they constitute but a fraction of the Mexican population and occupy what is generally described as *tierras nacionales*. It would perhaps be
more accurate to classify the lands occupied by these
Indian groups as tribal lands, as their rights would
seem certain to be protected under present legislation. This part of the rural population, occupying
national lands, represents one extreme of the Mexican rural community. The peons located upon the
haciendas represent the other extreme. Between
these two is the free village community.

*Free village communities of the congregate type
comprise more than half the total rural population,
but own much less than half of the privately-held
lands of Mexico*. We have already seen that in 1910
the free villages contained 51 per cent of the total
rural population. Unfortunately there are no adequate statistics of the area held by villages. However, if we examine the figures for size distribution
of rural land holdings and correlate them with the
population occupying free villages, we can get an
approximate picture of the basis of landholding upon
which the free village community is built.

Mexico had, at the last land census, 622,213 [26] individual pieces of rural property. These properties,

[26] For general table and for method of securing figures, see
Appendix C.

constituting the "producing units" of Mexican agriculture, were distributed as follows: [27]

Size (In hectares)	Number	As percentage of all properties
Less than 1	151,264	24.3
1 to 5	216,152	34.7
6 to 10	65,958	10.6
11 to 50	109,936	17.7
51 to 100	25,197	4.1
All properties under 100 hectares ...	568,507	91.4
101 to 200	17,720	2.8
201 to 500	15,722	2.5
501 to 1,000	7,482	1.2
All properties 100 to 1,000 hectares ..	40,924	6.5
1,001 to 5,000	9,506	1.5
5,001 to 10,000	1,678	0.3
More than 10,000	1,598	0.3
All properties over 1,000 hectares	12,782	2.1

Mexico thus had nearly one-fourth of all its rural properties in units of less than 1 hectare,[28] nearly 60 per cent in units of less than 5 hectares, and nearly 90 per cent in units of less than 50 hectares. In eight states more than 90 per cent of all pieces of property are under 50 hectares each.

Practically all of the parcels of 1,000 hectares and more represent hacienda properties, whereas the village holding is typically less than 10 hectares, and in practically no case exceeds 100 hectares. This

[27] *Anuario Estadístico,* 1923, pp. 107-108, Appendix C.
[28] One hectare equals 2.47 acres.

makes it clear that the large number of small holdings representative of village land ownership could
not make up as much as one-half of the privately-
owned rural land of Mexico. The 609,431 properties of less than 1,000 hectares listed in the table on
page 54 constitute approximately 98 per cent of the
individual property holdings in Mexico, but comprise an area less than that of the 12,782 properties
of 1,000 hectares and over.

If we now examine the distribution of the villages
and compare them with the percentage distribution
of the parcels of less than 10 hectares in the different
states we get a further insight into the structure of
the rural community.

We can see from the table on page 56 that in
Oaxaca, where approximately 85 per cent of the total
rural population was located off the haciendas and
ranchos, 67 per cent of the communities in the state
were free villages, 72 per cent of all pieces of property were of 10 hectares each or less, and only 10.7
per cent of the area of the state was held in sections
of more than 5,000 hectares. If in contrast we take
a state like Coahuila, where only 30 per cent of the
population is to be found off the hacienda, only 12
per cent of the villages are free, only 16 per cent of
the pieces of property are under 10 hectares each,
and 90.7 per cent of the total area of the state is
held in parcels of over 5,000 hectares each. Many
factors enter into determining these combinations
and the correlation is not always as simple as the

DISTRIBUTION OF RURAL POPULATION AND LAND BETWEEN FREE
VILLAGES AND HACIENDAS *

State	Percentage of Rural Population in Free Villages (1910)	Free Villages as a Percentage of All Rural Communities (1921)	Rural Properties Under 10 Hectares as Percentage of All Rural Properties (1923)	Area of Properties of 5,000 Hectares or Over as Percentage of All Privately Held Lands (1923)
Oaxaca............	84.9	56.9	72.4	10.7
México............	82.1	62.6	88.9	20.5
Hidalgo...........	78.2	62.3	92.2	10.8
Puebla............	77.2	66.5	86.9	3.5
Veracruz..........	75.8	64.0	57.9	28.4
Morelos...........	74.1	87.7	95.3	....
Tabasco...........	67.7	12.2	35.9	19.2
Tlaxcala..........	65.0	41.5	55.1	9.8
Sonora............	54.4	29.2	42.1	41.7
Yucatán...........	54.0	24.7	41.7	30.0
Baja California....	52.0	18.6	16.3	77.7
Guerrero..........	49.8	60.7	49.7	10.7
Campeche.........	49.4	22.1	24.1	81.7
Michoacán a......	39.4	6.7	82.8	15.9
Colima............	39.1	24.0	12.7	69.0
Nuevo León.......	37.3	10.4	59.2	29.5
Chiapas...........	36.2	18.3	52.8	19.9
Nayarit...........	34.7	9.3	56.9	75.8
Aguascalientes a...	33.6	16.3	68.3	44.9
Jalisco a..........	33.4	7.9	76.6	16.9
Chihuahua........	33.0	26.4	35.2	86.5
Querétaro a.......	33.0	11.7	80.0	32.0
Coahuila..........	30.4	12.5	18.8	88.1
Durango..........	29.5	22.7	51.0	74.5
Sinaloa...........	26.4	8.8	37.5	30.9
Tamaulipas.......	23.2	5.5	22.6	46.8
Zacatecas.........	21.1	5.7	19.3	93.4
San Luís Potosí....	17.8	12.6	28.0	71.2
Guanajuato a......	13.3	5.1	59.6	25.1

* The data used in columns 2, 3 and 4 are not available for 1910, but it is
clear that if the detailed figures were available they would only tend to
sharpen the relationship here indicated.
a The five states of Michoacán, Aguascalientes, Jalisco, Querétaro, and
Guanajuato, in which there are a comparatively small number of free villages
and free inhabitants but a large number of small-sized properties, are all
located in what is the best developed agricultural section of Mexico. They are
the states in which the "rancho" has taken firmest root and therefore combine
a heavy proportion of the population in resident communities and a small
percentage of the total area of the state in large holdings.

discussion above might seem to imply. But as a general rule, the states having a preponderant portion of their area in haciendas have the greater part of their rural population located upon them with few independent villages and with a small proportion of properties under 10 hectares, while the states where the haciendas embrace a comparatively small area tend to have a large proportion of the population living in free villages, to have villages of considerably greater size, and to have a considerable proportion of all individual pieces of property in the state under 10 hectares each.

Generally speaking, the free rural villages have insufficient lands. This broad generalization seems to be the inevitable conclusion from any survey of the Mexican rural community. The study of Gamio in the Valley of Teotihuacán,[29] some 30 miles from Mexico City and in a rich agricultural region of Central Mexico, is illustrative of the general conditions. The Valley has 10,500 hectares of land and 8,339 inhabitants. It contains 22 villages. Seven haciendas occupy 9,450 hectares or approximately 90 per cent of the land in the valley, while 416 individuals scattered in the 22 villages own 1,050 hectares. There are 7,097 individuals who are without any lands at all.[30] These villages, it must be remembered, repre-

---

[29] Gamio, *La Población del Valle de Teotihuacán, Secretaría de Agricultura y Fomento, Dirección de Antropolgía,* Mexico, 1922, 3 vols. in 2.

[30] *ibid.,* Vol. I, Intro., p. xiv.

sent either the old habitations of the conquered
Indian races that remained where they were
found by the Spaniards or the communities into
which "the more submissive ones were gathered
. . . preserving as far as possible their traditional
and picturesque city arrangements with irregular
streets, their houses standing alone in a garden or vegetable patch. . . . " [31] The author should
have added that they have frequently no lands beyond those that make up their little garden patches.
"Between 1896 and 1906 the small rural properties
had increased from 89,724 to 139,804, and of the
last, 93,893 had a fiscal value of less than 50 pesos
each. They were of half a hectare or less and were
destined for the production of the indispensable
products for physical needs." [32] These properties
are so small that in some cases one can only plant 10
litres of maize in them,[33] or they are so small that
an individual owner may only plant from six to ten
orange trees upon his property.[34] In one village in
Puebla [35] one owner is reported owning 17 individual
parcels of land, the total value of all the pieces being
312 pesos, or an average of 18.3 pesos each. We can

[31] Gamio, *Aspects of Mexican Civilization,* p. 116.

[32] Puest, Otto, *La Agricultura Pequeña de Familias y El Crédito
Hipotecario,* in *Boletin de la Dirección General de Agricultura,*
Part II, p. 502, No. 6, Mexico, 1911.

[33] Municipio of Tuzamapan in reply to *Oficio* No. 145, Aug. 6,
1926. (Manuscript.)

[34] *Agránomo Regional Zona 13,* Aguascalientes, Oct., 1925,
Mun. de Cavillo. (Manuscript.)

[35] *Mun. de Coronanco.* (Manuscript.)

further illustrate this point by the figures for 69 villages in four different states.

AVERAGE SIZE OF LANDHOLDINGS IN 69 VILLAGES *

State	Villages Reporting	Villages Classified by Average Size of Holdings in Hectares								
		Under 1	1 to 2	2 to 3	3 to 4	4 to 5	5 to 10	10 to 25	25 to 50	50 to 100
Chihuahua	6	..	..	..	1	..	..	..	2	3
Durango..	18	..	1	5	2	5	5	..	..	..
Oaxaca...	31	15	2	2	2	2	5	3	..	..
Puebla....	14	4	4	1	1	..	1	2	..	1

* Compiled from replies to letters sent out by the *Oficina Investigadora Agrícola* during 1926. Manuscript copies.

Of the sixty-nine villages for which information was secured the average holding was of less than 1 hectare in nineteen villages; of less than 2 hectares in seven villages; of less than 3 hectares in eight villages; of less than 4 hectares in six villages. In other words, more than 50 per cent of the villages reporting had on the average less than 4 hectares per inhabitant owning land.

Ownership of land is unevenly distributed among the village inhabitants. This is especially true of these villages that have lost their communal character. Among those there have developed landowners and landless proprietors and laborers, some inhabitants owning a number of properties and others owning none.

We have already seen that the total number of inhabitants in the rural village is 12.9 times greater than the total number of landowners in the Republic

of Mexico. We will now glance at the picture in a
little more detail. Gamio points out that only 416
people scattered in 22 villages had land in the Valley
of Teotihuacán and that over 7,000 people were landless. This may be an extreme picture and we can
not set the figures right for each village for the whole
Republic. We can further detail this story by quoting a few typical reports of educational missionaries, regional agronomists, and letters from local officials describing conditions between 1922 and 1926.

One educational missionary from Guerrero reports
that "many of these villages have no lands. They
pay rent for the miserable existence which they
lead." [36] "Some of the inhabitants cultivate tiny
pieces of land and others live from their wages.
Properly speaking, this village has no lands. The
large areas that exist belong to a few owners of the
neighborhood." [37] "This village is composed of Indians who speak a pure native tongue although there
are a few who can read and write Spanish. This
village is notoriously poor. The greater part of its
inhabitants dedicate themselves to wage work although a few cultivate tiny fractions of land." [38]

*The lands held by the villages tend to be the
poorer lands.* The haciendas have pre-empted the
valleys, and the villages have receded into the mountains. This in part was a natural result of the development of the large estates. Generally speaking,

[36] *Edu. Púb.* Guerrero, 1922 *Exp.* 150, pp. 33-34. (Manuscript.)
[37] *ibid.,* Hidalgo, 1922, Exp. 347, p. 1.
[38] *ibid.,* Hidalgo, Exp. 337, 1922, p. 5.

therefore, it has meant the village has been compelled to content itself with the least desirable lands.[39] Where not located in mountain pockets and permitted to continue residing on the plains, the villages have been crowded onto the poorer lands. The irrigated or irrigable lands have generally been absorbed by the haciendas, even the better class of non-irrigable lands (temporal) usually belonging to the large estates. On the plains the villages have not only been crowded into the worst lands, but have been confined within very narrow limits.

The villages tend to be confined within the boundaries of the haciendas and therefore to be dominated by them. The villages, especially of the central plateau, are bounded by or located within the very limits of haciendas. To such an extent is this the case that in some parts of Mexico the haciendas begin just outside the very streets of the villages. "Generally the inhabitants of the State of Morelos are up in arms because the villages have absolutely not a single piece of land. In the village of Jonacatepec the hacienda of Santa Clara begins eight meters from the last street so that the unhappy Indians prefer to live in the mountains. They are scattered even in the most broken mountain tops or in the forests where they may find a piece of land." [40] In some of the villages the inhabitants could not keep an ass or a goat because the gates of

[39] Molina Enríquez, p. 81.
[40] *Diario de los Debates Del Congreso Constituyente,* Vol. II, p. 444.

the haciendas closed in the streets.[41] In the state of Hidalgo for example, the hacienda of San José el Zoquital had 36,294 hectares and either surrounded or bounded 10 villages. The hacienda of Tlahuelilpa Ulapa y Anexos had 31,926 hectares and had 22 villages within its confines while the hacienda of San Antonio y Anexas y el Marquez had 27,000 hectares and dominated 17 villages.[42] This physical dominance led to a political and social control of the villages. Two of Mexico's most distinguished students of the agrarian problem note that: "When an hacienda did not cover a complete municipio (county) or more than one, there were two or three that covered it and in consequence the *Jefes Políticos,* the *Presidentes Municipales,* and the *Ayuntamientos* were as subject to the large landholders as were the authorities of even the smallest villages."[43] Most of the examples we have cited record a story of the days before the revolution, but as we shall see, land distribution is but little changed. The picture drawn by Gamio of the Valley of Teotihuacán was for 1922 and not for 1910.

One could go on like this indefinitely. But we have probably said enough to make the point that either the villages have no lands or insufficient lands, or they have the poorest lands, and that, broadly speaking, the free rural villages have to depend

[41] Roa, *Las cuestiónes Fundamentales de Actualidad en México,* p. 166.

[42] *El Problema Agrario en el Estado de Hidalgo,* 1926, p. 38.

[43] Roa and Covarrubias, *El Problema Rural de México,* p. 63.

upon the hacienda for access to tillable soil for their means of existence either as renters, croppers, or workers. The free village exists but its economic life is dominated by the haciendas. That is true as a general statement though it must always be remembered that some Indian groups such as we have described under the term "scattered community," are free from domination by the large estates and also that a number of congregated communities have an abundance of land for their needs, more than they can or do utilize. These groups, however, are clearly in the minority. An example is the municipio of San Pedro Mixtepec. "The municipio possesses over 20,000 hectares of very fertile lands which, except for a cultivated area of not over 500 hectares and another portion of grazing land of not more than 100 hectares, remains uncultivated." [44]

Confinement and poverty have in certain sections given rise to conflicts between villages that have lasted for generations. These conflicts arise over the use of both land and water. Space will permit only a few examples: "The lands of this community which from time immemorial have been owned by this municipality are 2,000 hectares of tillable and 6,000 hectares of mountain land of which it was robbed by the village of San Juan Azompa during the years 1873, 1874, and 1879. For this reason we are now trying to reclaim them through the National Agra-

[44] *Zona 33*, Oaxaca, July, 1923, *Municipio S. Pedro Mixtepec.* (Manuscript.)

rian Commission." [45]   "The waters of the River
Alseseca are in dispute among 7 villages not counting
Cholula." [46]   The governor of the State of Guerrero
reports that through his mediation five villages have
settled their disputes over lands, and continues,
"Through my mediation, calm has been established
between the inhabitants of Temaxcalapa and Teu-
cizapón who for 47 years have carried on a struggle
over some land that had led to the loss of a considerable number of lives and much property." [47]   Such
reports could be duplicated from many other sections. We are now in a position to move on to a
consideration of the different systems of land tenure
that are to be found within the villages themselves.

*The complex system of land tenure that exists
among the villages ranges from communism to individualism.*   Here we enter into a cultural problem
that has its origin in the racial traditions of the different groups existing in Mexico. We are obviously
not in a position to describe these systems in detail.
But for an understanding of contemporary Mexico
and the problems that it presents it is essential to see
that such systems of land tenure do exist and they
help shape the very nature of the agricultural and
the agrarian organization of Mexico.

[45] *Presidente Municipal de Huatlatlanca*, July 27, 1926, in
reply to *Oficio* no. 145. (Manuscript.)
[46] *Agrónomo Regional, Zona 28*, Puebla, *Mun. de Cholula*,
August, 1923. (Manuscript.)
[47] *Periódico Ofical del Gobierno del Estado de Guerrero, Año.*
IX, *Num. 36, Chilpancingo*, Sept. 4, 1926, p. 2.

The Indians in Mexico have since the conquest striven to preserve their communal lands and where they have succeeded they show the greatest fear and jealousy of all outsiders and strive to prevent strangers from acquiring permanent land rights with the community.[48]

"It is dangerous to travel through the forest because the Indians consider it as their only patrimony and fear that strangers will take possession of it and leave them in complete misery." [49] Where they have preserved their lands the system of actual possession and tillage tends to vary in almost every community. We are told that "every little property has two or three owners." [50] But ownership does not necessarily involve title. "The lands in general belong to the community. Of the 888 people having

[48] "Zacatepec is a community of 1,500 inhabitants of almost pure Mixteca Indians who speak their native tongue and among whom very few speak Spanish. They refuse as far as possible to have any dealings with the Mestizos. They live under a system of absolute communal property and the whites and Mestizos are received with all caution and lack of confidence. Outsiders may be permitted to construct houses without that implying that they become owners of the land on which they construct the house for any longer time than they themselves inhabit it. They can never sell or pass this land and when they leave it is returned to the village. Only the pure Indians are allowed to plant perennial crops, such as fruits, or sugar cane, or cocoa, or bananas; but the strangers, that is, the whites and Mestizos, are only conceded permission to plant a crop that takes one year, such as maize, cotton, or rice." *Zona 33, Oaxaca,* September, 1923, *Mun. de Zacatepec.* (Manuscript.)

[49] *Edu. Púb.,* Puebla, *Exp.* 979, p. 2. (Manuscript.)

[50] *Presidente Municipal of Huetamalco,* Aug. 11, 1926, in reply to *Oficio* No. 145. (Manuscript.)

rights in the land 619 possess no titles of property." [51]   Or use is secured by doing certain required work for the community, such as the local communities require.   "Because of the existence of this forest it is easy to secure wood (for a school) at a relatively low price or even free by means of *faenas* or unpaid labor ordered and directed by the local authorities. The Indians do not resist, for even the women participate without showing indignation." [52]   "Or the lands are communal and any individual has a right to plant where he finds it convenient without any obligation of payment of any rental except that of serving the community in those collective works in which all citizens participate, the repairing of roads or the streets of the village, the municipal building, the school, or the prison.   They prorate all the expenses of the village community among all the members." [53]   "We have 1300 hectares of second class non-irrigated lands and 600 hectares of mountain land to which there are 585 proprietors with rights to the land among men, women, widows, and orphans —all in equal parts in proportion to the possibilities of each." [54]   In many villages there is the form of electing a guardian of lands.   "From time immemorial it has been the custom among the Indian villages of the Republic annually to name a *guardia*

[51] *Municipio of Huehuetla,* Puebla, July 19, 1926.   (Manuscript.)

[52] E. P. Puebla, 1922, *Exp.* 979, p. 2.   (Manuscript.)

[53] *Agrónomo Regional, Zona 33,* Oaxaca, July, 1923, *Num. S. Pedro Mixtepec.*   (Manuscript.)

[54] Puebla, *Municipio de Ocotepec Presidente Municipal* in reply to *Oficio* No. 145, April 15, 1926.   (Manuscript.)

detierras to distribute among the cultivators a parcel of land which that individual is to cultivate during that year." [55]

In many villages, especially in such states as Mexico, the lands are held by a *cacique* in whose hands the titles were deposited by the Indians when they were compelled to accept individual deeds to their lands under the Diaz regime, but after depositing their titles and forming a sort of anonymous cooperative they continued their old communal system of land holding." [56] Or the lands which belong to the village or to the *ayuntamiento* may be rented to the individual who works it at a stipulated price per hectare. He may even have the right to transfer the use but not the title of the land to someone else. If the land is abandoned it returns to the community. "Here the lands of the villages are to this day administered by the *ayuntamiento* of Ixcuintla which rents the lands to the neighbors who pay annually for the right to exclusive cultivation of this or that piece of land, and when one wishes to purchase a piece of land he secures from another cultivator the right which that one has to cultivate but without being able to acquire the actual ownership of the piece of land he is occupying and cultivating." [57]

In spite of the wide extent and the varied charac-

[55] *México Revolucionario,* p. 54.

[56] Manero, Antonio, *The Meaning of the Mexican Revolution,* quoting from Luis Cabrera, pp. 23-24.

[57] *Agrónomo Regional Zona,* No. 18, Nayarit *Municipio de Venado,* July, 1922. (Manuscript.)

ter of the communal village ownership of lands and waters it is probably true that they represent a minority rather than a majority of the free villages. Until the breakup of the common lands as a result of the legislation of 1857 and as a result of the activities of the Diaz regime this method of land ownership and land use was probably the predominant one. But at present it seems doubtful whether the villages of the Republic that have preserved their communal character of land administration constitute a third of the total free villages. This estimate is largely speculative and has the basis only of observation in many different parts of the Republic. Under a more common system of land tenure, found in perhaps the majority of the villages, the tillable lands are held in individual ownership, while the mountain, forest, and pasture lands are held in common. This is the form in which the lands are given by the Federal Government to villages under the recent agrarian legislation.[58] No figures can be given, but further citations from any part of the Republic would merely be a repetition *ad infinitum* of the same fact. "There are many small properties . . . worked individually and only the pasture lands are held and used in common." [59]

Another type of land ownership is one where both tillable and pasture lands are held individually by

[58] See Chapter IX.
[59] *Agrónomo Regional Zona,* 3, November, 1925, Coahuila, *Mun. de Monclova.* (Manuscript.)

the village inhabitants. But as we have already said
there is no way of telling the distribution of the type
of village land tenure that exists in Mexico by the
number of villages or even in detail by the type of
tenure which prevails in different places. These
problems are encrusted with generalizations and theories, but there are practically no extensive studies
that would answer the simple question of what proportion of villages have these different forms of land
ownership or of what the land ownership and its
varied tenure is like. It is for this reason that we
have given so much space to some contemporary
examples of prevalent types without hazarding more
than a guess as to their extent and variety.

*The large mass of the village inhabitants depend
primarily but not exclusively upon agriculture as a
means of livelihood.*[60] This is perhaps already clear
from the previous discussion but it deserves emphasis and differentiation because not all villages live
by agriculture and because the relation of the villages to the soil differs so widely. Many villages

[60] "All the men and a large part of the women from the age
of 14 years devote themselves exclusively to agriculture working
as peons in the neighboring *haciendas*. In addition, each head of
family with a very few exceptions possesses a small fraction of
land in which he cultivates maize, from which is derived the
necessary food for the year, dedicating the wages which they earn
to the periodical feasts that are organized for religious or family
purposes, while for clothing they only buy the cloth. The
cotones which they use as coats are manufactured in the family
from the wool which they themselves spin upon homemade instruments." Comaltepec, Puebla, *Edu. Pub.*, 1921, *Exp.* 982. (Manuscript.)

have a sufficiency of land and raise enough of their own products to last them the year around, and even sell some of their agricultural products in the neighboring markets. But the largest number of villages seem to have to depend upon other land in addition to their own to secure their means of subsistence for the year.[61]

In some villages the inhabitants having no lands are entirely dependent upon wage labor in the haciendas that lie below them in the valleys or that surround them.[62] Other villages tend to avoid wage labor and to practice crop-sharing or renting of the lands of the neighboring haciendas.[63] This is especially true of those villages where the inhabitants happen to have some work animals and tools. Other villagers combine work as little landowners, as

[61] "They devote themselves to agriculture, a large majority of them having a fraction of land for each family which they cultivate for their personal consumption and work as *peons* on the *haciendas* spending the cash which they earn on feasts and clothing, the clothing being very deficient because they are native women who only cover themselves from their waist to their thighs, leaving the rest of the body uncovered." Pueblo, *Edu. Pub. Exp.* Num. 12-1-5-61, 1922.

[62] "San Andrés is a village of 772 inhabitants who have no sort of industry and are all occupied as day laborers." Oaxaca, Class. 12-2-5-313, *Edu. Pub. Exp.* 1826, pp. 35-36.

[63] "The majority of these four small communities have their own burros which they use in carrying charcoal and wood from the mountains. These little communities are completely surrounded by the *hacienda* of El Saucillo, which has 35,000 hectares. They work independently, depending upon their burros or work as share croppers but not as wage workers. The villagers live in their own houses." Aguascalientes, *Comisión Nacional Agraria,* January 31, 1924, *Municipio Rincón de Ramos,* Circular 15.

renters, as croppers, as wage workers, and as small pedlers and merchants. They dedicate themselves to agriculture in part and in part to pottery,[64] mat-making, manufacture of *pulke,* acting as mule drivers [65] and the making of all sorts of toys and native arts, and generally carry these products on their backs to the markets during the local feasts in the neighboring villages or in some cases over miles of weary mountain travel of days or even weeks to sell the little things they have at an insignificant price.[66] Others having no lands and no raw materials and no skill for the development of any special craft and not having sufficient lands within their means even as wage workers, if they are fortunate enough to have a forest to exploit, give themselves over to making

[64] Santo Domingo Tonaltepec, *Edu. Pub. Exp.* No. 12-4-1-92. (Manuscript.)

[65] "Most of the inhabitants of this town live as mule carriers, that is to say, the majority of the inhabitants either own mule pack saddles or drive the animals." *Zona,* 18, *Navarit,* October, 1922, *Mun. del Rio.* (Manuscript.)

[66] "The Indians of the State of Jalisco near the lake of Chapala undertake voyages of 15 or 20 days to Michoacán where they buy a bundle of palm leaves which they call *soyate.* From this they fabricate hats which they later sell at six *centavos* apiece. Those from the State of Michoacán make trips of 20 and 30 days with loads of shingles which they carry to sell in Guadalajara at a price that does not cover half of the rent of the mules. Those from Guerrero manufacture chairs covered with *tule* and carry them 30 *leguas* upon their back to sell them in Ometepec, while those of this state in the Sierra of Tlaxiaco carry through services as if they were beasts of burden, being satisfied with 18 *centavos* a day with which they feed themselves." General Carlos Pacheco, *Ministerio de Fomento, Memoria México, Enero 1883-Junio 1885, Tomo* III, p. 508.

charcoal,[67] which they cart to the neighboring towns and cities.

It is difficult to generalize and no statistical studies are available. But as a rule the small village has at best remained a self-sufficient unit. It rarely produces agricultural products for more than its immediate purposes. It finds itself dependent upon outside sources of soil and implements to eke out its needs, or has frequently to supplement that by some semi-industrial undertaking. The inhabitants of communities that happen to be near some mine will spend a portion of their time in the mines and return for the tilling seasons if they have lands of their own.[68] A thumb-nail description of eleven villages in one district in the State of Hidalgo will give a good indication of the complexity and variety of types of villages that may be encountered close together.[69]

Barrio de El Maye	Lives from agriculture and is very well off.
Barrio de El Mando	Lives from agriculture and by wage labor.
San Nicolás	Lives well from agriculture and makes coats and serapes from wool.
Maguey Blanco	Exploits the *maguey*, making *pulque* and articles from the fibre.

[67] *El Rancho de Sombrerete*, Querétaro, *Edu. Pub. Exp.* Num. 12-4-3-128. (Manuscript.)

[68] *Zona* 33, Oaxaca, March, 1923, *Municipio de S. Mateo Tepantepec.* (Manuscript.)

[69] *Estudio de la Zona de Ixmiquilpan,* Hidalgo, etc. (Manuscript.)

Remedios	Lives from little industries, depending upon the *maguey* plant. Some of the inhabitants have a few hogs and chickens.
Portezuelo	This village is very poor. They live as carriers. They buy earthenware in Chapaltongo, a distance of 20 kilometers, and carry it on their backs to the mountains, Jacala, etc., 50 kilometers. They carry their provisions with them and eat in addition fruits that they find on the road, such as prickly pears.
Panales	Like the previous one. In this place they are famous as highwaymen.
Orizabita	They are very revolutionary and active. They make *pulque* and carry it for sale 30 kilometers and return in the same day. In this place they make very acceptable guitars, bassoons, and violins. They also fabricate very curious miniatures.
Barrio de Tepe	Very barren. Live as wage workers and very poorly, helping to eke out their existence by the products of the *maguey* plant.
Alberto	This community is located on the banks of the river and benefits by its use.
El Ni	Very barren. In this place and in the county seat there are very skillful pyrotechnians who make

> fireworks for the numerous re-
> ligious feasts in the neighbor-
> hood.

We can, however, secure a more detailed picture
of the agricultural structure of these communities
by examining their agricultural technique and by
noting the tools they use, the number of animals
they have, the amount of land they can cultivate
with their resources, and the kind of crops they
grow.

*In addition to having insufficient lands the rural
villages suffer from an insufficiency of work animals
and agricultural implements.* Here again no satisfactory statistical material is available. We have
not the means of drawing a picture for even a good
sample of Mexican villages in the different states.[70]
Fortunately, we can give the distribution of animals
and tools per capita for the inhabitants of 59 villages in the State of Tamaulipas.[71] In one sense this
is not a good sample, as it is drawn from the towns
that have received lands from the government within
the last few years and the policy is to give lands
only to those who have less than a thousand *pesos*
worth of possessions either in lands or goods, so that
our picture is of the poorest groups in the rural community. But the material we give represents 25,730

[70] The material for such a study is available in the National
Agrarian Commission, but it has not been tapped and organized.

[71] Compiled from the statistical tables at the back of *Primera
Convención de la Liga de Comunidades y Sindicatos Campesinos
del Estado de Tamaulipas,* 1926.

people, or 57.8 per cent of the total population living within free villages in the State of Tamaulipas in 1921.[72] These 59 villages had received 98,292 hectares, or 26.2 hectares per capita, in provisional possession.[73] Of this total the cultivatable lands were 25,536 hectares, of which 7,115 hectares, or 34.7 per cent, were under cultivation.

The reasons given for the small area under cultivation vary, but the insufficiency of animals and tools is one that is frequently repeated.[74] Other equally illuminating reasons are the lack of wood for fences and the lack of means to purchase wire fence, the absence of seed, the lack of subsistence while the crop is maturing and the necessity therefore to seek work in the neighboring haciendas.

These 59 villages, with their 25,730 inhabitants, had the numbers of animals and agricultural machines as shown in table on page 76.

This table is illuminating and needs little comment. It shows 10 persons to each ox, 56 to each mule, 13 to each horse, and 15 to each ass. Nor is there greater sufficiency in food animals, for there are approximately 2 people to each chicken and 7 to each hog. But poorest of all is the showing for agricultural machinery. There are over 100 persons to each cultivator, over 1,000 to each thresher and over 50 to each cart. Of these 59 villages 9 have no oxen, 20 have no mules, 7 have no horses, 6 have no hogs,

[72] See Appendix B.
[73] See Appendix C.
[74] *Primera Convención,* pp. 89-186.

ANIMALS AND AGRICULTURAL MACHINERY IN 59 VILLAGES IN THE
STATE OF TAMAULIPAS *

Item	Number	
	Total	Per 100 Population
Work Animals		
Oxen..........................	2,714	10.55
Mules.........................	460	1.79
Horses........................	2,002	7.78
Asses.........................	1,771	6.88
Food Animals		
Cows..........................	2,144	8.33
Calves........................	1,778	6.91
Goats.........................	7,740	30.08
Hogs..........................	3,746	14.55
Chickens......................	17,065	66.32
Agricultural Machinery		
Cultivators....................	236	.92
Sowing machines...............	77	.30
Tractors.......................	1	....
Threshers......................	18	.07
Carts.........................	459	1.78

* Compiled from the statistical tables at the back of *Primera Convención
de la Liga de Communidades y Sindicatos Campesinos del Estado de Tamaulipas*, 1926.

5 have no chickens, 47 have no threshers, and so on
down the list.

The tale told by the statistics for these few communities in the state of Tamaulipas may be duplicated for other parts of Mexico [75]—perhaps for most

[75] For instance, we read concerning the state of Guerrero
(*Zona 19, Mun. de Teposotian*, March, 1925): "Because of the
lack of work animals the greater part of the agricultural work
must be done by hand. . . . The work is very difficult and one
individual working by hand can barely cultivate a hectare of land
during the agricultural year"; and concerning Oaxaca (*Zona 33*,

agricultural villages. It depicts an agriculture depending for its motive power upon human hands—a hoe agriculture. The absence of animals and machinery has shaped the whole agricultural technique of the free rural villages; agriculture depends upon hand tools, and even hand tools are scarce and primitive. The pick, the iron bar, a long pointed wooden stick, the hoe, the machete, and the ax are the most common and most widely-used agricultural tools. The plow used is of wood, only occasionally rimmed with an iron band.[76] Still more rarely does one find a modern steel plow in the free rural village. Great sections of territory in Mexico are under cultivation by the free rural villages where the plow—even the old single-handed wooden plow that can barely scratch the soil—is absent,[77] and in some places is opposed because of the belief that it spoils the land.[78]

Mun. de Santiago Etla, April, 1923) : "The agricultural work is much more difficult as three-fourths of the neighbors lack work animals." Such citations could be extended in great number.

[76] "The chief crops cultivated are maize, cotton, tobacco, beans, sugar cane, coffee, chili and rice, and also forages. The maize, beans, chili, and rice are planted in June, and the only cultivation they receive in their growing season is one or two cleanings with the machete of the weeds, and the crop is gathered from November on. All the work of preparation of the land consists of cutting the trees and vegetation, all of the work being done with the machete and an ax. They are beginning to use the wooden plows in some places." *Zona 33, Oaxaca, Municipio de Cacahuatepec,* August, 1923. (Manuscript.)

[77] "In the Costa Grande, an area of over 250 kilometers, the wooden plow is barely known and there are only about a hundred wooden plows in use." *Zona 19,* Guerrero, *Municipio de Costa Grande,* August, 1925. (Manuscript.)

[78] *ibid.*

The methods of cultivation and rotation differ with the crops, and over great areas there is no rotation at all. In the coastal region and in the upper mountains, the common method of preparing the soil is to cut down the forest during the dry winter season, burn the fallen timber toward spring, later clean the underbrush with a *machete,* and before the first rains break the ground with a long pointed stick sometimes tipped with iron. A hole is made in the ground and seed is placed in it. The rain is then expected and prayed for and the crop harvested at the end of from four to six months.[79] There may, during the growing season, be one or two clearings of the weeds. This is a widely spread system for maize, the almost universal crop. It is not seen in the neighborhoods of the better plateau lands which have so largely been pre-empted by the hacienda, but away from the crowded village sections and in the tropical coasts and up in the mountain regions this is a very common method.[80]

Even more popular than the stick, the almost universal tool is the *machete,* a large slightly curved

[79] "The rain, of course, does not penetrate far into the unploughed ground, but runs off the steep declivity; and it is only by continuous soaking during weeks of rain that the plants are saved from being dried up by the intense heat of the sun. During the dry season and a part of the wet—that is to say, from the beginning of April to the end of August—the Huichols are constantly making feasts to produce rain." Lumholtz, *Unknown Mexico,* 1902, Vol. II, pp. 9-11.

[80] "This method of planting is found scattered in different parts of the states of: Nayarit, Guerrero, Michoacán, Jalisco, Oaxaca, Chiapas, Campeche, Tabasco, and Veracruz.

knife which is the instrument for nearly all purposes. It serves as an ax, a hammer, a knife, a sickle, a scythe, and last but not least, as an instrument of battle and defense against the animals of the forest, or in a feud. The hoe, too, is widely used, especially in settled agricultural regions where the ground has been made easily tillable.[81]   The wooden plow drawn by two oxen, and more rarely still by mules, is seen in most parts of Mexico, but generally speaking, chiefly on the lands of the haciendas. The villages, as we have already seen, frequently lack sufficient lands for the use of plows, and where they have the land they often lack the animals. Where they do have enough land these are generally mountainous, forested, or broken and rocky. Here, as we have seen, they burn the forest and frequently, after one crop, leave the land fallow for six years.[82] Six years in a tropical section of the country may well make the land a jungle again.

The free rural villages are not only poor in worldly goods but primitive in their technique. We have perhaps already said enough to indicate the great poverty of the free rural villages in Mexico, a poverty of land, animals, tools: the basic essentials for any agricultural community. This poverty, how-

[81] "It is to be noted that they only use the wooden plow in the least broken parts of the mountainside but in general they plant with a stick without animals, and in the planting of maize, which is their chief crop, they use the hoe." *Zona 33, Oaxaca, Mun. de S. Mateo Tepantepec*, March, 1923, p. 38. (Manuscript.)

[82] *Zona 31, Guerrero, Mun. de Taxco*, April, 1923. (Manuscript.)

ever, is but part of a greater poverty, a poverty in technique, in cultural equipment. This greater poverty is more than a part of economic insufficiency. It goes back to cultural, historical, and traditional patterns. It is in part the result of four hundred years of oppression, in part the result of the tenacious hold of traditional mores, ancient ways of living and doing.[83]

Further light is thrown upon the general problem of the cultural status of the Mexican rural community by the replies submitted by 271 villages, scattered over 10 states, to a questionnaire filled out by educational missionaries, sent out by the Mexican Department of Education between 1922 and 1924.[84] For these 271 villages we find that 49.2 per cent are occupied by *mestizos,* 57.7 by Indians, and 3.1 by both Indians and *mestizos.* In spite of the fact that nearly 60 per cent of the villages are described as Indian, only 11.2 per cent are given as speaking purely or preponderantly native tongues,[85] confirming what Gamio has described for Teotihuacán. The Indian population has learned to speak Spanish without necessarily taking over the other cultural habits of their white neighbors and masters.[86] The figures for language are as follows: Native 11.2,

[83] Gamio, *Teotihuacán,* Introduction, p. 27.

[84] See above, page 423.

[85] "I have been in towns of six thousand Indian population where there were not, perhaps, a dozen who could talk Spanish, and I have been in many Mexican towns where there was only one man who could talk Spanish." Starr, *Mexico and the Caribbean,* p. 17.

[86] "The Teotihuacanos adopted the new language and the new

Spanish 55.4, and communities speaking both, 39.4 per cent.

If we now turn to a related factor, that of schools, we secure a further confirmation of the general picture drawn by students and observers of Mexico. We are told that in the Valley of Teotihuacán the percentage of illiteracy is 25.6,[87] while of the 25,000 inhabitants in the 59 towns in Tamaulipas the percentage of illiteracy was found to be 15.8.[88] In our figures for schools in 1922 for the towns for which we have replies the figures showed that at that time there were schools in only 40.3 per cent of the villages. The table on page 82 summarizes the race, language, and school distribution for those of the 271 villages in the 10 states for which we have information.

These questionnaires bring out another important phase of the Mexican rural community, namely, its great poverty in professional service. Gamio pointed out that altogether there were only 22 *profesionales* serving the population of over 8,000 people in the valley of Teotihuacán, and to get this number he counted teachers without professional title, native medicine men using herbs, and priests.[89] That is, in this valley, located within 30 miles of Mexico City,

religion, but at bottom preserved themselves from being reduced to European culture. During the nineteenth century they definitely lost their language, but not their customs." Gamio, *Teotihuacán*, Vol. I, p. 772.

[87] Gamio, *Teotihuacán*, Introducción, p. 22.

[88] *Primera Convención de la Liga de Comunidades.* Statistical Appendix.

[89] Gamio, Teotihuacán, Introduction, p. 36.

RACE, LANGUAGE, AND SCHOOL STATUS IN 271 VILLAGES, 1922 *

State	Villages Reporting	Race			Language Spoken			Villages Without Schools
		Mestizo	Indian	Mestizo and Indian	Native	Spanish	Native and Spanish	
Jalisco.........	17	10	1	5	..	16	..	2
Morelos........	11	6	2	2	..	8	3	10
Veracruz.......	7	7	...	..	..	6	1	6
San Luis Potosí..	9	9	...	..	..	9	..	4
Michoacán.....	7	3	3	..	3	3	..	4
Tabasco........	8	...	6	..	..	...	8	3 a
Puebla.........	19	4	15	..	1	2	14	3
Hidalgo........	32	15	16	1	5	18	9	24
Oaxaca........	82	22	60	..	18	27	37	51
Guerrero.......	79	55	24	..	3	59	17	22 b
Total........	271	131	127	8	30	148	89	129

* Compiled from the replies to questionnaires. (Manuscript.) The apparent discrepancy between the details and the totals for certain items is due to the fact that some of the questionnaires were not fully answered.
a No reply from 3 villages.
b No reply from 52 villages.

there was not a single doctor, dentist, lawyer, engineer, architect, or veterinarian—apparently not a single human being in all the 22 communities who carried something of the cultural equipment of the contemporary scientific world, and who could apply it to the needs and problems of the rural community. Our figures, derived from answers to the questionnaire filled out by the educational missionaries, are of similar import. Of the 271 towns filling out the questionnaire, only 206 answered the question about *profesionales*. Of these, only 22 replied yes to the question, "Are there any *profesionales?*"; 184 answered no; and 65 gave no answer. The details are as follows:

State	Villages reporting	Villages without profesionales
Jalisco	17	15
Morelos	11	11
Veracruz	7	7
San Luis Potosí	9	9
Michoacán	7	7
Tabasco	6	6
Puebla	19	11
Hidalgo	24	23
Oaxaca	78	67
Guerrero	28	28
Total	206	184

Of the villages for which we have information, 89.3 per cent had no professional service. In many of the replies to this question there appears the phrase *"de ninguna clase,"* of no sort whatever. Only 10.7 per cent of the communities reported *profesionales*. We cannot tell how many or what sort. We do know, however, that as a general rule the professional, in the sense of a trained person having modern technical equipment at his disposal, is very rare indeed in the rural Mexican community, whether Indian or Mestizo. Even more than in the United States, the professional and skilled workers tend to crowd into the large cities.

Another way of approaching the problem of technical equipment of the communities is found in the answer to the question, Can they make school furniture? That is, are they a community having carpenters? For the wood is generally, if not always, available, and the furniture asked for in the small rural village consists of a table and a bench requiring the simplest sort of mechanical competence. The answer for the 271 villages was no in 68.4 per cent of the cases. That is, the majority of the communities are without nails, saws, and hammers. They are without tables and chairs. Those who have traveled in Mexico know that in many a community the only place of rest is on a mat on the floor or, in warmer regions, in a hammock. But it is only by seeing that nearly 70 per cent of the communities replying to the question had to answer it in the negative that we get a sense of the technical poverty of the Mexican rural community. In detail, the answers to the question on whether school furniture could be made in the communities are as follows:

State	Villages reporting	Villages unable to make school furniture
Jalisco	14	2
Morelos	4	2
Veracruz	3	3
San Luis Potosí	9	9
Michoacán	7	5
Tabasco	3	3
Puebla	16	13
Hidalgo	24	16
Oaxaca	81	49
Guerrero	26	26
Total	187	128

The cultural backwardness of the Mexican rural community is in large part due to scanty transporta-

tion facilities.[90] The whole question is basically tied up with the inaccessibility of the rural community, its means of communication, its contact with the world. Mexico is predominantly a country of the mule path,[91] mountainous, and with a rainy season lasting in some parts of Mexico for the whole summer, practically isolating the community, cutting it off in many places [92] from postal and even telegraph communication.[93] Rural Mexico is a country without books, newspapers, or magazines, without teachers or doctors—an inaccessible, cut-off little world, set apart from the rest, and upon occasions still

[90] If we discount the people and the transportation facilities of the Federal District, which are largely urban in character, Mexico had, in 1925, 422 people for each automobile, 3,697 for each bus, 2,138 for each truck, 30,090 for each motorcycle, 1,540 for each coach, 159 for each cart, and 591 for each bicycle. It should be remembered that most of the automobiles, trucks, motorcycles, buses, and bicycles are to be found in the large cities and not in the rural districts. Compiled from *Estadística Nacional,* Nos. 58 and 59, June 30, July 15, 1927.

[91] "When the railway was introduced into Mexico, it came as a rival of the half-starved donkey and the not overfed Indian." Moses, Bernard, *Railway Revolution in Mexico,* San Francisco, 1895, p. 10.

[92] "This village, like all similar ones, lacks all means of communication, and they only receive correspondence in the city of Oaxaca, where they have to send for it by special messenger." *Zona 33, Oaxaca,* March, 1923, *Mun. de S. Catarina Estla.* (Manuscript.)

[93] "Communications are completely deficient. They lack postal service, telegraph, and telephone. I wanted to distribute a picture of the children among them, as they have never been photographed, nor is there a scale in the village upon which to weigh the school children." *Edu. Pub. Exp.* No. 12-3-4-54, *Campeche.* (Manuscript.)

(1926) using barter.[94] Of the communities we are considering, 64.2 per cent reported that the only means of access to the village was foot or horseback, while 27 per cent reported horse and cart transportation. One must remember, however, that the Mexican country cart is frequently an ox-cart on two wheels, used to haul agricultural products over impossible roads. And the cart itself is often carried on wheels cut solidly from the trunk of a large tree —the old Egyptian model. Only 4.9 per cent of the villages could be reached by railroad, 1.2 by water,[95] and 2 per cent by auto. These figures are for 1922 to 1924 inclusive. There has certainly, in some parts of the Republic, been considerable improvement since then. But even if our figures tend to overstate the actual situation, they reveal an isolation of the rural community which in itself would be held to explain many of the problems of Mexico.

The table on page 87 summarizes the preceding discussion of the transportation facilities for the 271 villages scattered over the 10 states for which we have information.

We are now in a position to give a summary description of the life of the free village. These communities, embracing more than half of the rural

---

[94] "They make their sales in the primitive form. It is interesting that they do not use money, only by means of exchanging maize, beans, dried chili, and tortillas." *Coyotepec, Tepexi, Estado de Puebla, 4 de junio de 1926, la Trabajadora Social de la Misión.* Raquel Portugal.

[95] All of these in Tabasco.

TRANSPORTATION FACILITIES IN 271 RURAL VILLAGES, 1922-1924

State	Number of Villages	Villages Answering	Means of Transportation				
			Mule or Horse-back	Horse and Cart	Rail-road	Water	Auto
Jalisco........	17	14	4	10	..	..	..
Morelos.......	11	9	3	4	2	..	..
Veracruz......	7	6	3	3	..	..	..
San Luis Potosí.	9	9	3	2	..	..	4
Michoacán....	7	7	7	..	..	..	..
Tabasco......	8	4	..	1	..	3	..
Puebla........	19	17	14	..	2	..	1
Hidalgo.......	32	25	22	2	1	..	..
Oaxaca........	82	78	30	41	7	..	..
Guerrero......	79	77	72	5	..	..	..
Total.......	271	246	158	68	12	3	5

population, have insufficient lands for their agricultural needs, and insufficient tools and animals to cultivate the lands they do have. Their agriculture is thus largely a hoe agriculture. Their lack of land and tools and animals compels them, in a large measure, to secure a portion of their income as wage laborers, as croppers, and as renters. Some of them fill out their economic needs by arts and crafts, and by acting as carriers, mule drivers, and petty merchants.

These little villages, generally under 300 souls each, are isolated from the rest of the world, and their only connections are mule paths, more rarely ox carts, and infrequently railroads. They have almost no professional service, frequently no postal, telegraph, telephone, newspaper, magazine, or book contacts. They have in the vast majority of cases no schools. Their food consists largely of maize bread, known as tortillas,[96] beans, and chili. Meat is a luxury that they eat but rarely. Milk is an almost unknown treat for the working and poorer peasant classes. Even the children are accustomed to the heavy diet of the elders—doubtless one of the reasons for an infant mortality in the rural community estimated at between 75 and 80 per cent of the children born.[97]

The houses are one-room shacks, made of adobe in the colder regions, and in the warmer climates made of bamboo sticks or reeds, of a great variety of more or less porous material that permits the wind to pass through.[98] The one room serves for the whole family, and sometimes for the animals that the family

[96] "They take two meals a day, which are composed of beans, tortillas, and chili for the first. For the second meal they add a few vegetables and very rarely meat. In Huejotzingo they slaughter only one beef every eight days and one hog every day, which is equal to a sale of 30 pesos a day for a population of 6,000 people." *Zona 28, Estado de Puebla,* August, 1923, *Mun. de Huejotzingo.* (Manuscript.) This indicates the food standards of even rural communities of 6,000. Gamio, *Teotihuacán,* Introduction, p. 28, points out that the food habits remain practically the same as they were before the conquest.

[97] Gamio, *Teotihuacán,* Introduction, p. xxiv.

[98] "Compared with these habitations, a Calmuck or even a Tartar tent is a palace. They are made of stones and mud, raised not more than five feet from the ground, and thatched with leaves of the yucca; the walls all black with smoke, for they have no chimneys; and the earth floors are covered with filth. I certainly never saw a negro-house in Carolina so comfortless. Any master, who, in our country, should lodge his slaves in this manner, would be considered barbarous and inhuman." Poinsett, Joel Roberts, *Notes on Mexico,* London, 1822, p. 254.

may have.[99] From the point of view of cleanliness, in spite of the fact that the Maya Indian in Yucatan is proverbially clean and neat, the situation is generally indescribable. There simply is no sanitation in large parts of rural Mexico. In part this is due to the lack of sufficient water, in part to the lack of knowledge and habits of cleanliness.[100] The water is so bad in some places that the natives avoid drinking it, drinking alcoholic beverages instead. This frequently leads to habits of drunkenness that in some parts of the rural community are very serious, and absorb all the earnings beyond the very minimum for the low standard of life to which they are accustomed. Clothing is of the most meager sort, and in some places remains unwashed from the time it is put on to the time it falls to pieces as a result of age and wear.

The rural community is poor, poorer than most Europeanized, city-dwelling Mexicans realize. In fact, Mexico comprises two civilizations, living side by side but with neither one fully conscious of the

[99] "The habitations of the people on the roadside are miserable indeed. The walls are of stone, piled up loosely, like the fences, and not much higher; and the roof is a wooden shed, kept down by a number of large stones, and sometimes ornamented by ranges of pumpkins." *ibid.*, p. 173.

[100] The water for many rural communities is derived from collectors in large artificial dugouts. During the long dry season the winds cover the surface of the water with sand. This is the only source of water for the animals who come both to drink and to bathe in it, and Gamio notes that even the carcasses of dead animals may sometimes be found in the water deposits. Gamio, *Teotihuacán*, Introduction, p. 39. This description can be repeated for other places.

other. In 1864 Pimentel drew a contrast between the upper and lower levels of Mexican civilization, between the whites and the Indians, which is still essentially true today. "The white speaks Spanish and French; the Indian has more than a hundred different languages in which to make himself known. The white is catholic or indifferent; the Indian is idolatrous. The white is a proprietor; the Indian a laborer. The white is rich; the Indian poor and miserable. The descendants of the Spaniards are within reach of all the knowledge of the century—all the scientific discoveries; the Indian is totally ignorant. The white dresses according to the best models of Paris and uses the richest fabrics; the Indian goes almost naked. The white lives in the cities in magnificent houses; the Indian is isolated in the fields, and his habitation is a miserable hut. That is the contrast which Mexico presents." [101]

With this condition as a base for a large part of the rural population, we are in a position to appreciate the meager character of Mexican agriculture and the great problem involved in the attempt to reconstruct Mexican agrarian and agricultural organization. We can now turn to a discussion of the hacienda.

[101] *Memoria sobre las causas que han originado la situación actual de la Raza Indigena de México, y medios de remediarla,* México, 1864, pp. 217-218.

CHAPTER IV

SIZE AND DISTRIBUTION OF THE HACIENDAS

The predominant agricultural organization of Mexico is not the little village which we have just described, but the large estate—the hacienda. This large agricultural unit has given Mexico some of its most typical features, and has laid the groundwork for some of the country's most serious problems. Just as the small village, with its petty agriculture, its primitive tools, its complex social structure, occupies a peculiar and deep-rooted place in the economic organization of Mexico, so likewise the hacienda, with its vast areas, its unified management, its political and social dominance, made Mexico a country of proverbial contrast—the *hacendado* and the peon. The hacienda is the mode, the type of Mexican agriculture, and until very recently it completely overshadowed the little village and the 6,000,000 people that found their abode in it.

While it is impossible to identify hacienda properties in the statistics, we cannot go far wrong if we classify all holdings of over 1,000 hectares as belonging to this category.[1] We have already seen

[1] This is admittedly an arbitrary division. Any other figure, however, would be equally arbitrary. The use of this figure

(page 54) that in 1921 there were 12,782 properties of this size or larger. This small number of large properties, making up 2 per cent of the total, embraces over half the area of the privately held lands of rural Mexico.[2] A striking comparison of this situation with that of the village properties, discussed in the previous chapter, is brought out in the following tabulation:

RURAL LANDS IN VILLAGE PROPERTIES AND IN HACIENDAS, 1923

| | | | Percentage of Total | |
Item	Village Properties	Haciendas	Village Properties	Haciendas
Pieces of property..	609,431	12,782	97.9	2.1
Area (in hectares)..	66,459,945a	92,646,420b	41.8	58.2
Value (in pesos)...	611,712,087	728,915,772	45.6	54.4

a Arrived at by deducting from total of all privately owned lands in the states all properties of 1,000 hectares or more.
b Of the 10,126 for which we know area.

Somewhat more than half of the 10,126 haciendas

makes it possible for us to dispense with the use of the term "rancho." "Rancho" and "hacienda" have both lost whatever significance as an area classification they may have had in the past. The 1,000 hectares as a classification for hacienda has been adopted by McBride. See McBride, George McCutchen, *The Land Systems of Mexico,* p. 25.

[2] Our information on this point, being collected from tax records which showed only properties valued at 5,000 pesos or over, omits 2,656 tracts which were included in the number 12,782. Even the remaining 10,126 properties of an area of 1,000 hectares or more valued at 5,000 pesos or over constituted 58.2 per cent of the area, and 54.4 per cent of the value of all privately held lands. It would seem certain, therefore, that a full count would indicate that properties of 1,000 hectares or over make up somewhat more than three-fifths of the total area of privately held lands.

for which we know the area fall within a range of 1,000 to 4,000 hectares. That is, 6,481 properties contained less than 4,000 hectares each, as compared with 1,530 properties of 10,000 hectares or over, and only 110 which run above 100,000 hectares.

On the average, the value (per hectare) of the 1,000-hectare hacienda is ten times as great as that of the hacienda having 100,000 hectares or more. The smaller hacienda in Mexico thus tends to be much more valuable as an agricultural property than the larger. We will see later that this is due to the many factors of climate and population density which, in part at least, have determined the geographic distribution of the different-sized haciendas. But the fact in itself is worthy of note, and it can be laid down as a rule in Mexican agricultural organization, that the great properties have a lower assessed valuation per hectare than the smaller ones. This is not entirely due to economic reasons. Political factors and traditions have helped shape the fiscal legislation so as to decrease the valuation of the larger properties. But even so, there is a striking regularity in the decreasing value of the hectare as we go from tracts of 1,000 to 2,000 hectares, where the average is 22.9 pesos, to those of over 100,000, with an average value of 2.4 pesos per hectare. The table on page 94 clearly shows this sharp difference in the average value of the hectare in the different-sized properties.

Size of Hacienda (in hectares)	Average Value per Hectare (in *pesos*)
1,000 to 2,000	22.9
2,000 to 3,000	21.0
3,000 to 4,000	19.2
4,000 to 5,000	16.3
5,000 to 10,000	11.7
10,000 to 20,000	7.7
20,000 to 30,000	7.5
30,000 to 40,000	4.4
40,000 to 50,000	6.5
50,000 to 75,000	4.0
75,000 to 100,000	3.3
100,000 or over	2.4

The smaller-sized haciendas, while greater in number than the larger ones, embrace a much smaller percentage of the privately held lands than do the larger ones. In fact, the 110 properties of over 100,000 hectares represent approximately one-third óf the total lands that are held in haciendas in the Republic of Mexico. These 110 properties have a combined area greater than the 8,596 haciendas that range between 1,000 and 10,000 hectares, but make up only 5.44 per cent of the total value of the haciendas. This general size distribution and its inverse relation to the distribution of value for the same properties are well brought out by the table on page 95.

In some of the northern and coastal states the haciendas contain over 80 per cent of the respective areas of the states. This general fact that the states in the North and on the coasts tend to have a greater portion of their areas in large estates is consistent

AREA AND VALUE OF PRIVATELY OWNED LANDS REPRESENTED
BY 10,126 HACIENDAS, 1923

Size of Hacienda in Hectares	Number of Properties	Area		Assessed Value	
		In Hectares	As Percentage of Area of all Private Rural Lands	In Thousands of Pesos	As Percentage of Assessed Value of All Private Rural Lands
1,000 to 2,000....	3,693	5,340,111	3.36	122,468	9.14
2,000 to 3,000....	1,781	4,330,638	2.72	90,873	6.78
3,000 to 4,000....	1,007	3,466,054	2.18	66,406	4.95
4,000 to 5,000....	651	2,906,081	1.83	47,238	3.52
5,000 to 10,000...	1,464	10,030,302	6.30	117,336	8.75
10,000 to 20,000..	804	11,105,392	6.98	85,931	6.41
20,000 to 30,000..	251	6,072,424	3.82	45,419	3.39
30,000 to 40,000..	145	4,967,995	3.12	21,946	1.64
40,000 to 50,000..	62	2,812,265	1.77	18,320	1.37
50,000 to 75,000..	106	6,339,267	3.98	25,043	1.87
75,000 to 100,000.	52	4,528,116	2.85	14,890	1.11
100,000 or over...	110	30,747,775	19.32	73,046	5.44
All..........	10,126	92,646,420	58.23	728,916	54.37

with the cheaper land values in those states and with
lower population density. Of the eight states where
the haciendas have approximately 80 per cent of the
total privately owned lands five are located in the
northern part of Mexico, two border on the Pacific
and one on the Gulf. On the other hand, of the
eleven states where the area held by the haciendas is
less than 40 per cent of the privately owned lands in
the state, eight are centrally located. Generally
speaking, therefore, the haciendas embrace the greatest
areas in the northern and the smallest in the central
and southern states.

The haciendas represent relatively greater values

in central than in the northern or coastal states. In the central parts of Mexico where the haciendas of over 1,000 hectares include the smallest portions of the areas of the states they at the same time show a very much higher proportionate value. This can easily be seen if we arrange the states according to the percentage of the area occupied by the haciendas. (See table on page 97.)

These figures show the wide difference in the values represented by the large haciendas in different states of Mexico. They also show that in the states of central and south central Mexico where the greatest part of Mexican population is concentrated the haciendas are more valuable per hectare than the rest of the lands of the state. That is, the large estates tend to have the best lands in the crowded sections of Mexico, whereas in the sparsely settled states the best lands are in the main in the smaller parcels. This fact has an important bearing on the Mexican agrarian problem and tends to make the solution of the problem more difficult in central and south central Mexico than in the northern parts of the Republic.

Every state in Mexico has single properties with areas of 10,000 hectares or more. That in itself tells us comparatively little about the average size of the haciendas in the different states, but it is one way of describing the size distribution of the Mexican hacienda in the different states. The smallest state in the Republic—Tlaxcala—contains haciendas of over 10,000 hectares, and one-half of the states have haciendas of 100,000 hectares or over. The figures on page 98, showing the number of states in which

AREA AND VALUE OF HACIENDAS,[a] BY STATES, 1923

Shown as Percentages of Respective Totals of All Private Rural Lands

State	Area	Value
Coahuila	93.6	73.9
Colima	92.7	67.7
San Luis Potosí	84.8	79.2
Zacatecas	84.5	57.9
Baja California	84.3	61.5
Campeche	83.8	72.0
Nayarit	83.4	74.2
Chihuahua [b]	82.2	....
Durango	79.9	85.2
Yucatán	57.4	56.9
Sonora	53.9	74.5
Guanajuato	51.7	39.1
Tlaxcala	50.1	51.8
Querétaro	49.9	71.4
Tamaulipas	47.3	72.1
Sinaloa	47.1	60.6
Aguascalientes	43.5	46.2
Veracruz	42.5	40.8
México	39.8	48.7
Morelos [b]	39.3	....
Nuevo León	38.4	45.2
Chiapas	38.1	48.6
Jalisco	32.8	42.2
Michoacán	25.3	41.7
Hidalgo	24.4	51.8
Guerrero	23.5	48.5
Tabasco	22.9	19.4
Oaxaca	18.2	59.1
Puebla	15.3	43.7
Quintana Roo [b]	....	....
All states	58.2	54.4

[a] See footnote, page 91, for definition of "hacienda" as used in this table.
[b] Value data not available, and data with regard to number and area are incomplete.

properties of a given size appear (Federal District not included), indicate the distribution of large land-holdings.

Properties of:	Number of States
100,000 hectares or over	15
75,000 hectares or over	17
50,000 hectares or over	20
40,000 hectares or over	21
30,000 hectares or over	26
20,000 hectares or over	29
10,000 hectares or over	30

It is interesting to note that the states which contain the very largest properties are all Northern and coastal states. Except the state of Tabasco, all of the coastal or border states have estates of over 30,000 hectares, and if we exclude also the little state of Colima they all have haciendas of over 50,000 hectares each.

In spite of the fact that all states have properties of over 10,000 hectares, the predominant agricultural unit is under 3,000 hectares. Geographical distribution has little relation to this fact. It is true that in the four Northern states of Chihuahua, Coahuila, Durango, and Nuevo León, one-half of the properties are of approximately 5,000 hectares or over, thus falling in with the general geographic distribution of the largest-sized properties. On the other hand, in such states as Sonora, Lower California, and Tamaulipas, the haciendas tend to be between 2,000 and 3,000 hectares each, while in the states of Yucatán, Tabasco, Chiapas, Hidalgo, Tlaxcala, and Puebla they tend to be of between 1,000 and 2,000 hectares.

Thus we see that in 20 out of 29 states the typical haciendas are under 3,000 hectares, and that in only 5 states is the typical agricultural unit over 5,000 hectares.

Most of the haciendas have resident populations of at least 100 people. This is the general statement that we can make of the larger haciendas. There is, however, no satisfactory answer of the question: What is the relation between the size of the hacienda and the population residing upon it? We can only guess at the reply. We know that in 1923 Mexico had 12,782 agricultural properties that were each of 1,000 hectares or more, and that in 1921 there were 11,354 agricultural properties with resident populations of 100 or over. By assuming that the large properties tended to contain the largest resident communities, we can say that at least 88 per cent of all the haciendas (properties of 1,000 hectares or over) had resident populations of at least 100 people.[3] On the basis of population, these 11,354 resident hacienda communities may be grouped as shown in the table on page 101.

It is clear that more than 50 per cent of the haciendas had resident populations of 100 or over, and that only about 1 per cent of the haciendas had resident populations of 1,000 or over. The resident hacienda communities of 100 or over as they existed in 1921 are given in the table which appears on page 100.

[3] See Appendix C for discussion of Population Census.

POPULATION CLASSIFICATION OF HACIENDA COMMUNITIES
OF 100 PEOPLE OR OVER

Classification	Number of Communities	Percentage of Total
100 to 200	6,373	56.1
200 to 300	2,460	21.6
300 to 400	1,113	9.8
400 to 500	562	5.0
500 to 1,000	732	6.5
1,001 to 2,000	105	.9
2,001 to 3,000	8	.1
3,001 to 10,000	1	. . . .
Total	11,354	100.0

An examination of this table will show but little
geographic explanation for size of resident hacienda
communities in different sections of the Republic in
1921. We know that the proportion of the total
population living upon haciendas differs widely in
different states, but to all appearances the hacienda
itself as a working unit had a population in 1921
that was determined by purely local conditions, to
discover which would require a much more detailed
analysis than is possible at this time.

It is clear that the Mexican hacienda is in the
large majority of cases under 5,000 hectares. The
very large properties are comparatively few in
number and are to be found chiefly on the Northern
border or in the coastal states. It should, however,
be remembered that while these large haciendas
represent smaller values and poorer land, they do
embrace nearly one-fifth of all the privately held
lands in the Republic. The smaller haciendas,

located in the central states where the population density is much greater, represent higher land values. This fact is important in its bearing upon the Mexican agrarian problem.

POPULATION CLASSIFICATION OF HACIENDA COMMUNITIES
OF 100 PEOPLE OR OVER, BY STATES, 1921

State	3000 to 7000	2000 to 3000	1000 to 2000	500 to 1000	400 to 500	300 to 400	200 to 300	100 to 200
Sinaloa	1	1	5	31	27	47	134	287
Coahuila	....	1	8	36	26	39	68	185
Durango	....	1	1	34	29	41	108	225
Guerrero	....	1	6	14	9	28	55	146
Michoacán	....	1	15	93	73	157	311	778
Nayarit	....	1	1	10	8	21	32	82
Oaxaca	....	1	4	15	13	25	65	144
San Luis Potosí	....	1	13	68	43	82	158	283
Chihuahua			1	15	15	35	100	243
Guanajuato			8	101	73	163	373	865
Hidalgo			1	18	20	31	62	155
Jalisco			16	73	49	104	260	895
México			9	27	16	30	60	135
Nuevo León			2	14	12	30	41	198
Puebla			1	14	18	39	75	136
Querétaro			2	35	17	39	92	187
Tamaulipas			1	7	4	21	40	154
Veracruz			1	6	6	8	25	112
Zacatecas			10	69	54	74	143	370
Aguascalientes				10	4	10	22	57
Campeche				1	2	4	5	17
Chiapas				17	18	32	74	298
Colima				6	2	11	21	44
Sonora				4	5	3	23	82
Tabasco				4	....	3	25	101
Tlaxcala				3	9	9	37	46
Yucatán				6	8	19	43	117
Dist. Federal				1	2	5	1	13
Baja California				....	....	2	3	10
Morelos				....	....	1	4	6
Quintana Roo				....	....	....	....	2
All States	1	8	105	732	562	1113	2460	6373

CHAPTER V

ECONOMIC ORGANIZATION OF
THE HACIENDA

The Mexican hacienda as we know it today is the result of a long period of evolution. As suggested earlier (see page 4), it is possible that there existed even before the Spanish conquest a type of large landholding of a somewhat feudal character. Whatever the precise nature of this institution, however, it was superseded by the new type of land tenure which was an outgrowth of the conquest and which, with some modification, persisted down to the close of the Diaz régime (1910).[1]

That it has thus maintained itself is doubtless due in no small degree to the fact that it was planted in a receptive environment. The sparsity of population and its primitive character, the fact that large sections of the country were best adapted to

[1] The present chapter, being part of a discussion of the background of the Mexican agrarian problem, deals primarily with the hacienda as it existed prior to the revolution. The changes in the system since 1910 are discussed in Part III of the book.

In *Estadística de la República Mexicana* (*Anexo Num. 3 a la Memoria de Hacienda*), 1877-1878, pp. 1-274, the reader will find detailed description of the economy of haciendas as given by their owners. These reports constitute a very rich source for an insight into the organization and the problems of rural Mexico.

grazing, while rainfall conditions in others called for irrigation works—these and possibly other factors combined to make it easy for the large hacienda to take root and to expand within the economic environment of Mexico, and to become established as the leading system of agricultural life and labor.

The political and economic results of the Spanish conquest forcibly brought the hacienda system into being. It superseded previous systems of landholding as a creation of the conquest and an instrument of political dominion. If one is to understand the place of the hacienda in the economic life of Mexico, he must perceive that it came as a military and political act, the forceful dispossession of a population already living under a well-established system of land ownership and utilization.[2]

The whole economic structure of Mexico was sharply influenced by the fact that Mexico began its career as a European colony under conditions that did not favor the rapid development of its agriculture. The Spanish conqueror was a soldier and not a farmer. His interests were in power and in gold to be had from the mines. The early land distribution was made with a view to a distribution of the Indians, rather than the land, among the conquerors, and little attention was paid to determining accurate boundaries. This failure to delimit

[2] Compare Orozco, Luis Wistano, *Legislación y Jurisprudencia, Sobre Terrenos Baldíos,* Mexico, 1895, Vol. 2, pp. 1078-1099.

the boundaries of the haciendas has been a continuous plague to Mexico ever since. It has made land titles insecure, and led to innumerable disputes between landowners, villages, and the government. It made sale and transfer of property an elaborate and expensive undertaking.[3]

These factors, both favoring the enlargement of the hacienda system and impeding the transfer or division of units, were strengthened by the fact that the landowners retained political power from the Spanish conquest to the end of the Diaz régime. In one form or another they bent the laws of the country to serve their ends.[4] The greater part of the lands of the country were early pre-empted by the Spaniards, and once in their possession the haciendas became feudal patrimonies. Generally only death or bankruptcy broke the landholder's grip upon the property.[5] In addition the great estates acquired by the church and held to the middle of the last century contributed to this immobility of ownership in land. The large estates were thus only in a limited way subject to the rules of economic enterprise, management for profit, and sale for gain. They were held because of family

[3] Andrés Molina Enríquez, *Los Grandes Problemas Nacionales,* México, 1909, p. 126.

[4] Orozco, *Terrenos Baldíos,* pp. 1095-1097.

"It is well known that our laws covering mortgages establish the principle of the indivisibility of the guarantee which is an impediment to the division of mortgaged property." *Ensayo Sobre le Reconstrucción de Mexico.*

[5] Andrés Molina Enríquez, pp. 85-91.

tradition, as means of social prestige, and managed
with as little risk as was possible.[6]

*The purpose of the hacienda seems to have been one
of security rather than profit.* The owner as a general rule lived in a city, in the capital of the state, in
Mexico City or, if his fortune permitted, in Europe.[7]
The property was therefore managed through an
administrator, and the owner asked only for a more
or less customary income.[8] Absentee ownership,
indirect management,[9] and security of income lay at
the root of the hacienda administration. The
administrator having little personal interest in the
property satisfied himself and the owner if he could
make the hacienda yield the customary income.
This led to the emphasis upon security as the basis
of the administration ideal. The whole organization
was pivoted about this object.

*The large estates were ordinarily too extensive to
be administered as single units,*[10] *and were divided*

[6] Orozco, p. 938.

[7] McBride, p. 29.

[8] Molina Enríquez, p. 92.

[9] "The system of renting practiced in Mexico is one of two
equally pernicious forms. Sometimes the proprietor rents his
whole property to a speculator and at other times he rents the
worst lands in fractions to poorer cultivators. In the first case
the renter destroys the property by trying to abstract from it all
he can during the time of the contract and the other system is
also bad because incapable people work the most sterile part of
the land and without resources to improve it." Pimentel, Francisco, *La Economía Política aplicada a la propiedad territorial en
México,* Mexico, 1866.

[10] "Roughly speaking, the hacienda is thirty square leagues in
extent. The nearest village, from which the simplest things, such

into ranchos. Each *rancho* had a subordinate *mayordomo* under general supervision of the administrator.[11] The lands of these *ranchos* were as a rule divided into five different classes: those cultivated directly, by croppers, by renters, by resident laborers working corn patches as a part of their wage bargain, and by non-rent-paying tillers breaking new ground.

This administrative division of the lands in the hacienda was also a division according to quality. The hacienda when it directly cultivated the lands —and it did not always do so—usually worked the best lands, those that were irrigated, or that had enough moisture or rainfall for a fairly certain crop.[12] The poorer lands went to the croppers, renters, resident laborers and non-rent paying tillers of new land.[13] But even with all of this subdivision the hacienda lacked the enterprise, the capital equipment, and the access to the markets to cultivate more than a fraction of the tillable soil.[14] It has been estimated that the haciendas did not, on the

as a box of matches or a packet of pins, had to be procured, was eight leagues off. The nearest post-office was thirty leagues away, and railroads or diligencia routes were far from this remote region." A. Gringo, *Through the Land of the Aztecs,* London, 1892, p. 206.

[11] Santisteban, J. B. de, *Indicador Particular del Administrador, Breve Manual basado sobre reglas de economía rural, enherentes al sistema agrícola en la República Mexicana, 2nd ed.,* Puebla, 1903, p. 175.

[12] Molina Enríquez, p. 91.

[13] *ibid.,* p. 177.

[14] McBride, *Land Systems,* p. 27.

average, cultivate more than a tenth of their arable lands,[15] and that the village lands were more fully cultivated.[16]

The hacienda strove to be as nearly self-sufficient as possible. The greater the internal resources of the hacienda, the greater the variety of raw materials, the more secure the labor force, the larger the number of things that could be done within the

[15] Orozco, Vol. II, p. 956.
[16] Molina Enríquez, p. 81

No material is available that would give the percentages of the different lands even on the largest haciendas. The following figures are a few that we have collected and show both the very small area under irrigation and the small proportion of land classed as non-irrigated but tillable (*temporal*).

In Morelos, 28 haciendas were reported at a total of 300,862 hectares, of which 31,757 or 10.6 per cent were irrigated, but of which only 10,458 hectares or 3.5 per cent were cultivated in any one year. (*Cuadro Comparativo* issued by the State Agrarian Commission, May, 1923.)

The area of all properties of over 100 hectares in the State of Tamaulipas, which is given as 5,176,422 hectares, is divided as follows: irrigated 0.3 per cent, *temporal* 0.3 per cent, pasture 93.8 per cent, fibre 1.1 per cent, and oil lands 4.5 per cent. (Typewritten copy of tax sheets giving size and classification of all properties of over 100 hectares, 1926.) In Durango for all properties of over 5,000 hectares given as 8,902,531, 0.66 per cent are given as irrigated, 1.06 as *temporal,* and all the rest as pasture. (Typewritten copy of tax register for all properties of over 5,000 hectares, 1925.) For Zacatecas we get: irrigated 0.2 per cent, *temporal* 3.2 per cent, pasture 73.8 per cent, and mountain 22.8 per cent. (*Extención y Clasificación de cada finca en el estado de Zacatecas* supplied by L. Robles, *Jefe del Dept. de Agricultura* to *Oficina Investigadora Agrícola,* April 28, 1926. This is an incomplete list.)

It should, however, be noted that most of these figures are for properties in Northern Mexico. The large estates in central Mexico would probably show a much larger percentage of *temporal.*

confines of the property itself, the more permanent was its income and the more secure the position of its owners.[17] The larger the hacienda, the greater is the variety of soil, the greater the security of its woods, pasture and watershed,[18] and the easier to protect the fruits and animals that the property contains. This self-sufficiency was sought in another fashion, that of reducing to a minimum the expenditure of money by the hacienda. As far as possible all improvements in the hacienda were made with resources available upon the property with home-made tools, and that meant the most primitive tools. It meant a home-made plow drawn by oxen raised upon the pasture of the farm. It meant a wooden harrow, if one was used, and the use of rawhide instead of nails.[19]

As far as possible the hacienda maintained a per-

[17] Orozco, Vol. II, p. 955.

[18] McBride, pp. 26-27.

[19] "They have but few tools, and, except possibly some contrivances for raising water, nothing worthy the name of machinery. Without being bred to any mechanical profession, the peons make and repair nearly every implement or tool that is used upon the estate, and this, too, without the use of forge or of iron, not even of bolts and nails. The explanation of such an apparently marvelous result is to be found in a single word, or rather material—rawhide—with which the peon feels himself qualified to meet almost any constructive emergency, from the framing of a house to the making of a loom, the mending of a gun, or the repair of a broken leg; and yet, even under these circumstances, the great Mexican estates, owing to their exemption from taxation and the cheapness of labor, are said to be profitable, and, in cases where a fair supply of water is obtainable, to even return large incomes to their absentee owners." Wells, David A., *A Study of Mexico*, New York, 1887, pp. 33-34.

manent labor force. Generally speaking, it may be said that the Mexican hacienda has suffered from insufficient labor supply. This is less true of the central part of Mexico than of the tropical coast states or of the North, but as a whole and even in the central parts of Mexico, there has been a general resistance on the part of the Mexican Indian and Mestizo to regular work upon the large estates. Where the Indians have been able to hold on to their lands, or where they have retained villages with even bare little plots upon which to grow maize they only work upon the haciendas intermittently and irregularly, preferring to till their own plots to raise enough for their own meager existence.[20]

The serfdom that existed in Mexico for some four hundred years must be looked upon as in part an attempt to overcome a labor shortage.[21] The reduction of the lands of the villages has been an attempt not merely to get lands but also to get permanent labor. It is generally agreed that the system of indenture was most fully developed in those sections of Mexico where labor was scarcest.[22] But all generalizations must be taken with caution. It is perfectly clear that the conditions of labor, especially in

[20] Roa y Covarrubias, *El Problema Rural de México,* Mexico, 1917, pp. 12-13.

[21] "Suitable farm-labor is very scarce. Strangers, from the nature of the climate, are useless, absolutely so, as farm-laborers." Quoted by Wells, *A Study of Mexico,* p. 145.

[22] "Yucatan does a trade with men from central Mexico that leaves nothing to envy the ancient trade in Negroes." Molina Enríquez, p. 202.

the proportion of workers kept in residence upon the haciendas, differed widely between states, and also differed as widely in the different counties of the same state. But the local customs,[23] crops, populations, were so varied from district to district that the labor contract of rural Mexico represents the intricacy of a cobweb which it is not our intention even to attempt to unravel. Broadly speaking, however, we can distinguish between two major labor systems: the indentured and the free laborers.

All haciendas seem to have had both indentured and free laborers working side by side. In some places, especially in the coffee and sugar plantations, the permanent resident laborers seem to have been comparatively few; in others, to have been numerous. Here again it is difficult to make any definite generalization. But we do know the total number of people that lived upon the haciendas and we know that the greater part of these were kept upon the hacienda by a system of debt. In addition to the indentured and free workers, the haciendas generally had renters and croppers. We can perhaps best indicate the type of labor that was to be found upon the typical large hacienda by the following outline. The average hacienda had:

An administrator
One or more mayordomos (superintendents for
    ranchos)
Clerks (*escribientes*)

[23] Kaerger, Karl, *Landwirtschaft und Kolonisation im Spanischen Amerika,* Leipzig, 1912, Vol. II, p. 521.

Priest (in the large haciendas)

Teacher (only rarely)

Foremen (in charge of different sections, such as cattle, special crops)

Cattle herders (*coporal* and *vaqueros*)

Heads of labor gangs (*capitanes*)

Resident indentured workers (*acasillados, acomodados*)[24]

Resident crop-sharers who were also workers

Resident renters who were also workers

Renters who had crop-sharers or sub-renters under them

Non-resident (temporary) renters

Non-resident (temporary) crop-sharers

Gangs of workers hired for the agricultural season (*cuadrillas*)

Workers hired by the month

Workers hired and paid by the week

Workers hired by the task system

Workers hired and paid by the day. In addition the hacienda might have a police force of its own, a magistrate [25] and a prison, special mule drivers (*arrieros*), sheep and swine herders (*pastores, maraneros*), smith, carpenters, and specialists of various kinds

While this skeleton outline of the labor organization of the hacienda may be accepted as descriptive

[24] "The inhabitants of San Benito are not vicious; they are peaceful workers and they like agriculture but they are lacking in cheerfulness which is displayed by those who have their own lands." Zona 18, Chiapas, August, 1925, M. Tapachula. (Manuscript.)

[25] "Generally the administrator of a hacienda is the local authority, being invested with the power all recognize as indispensable for the purpose of conserving order in a community of some hundreds of people." "*El País del Henequén,*" por H. L. Daniels, *Boletín de la Dirección Agricultura,* June, 1911, Pt. 2.

of all Mexico, the proportional distribution between the classes of labor, as we have already said, differed widely. The henequen plantations of Yucatan,[26] the coffee plantations of Veracruz and Chiapas and the sugar plantations of Morelos used large numbers of workers who came in "cuadrillas"—gangs from long distances. These haciendas also had a proportion of their workers in permanent residence, kept upon the place by debt. The typically agricultural states, those of the upper plateau, and the others as well, when not cultivating tropical crops, used fewer "gangs." Most of the work upon these, the cereal crop haciendas, was done by resident workers, crop-sharers, renters, or by such workers as came from nearby villages.

As far as possible the work of the hacienda was done by unremunerated labor. The internal economy of the hacienda lent itself to a variety of privileges and prerogatives on the part of the owner or his administrator, which made it possible to get a considerable portion of the work done without any expenditure of money or even of direct compensation. The almost universal system was one of *dar faenas* (literally "give tasks") by which each resident upon the hacienda for the privilege of occupying the place did a certain amount of work before the regular day's labor began and after it concluded.[27] This was a method of getting most of the chores done. In this work both the women and the

[26] Kaerger, Vol. II, p. 478.

[27] Gamio, Teotihuacán, Vol. II, p. 453. *Comercio Interior y Exterior, No. 12,* June, 1886, p. 31. *Mun. Cuautla,* Morelos.

children participated. It included making *tortillas* for the "big house" on the hacienda, cooking, washing, cleaning, bringing in the animals from and driving them to pasture.

In addition to the system of *faenas,* croppers and renters had frequently to give a work rental for the right of pasturing their work animals. This was a certain number of days' work during the year with the work animals, apart from the crop or money rental for raising the crop. The cropper and renter were also expected to give in addition to a work rental for the animals, a work-rental [28] for occupying the land. This system had many variations, but it was widely spread all over the haciendas of Mexico and resulted in providing the hacienda with a considerable portion of its labor free of any charge. The author found a variation of the system still existing in Chiapas in 1926. The worker upon the hacienda had to pay what is called *baldiaje,* that is, work a given number of days with each animal that was allowed to pasture on the hacienda grounds. And there were some haciendas where all of the animals on the place were in the hands of renters or croppers and by this means, as payment for grazing, all the work animals were provided free of any cost to the hacienda. In the same state, all of the human labor for some of the haciendas, especially near the city of Comitan, was secured by a rental (*baldiaje*) for each hectare of land the cropper tilled for himself. In one extreme case, on the haciendas

[28] Kaerger, Vol. II, p. 639.

surrounding the village of Amatanango, the croppers had to pay 8 days' *baldiaje* a month for each hectare that they planted for themselves. That meant that if the worker cultivated two hectares he had to give the hacienda 16 days' work a month during the agricultural season. This was more than was usual in the same section of the state, and the nearer to the national lands one came the fewer the days per hectare that a worker had to give for the right to cultivate a hectare.[29]

Even when wages were paid, they were small in amount. The normal daily wages received in money about 1887 ranged between 12½ centavos and 1 peso.[30] (See table on page 115.) The wage structure of Mexico was exceedingly complex, as it was to a large extent a local, traditional, and customary wage structure independent of outside factors.

[29] "They are obliged to work two days a week and are free to work in other haciendas the rest of the week. In return for this they are permitted to plant some land on the hacienda." *Edu. Púb.*, Hidalgo, 1922, *Exp.* 348, p. 1.

[30] "The hot region, which embraces the coast on both oceans and the low valleys situated in the interior of the country, is very sparsely inhabited; labor is therefore very scarce, and wages are higher here than in any other region. While in the high and cold regions wages were often 12½ cents a day and rations, on the coast they are sometimes $1.00 a day. The inhabitants of the cold and temperate regions do not like to descend to the warm zone, because they are exposed to maladies prevailing there, such as yellow fever and intermittent and remittent fevers, and because they are terribly annoyed by mosquitoes, and they can hardly endure the heat. If at any time they do go down there, it is only to remain a few days." Matías Romero, *Mexico and the United States,* New York, 1898, Vol. I, p. 509.

RURAL WAGES IN 685 MUNICIPIOS, IN 28 STATES, 1885-1887*

State	Number of Municipios	Municipios with Specified Average Wage (In centavos)											
		1-12½	12¾-18¾	19-25	25¼-31¼	31½-37½	37¾-43¾	44-50	50¼-56¼	56½-62½	62¾-68¾	69-75	75-100
Veracruz	128	1	2	22	26	50	7	14	1	3	1	1	
Chiapas	76	12	36	18	4	3	2	1					
Durango	19			3	4	6		3				3	
Jalisco	23		3	16	3	1							
Morelos	22		2	4	6	8	2						
Nayarit	23			3	2	15	2	1					
Nuevo León													
Michoacán	3			2		1							
Oaxaca	74	4	45	24	1								
Puebla	15		1	10	4								
Querétaro	1										1		
San Luis Potosí	1						1						
Sonora	43					2	2	28		3	1	5	2
Tabasco	7					1	2	2		1		1	
Tamaulipas	15		2	7	3	1	1	1					
Yucatán	1				1								
Guerrero	40	1	5	18	9	4	1	2					
Zacatecas	19		3	5	4	5	1						
Guanajuato	39		18	21									
México	54	2	17	17	15	3							
Tlaxcala	32			24	6	2							
Hidalgo	38		13	21		4							
Baja California	1	1											
Aguascalientes	1	1											
Distrito Federal	1			1									
Colima	2			1	1								
Coahuila	7									1			
Chihuahua													
Totals	685	22	147	218	93	106	21	54	1	8	3	10	2

* Compiled and organized from *Informes y documentos relativos a comercio interior y exterior, agricultura é industrias,* 1885-1887. This may be taken as a fair average for all Mexico.

We know that wages had remained more or less stationary from the beginning of the century, and that broadly speaking rural wages were not much changed between that time and 1910.[31] We know that in spite of the general rise in wages as a result of the revolution there are still places in Mexico where they have remained comparatively stationary.

In August, 1926, wages in the Municipio of Huimilpan in the State of Querétaro, in the very center of Mexico's richest agricultural zone, were reported as 25 *centavos* or 2 *cuartillos* [32] of maize.[33] Other reports from the same state are of a similar import,[34] while from some place in Jalisco in 1924 wages were reported to be between 12 and 20 *centavos* per day and 4 litres of maize.[35] We merely cite these figures as testimony for the static character of the Mexican rural wage structure, especially before the revolution.[36] But it would be a mistake

[31] See Chapter VI.

[32] A *cuartillo* equals 1.38 litres.

[33] *Agrónomo regional Zona 26,* Querétaro, August, 1926, M. de Huimilpan. (Manuscript.)

[34] *Zona 22,* Querétaro, May, 1923, *Mun. de Colón,* 25 to 50 cents, *Mun. de Cadereyta* 40 cents, July, 1923, *Mun. de Villa Bermal* 50 cents, and August, 1923, *Mun. de Querétaro* 20 cents, and 1 *cuartilla* of Maize. (Manuscript.)

[35] *Agrónomo Regional Zona 24,* Jalisco, October, 1924, *Mun. Lagos de Moreno.* (Manuscript.)

[36] As late as 1921 one of the speakers before the Catholic Social Conference in Guadalajara, reported that: "I have examined one of the statistical tables provided by the *Confederación Católica del Trabajo* in which is to be noted that in some parts the wages are so low that it is difficult to understand how the workers live . . . where the agricultural laborers are paid 15 to

to consider the money wages as an actual description of either the amount of wages paid or of the form in which they were paid. The money wage must be looked upon as nominal rather than real—mere symbols recording the income´and expenditure of the hacienda laborer made through the hacienda store,[37] the *tienda de raya*.[38]

The haciendas held wage payments to a minimum by the very common practice of payment in kind or by token rather than in cash.[39] The laborer did receive a certain amount of money three times during the year—3 to 5 *pesos* during Passion Week, perhaps 6 to 10 *pesos* on All Saints' Day, and a further gift at Christmas,[40] with special payments in case

18 *centavos* a day." Sr. Lic. D. José Gutiérrez Hermosillo, *Comité Diócesi de Acción Católico Social, Curso Social Agrícola Zapopano, Guadalajara,* 1921, p. 92.

[37] "The pay per day of an ordinary agricultural laborer is one *reale* and a half, or 18 and three-quarters cents. Those employed on large haciendas are paid off in part by store-orders, which of course greatly reduces the cost to the employer, and correspondingly swindles the luckless laborer out of his just due. Then the produce of the land is sold to him at a very exorbitant price, so that the peon's nominal pay of 18 and three-quarter cents per day does not in reality amount to much more than half that sum. Meek in his disposition, with few wants, he submits to this, and indeed to any other species of imposition without complaint." Conkling, Howard, *Mexico and the Mexicans,* New York, 1883, p. 122.

[38] "The four *pesos* and rations, the monthly wage of the worker, was converted into a series of notations that the worker neither does nor can understand." Orozco, Vol. II, pp. 1096-1097.

[39] Pres. Silviano Carrilo, *Trabajos Presentados en la Cuarta Semana Social Mexicana,* September 23-28, Zacatecas, 1912, p. 110.

[40] Luis Cabrera quoted in Félix Palavicini, *Los Diputados,* 1915, Vol. I, p. 169.

of illness, death, the birth of a child, or some festive occasion.[41] Otherwise he would draw from the hacienda store such goods as met his simple needs, derived as far as possible from the estate itself. Such supplies consisted chiefly of maize and beans and salt. In a minor degree they included candles, plain white cloth for clothes, *pulque* (alcoholic beverage), lard, brown sugar, large straw hats, cheap print cloth, sandals, dried meat, red peppers, large colored handkerchiefs, string, tobacco, and flint.

Free commerce was excluded from the haciendas, and the *tienda de raya* (the truck store) managed by the administration was the chief and frequently the only source of supply. The ideal of good administration was to make such money as was paid out in wages return to the hacienda through this store at a profit.[42] The goods (when not raised locally) were bought wholesale by the hacienda and sold retail either as advances against wages or for the money that had been paid out in wages.[43] And

[41] Alberto Gracía Granados, *El Crédito Agrícola en México*, 1910, p. 6.

[42] *Santisteban,* p. 91.

[43] Labor established and employed on large estates, bound to the land by an ever-increasing debt to the owners, incurred by advances in the necessities of life, with a nominal wage that does not vary. Though illegal, these debts are in some cases carried from father to son, and such labor has been known to be transferred by sale with the property. Labor contracted and obtained through the local authorities. Such labor is subject to losses through advances and expenses of transport. Wages actually earned are low and desertion frequent. Great Britain, Diplomatic and Consular *Reports,* Annual Series, 1895.

in a good many of the haciendas, purchase at the *tienda de Raya* was compulsory.[44] As a part of its wages the hacienda extended housing and a piece of land. The hut was ordinarily built by the worker

[44] A picture of the agricultural labor in Mexico as it existed between the '70's and the end of the nineteenth century and in a general way up to the end of the Diaz regime may be gotten from the following reforms which a group of interested people suggested as a basis of a law in 1866. It is interesting to observe that the very influential and able Mexican publicist and economist, Dr. Francisco Pimentel, opposed these reforms on the grounds that they were contrary to the laws of economics and therefore unnecessary. Some of the more important of these suggested reforms are as follows:

1. That workers may leave the hacienda at any time when they have no debt or have paid it.
2. Work from sun to sun with two hours' intermission.
3. Cannot be compelled to work on Sunday and holidays.
4. Children under 12 can only be compelled to work half day.
5. Payment must be in money and workers cannot be compelled to make their purchases in the *tienda de raya*.
6. That after the decree the workers cannot be held responsible in law for debts above 10 pesos.
7. The owners must not prevent traveling merchants from coming to the hacienda.
8. Water and habitation to be provided for all workers.
9. All haciendas are prohibited from maintaining prisons, stocks, whippings, and in general all corporal punishment.
10. That debts be paid by deducting one-fifth of wages.
11. That the children shall not be held responsible for the debts of their parents except to the amount of their inheritance.
12. That the owners shall give each worker a book within which he is to note the account.
13. Parents are forbidden to bind their children.
14. Obligation to provide medicine in case of sickness, at request of worker, with deduction of one-fourth from wages.
15. Schools for all haciendas having 20 families.

Pimentel, Francisco, *la Economía Política aplicada a la propiedad territorial de México*, 1866.

himself,[45] with the materials available on the hacienda and the piece of land was looked upon as a means of increasing the yield of the hacienda without it assuming any of the responsibilities for its cultivation, except perhaps the right of the worker to use its instruments and animals on the days when they were not needed.[46] Not infrequently the peon was charged a rental for this piece of land. All of the goods that passed to the peon were charged against his account, and as long as he was in debt he could not leave the estates.[47]

Generally speaking, the resident laborer was tied to the hacienda by debt. This debt [48] he incurred in a great variety of ways. He might have received a sum for the celebration of his marriage.[49] His

[45] "In such houses of the common people there is rarely anything answering to the civilized idea of a bed, the occupants sleeping on a mat, skin, or blanket on the dirt floor. There are no chairs, tables, fireplace, or chimney; few or no changes of raiment; no washing apparatus or soap, and in fact no furniture whatever, except a flat stone with a stone roller to grind their corn, and a variety of earthen vessels to hold their food and drink, and for cooking, which last is generally performed over a small fire, with a circle of stones outside, and in front of the main entrance to the dwelling." Wells, David A., *A Study of Mexico,* 1887, pp. 96-97.

[46] Santisteban, p. 194; Kaerger, Vol. II, pp. 635-641.

[47] "But the peonage system has no legal existence in Mexico, because Article V of our Constitution of 1857, enacted for the purpose of abolishing it, provides that 'nobody should be obliged to render personal service without proper compensation and his full consent.'" Matías Romero, *Mexico and the United States,* 1898.

[48] McBride, p. 32.

[49] Matías Romero.

parents might have accumulated debts while he was growing into manhood. He might personally have transferred his labor from one hacienda to another by finding some *amo* (master) to assume his debt to his previous employer.[50] This debt generally kept increasing with the years. Nominally there would be a settling up of accounts each year, generally during Holy Week. But by and large, the worker upon the hacienda found himself in arrears,[51] and as he ordinarily could not pay he could not leave the estate.

The hacienda tended to shift the risk of raising the crop upon renters and croppers.[52] Generally speaking the hacienda cultivated only the irrigated or

[50] Wells, *A Study of Mexico*, pp. 28-30.

[51] These conditions, generally true for the permanent workers, were modified in one way or another for the rest of the laboring force. The cropper frequently found himself in debt at the end of the year. The day laborers, the week, month and task laborers, were as far as possible paid in kind, or in tokens only acceptable in places where the administration had an interest.

[52] It has been impossible to secure more than a few examples of the distribution of crop-sharers and *peons* in the different states and these are for the period after the revolution. These figures were supplied upon request by the governors of states.

	Peons	Renters and Crop Sharers
Durango	85,243	15,100
Nuevo León	14,478	14,828
Aguascalientes	22,240	4,075
Tlaxcala	29,509	13,304
Chihuahua (incomplete)...	4,487	9,780

In reply to a request for this information the governor of Queretaro said: "It is not possible to supply this information as we have no source from which to get it."

humid lands. The crops it raised were the commercial crops—wheat, sugar, coffee, and so forth; or it planted and raised directly the fibers (*maguey*) plants which involved comparatively little risk [53] and required considerable capital because of the long maturity period of the crop. On many large cereal-growing haciendas the only direct undertaking was in the raising of livestock, leaving the cultivation of the soil to renters and croppers.

The large haciendas either were rented outright [54] to renters who in turn sublet fractions of from 4 to 100 hectares to others, or themselves directly sublet fractions. [55] Even in some of the non-cereal crops like tobacco subletting and cropping were common, and for maize and beans the system was almost universal, especially so for maize. [56] We thus have a system where wheat and barley, for instance, would either be grown directly [57] or through renting,

[53] Molina Enríquez, p. 91.

[54] "The system that is followed in cultivating the land in this *Municipio* is generally on the basis of crop-sharing. There are few proprietors who cultivate directly their own lands." *Zona 8,* Estado de Nuevo León, *Mun. de Zuazua,* June, 1925. (Manuscript.)

[55] *El Problema Agrario en el Estado de Hidalgo, Imprenta de la Dirección de Estudios Geográficos y Climatológicos,* 1926, pp. 3-8.

[56] "The *hacienda La Gavia* in the State of Mexico comprised 120,000 hectares which was divided into 7 ranchos and had before the revolution some 2,000 renters and croppers." *Memorandum sobre la organización de la Hacienda de "La Gavia,"* Gilberto Fabila. (Manuscript.)

[57] *Agrónomo Regional, Zona 14,* Querétaro, October, 1925. (Manuscript.)

but where maize would be grown through crop-sharing.[58]

The systems of crop-sharing and renting differed widely between sections of the country, between crops.[59] Frequently the hacienda would provide the land, the tools, the seed and the animals, as well as *habilitación* (keep) during the growing season. The crop would be divided in half,[60] the cropper having to

[58] "Maize is not sown at the cost of the hacienda but through a system of crop-sharing." *Zona 18,* Estado de Nayarit, *Mun. de Compostela,* September, 1922. (Manuscript.)

"Agricultural work in a general way, at least that which concerns itself with the cultivation of non-irrigated lands, is made upon a system of crop-sharing." *Zona 9,* Estado de Zacatecas, *Mun. Jerez,* December, 1922. (Manuscript.)

"Crop-sharing is the method used for the cultivation of maize and beans on all the haciendas." *Zona 22,* Estado de Querétaro, *Mun. Querétaro,* June, 1923. (Manuscript.)

"The cropper who limits himself to cultivating maize very rarely succeeds in emancipating himself from the condition, because as a general rule, which has few exceptions, and only when using very good land and in very rare years covers the costs and pay the debts to the hacienda. The result is that the cropper is almost always in debt." *Informe de la Cámara Agrícola Nacional de León, Boletín de la Dirección General de Agricultura, Part II, Número 2,* February, 1912, pp. 140-141.

[59] "In case of the death of an animal by lightning it is charged to the owner of the animals but in all other cases the crop-sharer has to pay for the animal. Rentings are so varied that it would be difficult to give an adequate description of them." *Zona 28,* Estado de Michoacán, *Mun. de Pátzcuaro,* October, 1924. (Manuscript.)

[60] "To the crop-sharer are given lands, animals, seed and half the cost for making the crop. All the rest is done by the cropper. If for some reason they lose an ox they have to pay for it. If during their work they need maize or beans for their own food they are given it by the hacienda on the condition that they return double the amount when the crop is harvested. It is necessary that the crop should be good indeed for the croppers to

return the *habilitación* (keep). On some haciendas the cropper could keep half the forage, on others all the stalks belonged to the owner. On some haciendas he would have to deliver the share of the estate to its barn, in others the division was made on the field and the hacienda would haul its own crop. In many places the tools and animals were provided by the croppers, the hacienda only giving seed.[61] In Oaxaca there used to be a custom that for each 100 furrows the croppers would in addition to all other payments give the hacienda a chicken.

We have probably said enough to point out the complexity of the rural organization and the fact that the burden of the risk for raising the crop tended in a large measure to be thrown upon the cropper,[62] renter, and resident worker whose little

be able to liquidate all their debts and have enough maize left to cover their needs for the rest of the year." *Zona 19,* Colima, *Mun. de Comala,* October, 1923. (Manuscript.)

[61] "The cropper is given the land, oxen and seed, the seed he has to return double at the end of the crop. If one of the oxen dies by lightning or for any other reason he has to pay for it. In addition he is charged for the oxen, and has to pay for a watchman who watches the crop, so that no one can even take a stalk for the animals. The cutting of the stalks is at his expense and the hacienda takes one-quarter of this. The hacienda does the gleaning and charges him one-half the cost. The hacienda shells the corn, charging the cropper 3 *centavos* for each *hectolitre,* keeping the cobs; the cropper receiving one-half of the maize after settling his accounts and costs indicated. As a result of these accounts, as frequently happens, instead of gathering maize he gathers a debt for the next year." *Zona 13,* Estado de Jalisco, *Mun. de Sayula,* May, 1924. (Manuscript.)

[62] "When the time of planting arrives many of the croppers migrate with their families to the piece of land which they are

maize parcel was looked upon as a means of increasing the yield of the hacienda without effort on its part, and was frequently bought by the hacienda while still standing [63] as a means of liquidating debts.

The hacienda had other sources of income in addition to those we have just described. If it had abundant pasture it ordinarily permitted the cropsharers and renters to graze their work animals for a fixed charge [64] and could, although it occasionally refused to,[65] permit the neighboring rancheros or villages to graze some animals at a given price per head. It could permit the neighboring villages to make charcoal from dead wood, or from sections of the estate that were being cleared, and charge a certain minimum for each load. It might draw a simi-

given to cultivate, making a little *cabaña* so as to live in it until the gathering of the crop, after which they return to the village from which they came for the rest of the year or if they do not happen to have any home, continue living on this piece of land, which for many of them is a great privilege." *Zona 21,* Zacatecas, *Municipio de San Pedro Ocampo,* November, 1924. (Manuscript.)

[63] Luis Cabrera, quoted from Felix Palavicini, *Los Diputados,* Vol. II, p. 170.

[64] "The two months during which they use the oxen the croppers are given the necessary feed which they have to return at the end of the crop, or if they are allowed to pasture these oxen they are charged a minimum of one *peso* a month per head. If unfortunately one of the animals dies during work they have to pay for it even if death is due to accident or epidemic, even such as death by lightning over which they have no control." *Zona 19,* Estado de Colima, *Mun. de Comala,* October, 1923. (Manuscript.)

[65] "The rest of the haciendas because of the autocratic caprice of their owners do not rent pasture to any one at any price even for a goat." Orozco, Vol. II, p. 914.

lar small income from rights to collect fruits, or dig clay for pottery, or hunt, or cut wood for sale. In short, if the hacienda was large enough, a number of money-producing by-products could be drawn upon without involving any considerable enterprise from the administration.

Six factors in the organization of the Mexican hacienda were responsible for its success. They made it possible for the institution to persist and retain its feudal form and structure to the end of the Diaz regime in 1910, and in some considerable degree to persist into the present. These economic practices may be summarized in the following six categories.

1. The economy of large areas
    a. Variety of resources
2. The economy of indentured labor
    a. Permanent labor force
3. The economy of unremunerated labor
    a. Work tasks for all residents and their families (*faenas*)
    b. Work rentals for grazing
    c. Work rentals for right to tillage
4. The economy of payment in kind
    a. By crops raised on the property
    b. By products purchased wholesale and sold as wage, at a profit in retail
    c. By payments in token coins acceptable only on the hacienda or in places where the administration had an interest and a profit
    d. By trying to receive back at the hacienda store the money paid out in wages

5. The economy of indirect tillage by passing on the risk of the crop to:
   a. Renters, for money or crop rentals
   b. Crop-sharers
   c. Workers having little maize plots
   d. Non-rent-paying openers of new land
   e. Neighbors or villages who pay rentals for grazing
   f. Workers who pay money rentals for the right to make charcoal, or collect fruits or other natural resources
6. The economy of low risk-bearing crops and products
   a. By tilling only the irrigated or best lands
   b. By planting fibre (*maguey* crops) which involved a very minimum of risk and a maximum of certainty
   c. By raising cattle (in the largest haciendas the only direct undertaking of the haciendas)

This system of administration gave the hacienda a surplus crop beyond all internal consumption, which was accumulated as far as possible without any direct risk or expenditure of money. This surplus crop was then loaded upon the backs of pack mules or in some instances upon the backs of men and carried to the nearest trading center, often days of travel away. More recently it has been delivered to the nearest railroad station.

It must be borne in mind that this general description of the Mexican hacienda was more completely true of some places than of others—depending in part on the crop grown, in part upon the sufficiency of labor, and in part upon local custom or tradition.

But as a whole it represents the method by which the hacienda was enabled to continue for 400 years with as little enterprise and initiative as it obviously exhibited. From this organization followed a number of definite by-products.

The hacienda kept Mexican agriculture from being modernized. It helped keep agricultural technique primitive. The landowner and the administrator had little interest in improving agricultural methods. Their interest was in the share of the crop, and the burden of cultivation tended to fall upon the cropper and renter who was least equipped for modern improvement, both financially and technically. It tended to prevent the development of a middle class as a very large proportion of all the "commerce" of the rural community was in the hands of the large haciendas. It tended to prevent the development of a self-sufficient peasantry or farming class. It prevented the investment of capital in agriculture. All of these factors combined help to explain both the economic condition of the Mexican rural population and the small place agriculture has played in the development of Mexican economic life. As we point out in the following chapter, page 147, in spite of the fact that a very large proportion of all haciendas were essentially dedicated to raising cereals and that practically all haciendas raised maize and generally also beans, Mexico has for a long time been importing maize, which is the essential food of the people. It ought to be repeated that the hacienda as a part of its economy threw the tax burden [66] upon the rest of the community by paying only a nominal tax [67] upon land, and insisted on high tariffs so as to raise the price of its products.[68]

It should be remembered that we are describing an organization that has persisted for 400 years. It is true that certain broad changes have taken place, especially in the spread of the market area in recent years [69] because of the development of railroad transportation; yet it should also be remembered that rail transportation was only made available within the last 50 years, that in general these railroads were built to meet the needs of the mining centers of the Republic and of international commerce, and that the two leading railroads crossed the greater part of

[66] "But the greatest obstacle in the way of tax reform in Mexico is to be found in the fact that a comparatively few people —not six thousand out of a possible ten million—own all the land, and constitute, in the main, the governing class of the country; and the influence of this class has thus far been sufficiently potent practically to exempt land from taxation." Wells, *A Study of Mexico*, p. 186.

[67] As late as 1911 it was possible for the official publication of the Department of Agriculture to say: "In practically all the states there are regions where agricultural production is very abundant, but due to the lack of communication or transportation, it is frequently impossible to carry them; or at least the benefits are almost nullified as a result of the exorbitant cost of the carrying charge. There are places where the corn crop cannot be liquidated unless first converted into fat by means of hogs capable of supporting the traffic charge and there are others where the transportation handicap cannot be overcome even by this resource." *Boletín de la Dirección General de Agricultura,* September, 1911, *Num. 5, Part II,* p. 437.

[68] Molina Enríquez, p. 94.

[69] See Chapter VI.

the Mexican desert and the sparsely populated sections. The railroads have to date in only a minor degree influenced the agricultural development of the country. In only a few favored spots has the agricultural organization shown any considerable response to the new influence. These are the Laguna district, where cotton has been developed on a large scale; the West Coast, where sugar and fruits and vegetables are grown; certain sugar, banana, and coffee haciendas on the Eastern slope and in Chiapas near the border of Guatemala. That is, the hacienda system persisted up to the Diaz regime as it had persisted for 350 years before it. The changes set in motion during this regime directly influenced industrial developments, manufactures, mining, railroads, and only indirectly agriculture. Since 1910 the internal revolution has profoundly stirred the social and political character of the country, but the agricultural organization has only been slightly modified for the better, and it can even be argued that the agriculture of the country has suffered instead of benefited.

We must conclude that the hacienda system was a feudal [70] political structure that did not contribute

[70] "The evenings closed in about six, and we generally spent an hour in the office, while the reports of the day were brought in by the head-men, and a portion of the laborers received their wages. It was a lively hour. The lord of the hacienda is *de facto,* if not *de jure* lord of his laborers. He has a prison in the hacienda, into which he puts them without ceremony, if he thinks it to their benefit. When the office work is completed, Tejira, or his administrator, holds a short court for dispensing

materially to the economic development of Mexico.[71]
For this perhaps the hacienda was in itself not entirely to blame. The policy of the Spanish government in preventing immigration, the lack of an
active middle class, the absence of capital for investment, the almost insurmountable difficulties in the
way of agricultural credit,[72] the usurious interest
that was charged when the credit was to be had, the
roads, "good only for birds and deer," the fact that
the *alcabala* (internal tariff), persisted up to nearly
the end of the nineteenth century,[73] the fact that the

small loans, doles of Indian corn, or advice, or medicine for the
sick; for granting licenses for marriage, christening, or other
festivities, for settling disputes, and for all such matters as may
naturally arise amongst a community of four hundred or five
hundred people." Brocklehurst, Thomas Unett, *Mexico Today*,
London, 1883, pp. 147-8.

[71] Molina Enríquez, p. 86.

[72] There has never been any adequate system of agricultural
credit in Mexico. Agricultural credit used to be supplied by the
church, but during the last half century that has been made
difficult. In addition the inadequate titles to land make credit
very hard to secure and very high. "In Guanajuato two-thirds
of the owners have no adequate titles and occupy their lands by
possession." (Gonzalez Roa, *Las Cuestiónes Fundamentales de
Actualidad en México*, p. 164.) There does not exist in the state
(Guanajuato) a single institution for the extension of credit to
agriculturists. *Boletín de la Dirección General de Agricultura*,
1912, Part II, No. 2. Typical examples of the reports of the
Agrónomos Regionales are the following:

Zona 22, Querétaro, August, 1923, Municipio de Querétaro:
interest at least 12 per cent a year.

Zona 33, Oaxaca, November, 1923, *Mun. Uicotlán*: Interest is
as a general rule 2 per cent per month. Not infrequently the
report is 2 and 3 per cent a month. (Manuscript.)

[73] "This practice of locally taxing interstate commerce is in
direct contravention of an article in the Mexican constitution of
1857. . . . The existence in a state of the new world of a system

greater part of the working population was kept at the very lowest possible means of subsistence and prevented from accumulating capital, the importance given to mining, the almost entire absence of education, the fact, in short, that Mexico was throughout all the colonial period a feudal aristocracy governing a serf population, and like a feudal aristocracy spending its income in luxurious and high living rather than in internal improvements, all combined to keep the hacienda system intact for so long a period in Mexican history. If we add to this the unsettled conditions of Mexico all through the period of the last century, when the only safe property was land, we can see why the *hacendados* held on to their estates,[74] made no improvements, developed no new agricultural techniques, built no roads, lived as well as the conditions would permit by drawing from their estates such income as they could,[75] and augmented that income by raising tariffs[76] and

of taxation so antagonistic to all modern ideas, and so destructive of all commercial freedom, is certainly very curious." Wells, *A Study of Mexico,* p. 173.

[74] Wells, *A Study of Mexico*, pp. 117-118.

[75] " During all the course of the history of Mexico until the time of General Diaz both the rural and urban properties were of comparatively little value. The yield from the land was insignificant." González, p. 161.

[76] "The principle upon which the sugar and coffee *hacendados* conduct their business appears to be to grow only sufficient for the demands of the neighborhood of their estates, and for this purpose they keep shops in the nearest large town, where they sell it to the small dealers. As the tariff is so high as to be prohibitory to the importation of foreign sugars, they can obtain highly remunerative prices, and it is a fact that poorly refined

lowering wages at the expense of the rest of the community. This hacienda system and the structure of the rural community (Chapter III) present the two sides of Mexican rural organization.

sugar costs in Mexico more than good loaf-sugar fetches in London." A. Gringo, *Through the Land of the Aztecs,* London, 1892, pp. 90-91.

. . . the Louisiana planters sell their sugar in New York with a profit at from six to seven cents per pound, while in the City of Mexico and other places in my country it commands twice and even three times that price. The same is the case with tobacco." Matias Romero, *Mexico and the United States,* New York, 1898, Vol. I, p. 524.

CHAPTER VI

CAUSES OF THE REVOLUTION

The eighteen years since the Madero Revolution broke upon an unexpectant Mexico have witnessed many changes. The persistent turbulence, however, has served to obscure the underlying shift of power and purpose. The continuous struggle between factions, the easy use of revolutionary slogans, the ready resort to violence, the unending stream of charges and countercharges, and the constant bias of the contending factions have made a description of the broader trend of these years of internal strife a difficult matter. And yet it is admitted by those who have watched Mexico during this period that a change has taken place—perhaps a fundamental and basic change, the import of which may lie beyond any immediate objective.

In a study such as this, it is obviously impossible to undertake a description of even the most important of these modifications excepting in so far as they influence the agrarian and agricultural organization of Mexico. But even here, it seems essential to note that the Mexico of today appears different from the Mexico of the Diaz regime.[1] It is clear that in some way the Mexican's attitude towards life is different, that in some way his spiritual and cultural values have been remodeled in the crucible of internal strife.[2] These changes in so far as they affect the problems here under discussion are largely confined to three major tendencies—agrarianism, social organization,[3] and nationalism. In the three

[1] "Their traditional, age-old sadness has been lighted by hope. They now play and laugh as they never did before. They hold their heads high." Pedro Henríquez Ureña, "Revolution and Intellectual Life," *Survey Graphic*, May, 1924, p. 168.

[2] "The Indian of today is not the Indian of yesterday in personality and standard of living. He is more likely to look down upon the aristocracy than to take off his hat as he passes on the street." Vasconcelos, Normal Wait Harris Memorial Foundation, *Report* of Round Table, June 28, 1926, p. 10.

[3] The most striking single example of the profound change taking place in the spiritual life of Mexico is to be found in the frescos of Diego Rivera, "that great and prolific Mexican master whose fame and works are at last—and how fortunately—seeping into the United States," drawn upon the walls of the Department of Education and of those of the Agricultural College at Chapingo. The work done during the last four years by this great artist has been compared with the greatest art of all time and is unique in the sense that it is an expression of the new Racial-Nationalism which has sprung from the revolution and which delights in being Mexican and indigenous.

While the work of Diego Rivera is the most striking and powerful, it is merely one of the varied influences which are indicative of a new national stirring. One must mention the rediscovery of the Indian folk songs and their introduction into the popular schools, the great interest in Indian art, the new methods of drawing based upon older Indian methods developed by Adolfo Best Mauguard. For a glimpse of the new values in things spiritual, see *Survey Graphic*, May, 1924, especially articles by Manuel Gamio, José Vasconcelos, Pedro Henríquez Ureña, Catherine Ann Porter, Diego Rivera, Esperanza Velázquez Bringas, and Dr. Atl; also *Mexican Folkways*—a magazine dedicated to

following chapters we shall trace the historical growth of these broader social policies and discuss what seems to be their import for Mexico.

the new interest in things Mexican; *Metodo de Dibujo, Tradición resurgimiento y evolución del Arte Mexicano*, by Adolfo Best Mauguard; Miguel Covarrubias, *The Prince of Wales and Other Americans*, New York, 1922, and *Negro Drawings*, New York, 1927; Ernestine Evans, "Frescoes Glorify Mexican Indian Life," *New York Times Magazine*, September 26, 1926, pp. 12, 21; Maximo Bretal, *La Nueva Pintura Mexicana Social*, Havana, April, 1927, pp. 40, 62; James C. Bardin, "Yucatan Develops a Truly American Art," *Bulletin Pan-American Union*, July, 1926, pp. 60, 676-685; Dr. Atl, *Las Artes Populares en México*, Volumes 1 and 2, *Publicaciones de la Seria, de Industria y Commercio, Mexico Editorial Cultura*, 1922, 2 vols.; Betram D. Wolfe, "Art and Revolution in Mexico," *Nation*, New York, August 27, 1924, pp. 207-208; Daniel Cosio Villegas, "La Pintura en México," *Cuba contemporánea*, Havana, April, 1924, pp. 331-339; "Un Pintor Mexicano, Diego Rivera Figueroa," Havana, April 19, 1914, p. 188; Diego Rivera, "Espíritu de Agremíación en el Arte Mexicano," *La Nueva Democracia*, New York, July, 1924, pp. 6-8, 30-31; Rosendo Salazar, *México en Pensamiento y en Acción obra ilustrada con muchedumbre de reproduciones de la colosal obra pictórica de José Clemente Orozco, Diego Rivera y Dr. Atl, y fotografías de prominentes representativos de nuestra revolución*, México, 1926; Guillermo Rivas, "The Artist Looks Backward," *Mexican Life*, Mexico, December, 1926, pp. 16-18; Miguel O. de Meudizobel, *Las Artes Aborígenes Mexicanas Imprenta del Museo Nacional de Arqueología, Historia y Etnografiá*, 1922; Manuel Gamio, *La Población del Valle de Teotihuacán*, Mexico, 1922; Gruening, Ernest, *Mexico and Its Heritage*, 1928, pp. 635-657.

"The most evident proof of my statement is the spontaneous offering of the peasants to take up arms in the defense of General Obregón's government. They are no longer the peasants who stick their heads in a well at the order of their master. Today they obey organization discipline, they think and work within the judgment of their syndicate." El Brazo de Obregón, *Ideario de la Revolucion Mexicana*, p. 83.

"It is absolutely necessary that we all persuade ourselves that the day of a profound and radical change in the economic and social organization of Mexico has arrived, and it is of no use

I. THE COMING OF THE REVOLUTION

The Mexican revolution of 1910 came at a moment of holiday-making over the centennial of Mexico's independence from Spain. It came at a time when Mexico seemed at peace with itself and secure in its relations with the world. The celebration of the centennial of independence had been made the occasion of an international tribute to Mexico. The governments of the world rivaled each other in decorating the aged ruler of Mexico, and the Mexican government lavished its public treasure upon entertainment and public feasting. And yet before the feasting and the merriment had died away, the seemingly impregnable government had fallen like a house of cards, and Mexico became a center of turmoil and international contention which made it a byword for disorder and banditry.[4]

It is true that there had been a few rumblings of discontent, but nothing serious seemed to be im-

to be forging illusions for ourselves or to be animated by a hatred that will carry us to anarchy and social disequilibrium. . . ." A Los Terratenientes de Nuestra Patria, La Paz Social, Revista Mensual, Organo del Secretariado Social Mexicano, Tomo III, Num. 2, p. 57.

[4] "Diaz was crowned a savior and ruler of Mexico, but even while the acclamations of vast throngs were reverberating through the palaces and streets of Mexico City, the hour of disaster was drawing nigh; the great structure which had been built up by the wisdom, sobriety, and patriotism of one man had not been built strong enough to stand the storms which presently broke forth. From the pinnacle which he had reached, Diaz fell to an abyss and with him fell his country." Wilson, Henry Lane, *Diplomatic Episodes in Mexico, Belgium, and Chile,* p. 190.

pending. Here and there a strike had occurred, here
and there an Indian uprising had been suppressed or
driven back into the mountains.[5] The only serious
trouble for a long period of time had been with the
Yaqui Indians in Sonora [6] and with the Maya Indians in Quintana Roo. But in both cases there was
the ready explanation that these were savages and
bandits, and it was understood that with them, as
with other recalcitrants, there was to be no peace.
It became in fact a war of extermination.[7] Apart
from these minor difficulties, the government seemed
strong, indeed impregnable. The continuance of its
policies was expected even in case of the death of
President Diaz.[8]

II. THE DIAZ REGIME

The rule of Porfirio Diaz, which came to this sudden and unexpected end, is the most remarkable in
the history of the Mexican republic. Coming to

[5] Manuel Maple Ard, *El Movimiento Social en Veracruz,* 1927,
pp. 1-10.

[6] "The recent attempts to survey the lands of the Yaqui and
Mayo rivers have been suspended, awaiting a petition from the
legislature of Sonora to the general government to supply a force
of 1,000 soldiers to keep the Yaquis in subjection during the
survey and location of certain government grants upon those
rivers. For this purpose, a return grant by the owners to the
general government of a portion of the lands is to be made to
cover the expense of maintaining the military in this district."
Leonidas Hamilton, *Border States of Mexico,* Chicago, 1882, p. 45.

[7] John Turner, *Barbarous Mexico,* 1910; Carlo de Fornan, *Diaz
Czar of Mexico,* 1909.

[8] "The policy of General Diaz will not disappear, cannot disappear, even should the man pass away." Maqueo Castellanos,
Algunos Problemas Nacionales, Mexico, 1909, p. 211.

office in 1876, this extraordinary ruler, excepting the
single presidential period of 1880-1884, when a recognized tool of Diaz was placed in the presidency,[9]
kept his power in Mexico until 1911.   He was re-
elected every four years, and as the elections recurred
they became more and more of a political formula
kept up for appearance sake and less and less compatible with the desires of the people.[10]   The power
of Porfirio Diaz was therefore dominant for 35 years.

These 35 years must be reckoned as the most constructive in the hundred years of the republic which
were celebrated just before the government was
overthrown.[11]   Diaz gave Mexico political stability.
The persistent military and factional turbulence
which had made any continuous political administration impossible was brought to an end.   Up to
that time Mexico had had on the average more than
one government per year; it now had one that lasted
35 years.[12]

*The Diaz administration made political peace and
stability the basis for a rapid industrial develop-*

[9] Priestly, H. I., *The Mexican Nation,* 1923, p. 378.

[10] *ibid.,* p. 390.

[11] "This great man possessed the wisdom and the statesman-
ship, the strong arm, and the steadfast purpose necessary to weld
the warring factions, to reconcile the antagonistic parties and to
lift Mexico from retrogressive chaos and launch it on a career
of unexampled prosperity." Lummis, Charles F., "The Awaken-
ing of a Nation," *Mexico of Today,* New York, 1898.

[12] "From 1821 to 1926 we have had 83 governments. If we
deduct the long period of General Diaz . . . we find ourselves
with more than one government per year." J. Silva Herzog,
Conferencias, Mexico, 1927, p. 53.

ment. The banditry that fattened upon the public disorders was sternly suppressed, and Mexico became one of the safest countries in the world.[13] The old bandits were either exterminated or enrolled into the *rurales*—the rural police—and their stern justice became a byword of fear and terror in Mexico.[14] With political stability and internal order came economic developments that soon placed Mexico in a favorable position in the family of nations. Internal revenue increased, the budget was balanced, railroad construction was pushed rapidly and rose from 691 kilometers in 1876 to 24,717 in 1911. Mining was developed with great intensity. The silver production rose from 522,820 kilograms in 1875 to 2,416,669 kilograms in 1910. Gold production jumped from 1,636 kilograms in 1875 to 41,420 kilograms in 1910. The economic development of Mexico under the

REVENUES FOR MUNICIPAL, STATE, AND FEDERAL GOVERNMENTS *
(In *pesos*)

Year	Municipal	State	Federal	Total
1881.......	6,155,356	8,328,125	25,879,312	40,362,793
1891.......	11,964,329	19,038,694	44,142,857	75,145,880
1901.......	18,424,486	20,760,556	63,283,196	102,468,238
1910.......	18,337,439	27,394,851	106,328,485	152,060,775

* *Boletin de la Estadistica Nacional,* January 31, 1927, p. 24.

Diaz regime was reflected in its international trade accounts. Exports and imports totaled 51,760,000

[13] Terry, *Mexico,* p. 65.
[14] Priestley, p. 393; Turner, *Barbarous Mexico.*

pesos in 1873 and rose to 499,588,000 pesos in 1910, exports exceeding imports by more than 87 million pesos.

These important economic changes contributed to and were part of the process that led to the abolition of the internal tax, the *alcabala,* which had persisted till a very recent date,[15] hampering internal trade and making tax administration a confusing and costly undertaking. These changes led to the establishment of the gold standard, the stabilization of Mexican exchange, the improvement of Mexican credit, the rapid inflow of foreign investments, the development of ports, the modernization of cities, and the harnessing of water-power. Much public money was expended upon the beautifying of the larger cities, and huge public buildings were constructed to serve the developing administrative needs of the government.[16] A summary of these varied achievements makes a striking citation of progress and change. It impressed the world out-

[15] Priestley, p. 383.

The *alcabala* was abolished by the Constitution of 1857, but persisted until towards the end of the Diaz regime, and as a matter of fact has not as yet been entirely uprooted.

"Halfway from the village of Cholula, while riding one morning, I found Employe Aporanlly from the Ayuntamiento of Puebla collecting *alcabala* for the introduction of articles of prime necessity of whatever kind." *Informe del Agronomo Regional, Zona 31, Estado de Puebla Municipio de Cholula,* August, 1924. (Manuscript.)

The author found traces of the system still in force in isolated and remote parts of Mexico as late as August, 1926.

[16] Vicente Lombardo Toledano, *La Libertad Sindical en México,* Mexico, 1926, pp. 29-30.

side, and Mexico "stood in 1910 as the fairest and brightest example of Hispanic American solidity." [17]

These evidences of progress and prosperity, especially impressive to foreign observers, concealed shortcomings that destined Diaz' work to early ruin. In its anxiety to give Mexico the benefits of modern industrialism, to open its resources to ready exploitation, to give it a place in the commonwealth of nations, the Diaz administration adopted the more obvious fiscal and industrial policies of modern nations without destroying the feudal structure that underlay Mexican economic organization. The assumption was that capitalistic individualism, given full and free reign, would in and of itself cure Mexico of its great ills.[18] The facts proved the contrary. Instead of destroying agricultural feudalism, the hothouse industrialism so rapidly introduced into Mexico merely aggravated the earlier evils and brought new ones of its own. It is possible to argue that if the Revolution had not occurred, modern influences following inevitably in the wake of railroads, factories, telegraphs, and good roads would have changed the face of Mexican economic life and brought it abreast of contemporary industrial nations. Such arguments, however, are beside the point. The Mexican people did not wait. They rebelled against this industrial feudalism and at-

[17] Priestley, p. 393.
[18] Roa and Covarrubias, *El Problema Rural de México*, 1917, p. 86.

tempted to change the structure upon which it rested.

This industrial feudalism, it must be remembered, was very complicated. It was a social and political structure that had been built up through force, conquest, and imposition. It was a social structure, at the bottom of which rested an Indian population that had never become fully Europeanized, that retained, in spite of 400 years of white domination, the essential racial and social organization of pre-Hispanic days.[19] This underlying Indian population and these Indian institutions had in a measure blended their racial and economic forms with that of their conquerors, and the *mestizo*, part Indian, part Spanish, had been injected between the conqueror and the conquered. But economically and spiritually the *mestizo* was closer to the Indian than to the white man.[20] In 1910, therefore, Mexico had a fundamental Indian tradition and culture, a medieval land-holding system introduced by Spain, a political constitution copied from France and the United States, and an industrialism taking rapid

[19] Manuel Gamio, Forjando Patrio, México, 1916; *Empiricism of Latin-American Governments and the Empiricism of their Relations with the United States,* Mexico, 1919.

[20] "Moreover, the *mestizo,* or half breed, born under these circumstances was educated by the mother, since the father abandoned the woman sooner or later, and he in turn increased in body and spirit the indigenous man—passive enemies of the white colonists." José Vasconcelos and Manuel Gamio, *Aspects of Mexican Civilization,* Lectures on the Harris Foundation, 1926, p. 110.

root in what proved to be recalcitrant soil. The Revolution broke out because remedy in the form of unrestrained individualism did not fit the disease. It aggravated it.

III. INDUSTRIALIZATION AND ITS RESULTS

It is difficult to explain just why the revolution began in 1910 rather than in 1909 or 1905 or some year after 1910. However, there is sufficient evidence taken all together to show that the revolution, when it did come, bore a logical relation to cumulative difficulties growing out of the effort to industrialize the country.

Industrialization was paralleled by a rapid increase in the cost of living without a corresponding rise in the wages of the masses. It is true that the money wages of industrial laborers increased somewhat, but that of the mass of the population, the agricultural laborers, remained comparatively unaffected. As a matter of fact, money wages in Mexico had apparently remained at a practical standstill for nearly a century. They seem to have changed but little from 1794 to 1891.[21] The wage data reported by von Humboldt for 1794, by Miguel Lerdo de Tejada for 1838, by Pimentel for 1861, and the data available for 1891 are approximately the same.[22] This stationary character of the money

[21] *Revista Quincenal Organo del Departamento de la Estadística Nacional,* May 31, 1925, No. 10, pp. 15-19. *La Curva de los Salarios y el Costo de la Vida.*
[22] *ibid.*

wage during so long a period does not, however, up to the Diaz regime, seem to have been seriously adverse to the standard of living to which the mass of the Mexican agricultural population was accustomed.[23] The practical isolation of Mexico from the rest of the world, the poor internal communication, the slow increase of its population, the almost complete absence of internal migration due to both the regional cultural groupings and to the great differences in climate, and the fact that the mass of the population was either tied by debt as peons to the large haciendas or lived within communal villages [24] made the country almost independent of the changes taking place in the outside world.

This isolation and sufficiency of internal economy was gradually broken down by the economic forces set in motion during the industrialization of Mexico taking place under the Diaz regime.[25] Until the opening up of the country by railroads, Mexico's international commerce consisted largely in the export of precious metals, especially silver, and the import of luxuries.[26] The long distance between the center

[23] ibid.
[24] See Chapters III and IV.
[25] Revista Quincenal, May 31, 1925, pp. 15-19.
[26] ". . . before railroads were built, in consequence of the broken surface of that country, and upon the results of such conditions which prevented any article from being profitably exported unless raised near the coast or unless it had a very high price and small bulk, like precious metals, these facts reducing the exports of Mexico practically to the precious metals, indigo, cochineal, and similar articles of high price and small bulk."

of Mexico's population and the American boundary, the fact that all imports either overland or by water had to be carried over the high mountains to get into the central plateau where Mexico's population is so largely concentrated, discouraged any imports excepting those of the greatest value. The railroads changed all of that. The railroads developed a free working-class population, stimulated the growth of cities, stimulated the development of mining and other industries, and expanded the market for and the price of food. The growing cities, however, could more easily be fed from the outside through rail transport than from the interior. The interior roads tended to deteriorate as the railroads developed because the government began to neglect the highways.[27]

In addition, a heavy protective tariff covering a large part of all the articles imported increased the cost of food and clothing.[28] The tariff served to raise

Matias Romero, *Mexico and the United States,* New York, 1898, Vol. I, p. 531.

[27] As a result of the abolition of a system of road tolls during the War of the Reform, the roads were neglected and became worse with the passing years. "From this has resulted what seems an inexplicable phenomenon. . . . The Mexican Republic which lives in full peace and which considers itself a civilized nation has its roads today in a worse condition than they were 50 years ago when it lived in perpetual revolution and was looked upon by civilized countries as a semi-barbarous nation." *El Crédito Agrícola en México,* Alberto García Granados, México, 1910, pp. 27-28.

[28] Wells, *A Study of Mexico,* p. 154.

"A population of ten million, poor almost beyond conception,

the cost of the basic articles without apparently effecting an upward change in the money wage of the mass of the population. But the tariff did not enable the Mexican agriculturists to reserve the market exclusively to themselves, for they did not raise enough to support the growing city populations, and where they did they could not transport it to the center of consumption.[29] This is suggested by the fact that the period of rising prices of corn and wheat was also a period of increasing imports.[30] Moreover, the imports, in addition to the heavy tariff entry at the border, had to contend with the

have therefore to pay from two to three hundred per cent more for the staple material of their simple clothing than needs be, in order that some other ten or twelve thousand of their fellow citizens, men and women, may have the privilege of working exhaustively from fourteen to fifteen hours a day in a factory for the small pittance of from thirty-five to seventy cents and defraying the cost of their own subsistence." *ibid.*, pp. 156-157.

Lauro Vidas, *Boletín de la Dirección General de Agricultura*, Part II, No. 6, October, 1911, p. 470.

[29] "The processes and tools used were exactly equal to those employed in Egypt more than 4,000 years ago. . . . The larger extensions . . . required enormous capital to cultivate adequately and our routine *latifundistas* did not possess this capital. They were not men of the field, but of the city; they were not residents, but absentees." J. Silva Herzog, *Conferencias*, Mexico, 1927, p. 73.

"The haciendas away from easy access to the railroads prefer generally to confine their production within the limits of the local market without undertaking any new production." Alberto García Granados, *El Crédito Agrícola en México*, Mexico, 1910.

[30] See table on page 30.

excessive railroad rates [31] and the internal tax, [32] which was not abolished until late in the nineteenth century. [33] The result of all this was to raise the price of the basic foods in Mexico, to fasten the grip of the large landholders upon their estates by assuring them protection from the cheap grains of the United States, [34] and at the same time to raise the value of their property. [35] This increase of the price of maize and wheat after the nineties was only a part of the general rise of prices in Mexico. [36]

[31] Granados, *El Crédito Agrícola en México,* pp. 28-29, 31-32.

[32] "But in Mexico each state of the republic has practically its own custom-house system, and levies taxes on all goods, domestic and foreign, passing its borders, and then in turn the several towns of the states again assess all goods entering their respective precincts. The rate of state taxation, being determined by the several state legislatures, varies, and varies continually with each state." Wells, *A Study of Mexico,* pp. 164-166.

"One reason why Mexican products were so high was that before they reached the markets they had to pay the local duty called *alcabala,* levied in coming into the cities. Unfortunately, the internal commerce of Mexico was not free, as in the United States, where such freedom has contributed very much, in my opinion, to the marvelous prosperity of the people. Our Constitution of 1857 prescribed the abolition, from the first of July, 1858, of the interior duties and custom houses throughout the country, but it was not until recently that this measure could be carried out." Matias Romero, *Mexico and the United States,* Vol. I, p. 526.

[33] Priestley, p. 389.

[34] ". . . Our maize and wheat are 40 per cent higher than in the United States or in the Argentine." Otto Peust, *Boletin de la Dirección General de Agricultura, El Movimiento del Valor Predial en México, Numero 1, Mayo, 1911,* p. 7.

[35] José Covarrubias, *La Trascendencia Política de la Reforma Agraria,* Mexico, 1922, pp. 88-89.

[36] "Corn, beans, chile, wheat, butter, meat, and cloth tripled at least in their value and resulted in a reduction to a third the miserable wage of the *peon.*" *ibid.,* pp. 88-89.

PRICES OF SELECTED ARTICLES OF FOOD IN MEXICO, 1891 AND 1908 *

Commodity	1891 (Pesos)	1908 (Pesos)	Percentage Increase of 1908 Over 1891
Rice, 100 kilos............	12.87	13.32	*3.5*
Sugar, 100 kilos...........	17.43	23.00	*32.0*
Flour, 10 kilos............	10.87	21.89	*101.4*
Maize, hectolitro.........	2.50	4.89	*95.6*
Wheat, 100 kilos..........	5.09	10.17	*99.8*
Beans, 100 kilos...........	6.61	10.84	*64.0*
Chile, 10 kilos............	27.13	57.94	*113.6*

* Compiled from *Estadística Nacional*, May 31, 1925, p. 15.

These rising prices in the face of what was practically a stationary money wage increasingly lowered the subsistence level of the Mexican wage earners. Mexican wage statistics for that period are not very good, but what we have to tell is embodied in the table on page 150.

From this table it is apparent that the wages in the central states of Mexico (marked by asterisks) where the greater portion of the population is located, remained almost stationary, undergoing a change of approximately 16 per cent in an area containing over 54 per cent of the total population at a time when basic food prices had in a number of instances at least doubled. A Mexican author summarizes the wage position of the Mexican agricultural laborer in the following terms:

The average wage in Mexico is 25 centavos (12½ cents) per day. In the United States it is $1.50. For the economist, the work of the American laborer valued

in wheat is worth 15 times as much as the work of the
Mexican laborer; valued in maize it is worth 12 times
as much; valued in cloth it is worth 19 times as much.
. . . . We can say that the purchasing power of the

AVERAGE DAILY WAGES OF AGRICULTURAL LABOR, BY STATES,
1891 AND 1908

(In *centavos*)

States	1891 [a]	1908 [b]
*Aguascalientes	18	31
Baja California	50	72
Campeche	37[c]	
Coahuila	53	..
Colima	31	..
Chiapas	50	30
Chihuahua	22	52
*Distrito Federal	31	..
Durango	50	..
*Guanajuato	25	31
Guerrero	35	..
*Hidalgo	25	27
*Jalisco	34	27
*México	25	32
*Michoacán	46	31
Morelos	50	..
Nayarit	38	..
Nuevo León	19	..
*Oaxaca	34	23
*Puebla	34	31
*Querétaro	28	31
San Luis Potosí	22	..
Sinaloa	75[c]	..
Sonora	65	86
Tabasco	44	..
Tamaulipas	38	..
Veracruz	44	43
Yucatán	31	..
Zacatecas	34	40

[a] Compiled from *Estadística Nacional,* May 31, 1925, p. 15.
[b] Compiled from *Estadística Nacional,* May 31, 1925, pp. 18-19.
[c] Taken from manuscript records on file in the *Estadística Nacional* and secured through the courtesy of José Covarrubias.

Mexican worker is 14 times less than that of the American worker, or, what is the same, that 14 days' work yield in merchandise to a Mexican worker what an American laborer obtains in one day.[37]

The difficulties produced by industrialization were intensified by the land policy of the Diaz government. The continued breakup of the village lands which was taking place, especially in the heavily populated centers of the republic, was increasing the relative strength of the hacienda as against the communal village group. The village inhabitants were being reduced to the position of wage laborers for the year around by having in ever greater numbers to become resident workers on the haciendas. This resident agricultural population that was working for wages upon the haciendas was tied to the soil by a system of debts, was paid largely in kind rather than in money, and had perforce to trade in the hacienda store. These years of rapid industrial development under Diaz did not contribute to improve materially the economic position of the agricultural laborer. He was being increasingly driven from his communal moorings into the position of an indentured wage worker, and his income was shrinking in the face of rising costs.

The government in its attempt to bring the natural resources into use further increased these difficulties by alienating the greater part of the national

[37] Alaman, *Memoria Sobre Agricultura en la República,* quoted by *Estadística Nacional,* May 31, 1925.

lands, giving concessions for the establishment of
industries with long-term exemptions from taxation
and in general favoring the foreigner against the
Mexican, the white man against the Indian, the
rich man against the poor.[38] These activities found
their sanction in an extreme form of doctrinal individualism. The ideals of competitive individualism
were being applied to a feudal country, the theories
of competitive enterprise and freedom to work were
used to justify the suppression of organization and
strikes. All attempts to improve wages were
declared to be contrary to the law and to economic
science.[39] Any state interference to circumscribe

[38] " Public opinion was being influenced from the professorial
chair and the press with the allegations of an apparently irrefuta-
ble science, the impudent European prejudice of the superiority
of the white race or, that is, of the inferiority of the Mexican
Indian and Mestizo. From this sort of materialism only the
foreigner and his by-products benefited. The people received, on
the other hand, the confirmation of their right as pariahs."
Vicente Lombardo Toledano, *La Libertad Sindical en México,*
p. 30.
[39] *ibid.,* pp. 33-34.
The penal code of the Federal District which went into effect
on April 1, 1872, and which remained in force until the recent
adoption of a new code in 1927, in Article 25 had this to say
about strikes: "From eight days to three months imprisonment
and a fine of from 25 to 500 *pesos,* or only one of these punish-
ments will be imposed upon anyone who creates a tumult or riot
or uses any other mode of physical or moral force with the
object of increasing or decreasing the salaries or wages of the
workers or to impede the free exercise of industry or labor." See
Código Penal del Estado de Morelos for similar provision.
The economists had written: "Some people believe that the
wage in Mexico is so small as not to be adequate for the subsistence of the laborer. We reply then that it is an axiom of
the science of economics that the wages never can fall below

the debts of the workers was frowned upon by the group in power.[40] Finally, in the name of the survival of the fit, the Indians were looked upon as an inferior race.[41] The theories of the struggle for existence were made the basis of justification for a policy that favored the white man against the Indian, the European against the Mexican. The Indian was a pariah in his own land.[42] The doctrines of the superiority of the white race were fruitful instruments of political and economic oppression. This policy was fostered by an administration which, outwardly complying with the forms of democracy, constitutional government, and an elective presidency, was in effect a political tyranny. Diaz, who

what is necessary to maintain the working class because they would perish, and as in Mexico the workers subsist with what they are paid, it may be inferred that they do not need more for their subsistence." Pimentel, *Obras Completas,* III, *La Economía Política, Aplicada a la Propriedad Territorial en México,* 1866.

[40] Alfredo Brondo Whitt, *Ley Sobre Jornales Precedida de la Iniciativa del Ejecutivo y Dictámen de la Comisión de Puntos Constitucionales y Legislación,* Monterey, 1908, p. 11.

[41] "The workers, because they belong economically to an inferior race, do not receive any more than 25 *centavos* daily and some means of subsistence." Otto Puest, *Boletín de la Dirección General de Agricultura,* Part II, No. 2, June, 1911, *"El Movimiento del Valor Predial en México."*

"The weaker classes were looked upon by the privileged ones as inferior animals." Roa and Covarrubias, *El Problema Rural de México,* 1917, p. 75.

[42] "The whites still look down upon the Indians. There are still people who on wishing to express the condemnation of an act say, 'It is unbecoming of a man with a white face.'" Pimentel, *Memoria Sobre las Causas que han Originado la Situación Actual de la Raza Indígena de México y Medios de Remediarla,* Mexico, 1868.

ruled Mexico for 35 years, had in each state a political satellite who did his bidding. Each state had its Diaz in the form of a governor, and each local district had a little tyrant in the form of a *jefe político* who ruled with an iron hand.[43] State and municipal powers had completely lost their independence.[44] The constitution of 1857 was a form and a formula. It existed upon paper.[45] The district and state officials were dominated and manipulated from the center by the coterie surrounding Diaz.[46]

The political dominance of a small group who were guiding Mexico towards rapid industrialization led to consequences which they did not foresee. The modernization of Mexico was coincident with lowering standards of life for the mass of the people, with the violent destruction of age-old village organization, with the alienation of great parts of Mexican territory, with persistent denial of the aspirations of large masses of the population. These difficulties were the less acceptable as industrializa-

[43] Vicente Lombardo Toledano.

[44] *Informe Leído por el C. Primer Jefe, ante el Congreso Constituyente de Querétaro,* Dec. 1, 1916, pp. 140-141.

[45] *La Revolución y Sus Héroes,* Antonio P. González (Kanta-Klaro) Y.J. Figueroa Domenech, Fifth Edition, 1912, *"Plan de San Luis Potosí,"* pp. 248, 260.

"Not even for half an hour has it been the fundamental law of our government. . . ." Antonio Caso, *Discursos a la Nación Mexicana,* Mexico, 1922, p. 125.

[46] *Mi Juicio Acerca de la Revolución Mexicana, Conferencia Dictada por el Sr. Antonio Hernández Ferrer, en el Teatro "Merino" de Villahermosa,* Tabasco, Mexico, June 16, 1920, p. 20.

tion brought with it new ideas, a comparatively free and increasing industrial working population, strong influences from the growing migration to the United States, and conflicts of competing foreign industrial groups in Mexico that stood to gain or lose by changing policies of the government. All of these factors wove a complicated web of play and counterplay that weakened the powers of the central government and made the Mexican revolution possible. It was against this background that the Mexican revolution of 1910 broke out.

CHAPTER VII

THE REVOLUTION, 1910-1928

The revolution initiated on October 5, 1910, by Francisco Madero was largely a protest against the continued power of Diaz.[1] Madero's program differed but little from other political *pronunciamentos* upon which previous Mexican rebellions had been made to hinge. To the agrarian problem—that problem which was to become central in the urge of the revolution—he devoted but a single and meagre paragraph,[2] while the labor problem, which next to the agrarian became one of the dominating issues in

[1] Priestley.

[2] Paragraph 3 of *Plan de San Luis Potosí* contained the following: "Abusing the law of unappropriated lands numerous small proprietors, in their majority Indians (*indígenes*), have been despoiled of their lands either by the *Secretaría de Fomento* or by judgments of the courts of the Republic. It would only be a matter of justice to return to their original possessors the lands of which they have been despoiled in such an arbitrary manner. These orders and judgments are, therefore, declared subject to revision. Restitution of these lands to their primitive proprietors on the part of their present owners or their heirs who acquired them in such an immoral manner will be required, to whom also they will pay indemnity for the damages suffered. Only in the case where these lands have passed to a third person before the promulgation of this plan will the ancient proprietors be indemnified by those in whose benefit the despoliation was carried through."

Antonio González y J. Figueroa Domerick, *La Revolución y Sus Héroes,* 5th Edition, Mexico, 1912, p. 254.

the revolution, received no mention at all.[3]   This scanty program is typical of the Mexican revolution. Even the so-called radicals had no more elaborate formula in their opposition to Diaz; they asked for land and freedom because "if our people can win for themselves industrial liberty they can work out their own salvation."[4]

[3] On June 24, 1911, Madero invited the *hacendados* "to enter frankly into the new way, understanding that justice will be inflexible for all; that the most miserable worker of their haciendas has the same political rights as they themselves and that he will be equal before justice and the law." *ibid.*

[4] "They have dispossessed us of our lands and rendered us homeless by the hundreds of thousands; they have left us the choice of exile or imprisonment in such hells as the Valle Nacional." In letter addressed to Mr. Samuel Gompers, signed R. Flores Magón. From *Junta Organizadora Del Partido Liberal Mexicano,* Los Angeles, California, March 11, 1911.

"After receiving your letter with request to me to enter protest [against the military maneuvers on the Mexican border] my first impulse was to refer the matter to the Executive Council of the American Federation of Labor for decision, but before doing so I should say to you that I have not seen concretely stated the principles and purposes for which the revolutionary movement in Mexico was begun. I do not refer to the negative side but to the affirmative. I think the American people should be told by the authorized spokesmen of the revolutionary movement of Mexico, what it aims to accomplish as a constructive power if entrusted with the powers of government. If the present régime is to be supplanted by another, the present revolutionary party, without fundamentally changing the conditions which shall make for the improvement of the workers' opportunities, and a greater regard for their rights and interests, then the American Labor Movement can look upon such a change with entire indifference." Letter to R. Flores Magón, from Mr. Samuel Gompers, March 18, 1911.

After repeating reasons for revolt and pointing out the close relationship between the workers of Mexico and the United States and approving of Gompers's attitude, the reply adds: "Accordingly our party adopted at the outset 'Land and Liberty' as its

I. MADERO

Madero himself was a rich landowner. His family was and still is one of the great landholding families of Mexico. He proved to be an impractical, weak dreamer—an apostle who lost much of his popularity, one who fell between two stools: [5] his personal and family connections on the one hand and the aspirations which he had instilled amongst the Mexican people on the other, aspirations that he could neither quench nor control. He had offered to return the lands taken from the villages. In reply to that promise the peons of the larger part of Mexico, especially northern and central Mexico, rose in rebellion and demanded its fulfillment. [6] The tide swept southward and by 1912 had reached even

motto, and our brief declaration of principles states that we are struggling for possession of the land, reduction of the hours of labor and increased wages. If our people can win for themselves industrial liberty, they can work out their own salvation." Reply of the Junta (no date) to Gompers' letter of March 18, 1911, signed, R. Flores Magon. In the files of the Pan-American Federation of Labor.

[5] "President Madero found it impossible to fulfill the reforms demanded by the people. First because within his own government there had remained encrusted nearly all of the personnel of the previous government and, secondly, because he had to dedicate himself to fight the old régime which rose in arms successively under Reyes, Orozco, and Félix Diaz and fomented the rebellion of Zapata." *Codificación de los Decretos del C. Venustiano Carranza*, 1915, p. 216.

[6] Otto Peust, *"Congreso Agrícola en el Estado de Guanajuato," Boletín de la Dirección General de Agricultura, Parte II*, p. 531, Number 6, Mexico, October, 1911.

José Covarrubias, *La trascendencia Política de la Reforma Agraria*, Mexico, 1922, p. 97.

such feudal states as Yucatan, Campeche, and Tabasco.[7]

II. ZAPATA

Indeed, even before Madero rode to power in the wake of popular acclaim an Indian had risen in rebellion in the State of Morelos—a poor peon who had been driven to despair by the despoliation of his native village lands by the large landowners. He demanded a return of the lands, their immediate return. He proved a powerful figure during the Madero revolution and while the crowds were still

[7] "Some time since our Secretary Señor Granados made a short trip to Yucatan and Campeche for the purpose of studying the situation of rural labor in those states that have also been struggling with the same difficulties. From his personal observations and conversations with governors, agricultural societies and some important agriculturists of those states he had learned that the intricate problem has been solved satisfactorily, because in general the *hacendados* have improved the wages of the peons and the conditions of their habitations, have given them absolute freedom to come and go from the estates, have granted them the privilege to give some time to their own work, Sunday rest, weekly pay and free medical treatment and in general a more humane treatment and work by the task. When the peons heard of these improvements they voluntarily returned to the work of the field. The same plan has been followed by some of our *hacendados* with good results, some few continue attached to the old routine methods." "*Informe del Presidente de la Junta Directiva de la Cámara Agrícola Nacional de Tabasco, en la Asamblea General de Abril de* 1912," *Boletín de la Dirección General de Agricultura, Parte* II, *Revista de Economía Rural y Socióloga,* No. 4, April, 1912, Mexico, p. 312.

[8] *México Revolucionario, A Los Pueblos de Europa y América,* 1910-1918 (a collection of documents, speeches and articles conderning the Zapata Revolution collected and edited by General naro Amezcua, Chief of Staff of Zapata), "*Plan de Ayala,*" 142.

cheering the new President, Zapata—that was the name of the Indian leader—visited Madero and asked that the lands taken from the villages be restored to them without delay. Madero argued that the land problem was a complicated one, that time must be taken to study the matter, that immediate action was impossible.[9]   Zapata, disillusioned and embittered, returned to his native mountains and repudiated Madero. He called upon the people to overthrow the false Messiah, declaring that "be it known to Señor Madero and with him to the rest of the world that we will not lay down our arms until we are put in possession of our village lands." [10] On the 28th of November, barely a month after Madero had been elected President of Mexico, Zapata issued the now famous Plan de Ayala,[11] ordering the people to take possession of and hold their lands, "with arms in their hands."

This Indian leader has since become a byword for praise [12] and condemnation in Mexico and stands

[9] *ibid.*, p. 122.

[10] Antonio D. Melgarejo, *Crímenes del Zapatismo,* Mexico, 1913, p. 140.

[11] "Article 6. As an additional part to the plan that we mentioned (San Luis Potosí) we insert that all lands, mountains, waters, which have been usurped by the *hacendados cientítcos* or *caciques,* under the shadow of tyranny and venal justice be immediately passed into the possession of the villages or citizens who have their titles to these properties of which they have been deprived by the bad faith of our oppressors and to maintain these at all costs with arms in their hands, while the usurpers who consider themselves possessed of rights to these lands present the[claims for special tribunals to be established upon the trium of the revolution." *ibid.*, November 28, 1911, p. 7.

[12] "Zapata regardless of what is said represented in the terr

today as the most powerful single influence in the shaping of the agrarian program of the revolution. No one was so reviled and hated, no one perhaps was so loved and followed, and the impress of no other Mexican leader has been greater upon the Mexican revolution. Beginning in 1910 Zapata fought against Diaz, against Madero, against Huerta, and against Carranza. He was finally killed by an emissary of Carranza in April, 1919. To this day the Indians of Southern Mexico gather in Cuautla, the place where Zapata lies buried, and make a sacred shrine of his grave. They will to this day tell a stranger that Zapata's spirit wanders over the mountain at night and watches over the Indians and that he will return if they are mistreated.[13] The importance of Zapata has been obscured by the fact that he never came to power, by the fact that he was branded as a murderous bandit, by the fact that the bitter struggle in Morelos led to the economic ruin

tory of Mexico the Indian who had been flouted in all of our revolutions; the noble saintly protests of an unhappy and disinherited race. Zapata is and will remain the symbol of a high ideal. When a few years have passed away, a very few perhaps, the children of those who today malign him will go to deposit wreaths of gratitude on the tomb of the hero." J. Silva Herzog, *Conferencias*, 1927, p. 77

[13] "At Cuautla, the little *población* where Zapata was murdered in 1919, a *fiesta* is held each year in the month of April, anniversary of the martyr's death. And the Indians tell you that there are shadows on the mountains that night, as Zapata leads his army of dead *agraristos* in a shadow march across the hills. All year round, the Indians say, he stands guard in the mountains, watching to see that no one comes to take away their lands." Norman Studer, "My Mexican Notebook," *The New Student*, Oct. 19, 1927, p. 84.

of the state. The importance of Zapata lies in the fact that he had but one basic aim and that he died fighting for it. He was one of the few Mexican revolutionaries who did not enrich himself.[14] The significance of Zapata is indicated by the fact that *agrarismo* has become almost synonymous with *Zapatismo*.

Another important phase of the Zapatista influence is what is known as *indianismo*. The present racial nationalism dates back to Zapata. While it is true that the struggle of the Indian for a place in the sun is an old tradition that can be pointed to over a long history of blind and impetuous uprisings, it was the fact that Zapata held Mexico at bay, that the Indian fought and won, that has given the present Mexican movement its strong racial flavor. Zapata wrote the Indian note into contemporary Mexican history [15]—and the discovery of the Indian by the Mexican intellectuals dates from the time the Indian proved that he could destroy governments, fight large armies, and remain unconquered.[16] It must be remembered that even after the death of Zapata when his followers made their peace with

[14] *Mexico Revolucionario*, p. 142.

[15] It was his desire to "redeem the forgotten mountain race, developing aspirations in it; making it feel that it is master of the land on which it treads and provoking in their soul the hunger for the ideal and the desire for improvement, creating, in one word, a nation of dignified human beings. . . ." *México Revolucionario*, p. 32, April 18, 1916. *Manifesto a la Nación*.

[16] The contrast in the influence of the Indian as effecting the Mexican revolution is indicated by the following notes:

"The Indian has shown complete indifference to the political

Obregon, it was on their own terms—land for the people.

III. HUERTA

The failure of Madero to satisfy the demands of the common masses of Mexico, his lack of decision, his continued compromises and political inexperience led to his early downfall. A *coup d'état* on the 9th of February, 1913, by the old military crowd in Mexico, headed by Victoriano Huerta and inspired by the influences that had surrounded Diaz and with the implicit consent of the then American Ambassador to Mexico, removed Madero from office.[17] He was later murdered on February 22, 1913.

struggles taking place in Mexico, as if 'the bronzed race sees with secret pleasure the destruction of the other races. . . .' "

"The Indians enter the army only through force, they fight without knowing the reason, and with the same ease fight today for one party and for another tomorrow without sharing in the opinions that are discussed by the whites and the mixed race." Pimentel, *La Situación Actual de la Raza Indígena*, 1864, p. 195.

"It was the humble ones of the race, it was the Indians, the Yaquis, the Tlaxcaltecas, those of the mountains of Puebla . . . who made the revolution." *Diario de los Debates del Congreso Constituyente*, Vol. I, 1916, p. 688.

[17] "Henry Lane Wilson was inimical to Madero throughout the Tragic Ten Days. The Embassy was the center of anti-government activity. Huerta and Diaz visited him there on the night of February 18, and talked with him concerning their pact for the division of the governmental powers they had seized. There the names of the prospective ministers were discussed and agreed upon. Wilson then submitted them to the foreign ministers, who were waiting in an adjoining room, and asked their comments, in case any of the appointments seemed inappropriate. The ministers merely took note of them, but made no comment. They then listened while Rodolfo Reyes read to them what is popularly known as the 'Pact of the Ciudadela.' Huerta and Diaz shortly thereafter left, singly. The members of the Corps, on taking their farewells, expressed solicitude for the lives of the imprisoned executives. Mr. Wilson seemed not deeply moved.

Huerta, who was "a strong man," failed to maintain himself in power for long, and merely stirred a civil and military strife that lasted five years. His record is one of a desperate struggle to keep office and one that looked to the consolidation and preservation of the old policies of the government.[18]

IV. CARRANZA

The military reaction headed by Huerta stirred immediate opposition. Venustiano Carranza, then governor of the state of Coahuila, a former Senator under Diaz, and a *ranchero* of middle-class family, rose against Huerta on February 19, 1913, and a few days later issued the Plan of Guadalupe,[19] demanding the restitution of constitutional government.[20] It is significant that the platform of Carranza gave even less attention than that of Madero to the aspirations of the masses of the Mexican people. It contained not a single item that reflected the economic and social problems that by now had become leading factors in the Mexican internal revolution.[21]

His associates noted that he had felt free to lend his influence to the destruction of a legitimate government and to listen to plans for the organization of the usurping faction, but when it came to proposals to save the lives of the prisoners, he had no plans, nor even suggestions to offer." Priestley, *The Mexican Nation, A History*, p. 415.

[18] *ibid.*, pp. 410-424.

[19] M. Aguirre Berlanga, *Revolucion y Reforma, Libro Primero Génesis Legal de la Revolución Constitucionalista, Imprenta Nacional, México 1918, apéndice*, pp. 34-39.

[20] Priestley, p. 420.

[21] "A plan *ranchero* that did not contain any revolutionary doctrine and whose only object was to re-establish constitutional order." J. Silva Herzog, *Conferencias*, 1927, p. 81.

Carranza, with the aid of Obregon, a small Sonora farmer who had risen to military office with Pancho Villa, a bandit who displayed extraordinary military energy, and with the moral support of the Wilson administration,[22] drove Huerta from power.[23] The passing of Huerta from office merely prepared the scene for further strife. Zapata had never officially joined the movement led by Carranza. The fall of Huerta was for him merely a signal to broaden his program and continue the struggle.[24] Villa for reasons that are not entirely clear broke away from the successful movement and started on a rampage through Mexico to drive Carranza from the field. Carranza was compelled to abandon Mexico City [25] and flee to Veracruz, and begin a fight to regain power.

It was only after the successful revolutionary movement had been divided, when Carranza needed the support of all the elements he could gather under his banner, that he awoke to the fact that the struggle was for those broader ends which are now recognized as having been the underlying motives of the Mexican Revolution.[26]   A program of land

[22] Priestley, pp. 420-425.
[23] July 4, 1914.
[24] *Acta de Ratificación del Plan de Ayala, México Revolucionario,* pp. 12-18.
[25] November 21, 1914.
[26] Of his program issued upon being driven to take refuge in Veracruz, Carranza himself says: "It . . . became indispensable to demonstrate to the nation and the entire world that in the new conflict the officials and chiefs that had remained loyal to the Plan de Guadalupe did not have mere personal ambitions to satisfy but to once and for all put an end to the evils of the

distribution had been suggested by Samuel Gompers.[27] Villa and Obregon had united to urge the formation of an agrarian policy.[28] But it was

past. . . . It was for this reason that it became my first care to make additions to the Plan de Guadalupe by the decree of December 12, 1914." *Informe,* C. Venustiano Carranza, Dec. 12, 1914, pp. 24-25.

[27] "And it is also earnestly hoped and respectfully suggested that some definite declaration be made not only upon the lines indicated (mercy and justice for the *Huertistas*), but should be coupled with an avowal of purpose that the constitutionalists will carry into effect a rightful and justifiable division of the lands of Mexico for the working people. . . .

". . . In our opinion such a declaration of policy would do more than ought else to bring peace, unity, and progress to the people of Mexico and the stability of their government." Letter from Samuel Gompers to M. R. Zubarán, U. S. Representative of the Constitutionalists, July 25, 1914. On file in Pan-American Labor Office.

[28] On September the 9th, 1913, more than a year before the split between Villa and Carranza, Obregon and Villa combined to urge upon Carranza the necessity of stabilizing the now successful movement upon a constitutional basis and also to undertake the solution of the agrarian problem. (Memorandum of Obregon and Villa, pp. 16-25.) Carranza replied on the 13th by calling a convention to be held in Mexico City (pp. 6-29). The acknowledgment of this call contains the following statement signed by both Obregon and Villa, on the 21st of the same month.

"It is manifest that the Plan of Guadalupe, inspired as it was, in the abnormal and urgent circumstances of the moment, could not even outline each and every one of the problems to be solved" (p. 31).

"Moreover, as the call does not specify what reforms shall be taken up, there is danger that the agrarian question, which may be called the very soul of the revolution, may be relegated to a secondary position, and its discussion even frustrated by the intrusion of other matters of lesser urgency" (p. 32).

"We shall proceed to the capital, with the understanding, however, that the following matters be given precedence: First,

not until he had been driven from Mexico City and forced to remove his government to Veracruz that Carranza took official notice of these broader aims, and issued the decree of December 12, 1914.[29]

the ratification of the title of President ad-interim of the Republic, in favor of the First Chief; secondly, the immediate calling of general elections; and thirdly, the passing of measures which shall forthwith result in the division of lands, subject to the subsequent approval by Congress" (p. 34).

Ejército Constitucionalista, División del Norte, Manifesto Del C. Gral. Francisco Villa a la Nación, y Documentos que Justifican el Desconocimiento del C. Venustiano Carranza como Primer Jefe de la Revolución, 1914.

[29] Carranza then issued a general statement of the object of the revolution which was a comprehensive enumeration of the variety of reforms contemplated. Article 20 of this program contains the following:

"The first chief of the revolution in charge of the executive power will expedite and put in force during the struggle all the laws, measures, and means destined to give satisfaction to the economic, social, and political needs of the land, effecting the reforms which are demanded as indispensable by public opinion for the purpose of establishing a regime that will guarantee the equality of the Mexicans among themselves; agrarian laws favoring the formation of small property, dissolving the large estates and restoring to the villages the lands of which they were unjustly deprived; fiscal laws destined to obtain an equitable system of taxation for rural property; legislation for the purposes of bettering the condition of the rural *peon,* of the worker, of the miner, and in general of the working classes; the establishment of free municipal government as a constitutional institution; a basis for a new system for the organization of the army, electoral reforms for the purposes of obtaining effective suffrage, organization of an independent judiciary in the federal as well as in the state governments; revision of the laws relating to matrimony and the civil status of persons; measures that will guarantee the strict enforcement of the laws of reform; revision of the civil, penal, and commercial code to make more expeditious and effective the administration of justice; revision of the laws relating

This was followed, early in 1915, nearly five years after the Madero revolution began, by two important steps which laid the foundations for the labor and agrarian program.

To recruit the support of the workers in his effort to destroy the power of Villa, Carranza authorized Obregon to enter into negotiations with the labor unions of Mexico City and later signed an agreement with them.[30]   The labor unions sent their members to the exploitation of mines, oil, water, forests, and other natural resources of the country for the purpose of destroying monopolies created by the ancient regime and to eliminate and to prevent the formation of others in the future; political reforms that will guarantee the true application of the constitution of the republic and in general all other laws that are necessary for the purpose of assuring to all the inhabitants of the land an effective and full enjoyment of their rights and their equality before the law."
    Codificación de los Decretos del C. Venustiano Carranza, 1915, p. 136.

  [30] "The pact . . . between organized labor and the Constitutionalist government reads in its agreements as follows:
    (As far I am aware, this is the first time in history that a national government has entered into a working agreement with a labor organization.)
      " 'Agreement Between the Constitutionalist Government
            and the *Casa del Obrero Mundial*
    " 'As the workers of the *Casa del Obrero Mundial* are supporting the Constitutionalist government headed by Citizen V. Carranza, we hereby declare that the following terms are to govern the relations between the said government and the workers and between them and it bearing on the manner in which the workers shall collaborate with the Constitutionalist cause: In witness whereof we subscribe our signatures to this document: For the *Casa del Obrero Mundial,* the citizens Rafael Quintero, Carlos M. Rincon, Rosendo Salazar, Juan Tudo, Salvador Gonzalo García, Rodolfo Aguirre, Roberto Valdez and Celestino Gasca nominated on a sub-committee appearing before the First Chief of the Constitutionalist Army and exercising executive power conferred upon it by the Revolutionary Committee of Mexico City, which

to the front in separate battalions—the so-called "Red Battalions." In return the unions were authorized to proceed behind the lines to agitate

in turn represents the *Casa del Obrero Mundial,* and by Rafael Zubaran Capmany, Secretary of the government and representing the above-mentioned First Chief:

" '1. The Constitutionalist government reiterates its decree of November 4 of last year to include the conditions of the workers by the means of appropriate laws, enacting, during the struggle, every necessary law to carry out the said resolution.

" '2. The workers of the *Casa del Obrero Mundial* with the object of hastening the triumph of the Constitutionalists of the Revolution and of disseminating its ideals touching social reform and avoiding unnecessary bloodshed wherever possible, hereby declare the resolutions they have taken to collaborate in an effective and practical manner toward the triumph of the revolution, taking up arms both to garrison the towns in possession of the Constitutionalist government and to combat the reaction.

" '3. In order to carry out the proposed undertakings set forth in the two former clauses, the Constitutionalist government will attend with all the solicitude it has used up to date, to the workers' just claims arising from their labor contracts with their employers.

" '4. In towns occupied by the Constitutionalist army, and, in order that it may be free to attend to the needs of carrying on the campaign, the workers will organize in accordance with the military commander of each place, to hold it and preserve order. In case of the evacuation of towns the constitutionalist government through the respective military commander will advise the workers of its intention, giving them every facility to reconcentrate in the places occupied by the Constitutionalist forces. The Constitutionalist government in case of reconcentration will help the workers either by remunerating them for work actually done, or, under the caption of "solidarity" aid whenever work cannot be provided, so that they may attend to their principal means of subsistence.

" '5. The workers of the *Casa del Obrero Mundial* will draw up lists in every town where they are organized, and immediately in the City of Mexico, which lists shall include the names of all their comrades who agree to comply with the undertakings stated in clause 2; these lists, immediately upon completion, shall be

and organize the workers in the districts that were reclaimed from the enemy.[31] It is to this fact that the present growth of organization of the industrial

sent to the First Court of the Constitutionalist government, so that this court may know the number of workers ready to take up arms.

" '6. The workers of the *Casa del Obrero Mundial* shall carry on an active propaganda to win sympathy for the Constitutionalist government among all the workers throughout the republic and the working-class world, pointing out to Mexican workingmen the advantages of joining the revolution inasmuch as it will bring about the improvement the working class is seeking through its unions.

" '7. The workers shall establish centers of revolutionary committees, in every place they deem it convenient to do so; these committees, besides doing propaganda work, will look after the organization of labor groups and toward their collaboration with the Constitutionalist cause.

" '8. The Constitutionalist government will establish, in case of necessity, labor colonies in the zones it may control to serve as places of refuge for the families of the workers who may have taken up arms or who may have in any other practical form shown their adhesion to the Constitutionalist cause.

" '9. The workers who take up arms in the Constitutionalist government, and also the female workers who perform service in aiding or attending the wounded, or other similar service, will be known under the one denomination whether organized in companies, battalions, regiments, brigades or divisions, all will be designated as "reds."

Constitution and reform.	Health and Social Revolution.
Rafael Zubaran Capmany	Salvador Gonzalo Garcia
Rafael Quintero	Rodolfo Aguirre
Carlos M. Rincon	Roberto Valdes
Rosendo Salazar	Celestino Gasca
Juan Tudo	

Veracruz, February 17, 1915.

Copied from John Murry's *Mexico's Armed Citizen,* manuscript on file at Stanford University, pp. 48-51.

[31] Rosenda Salazar y José G. Escabeda, *Las Pugnas de la Gleba, Historia del Movimiento Social Mexicano,* pp. 116-119.

and agricultural workers in Mexico is partially due.[32] It established a relationship between the Mexican government and the organized workers of Mexico which has never been completely broken and which at this date seems closer than it ever has been in the past.

It was also at this time that Carranza issued his now famous decree of January 6, 1915, ordering the return of the lands to the villages and erecting the machinery for organizing and supervising the process of land distribution.[33] The decree of January 6, 1915, because the Carranza movement ultimately established itself in power, became the first legal source of the agrarian program. It was later in essence embodied in Article 27 of the Constitution of 1917. This decree of January 6 was followed on the 29th of the same month by a decree assuming federal jurisdiction over labor legislation.[34] It is recognized that the success of Carranza is due largely to the support gained by these various attempts to win the allegiance of the agrarian and labor groups.[35]

[32] ". . . and in this way was cousummated a fact which up to date has not been followed in any part of America and which symbolizes the birth of contemporary Mexico and its true popular characteristics, truly proletarian." *Méjico y su Legislación Social*, Don Carlos L. Gracidas, pp. 12-13.

[33] *Codificación de los Decretos del C. Venustiano Carranza*, 1915, pp. 151-157.

[34] *ibid.*, pp. 165-166.

[35] ". . . The decree of January 6, 1915, which was one of the greatest promises of the revolution and one of the documents which in the historical moment served as the fundamental base

V. THE CONSTITUTION OF 1917

The sweep of the revolution as it developed under Carranza led to the adoption of the Constitution of 1917. Carranza had not originally planned to give Mexico a new constitution. The decree of December 12, 1914, which outlined the various reforms the revolution seemed to demand,[36] provided for the election of a Congress and President to re-establish constitutional order,[37] and this was reaffirmed as late as June 11, 1915.[38] It was only on September 15, 1916, nearly five years after he took the field against Huerta, that Carranza finally issued a proclamation for a convention to reform the constitution of 1857.[39]

The convention which gathered in response to the call of Carranza was made up of one elected delegate to each 60,000 inhabitants or major portion thereof [40] and represented 221 out of 248 electoral districts. Representatives were present from all of the states, and only from Chihuahua and Guerrero were a

upon which the true revolutionists sought to find justice. In my opinion the decree of January 6, 1915, was one of those that brought the greatest contingents into the heart of the revolution precisely because it was one of its consequences, one of the replies to the eternal question of the villages that had lost their ajidos." *Congreso Constituyente,* Vol. II, p. 785.

[36] See note, page 167.

[37] *Codificación de los Decretos del C. Venustiano Carranza,* 1915, pp. 131-138; especially articles 4, 5, and 6, pages 137-138.

[38] *ibid.,* pp. 215-222.

[39] *Decreto* of September 15, 1916, republished in M. Aguirre Berlanga, *Revolución y Reforma,* 1918, pp. 95-107.

[40] *ibid.,* p. 104.

majority of the electoral districts unrepresented.[41] The constitutional convention met in the old city of Queretaro while the struggle with Villa and Zapata was still on. The Constitutionalists had won the fight, but civil war was smouldering. The convention met on the 21st of November, 1916, and closed on the 31st of January, 1917, lasting over two months.

Carranza in calling the constitutional convention declared its purpose to be the reform of the Constitution of 1857.[42] In a report to the delegates he discussed the details of the proposed changes [43] and submitted a complete form of the amended document.[44] An examination of this instrument

[41] The states having incomplete representation at the Constitional Convention were as follows:

State	Electoral Districts	Number Delegates Missing
Chiapas	7	2
Chihuahua	6	5
Guerrero	8	5
Hidalgo	11	2
México	16	2
Oaxaca	16	6
San Luis Potosí	10	2
Zacatecas	8	2
Veracruz	19	1

[42] Vicente Lombardo Toledano, *La Libertad Sindical en México*, Mexico, 1926, p. 52.

[43] *Diario de los Debates del Congreso Constituyente*, Vol. I, pp. 250-270.

[44] M. Aguirre Berlanga, *Revolución y Reforma* 1918 *Apéndice*, 182-269. *Proyecto de Reformas a la Constitución de 1857. Presentado por el c. Venustiano Carranza, Primer Jefe del Ejército Constitucionalista y Encargado del Poder Ejecutivo de la República al Congreso Constituyente de Querétaro.*

reveals an almost complete absence of those items which have since distinguished the constitution of 1917. Article 123, which embodies the present labor program, is entirely missing, and the only reference to labor is a suggestion that under Article 73 [45] the federal Congress be given authority to legislate on labor matters, while the agrarian article (27) is drawn on a much narrower scale and lacks some of those features that have since made this article the source of national and international controversy.[46] Most of the reforms suggested by Carranza are political in character, having to do with the administrative, judicial, and political structure of the government. Whatever is really new in the constitution comes largely from the constitutional convention itself.

The constitution of 1917 was heavily influenced by the fact that it was written during a period of intense national and international conflict. The convention met when the passions stirred by the Great War were encircling the globe, when the cry for social justice and the "rights of small nations" had a wider echo than at any previous time. The common people were everywhere securing and wielding powers that they had barely aspired to, and although the Russian revolution had not then startled the world, labor and labor organizations were making great strides all over Western Europe. The exigencies of the war had also forced govern-

[45] *ibid.*, Article 73, paragraph 5-a, fraction 10, p. 225.
[46] *ibid.*, pp. 196-199.

ments to assume extensive control of the economic organization of the different countries; they exercised wide discretionary powers over the development of natural resources, over exports and imports, over production and price, and were in many ways influencing both the use and the distribution of wealth. These broad changes in the social and political structure of the warring nations left their impress upon both the convention and the constitution which it gave to Mexico.

This period of the Great War was also a time of non-recognition of Mexico by the United States and by the more important European countries. Mexico, because of the war, the revolution, and non-recognition, found itself isolated from the world. It was compelled to seek spiritual, economic, and social sufficiency within itself. This isolation on one hand and the abundant energy and aggressiveness of the indigenous population on the other, led to a discovery that Mexico was a nation, a people with problems and possibilities. The passions of the conflict stirred a nation into self-consciousness."

⁴⁷ "With amazing optimism we discovered unsuspected truths. Mexico exists. Mexico is a land with possibilities, with aspirations, with life, with characteristic problems. This was not only a fortuitous accumulation of human beings who came from a distance to exploit certain of its riches or to view certain of its curiosities and to depart once more. It is no longer a transitory or permanent geographical extension of a body, the spirit of which resideth on the outside. The Indians and the *mestizos* and the *criollos,* live realities, human beings with all the attributes of human beings. The Indian no mere material for war and for work, nor the *criollos* the product of the outcasts of other lands, nor the *mestizo,* the occasional fruition of unconfessible

Thoughtful Mexicans make 1915, the year of bitterest internal strife, the year when this great discovery dawned upon Mexico. It was during this year that Mexico most surely turned its eyes upon itself.

In addition to the influence of the Great War, the revolution, and the emerging Indian, the constitutional convention had to count with the changes wrought in Mexico between 1857 and 1917. The Constitution of 1857 had been modeled and shaped by three major influences—the French Revolution, the liberal Spanish Constitution of 1812, and the Constitution of the United States. The anti-clericalism and the hostility to corporations of the Constitution of 1857 represented the French influence, while American influences were shown in the fact that it was presidential rather than parliamentary, with a strong federal tendency, and that in full accord with the doctrines of Montesquieu it incorporated the distribution of power between the executive, legislative, and judicial branches of the government. It was an English, French, American political document applied to a feudal economic and social structure and was, as already stated, unenforced and unenforcible. Certain aspects, however, of the doctrine which this constitution embodied made it a destructive instrument for the age-old Indian corporate groups that lie embedded in the

unions. There existed a Mexico and Mexicans. The colonial politics of *porfirismo* had led us to forget this elementary fact." Manuel Gomez Morín, *1915*, Mexico, 1927, pp. 8-9.

body politic of Mexico.[48]   The denial to corporate bodies of the right to own property became the legal basis for the despoliation of the lands of Indian villages which in their turn became a source of discontent leading towards the revolution of 1910.

The Convention of 1917 was faced with the fact that the Indians had risen against this despoliation. ". . . it is clear to the conscience of all the revolutionists that unless the problem is definitely solved the war will continue." [49]   It was the promise of lands that brought the greatest contingents to the constitutional cause, and the constitutional convention could neither blink nor sidetrack that fact. The Constitution of 1857 had, by its emphasis upon individual freedom, made it possible to declare labor organization, strikes, and agitation for economic

[48] "In none of the (civil legislation of the republic) is there a single provision that can regulate the existence, the functioning, or the development of the innumerable (*todo ese mundo*) communities that throb at the source of our social structure; the laws ignore the fact that there are *condueñazgos, rancherías, pueblos, congregaciones, tribus,* and so forth. It is truly shameful that when a matter referring to one of these communities comes up for consideration, one has to search for the relevant laws in the compilations of the colonial period. And there are not five lawyers in the whole republic that know these compilations well." *Iniciativa sobre el artículo 27 del proyecto de constitucion, referente a la propiedad en la República, presentada por varios CC. diputados en la sesion celebrada el dia 25 de enero, Diario de los Debates del Congreso Constituyente,* pp. xxxii.

[49] "I wish to say that the agrarian question is the important problem of the revolution and the one which interests us most, for it is clear to the conscience of all the revolutionists that unless this problem is definitely solved the war will continue." *Congreso Constituyente,* Vol. II, pp. **783-784.**

improvement contrary to law.[50]   Between 1857 and
1917, however, the rapid increase of foreign investments had stimulated the growth of industrialism,
and this industrialism was utilizing the feudal
heritage as an instrument of exploitation.   Mexico
found itself in 1910 with an increasing industrial
development but with practically no industrial labor
legislation and with all the forces of both political
and economic interests opposed to its enactment.
All or nearly all of this industrialism was foreign
to the spirit of a feudal country and foreigners were
largely manipulating it and benefiting from it.   As
a part, moreover, of the industrialization program
under Diaz, Mexico had seen very nearly all of the
nationally owned lands turned over to foreigners as
well as an increasing use of special concessions which
gave to foreigners in Mexico a prerogative and privilege seemingly contrary to the best interests of the
country.   All of these influences taken together
gave the constitutional convention of 1917 an altogether different setting from the one which prevailed
when the Constitution of 1857 was drawn.

To this must be added the further fact that during
the greater part of the Diaz period the intellectuals
of Mexico were under the dominance of Comte.   It
was in the name of positivism that many of the
things which a later generation repudiated were
done,[51] but it was also to this positivism that the

[50] See note, page 152.
[51] "Positivism formed a generation of men attached to material
well-being, jealous of their economic prosperity, who during 30

authors of the social program of the Constitution of 1917 turned for support when they were seeking an intellectual justification for their land and agrarian programs. It was in Comte's emphasis upon society, it was in his subordination of the individual to the organic group, that they found an intellectual justification for their platform. They saw in Comte's sociology the great discovery that society, instead of being made up of individuals in which the individual took precedence, was an organic group[52] which gave the individual whatever personality he enjoyed and which could and did shape individual destinies in terms of this organic group purpose.[53] This seems to have been the underlying intellectual basis of the authors of the Mexican constitution. While the writings of Karl Marx, Henry George, Peter Kropotkin, and other authors of social economic literature were known to some of the members of the constitutional convention, they seem to have

years collaborated in the political work of Porfirio Diaz. Against this porfirian positivism there arose the revolution." Antonio Caso, *Discursos a la Nación Mexicana,* 1922, p. 71.

[52] "The modern social sciences have demonstrated that the concept of property was erroneous and today no one any longer doubts that individual property is of a social nature because it is society which creates the right of private property and not the individual that creates society." Andres Molina Enriquez, *Boletín de la Secretaría de Gobernacion, Artículo 27 de la constitución federal,* Mexico, September, 1922, p. 85.

[53] "At the moment in which the Constitution of 1857 was elaborated the scientific theory of evolution had not yet been fully developed. The concept of society as a large organism had not yet been formed and the true nature of society was not known." *ibid.,* p. 6.

relied upon Comte's sociology for their chief support, a fact to be explained perhaps by the heavy French influence [54] in Mexico all through the Diaz regime. The author of Article 27 turns directly to Comte for his justification. Comte seems to have played in the Mexican scene in a more general way the rôle that Locke and Montesquieu had played in the American and French revolutions of an earlier date. [55]

This does not mean that the Constitution of 1857 lost its original structure or that it was emasculated of its earlier features. [56]   The older tradition was

[54] ". . . Positivism had replaced scholasticism in the official school, and truth did not exist outside of it. For political theory and economics, eighteenth century liberalism was accepted as final. In literature, the tyranny of the classics had been replaced by the domination of modern France. In painting, in sculpture, in architecture, the admirable Mexican traditions had been forgotten, and the right thing was to play the sedulous ape to Europe." Pedro Henriquez Ureña, "The Revolution in Intellectual Life," *Survey Graphic,* May, 1924, p. 165.

[55] "Speaking of the influence that formed the earlier constitution Andres Molina Enriquez says that: 'The then new ideas, today practically in disuse, formed the judicial atmosphere. The chief social sciences had barely commenced to appear. Comte had finished the science of sociology but nobody in Mexico then knew the work of this illustrious philosopher.'" *Boletín de la Secretaría de Gobernacion, El Artículo 27,* p. 6.

[56] "The constitution of the 5th of February, 1917 . . . is not a law made up of materials that are distinct from that which formed and composed the Constitution of 1857 or constructed upon a plan in which the former constitution could not be recognized. On the other hand, the Constitution of 1917 has conserved from its earlier model the general plan of its construction raised upon fundamental individual guarantees, the system of political organization of the nation giving form to the governments of the States and super-imposing upon them the federal government.

too strong and the number of well-known old lawyers in the constitutional convention itself made that impossible. What did, however, happen was that to the older doctrines new ones were added in the form of Article 27, which is an enlargement of, and an addition to, the Constitution of 1857, and Article 123, which is entirely new. The Constitution of 1917 retains the form of the older doctrine. It retains the separation of powers between the executive, legislative, and judicial branches of the government; the state and federal governments; the presidential form; and it incorporates universal suffrage, periodic elections, and in general the essence of our Bill of Rights. It merely adds in Articles 27 and 123 a recognition of some of the ideas and doctrines that had been generated in Mexico since 1857.[57]

It has conserved from the older constitution the distribution of authority between the states and the federation, between the powers of the government idealized by Montesquieu; it has conserved from the other also the supremacy of the executive over the legislative and the judicial in the federation as well as in the states. It has also conserved from the other one as a means to tie all the parts of the system the recourse to the injunction. It has in the same way taken from the previous one all that is substantial. Even the numbering of the articles in the new constitution is almost like that in the old." *ibid.*

[57] "When the constitutional congress of Querétaro met the ideas were completely different from those that existed in 1857. The concept of the organic structure of society had already been formulated. The concept of sovereignty as representing the will and the power of the social group had already been formulated. The right of property as originating from the existing social organization was already defined. The necessity of solving the conflicts between rights of property which belonged to society

Without the comprehensive character of Article 27 and the entirely new features of Article 123 the Mexican constitution of 1917 would remain little changed from its earlier model of 1857. These two articles have modified the very nature of the document. As expressed by Andres Molina Enriquez: "Although in substance there is little that the Constitution of 1917 has modified in that of 1857, there is something completely different in them and that is their spirit; both are practically the same law but from one to the other there has been a very important change; and that is the principle which dominates each. In one the principle that dominates is that the individual must be before and more than society; in the other the principle that dominates is that society must be before and more than the individual."[58]

and those which might belong to individuals was already clear. It was only necessary to find a fundamental principle that could unite the recognition of the rights acquired and sanctioned in the past and the provision for those new rights that might be acquired in the future to give form to the satisfaction of the desires that might seek their realization in the time to come. The wise colonial legislation made it easy to find the principle sought. The Constitution of 1917 performed the miracle of filling the gap that a bad observation of the facts had opened in our land between the past and the future of our institutions by forming the first paragraph of Article 27." *ibid.*, p. 7.

[58] "(1) The spirit of the Constitution of 1857 was essentially individualistic. That of 1917 is eminently collectivistic.

"(2) In conformity with the Constitution of 1857 in conflicts between the individual and society or between the individual and the state the first had to win. In the Constitution of 1917 the second wins.

"(3) In conformity with the Constitution of 1857 in conflicts between interests and persons the interests had to win. In con-

This social tendency has not become characteristic of contemporary constitutional influence without many a bitter struggle. Every legislative clause that has involved the rights of the individual and the newer sense of the rights of the community has had to be fought over again in the legislative assemblies. The older doctrines carried over into the new constitution in Articles 4 and 5 have frequently been opposed to the newer concepts embodied in Articles 27 and 123.[59] If the latter articles are those that have given contemporary Mexican legislation her characteristic notes it has been because those who were passing the legislations were ready to fight over the issues again,* if necessary, as they had proven themselves ready to fight originally to embody those doctrines into the new constitution.

The completion of the constitution and its adoption on February 5, 1917, and the elevation of Carranza by election as constitutional president of Mexico, officially inaugurated the new era. But unfortunately, Carranza seems to have been out of sympathy with both the agrarian [60] and the labor

formity with the Constitution of 1917 it is the persons who must win." *ibid.*, p. 11.

[59] *ibid.*, p. 6.

[60] Vasconcelos tells the following as indicative of Carranza's attitude: "It was at a dinner given by the then governor of the State of Nuevo León, General don Antonio I. Villarreal. It was then that Señor Carranza said: 'that he couldn't explain to himself why people talked so much about the agrarian problem; that that was not the real problem of Mexico because we aren't all going to be agrarians and declared that what Mexico needed was physical reforms. . . .' "

principles embodied in the constitution.[61]   His presidential regime is a record of continual neglect of the agrarian and labor demands of the new groups that had come to power with the revolution.[62]   He had earlier narrowed the powers of the decree of January 6, 1915, by prohibiting provisional grants of lands and thus retarded by four years the development of an active land program.[63]   He interfered with labor organizations and tried to make strikes upon public industries compatible with treason.[64] While the constitutional convention was still in session his soldiers had court-martialed and killed workers on strike, and he gradually permitted himself to be more and more surrounded by an irresponsible military group.[65]   He did, however, defend Mexico's international position and to a greater extent reclaimed the national lands being held in contravention of contracts under which they had been granted.[66]

[61] Carlton Beals, *Mexico,* 1923, pp. 58-68.

[62] Priestley, pp. 442-443.

[63] *Informe del C. Venustiano Carranza,* April 15, 1917, pp. 117-118.

[64] Beals, p. 60; Toledano, *La Libertad Sindical en México,* p. 237.

[65] *ibid.,* p. 58.

[66] "The politics followed by the constitutional government in agrarian matters has been to revindicate the larger part of the lands of the nation that former governments had ceded without any study and without any prevision to a few favorites. . . ." *Informe del C. Venustiano Carranza,* April 15, 1917, p. 113.   See Chapter XIII, p. 317, for area reclaimed.

VI. OBREGON AND CALLES

The internal administration became more and more oppressive and more and more corrupt.[67]   The final straw came when Carranza tried to place in the presidency a man practically unknown to Mexico, the then Mexican Ambassador to the United States, one who had lived most of his life in the United States and who had no personal and, so far as could be discovered, no idealogical sympathy with the program embodied in the new constitution.   It was under these conditions that the popular and almost bloodless movement known as the "Revindicating Revolution" [68] was led by Obregon against Carranza.[69]

Before the new election could take place Adolfo De La Huerta held provisional power for a few months, and it is significant that amongst the first things the new administration did was to reaffirm the decree of January 6, 1915, in its original scope authorizing the granting of lands provisionally to villages needing them,[70] and that soon after an "idle lands law" was issued.[71]   This law placed lands at the disposal of landless villages and made them

[67] *ibid.,* p. 58.

[68] April 23, 1920, under the *Plan de Agua Prieta.*

[69] *ibid.,* pp. 61-74.

[70] "The government in my charge has re-established at full import the decree of January 15, 1915, which authorized provisional possession for the villages after their demands have been reviewed by the local executives." *Informe rendido por el C. Adolfo de la Huerta,* Sept. 1, 1920, p. 35.

[71] June 23, 1920.

available for immediate use without having to go through the long drawn out process of a legal land distribution.[72]

With the inauguration of Obregon on December 1, 1920, the Constitution of 1917 really first entered into force. Most of the labor and agrarian legislation dates from after 1920.[73] The recent administration, that of General Plutarco Elías Calles, which commenced on December 1, 1924, followed and expanded the program of adapting the Constitution of 1917 to Mexican social and economic problems. His administration became the source of a great body of legislation covering wide and manifold aspects of the agrarian and industrial problems.[74]

VII. SUMMARY

The Mexican revolution which began in 1910 may be divided into two periods—that between 1910 and 1920, and that between 1920 and the present. The period between 1910 and 1920 was characterized by popular revolution. The movements headed by

[72] See pp. 261-271 for a detailed discussion of this legislation.

[73] "In the Constitutional Party which has just obtained a complete victory in its titanic struggle against tyranny and reaction, our workers amongst whom I have the honor to count myself are in the vast majority. This party will continue to struggle without tiring and without ceasing until a complete consolidation of its government, because in it it will find the salvation of its principles and the complete improvement for all men who by their morality are worthy of receiving its benefits." Letter from General Obregon to Samuel Gompers, dated Mexico, June 10, 1916.   Vicente Lombardo Toledano, *La Libertad Sindical en Mexico*, p. 72.

[74] See Chapter XI.

Madero, Zapata, Carranza, and Obregon were essentially popular uprisings against military tyranny and feudal aristocracy, with a program at first shadowy but constantly growing more definite—a program that gradually laid more and more emphasis upon a change in the position of the large mass of the common people of Mexico. Since 1920 all of the revolutions have been essentially military rebellions against the continuance in power of those groups that had fought the earlier revolutions of 1910 and 1920, and had for their objectives the modification of the agrarian and industrial features embodied in the Constitution of 1917. The upheavals from 1910 to 1920 were democratic and popular. Those between 1920 and 1928 were military and reactionary.

This revolution, reaching over a period of 18 years, that has surged over Mexico like a turbulent sea, seemingly planless and without any idealogical formulation, has thus finally crystallized into a constitutional order, the application and enforcement of which is the present source of Mexico's external and internal difficulties.

CHAPTER VIII

THE CONSTITUTIONAL PROGRAM

The program of the revolution as it has grown and developed under the stress of armed conflict may be described as agrarianism, social organization, and nationalism. The agrarianism centers around the conflict to destroy land-feudalism and is embodied in Article 27 of the Constitution of 1917 and in the laws to which that article has given rise. Social organization, that is, the attempt to build protective organizations for the purpose of enabling the individual Mexican, peon or industrial laborer, to meet his agricultural employers on a more equitable basis, "to balance" the powers of the worker and owner, is embodied in Article 123 of the same Constitution and in the laws based upon it. Nationalism—racial and political reawakening—underlies and is a part of both the agrarian and the labor movements and has dictated some of their most important features. This nationalism is the thread that makes the contemporary Mexican revolution a part of the wide-spread movement for social reconstruction and national self-assertion.

I. ARTICLE 27

The Mexican revolution has found its most significant and far-reaching expression in Article 27 of the Constitution of 1917. This article summarizes and condenses the juridical principles that underlie the attempt to satisfy the aspirations that have governed the strife in Mexico since 1910.[1] It contains the ideas, the principles, and in some respects the detailed items of all the laws about landholding that have been placed upon the statute books since 1917. Not only has this article conditioned the form and the character of the land distribution that has been a source of so much conflict in contemporary Mexico, but from its precepts have been drawn the ideas that have lain at the root of Mexico's major international disputes since its adoption. The oil legislation, the legislation governing the use of water, the new mining and forestry law, as well as those determining the conditions under which foreigners may hold agricultural property, are all based upon Article 27.

Whether considered as a purely juridical summation of a great popular movement or as a source of ideas for the governing of foreign investments or as a contribution to a system of landholding and land tenure, Article 27 is one of the great political docu-

[1] "Of all the articles contained in the constitution, surely the most important one is Article 27." Andres Molina Enríquez, *Boletín de la Secretaría de Gobernación. El Artículo 27 de la Constitución Federal,* Mexico, September, 1922, p. 1.

ments that has appeared in the last two decades. An understanding of its scope and consequences is essential for an insight into not only what is surging beneath the surface within Mexico itself, but for a better measure of the currents that underlie popular movements in other parts of the world—for in spite of the fact that Article 27 is fundamentally an indigenous product, it was not entirely uninfluenced from outside sources, nor has it remained without influence in other countries.

For our purpose it is perhaps best to group the contents of Article 27 under three headings: (1) the definition and limitation of private real property; (2) the definition of the persons who may or may not hold private real property; and (3) the formula for the solution of the agrarian problem. Such a grouping is made difficult by the great variety of the concepts embraced in the article, by the number of different things it provides for, and by the fact that some of its provisions are overlapping and that others are obscure and ill defined; but it provides a basis for the description of the nature and import of this constitutional mandate.

Nature and limitation of private property. Article 27 of the Constitution lays down the principle that the nation has had and still has original ownership in the national territory.[2] Of this territory the

----

[2] *ibid.,* p. **7**. Supplement to the *Annals* of the American Academy of Political and Social Science, May, 1917. *The Mexican Constitution of 1917 compared with the Constitution of 1857, Art. 27, par. 1.*

subsoil and the waters are of such a character that they belong to the nation as *dominio directo* and can never be alienated or prescribed.[3] Private ownership in either the water or the subsoil cannot be established under present Mexican law. Their use only may be had under concession, provided that they "be regularly developed."[4] That leaves the surface of the land and its appurtenances[5] as the only matter that may become private property.[6] Ownership therein is created by the nation when it passes title to the individual for a portion of the area which originally belonged to it[7] and over which the nation retains, even after it becomes private property, certain powers and rights.[8]

These rights and limitations are varied and not fully defined. Article 27 sets up certain specific re-

[3] *ibid.*, Art. 27, paragraphs 4, 5, and 6.
"In treating of the products of the subsoil, the constitutional congress wished that the rights of the nation should be even more precisely expressed, and for this reason employed the words '*Dominio Directo.*' . . . That is to say, the complete proprietorship that it has over these products is inalienable and imprescriptible, and only by means of concessions and subject to determinated conditions may it cede the use of these to private individuals." Letter from Pastor Rouaix, March 13, 1918, *Secretaría de Industría, Comercio y Trabajo, Documentos Relacionados con la Legislación Petrolera Mexicana,* p. 390.

[4] *Article 27 of the federal constitution, par. 6.*

[5] Water confined within a private property and having no outlet is privately owned.

[6] *El Artículo 27 Constitucional, Dictámen de la Comisión Nombrada por el Primer Congreso Nacional de Industriales,* Mexico, 1917, p. 44.

[7] *Article 27 of the federal constitution, par. 1.*

[8] *ibid.*, par. 3.

strictions in the constitutional mandate itself, and
leaves room for the development of an unlimited
variety of other types of limitations in the future.[9]
The private property which is established by the
nation is limited by the right of expropriation for
public utility.[10] The state and federal governments
may declare when an expropriation is to be considered for purposes of public utility, and all lands taken
for grants to villages come under this heading. The
taking of such lands is to be through administrative
rather than judicial proceedings.[11] For purposes of
public utility, all lands are to be valued at their
assessed value plus 10 per cent. The only
possible judicial determination would cover the
values of any improvements made since the last
evaluation for tax purposes.[12] These properties
are to be taken over by means of "indemnification."[13]

In addition to the limits established under the
heading of "Public Utility," private property is subject to such "limitations as public interest may de-

[9] *ibid.*, par. 3; *Dictámen Primer Congreso de Industriales*, 1917,
p. 48.

[10] *Article 27, par. 2.*

[11] *ibid.*, par. 8.

[12] *ibid.*

[13] *ibid.*, par. 2.

Much of the controversy over the agrarian program has, during the last few years, centered around the precise meaning of
"by means of indemnification." The Mexican government, sus-
tained by the courts, has held that by "means of" compensation
can take place after the fact of expropriation. The Constitution
of 1857 had required "previous" compensation. See Chapters IX
and X.

mand." [14] The full extent and character of "public interest" is not defined. It is suggested, however, in the general rights established in the same paragraph. These general rights to limit include the purposes "to regulate the development of natural resources . . . to conserve them," and "equitably to distribute the public wealth, [15] . . . to encourage agriculture, . . . to prevent the destruction of natural resources," and "to protect property from damage detrimental to society." [16] Under this provision, specific limitations not embodied in Article 27 have been enacted, and others may be at any time. [17] The article, however, itself establishes a number of limitations with a view to solving the agrarian problem. These are specific rather than general, and they must be considered as a part of the possible limitations to which private property may be subjected without at all exhausting the possibilities of future developments of this doctrine. It should also be noted that "limitation" may be had without compensation as it is distinguished from and different from direct expropriation for "public utility" by "means of compensation."

[14] *Article 27, par. 3.*
[15] "The distribution of the territory must be made for the benefit of the individuals that compose the nation in relation to the evolution of these individuals or in relation to the capacity of those same individuals to have, use, and defend the real estate in which their respective portion consists." *Boletín de la Secretaría de Gobernación, El Artículo 27 de la Constitución Federal,* Mexico, September, 1922, pp. 1-2.
[16] *Article 27, par. 3.*
[17] See Chapter XI.

The specific limitations imposed upon private property by this part of the article include the following: a right on the part of the states to limit the area that any one individual may hold,[18] and to compel the sale of the excess of that area [19] under specific conditions of valuation and means of payment. In addition to these limitations of private property and its uses, the article establishes a "family patrimony" which is to be fixed by each state and which becomes in law subject to no kind of lien or mortgage.[20] This "family patrimony" the family cannot alienate. These, then, are the definitions of private property and their limitations. The other sections of the article throw further light upon the nature of private property under Mexican constitutional law.

Persons who may or may not own private property. The article under discussion, in addition to sharply circumscribing the character of private property, recognizes a number of different types of persons as possible owners in private property and determines the kind of ownership these different persons may have. Ownership in lands and waters and their appurtenances, or the right to acquire concessions to exploit mines, waters, and mineral fuel, may only be enjoyed by Mexican citizens.[21] Foreigners may be given the same rights by the government of Mexico if they previously agree to be considered

[18] *Article 27, par. 11, fr. a.*
[19] *ibid.*, par 11, fr. *c.*
[20] *ibid.*, par. 11, fr. *f.*
[21] *ibid.*, par. 7, fr. 1.

Mexicans in regard to the specific property in question and agree further not to invoke the protection of their governments in regard to the same, under penalty of forfeiture of the property in question.[22] Foreigners, however, may under no circumstances acquire direct ownership of lands and waters within 100 kilometers from the border and 50 from the sea.[23]

Churches of whatever creed can neither acquire, hold, or administer real property or loan upon such property. All such ownership as they have at present vests in the nation. The church buildings used for worship belong to the nation, "which shall determine which of them may continue to be devoted to their present purpose." All other buildings under church control, whether of a charitable or educational nature, belong to the nation and are to be "used exclusively for the public services of the Federation and the state." [24]

Institutions of a public or private character dedicated to charitable, scientific, educational, or mutual aid purposes may only acquire and hold mortgages on real property if such mortgages do not exceed ten years. Such institutions must under no circumstances either directly or indirectly be under the patronage of religious institutions.[25]

A different limitation of the right to acquire real

[22] *ibid.*
[23] *ibid.*
[24] *ibid.*, par. 7, fr. 2.
[25] *ibid.*, par. 7, fr. 3.

property is applied in the case of commercial stock companies. Such companies may hold the land essential for their industrial or mining needs, but they must not hold agricultural properties or administer them. The extent of their needs shall be specifically determined in each case by the executive of the union or of the respective states.[26]

Banks,[27] while they may make loans upon rural and urban property, can permanently own and administer only such property as is essential for their direct purposes.[28] They may also, under the conditions to be fixed by law, hold temporarily such real property as may be adjudicated in their favor in execution proceedings.[29]

Still different restrictions upon the ownership of real property are applied in the case of village communes. Villages that have retained in law or in fact their communal character may hold and exploit lands, waters, and forests in common. This right is extended both to those who have retained their lands from the past and to those who have been given lands as a result of the revolution. This communal ownership and use is, however, of a temporary character, and is to last only "until such time as the

[26] *ibid.*, par. 7, fr. 4.
[27] "In regard to corporations, it is a theory also generally admitted that they cannot acquire a real right in property because their existence is founded in a legal fiction." *Boletín de la Secretaría de Gobernación, El Artículo 27 de la Constitución Federal*, Mexico, September, 1922, p. 19.
[28] *Article 27, par. 7, fr. 5.*
[29] *ibid.*

manner of making the division is determined by law." [30]

With the exceptions described, no institutions may hold real estate or mortgages upon real estate, except buildings designed to serve the immediate needs of the institutions themselves. [31] We thus have different types of rights of ownership for Mexicans, foreigners, Mexican companies, foreign companies, commercial corporations, banks, churches, public and private institutions, communal villages; differences in the rights of ownership between real estate and agricultural properties and mortgages; and between direct ownership, surface and subsoil utilization through concessions; and finally the recognized rights of governmental administrative units to own and use the property essentially for their own needs.

The formula for the solution of the agrarian problem. In addition to defining the character and scope of private real property and determining what persons may acquire, hold, and administer such property, Article 27 provides the legal basis for the solution of the agrarian problem. [32] All the grants of

[30] *ibid.,* par. 7, fr. 6.

[31] *ibid.,* par. 7, fr. 7.

[32] Carranza had promised that in the solution of the agrarian problem there would be no confiscation. "This problem will be resolved by the equitable distribution of the lands which the government still retains, by the "revindication" of those lots of which individuals or communities have been illegally despoiled by the purchase and expropriation of large lots if they are necessary, and by other means of acquisition which are authorized by the laws of the land." Venustiano Carranza, *Codificación de los Decretos del C.,* pp. 220-221.

lands distributed in Mexico since 1915, and all the laws that have become the legal basis for such distribution, derive their authority from Article 27.[33] The scope of the agrarian program as developed and prescribed has two major phases: the part for which the federal government assumes responsibility, and the part left to the states. The line drawn between these is not sufficiently definite to assure that the program will ultimately be worked out in this fashion,[34] and as a matter of fact conflict and overlapping have already arisen, but in general it is assumed that the states have one function and the federal government another, and the legislation since 1917 has in a measurable degree followed this form.

The federal legislation aims mainly to provide land for communities either through donation or through restitution. For the purpose of giving legal sanction to a restitution of properties to villages that have lost them, all alienation of village lands that took place after June 25, 1856, is declared null and void, while those that cannot prove title to lands are to be given such lands and waters as they need. The grant of lands is declared to proceed as a matter of public utility and therefore comes under administrative rather than judicial authority. Compensation

[33] It is to be remembered that this article includes and sanctions those acts of distribution that took place under the decree of January 6, 1915, before the new constitution became the basic law of the land.

[34] Gilberto Fabila and Francisco A. Ursúa, *Reglamento del Artículo 27 Constitucional, Fraccionamiento de Latifundios. Bases para la Ley Federal sobre esta materia,* Mexico, 1925.

for such lands is fixed by law as at assessed value plus 10 per cent.[35] Returns of land already made under the law of January 6, 1915, are confirmed.[36] The only exceptions to these rules relate to the lands acquired under the law of June 25, 1856, which do not exceed 50 hectares and lands of the same area which have been held in undisputed possession for ten years. Any area in excess of 50 hectares shall be returned to the community, and for this the owner shall be indemnified. Properties held by the village from the past or returned by way of restitution or given by way of grant may be held in common and used in common until such time as the laws determine the means of the subdivision. Rights in these village lands are reserved solely to members of the communities that benefit from the law and is inalienable.[37]

These are the general terms of the laws determining land distribution on the part of the federal government, and a large part of the land distributed has followed these provisions. But under the authority to place limitations upon private property contained in this article, the federal government has largely expanded and amplified its agrarian program. Under these general provisions, legislation has been placed upon the statute books governing the utilization of idle lands, the irrigation of lands for which nationally-owned waters are available, and laws governing colonization, rural credit, co-operatives, and

[35] *Article 27, par. 8.*   [36] *ibid.,* par. 9.   [37] *ibid.*

agricultural education.   These laws are discussed in later chapters of this book.[38]

The states have been given the duty of undertaking the destruction of the large haciendas.   This was done on the ground that conditions in the different states are so varied that a general program for the breakup of the large estates did not seem feasible. In consonance with the general spirit of Article 27, this prerogative of the states is sharply defined as to method.[39]   Each state is to determine the extent of the area any one individual may own.[40]   But all of the states must carry out this provision in conformity with the following stipulations.   They must set a date within which the owners of an area in excess of the one permitted by the states shall be required to reduce their estates in accordance with the stipulations of the law.[41]   Failing to do so, the state is to carry out the forcible division of the properties in question.[42]   This forced reduction in size is to be by means of expropriation proceedings.   The expropriated areas shall be sold under conditions stipulated by the state governments.[43]   The owners shall be required to accept agrarian bonds carrying a 5 per cent interest to be redeemed in not less than 20 years.[44]

[38] See Chapters XI and XVII.
[39] Constitution of 1917 compared with Constitution of 1857, *Art. 27, par. 11.*
[40] *ibid.*, par. 11, fr. *a.*
[41] *ibid.*, par. 11, fr. *b.*
[42] *ibid.*, par. 11, fr. *c.*
[43] *ibid.*, par. 11, fr. *d.*
[44] *ibid.*, par. 11, fr. *e.*

During the period of amortization, these properties cannot be alienated by the person acquiring them.[45] The local laws shall also govern the extent of the family patrimony which may neither be mortgaged nor attached in any form.[46]

In addition to the provisions here cited, the states have in their legislation also assumed the functions of developing small holdings, protecting the small village zones by creating surrounding areas within which only very small properties may be held. These general constitutional provisions have become the source of a considerable body of state legislation, some of which has been applied. The detailed discussion of this specific agrarian legislation and the machinery developed for its enforcement is discussed in the following chapters.[47]

II. CONDITIONAL OWNERSHIP

Article 27, it is obvious, has created a variety of new legal forms of landholding, and in its structure lies embedded the possibility of many other types and systems of land tenure. In fact, every new law, every new limitation, creates a special form of ownership in land. It seems true that the formula was developed to meet the special social and legal needs of the multifarious groups of different cultural levels that make up the Mexican community. They needed a property concept that would be broad

[45] *ibid.*, par. 11, fr. *d.*
[46] *ibid.*, par. 11, fr. *f.*
[47] See Appendix A.

enough to include the primitive notion of ownership characteristic of a wandering Indian group, knowing temporary possession, but having no notion of legal ownership, as well as one that could cover the needs of modern corporate and private ownership. The notion of specific limitations has thus become an instrument sufficiently flexible to cover present needs, and its flexibility makes it available for the creation of future specific types of land tenure.

This formula is broader in scope than any one of our current general property concepts. It obviously retains private property, and makes its expropriation dependent upon compensation and subject to general rules of public utility. It permits communal ownership, excludes certain types of ownership from lien and mortgage liability, limits its use in certain directions, and makes it subject to requirements for use in others. It also makes certain types of property, like subsoil and water, subject to concession. The emphasis seems generally to fall upon use, upon exploitation. The formula seems generally to favor the small owner against the large one, the native against the foreigner, the individual against the corporation, but it permits all of these to use and enjoy property under specific conditions.

What Mexicans have established cannot be described as socialism or nationalization or communism, nor is it private property in the accepted use of that phrase. It is more inclusive than any one of these descriptions. The limitations already developed could perhaps be duplicated in American property law that has arisen in one or another form of the exercise of the police powers. But here all of these forms co-exist on one equal basis and require no special justification or legal defense. They are all constitutional, and any other form that may be established by the legislature in the name of public interest will be equally constitutional within the concept as contained in Article 27. This attitude toward property may perhaps be described as conditional ownership—ownership in a variety of forms existing side by side, limited in different ways, but meeting the general requirements of "public interest." It seems that "given the protean right of property, all forms of exploitation are possible." [48]

III. ARTICLE 123

Article 123 has no precedent in Mexican constitutional law.[49] It contains a series of concepts and

[48] "The spirit of Article 27 of the Constitution of Querétaro is so powerful, so high, and so liberal that even if it breaks with the Roman tradition of the origin and inviolability of private property, it socializes these and submits them fundamentally to limitations required by public interests, social interests, or, still better, the majority and permits a diversity of limitations, adapts itself to the diverse groups that compose the national population . . . according to the necessities, the capacities, and the means of action of each. At the present time no country has achieved such an ample and just notion of this right, a notion that all the peoples are seeking, and one that Russia will undoubtedly arrive at some time in the future. Given the protean right of property, all forms of exploitation are possible." *Convocatoria General, de la Confederación Nacional Agraria, para la celebración de una Convención Nacional Agraria, que deberá celebrarse en esta ciudad del 10 al 20 de Septiembre del año en curso, p. 2, no date.*

[49] Compare Constitution of 1857 and 1917, pp. 94-102, in Supplement to the *Annals* of the American Academy of Political and Social Science, May, 1917.

imposes a body of mandates which are entirely new in Mexican legislation,[50] and may therefore be considered as one of the direct consequences of the revolution begun in 1910. This article is of fundamental importance to Mexico. Changes which have been made to hinge upon it and others in prospect make it next to Article 27 the most noteworthy constitutional document that has been developed by the Mexican revolution.

Article 123 contains the formula for an attempted solution of the labor problem just as Article 27 does for the agrarian one, and as Article 27 has become legal foundation for all contemporary Mexican agrarian legislation, so Article 123 is the source of all the labor legislation in the Republic. Just as Article 27 has become the source of land distribution, so Article 123 has become the base of labor organization. The first tries to place limitations upon real property, the second upon personal property. The argument runs to the effect that if the nation can as a matter of public interest limit that most solid of all personal rights—rights in land— then surely it is justified in placing limitations upon the more ephemeral and less ancient forms of property represented so largely by modern capitalism and its corporate forms.[51]   The justification for

[50] *Provecto de ley sobre Contrato de Trabajo, presentado al Primer Jefe del Ejército Constitucionalista, Enrargado del Poder Ejecutivo de la Nación, Ciudadano Venustiano Carranza, por el* Lic., Rafael Zubaran Capmany, *Secretaría de Gobernacion, 1915, Imp. Del. Gobierno Constitucionalista,* Veracruz, p. 16.

[51] "For it is clear that if treating of landed property which represents the crystallization of the major solidity of the rights

Article 123 is further found in the fact that the large landholding system has continued the relation between the landowner and his worker upon a basis not materially different from that which existed between the Spanish conqueror and the subjugated Indian.[52] So low, in fact, is the position of the laborer conceived to be that the government must defend and support him in his dealings with his large agricultural or industrial employer on the same grounds that it defends minors in contractual relations. Only thus can an equilibrium be established between the workers and their employers and only thus can justice be had.[53]

Article 123 is therefore looked upon as a declaration of the rights of the workers. The Mexican constitutional convention had promised to itself the glory of being the first to establish the rights of labor

of human beings social action could make itself felt up to the point of modifying the forms of those crystallizations, then with more reason could it make itself felt in personal property which is the matter with which industrial companies are constructed, seeing to it that these properties operate under conditions that satisfy not only the interests of the capitalists but also the laborers." *Boletín de la Secretaría de Gobernación, El Artículo 27 de la Constitución,* Mexico, September, 1922, p. 9.

[52] ". . . The historical antecedents of the concentration of real estate have created between the landowners and the workers a situation that at the present day:has many points of similarity with the relationship established during the colonial epoch between the conquerors and the Indians." *ibid.,* pp. 29-30.

[53] "The workers were in such a condition of inferiority that it was indispensable that official action should make itself felt for the purpose of balancing the forces [for the purpose] of full justice, official action occupying the same place that is occupied by the public officer in all the affairs to which minors are a party." *ibid.,* p. 9.

just as the French have the glory of consecrating the rights of man. In fact, Article 123 "constitutes one of the nicest pages in the new Constitution." As one of the members of the constitutional convention said: "Neither the American laws, nor the English, nor those of Belgium concede to the workers of those nations that which this law concedes to the Mexican workers." [54]

The introductory paragraph [55] of Article 123 is of

[54] *Diario de los Debates del Congreso Constituyente,* Vol. I, p. 720. *ibid.,* Vol. I, p. 702.

[55] As was indicated above, the program submitted by Carranza to the constitutional convention contained no special article devoted to labor. The only reference was a suggestion that under Article 73 the federal congress be empowered to pass labor legislation. All of Article 123 comes from deliberations of the constitutional convention and the influences that played upon it. Because of the fact that the constitutional convention left most of the elaboration of this article to a committee, it is difficult to get at the source of all of the paragraphs of this article. We can, however, reconstruct the source for most of the ideas in Article 123 from material available in the form of pamphlets, previous laws, especially in Yucatan, Jalisco, and Durango, from the project of a law elaborated in 1915 but never adopted, and from the debates on Articles IV and V in the constitutional convention.

A large part of the preliminary work of Article 123 seems to have been done in the preparation of the *Proyecto de Ley, sobre Contrato de Trabajo, Imp. Del Gobierno Constitucionalista,* Veracruz, 1915. This law was never promulgated, but it contains a major portion of the items to be found in Article 123. And it is interesting to note that the people who prepared the *proyecto* later contributed to its development and acceptance into the Constitution of 1917. Into the preparation of this projected law, we are told, went the experience of Mexican employees and workers, Mexican and foreign statesmen, and the legislation of many of the industrial nations. Specifically mentioned is the legislation of Holland, England, France, Germany, Belgium, Spain, Italy, and the United States. Foreign statesmen, publicists, and judges who were mentioned by name are Judge Higgins, of Australia, Justice Brandeis in connection with the Oregon

the nature of an enabling act, providing that the
state legislatures "shall make laws relative to labor
with due regard for the needs of each region of the
republic and in conformity with the following principles, and these principles and laws shall govern the
labor of skilled and unskilled workmen, employees,
domestic servants, and artisans, and in general every
contract of labor." The word "agriculture" does not
appear here, but the phrase "every contract of labor"
would be sufficiently broad to include the agricultural laborer even if he were not specifically mentioned in an early paragraph [56] as one of the classes
of labor for which a minimum wage is to be established.

The various provisions of Article 123 can be con-
veniently grouped under the following six headings:

1. Time limit on labor
2. Housing and community provisions
3. Wages and financial provisions
4. Organization and disputes between employers and
employees
5. Accident and disease
6. General provisions

minimum wage law, Father John A. Ryan's study of the minimum wage, the projected law of M. Gaston Doumergue introduced before the General Assembly in 1906, the Swiss law of
1910, and the law of M. Viviani presented in France in the same
year.

Ley del Trabajo, Del Estado de Yucatán, Mérida, 1915.

*Informe del C. Lic. Manuel Aguirre Berlanga Gobernador
interino al C. Venustiano Carranza Guadalajara,* 1914-1916.

*Proyecto de Ley sobre Contrato de Trabajo, Imp. Del Gobierno
Constitucionalista,* Veracruz, 1915.

[56] The Mexican Constitution of 1917, Article 123, par. 6.

Time limit on labor. The article provides for an eight-hour day,[57] a seven-hour limit on night work,[58] while overtime work is limited to three hours in any one day, and may not be repeated for more than three successive days. Women and children under 16 are barred from engaging in any overtime work.[59] One day's rest for every six days' work is mandatory, and working mothers must be allowed two half-hour rest periods during the day to nurse their children.[60] Children under twelve cannot become subject to a contract, and those between twelve and sixteen may work only six hours per day.[61]

Housing and community provisions. Employers, whether engaged in agricultural, industrial, mining, or other work, must provide their laborers with sanitary dwellings at a rental not exceeding "one-half of one per cent per month of the assessed value of the properties." They must do this even within inhabited places if employing more than 100 persons.[62] They are, in addition, responsible for the establish-

[57] *ibid.*, par. 1.

[58] *ibid.*, par. 2.

[59] *ibid.*, par. 9.

[60] *ibid.*, par. 5. This article also provides that "women shall not perform any physical work requiring considerable effort during the three months immediately preceding parturition; during the month following parturition they shall necessarily enjoy a period of rest and shall receive their salaries or wages in full and retain their employment and the rights they may have acquired under the contracts."

[61] *ibid.*, par. 3. Paragraph 2 also forbids night work in factories for women and children under 16 and in commercial establishments after ten o'clock at night.

[62] *ibid.*, par. 12.

ment of schools, dispensaries, and other community services. Every labor community having a population in excess of 200 must be provided with a "space of land not less than 5,000 square metres" for public markets, municipal buildings, places of amusement, and "no saloons or gambling houses shall be permitted in such labor centers." [63] Houses "designed to be acquired in ownership by workmen" through workmen's co-operatives for their construction shall be considered as "social utility" and therefore entitled to such help and assistance as the state and communities may provide to undertakings so designated. [64]

Wage and financial regulations. The minimum wage is embodied in the principle of the Constitution. The concept of a minimum for all labor in the republic is clearly and fully brought out. There is, however, no attempt to equalize the minimum for all sections of the country. On the contrary, "the minimum wage . . . shall be made by special commissions to be appointed in each municipality and to be subordinated to the central board of conciliation to be established in each state," [65] and shall be considered sufficient, according to the conditions prevailing in the respective regions of the country, "to satisfy the normal needs of the life of the workman, his education, and his lawful pleasures, considering

[63] *ibid.,* par. 13.
[64] *ibid.,* par. 30.
[65] *ibid.,* par. 9.

him as the head of a family." [66] These two provisions, therefore, in addition to providing for a minimum wage, create a local machinery for the determination of a minimum family income according to the needs of the varying local conditions, and set up a central agency in each state to which these local boards are to be "subordinated."

These same two paragraphs [67] that set up the minimum wage also provide that "workmen shall have the right to participate in the profits . . . in all agricultural, commercial, manufacturing, or mining enterprises." [68] The machinery created for the establishment of the minimum wage is also charged with the responsibility of determining the rate of profit-sharing "provided in the law." [69]

The minimum established by law is protected from "attachment, set-off, or discount." [70] This hedging about of the minimum and exempting it from legal attachment is carried a step further by the declaration that "the law shall decide what property constitutes the family patrimony. These goods shall be inalienable and shall not be mortgaged or attached." [71] All wages must be paid in legal tender and not in "substitute money." Overtime work must be paid double time,[72] and for the same work there shall be no discrimination in payment because of sex or nationality.[73] All labor contracts which

[66] *ibid.*, par. 6.
[67] *ibid.*, pars. 6 and 9.
[68] *ibid.*, par. 6.
[69] *ibid.*, par. 9.

[70] *ibid.*, par. 8.
[71] *ibid.*, par. 28.
[72] *ibid.*, par. 11.
[73] *ibid.*, par. 7.

are to be fulfilled in foreign countries must be viséd before the local consul of the country to which the laborer is to go and must include provision for "repatriation." [74] Nor can any private agency or public office exact a fee for finding employment for workmen.[75] In case of bankruptcy or "composition," the claims of workers for wages and salaries shall take preference above all other claims.[76]

The income of the worker is further protected by the provision that debts contracted by workmen in favor of their employers may only be charged against the workman himself, and under no circumstances against the members of his family. Nor can such debts be paid by the taking of more than the entire wage of the workman for any one month.[77] This is a very important provision. It is aimed at the abolition of the system of debts which for so many generations governed the relations of workmen to their masters, not merely in agriculture, but in practically all employments.

This question of the debts of the peons is one that has played an important part in the labor legislation of Mexico both present and past, as well as in the discussion of the relations existing between the agricultural laborers and their masters. The whole question was discussed in detail in Chapter V, "The Economic Organization of the Hacienda." Here we merely wish to call attention to the fact that the

[74] *ibid.*, par. 26.
[75] *ibid.*, par. 25.
[76] *ibid.*, par. 23.
[77] *ibid.*, par. 24.

revolutionists felt that they were doing one of the important works of the revolution when they decreed that "all debts contracted by workingmen on account of work up to the date of this constitution with masters, their subordinates, or agents are hereby declared wholly and entirely discharged." [78]

This general body of standards and limitations, protection, and privileges which is thrown about the financial position of the worker also includes a provision for the encouragement of "institutions of popular insurance, for old age, sickness, life, unemployment, accidents, and others of a similar character." These institutions are declared of "social utility" and are to receive all help which the law provides for such institutions. [79]

Organization of workers and settlement of trade disputes. The law provides not only for the right to organize on the part of workers and employers, [80] but also recognizes strikes and boycotts as legal under certain conditions. [81] The strike is considered a legal weapon when peaceful and when it tries to "harmonize the rights of capital and labor." In case of public services, the workers are to give ten days'

---

[78] The Mexican Constitution of 1917, Supplement to the *Annals,* Transitory Article No. 13, p. 113. This article is looked upon as the declaration of the freedom of the Mexican *peon*. The fact that it became one of the reasons for counter revolution, especially in southern Mexico—Chiapas, Tabasco, and Yucatan—gives it an historical significance of considerable importance.

[79] The Mexican Constitution of 1917, Article 123, par. 29.

[80] *ibid.,* par. 16.

[81] *ibid.,* pars. 17, 18, and 19.

advance notice to the boards of conciliation and arbitration. Strikes are unlawful when the majority of workers resort to violence—in case of war, in industries under government direction, or in the case of military establishments that make supplies for the army. Lockouts are lawful when they are declared with the consent of the boards of conciliation and arbitration and are for the purpose of maintaining a reasonable price "above the cost of production." [82]

Differences between capital and labor shall be submitted to a board of conciliation and arbitration to consist of an equal number of representatives for each party and one representative of the government. [83] Refusal to submit on the part of the employer or refusal on his part to accept the award subjects him to the penalty of having to pay three months' wages to all of the employees in the dispute, in addition to any liability incurred during the dispute, as well as to the termination of any contract that he may have had with his employees. On the part of the workers, a refusal to accept an award places them in the position of having their contract terminated. [84] The discharge of a worker because of union affiliation, for having taken part in a legal strike, or without "proper cause" makes the employer liable for three months' payment, and at the option of the worker to reinstatement for the performance of the contract. If the worker abandons his work because of mistreatment, or because of the

[82] *ibid.*, par. 19.   [83] *ibid.*, par. 20.   [84] *ibid.*, par. 21.

misuse of any member of his family, the employer remains liable for the payment of a three months' wage, even if the injury was inflicted by subordinates and agents, providing they were acting with his knowledge.

Accident and disease. Employers are made liable for accidents and occupational disease "arising from work" and responsibility for "proper indemnity," [85] even if they "contracted" their work "through an agent." There is also under the general law a very broad provision for regulation and supervision of work places in regard to sanitation and machinery protection. [86]

General provisions. In addition to the provisions outlined and described above, the federal law contains a series of "stipulations" which cannot be made subject to contract and which are void even if embodied in a contract. Any contract is declared null and void that provides for "an inhuman day's work," for a wage which is not remunerative in the "judgment of the board of arbitration and conciliation," for a span of "more than one week before wage payment," for the use of places of amusement, cafes, saloons, or shops as places for the payment of wages, for any "obligation" to buy in "specified" places, for deduction from wages as payment for fines, for any waiver of indemnities that may arise from disease,

[85] *ibid.*, par. 14.

[86] *ibid.*, par. 15. This provision, like many others, is still in general terms, as it has been impossible so far (December, 1927) to pass a federal "regulatory" law for Article 123.

accident, breach of contract, or discharge, and finally any "stipulation" waiving any right derived from labor legislation.[87] It is interesting to observe the large proportion of these limitations of the contract that center about the protection of the wages of the worker and strive to make impossible the reappearance of payment by "substitutes" for "legal tender," or that open the way to a re-establishment of the *tienda de raya* and its consequent debt relationships.

In the legislative and administrative development of Article 123 since its adoption, there has developed a strong tendency towards compulsory trade unionism.[88] The conflict has raged mainly over the boards of conciliation and arbitration that are created by this constitutional mandate.[89] The courts in early days of the new constitution, and under the general hostility of the Carranza administration to trade unionism, gradually whittled away the powers of these boards.[90] With a change in the political ad-

[87] *ibid.,* par. 7.

[88] For a discussion showing tendency towards compulsory trade unionism, see *Diario de los Debates de la Cámara de Diputados de los Estados Unidos Mexicanos,* 31st Legislature, 1925, September 2, 28, 29, and 30, October 1, 8, 13, 20, and 22, November 3, 5, 6, and 9.

[89] Lic. Maxmiliano Camiro, *Ensayo sobre el Contrato Colectivo de Trabajo,* Mexico, 1924.

[90] "Mexico is a country of presidential government. . . . His [the president's] ideas, his declaration, or that of his group or party tend gradually to shape the official doctrine of all the organs of public power; a question of fundamental psychology." Vicente Lombardo Toledano, *La Libertad Sindical en México,* Mexico, 1926, pp. 56-57.

ministration under Obregon, with the growth of
labor power, with the resignation and death of the
older members of the Supreme Court, there has been
a complete reversal of the judicial interpretation of
these paragraphs of Article 123, and the boards of
conciliation and arbitration have largely been made
independent legislative tribunals capable of declar-·
ing industrial law.[91] The sum total of these various
activities has been to lay the foundation for compul-

[91] The history of the boards of conciliation and arbitration
after 1917 is a revealing paragraph of what is taking place in
contemporary Mexico. The following note, which is taken from
Vicente Lombardo Toledano, *La Libertad Sindical en México*
(pp. 67-69), gives a summary of the Mexican Supreme Court
decisions dealing with these boards, and we think it worth while
to quote the note in full.

"During the six consecutive years from 1917 to 1923, the decisions of the Supreme Court advanced the doctrine that 'the
boards of conciliation and arbitration lack jurisdiction and do
not constitute a tribunal. They are solely an institution of public
law, which has for its object to avoid the great commotions
produced by the conflicts between capital and labor'; that 'the
boards are not established to apply the law- in each concrete
case and to compel the condemned to submit to its control, nor
do they have the power to apply the law for the purpose of
settling conflicts of right, nor to oblige the parties to submit
themselves to their judgments'; that 'in conformity with the
constitution both the workers and the employers have the right
to refuse to submit their differences to the board'; that 'section 21
of Article 123 of the constitution implicitly declares that the
judgments of the boards do not have any force [over] the thing
judged and establishes in itself a method not only to modify or
reform the judgment, but even to leave it completely without
effect'; that 'in not having the power to execute its judgments
in an obligatory manner against the acts to which it refers [it
may] proceed by injunction'; and that 'the attempt to forcibly
execute its resolutions constitutes a procedure lacking legal force
and violative of the individual guarantees.' Judgments of August 23, 1918; November 2, 1917; January 23, 1919; February 15,
1919.

sory trade unionism, a tendency which is entirely conscious on the part of the leaders of labor and their legislative friends.

The *Mexican* Press is at this time describing a

"At the beginning of 1924 the Supreme Court changed its decisions. 'Labor arbitration is an efficient institution which has two objects: first, to prevent the conflict between capital and labor and, secondly, to present to the parties a basis upon which these conflicts may be settled if they are accepted. It has the character of public and not of private arbitration. It is not the will of the parties that organize and establish it [the board of conciliation], it is the disposition of the law.' 'If Section 21 of Article 123 were not interpreted in this sense, the functions of the board of conciliation would be incompatible, for the workers in each case would have to resort to the common tribunals for the purpose of settling with their masters the differences relating to their work. The spirit of these legal provisions has been to obviate the long drawn-out procedure subjected to innumerable formulas, for the purpose of saving social upheavals, for otherwise the labor questions, because they are so numerous, would remain within the old antiquated canons subject to the delayed resolutions that would result in impoverishing rather than improving the condition of the worker, which is what the constitution desired in establishing these boards. Because of this [fact], they have come to constitute true tribunals that have to solve all that is relative to the labor contract in all of its aspects, either collectively or individually, for it is for that that they were created by Article 123 of the constitution.' 'The boards could execute their judgments from the moment that the constitution gave them the character of authorities, entrusting them with application of the law in relation to labor contracts and conferring upon them the power to decide and declare the law in the individual items specified in these contracts in which they act as tribunals. Their functions being public and operating in virtue of a law, it is indisputable that they have the power necessary to enforce the judgments or sentences whch they declare, for otherwise they would come to be consulting bodies capable only of making a declaration of law, in which case their functions would be civil [private] and would not achieve their object.' Section 20 of Article 123 of the constitution orders that the conflicts between capital and labor be subjected to the decisions of the boards, that is to say, establishes forced arbitration, confirming this thesis

comprehensive system of Industrial Courts which are being proposed by the newly elected President Portes Gil.

This tendency manifests itself not only through a direct mandate that the workers organize, but through the increasing insistence that collective bargaining have legal force.[92]   The state legislature of Veracruz by decree issued on January 15, 1925, makes collective contracts compulsory.   The same tendency is manifested in the federal labor law, which to date (December, 1927) has only passed the House of Deputies.   Article VIII of that law makes

with the sanction contained in Section 21 of the same precept.' 'By capital must be understood not various capitalists nor all of them, but only one, and by labor Section 20 of Article 123 of the constitution desires to signify various workers, many of them and not one.' 'The conflicts which may develop from the labor contract are collective or individual and if conciliation does not bring an end to the difficulty or conflict, they are submitted to arbitration, and the boards can resolve these conflicts whether they are individual or collective.' Judgments of January 24, 1924; August 21, 1924; September 23, 1924."

These decisions have thus moved from denial of any power to the boards to that of giving them power of compulsory arbitration in industrial conflicts.   In other words, we seem to have moved to an independent judiciary in industrial matters capable of pronouncing and enforcing industrial law independent of and outside the control of the regular judicial channels of the country. (Don Carlos L. Gracidas, *Méjico y su Legislación Social, Conferencia pronunciada por el Agregado Obrero a la Embajada de Méjico en Buenos Aires, Direccion General del Trabajo de la Provincia de Mendoza.*)   This at least would seem a warranted conclusion, assuming that the statement of the last author is correct.   This last point is apparently still in dispute, for a demand has just been made that injunction proceedings against the decisions of these tribunals be invalid.

[92] Puebla: *Código de Trabajo,* 1921, par. 112.

collective contracts compulsory for undertakings
lasting more than ten days and involving more than
1,000 pesos. This legal enactment in the direction
of compulsory unionism is further strengthened by
Article 113 of the same law, which makes it impossible for the boards of arbitration and conciliation
to recognize more than one organization in any one
industry, and makes it impossible for employers to
sign contracts with more than one union in a given
trade or profession, and that union must be the one
that has the majority of workers in active service (in
the given enterprise).[93] The law of the state of
Yucatan, while giving all people the right to organize
in defense of their interests, provides that the unor-
ganized workers have no right to claim the gains in
higher wages or other benefits which the organized
workers have achieved, thus giving legal sanction
and benefit to organization.[94]

These formulas, codes, and concepts constitute the
second basic outcome of the new constitution. They
have given rise to a great deal of organization
amongst both agricultural and industrial workers

[93] See Vicente Lombardo Toledano, *La Libertad Sindical en
México,* pp. 149 and 183.

[94] Yucatan: *Código del Trabajo y sus Reformas. Edición
Especial del Diario Oficial,* 1922. Mérida de Yucatán *Talleres
Tipográficos del Gobierno del Estado,* Arts. 2 and 3.

"The right to work is guaranteed [in the proposed federal law]
as long as it does not prejudice the right of a majority to strike."
Diario de los Debates, de la Camara de Diputados, September 2,
1925, p. 18.

See also Toledano, *La Libertad Sindical en México,* 1926,
pp. 75-76.

and have become the source of a great body of specific federal and state legislation looking in the direction of enforcing the provisions of Article 123.

IV. NATIONALISM

A strong national urge underlies the whole constitutional program and the legislation which rests upon it. "These laws," we are told, "guarantee not only Mexico's economic independence but at the same time constitute the basis of its sovereignty." [95] This urge is, as has been pointed out before, both racial and political. It aims at incorporating the Indian into the contemporary political organization and making him feel himself a member of a larger community. All through the revolution and its legislative by-products, one can see the workings of this desire to mould a nation out of a heterogeneous population. [96]

It is this self-consciousness, this feeling of becoming a nation, this striving for internal unity, that has been one of the dominating motives in the attempt Mexico is making to build barriers against too rapid industrialization and against the possible dominance of foreign investments in the country. The leaders fear the possible consequence of foreign investments. [97] "I see clearly that sooner or later, in one

[95] *Principales Leyes de la Secretaría de Agricultura y Fomento,* December, 1924, to January, 1927, Mexico, 1927, p. 457.

[96] Manuel Gamio, *Forjando Patria,* Mexico, 1916.

[97] "I have been in towns which, a little before my visit, were towns of hundreds of people, which were practically depopulated or left with but a few women and children in the place. What

year, in two, in three, in five, or in ten, there will come much European and American capital; there will come enormous anonymous companies, a mass of tremendous negotiations. In one word, the regime of large industry and large-scale commerce, the industrialization of Mexico, the foreign companies will come to be the economic masters of Mexico. The Mexicans in the midst of all these riches will not be the owners of the companies, of the large factories, of the mines, or of the large commercial establishments. We Mexicans will be here the employees, the dependents, the laborers of the large foreign masters." [98] To build some sort of protective organization against this present and future invasion of foreign capital—to modulate, to protect, to limit the reach and the power of the outsider in the moulding and development of the nation—that must be conceded to have been during the last 18 years and to be at present a dominating ambition of the new national consciousness that the revolution has brought in its wake.

had happened? American investors who wanted to try a futile experiment in raising rubber or in developing coffee plantations needed help. Do you get the idea? American investors, German investors, French investors, people who wanted agricultural labor where there was none available needed hands, and whole towns were depopulated against the wishes of the townsfolk in order to supply contract laborers to neighboring foreign plantations. Well, that is one way of lifting and improving, teaching, giving the results of Western culture to the Mexican people." Starr, *The Mexican People, Mexico, and the Caribbean,* p. 29.

[98] From speech of Soto y Gama, quoted in *Principales Leves de la Secretaría de Agricultura y Fomento,* 1927, pp. 75-76.

The whole world knows that [our] industry is in the hands of foreigners, the whole world knows that mining is in the hands of foreigners, all the world knows that the petroleum is in the hands of foreigners—in sum, the whole world knows that the life of commerce and industry in our land is in foreign hands. What is it that we Mexicans have? We have only the land that is exploited by foreign capital. The only thing that belongs to us, the only thing real, the only thing Mexican, is the human being, the individual. It is the only thing we have left —the human factor. . . . And precisely today, when there is no large industry, we must foresee the future . . . and subject capitalism to a strict and full regulation that will lead it along human ways and that will lead it towards making moral commitments with human beings. . . .[99]

[99] Lombardo Toledano, *Diario de los Debates del la Cámara de Diputados*, November 3, 1925.

See Chapter XV for detailed discussion of the influence of the revolution upon foreign holdings in Mexico.

CHAPTER IX

LAND GRANTS TO VILLAGES

In examining that part of the program of the Mexican revolution which provides for the distribution of land to the free rural villages, we must note first the machinery that has been set up for carrying this into effect. A clear understanding of this phase of the matter will help bring out fully the character of the legislation and the specific effects of these laws upon the contemporary rural community.

It is important to remember that these administrative organs have developed and grown as the years have passed, assuming impressive proportions as a series of distinct institutions. Instead of tracing their historical development we shall, for the sake of simplicity, confine ourselves to a description of their contemporary range and character.[1]

[1] The complicated and confusing agrarian legislation which in an unending stream has poured forth from or through the inspiration of the National Agrarian Commission may be divided into two parts. The first began with the decree of January 6, 1915, and continued under Article 27 of the federal constitution, which with various regulatory laws, decrees and circulars, constituted the legal basis for land distribution up to the end of 1926. The second phase, beginning with the Calles administration and coming to a head in 1927, has so broadened the scope of the legislation as to change sharply the character and the possible extent of the land distribution now being carried out in

I. LEGAL MACHINERY FOR LAND DISTRIBUTION

The National Agrarian Commission is the central agency created by the agrarian legislation. It plays the major rôle in carrying out the laws dealing with either the restitution or the donation of lands to villages. As such, it has wide administrative and executive powers, and has in fact assumed the proportions and influence of a great department of government.

Its dictates touch the fortunes of every landowner in the Republic, and fulfill or deny the aspirations of thousands of little Indian villages that lie scattered over the mountains and plains of Mexico. It has by its defense of the Indian villages, and by being the instrument used for carving the central revolutionary program upon the rural community,

Mexico. For the purposes of exposition we will first describe the legislation as it continued through 1926, as that was the legal foundation of the land distribution that took place since 1915. Then after summarizing the various criticisms and objections which were developed against that legislation, we shall detail the more important changes which the new laws have made.

The two best compilations of the agrarian legislation are (1) *Catecismo Agrario* by Julio Cuadros Caldas, *Recopilación de leys, reglamentos, circulares, jurispudencia,* etc., *relativos al asunto agrario e instrucciones a los pueblos para la tramitración de sus expedientes,* 1924, and (2) *Codificación Agraria* by Gaspar Bolaños V., (*Con Recopilación Anexa*). This latter collection of agrarian legislation, though not complete, is the fullest available in any single volume, and is especially valuable for the circulars and decrees issued under the auspices of the National Agrarian Commission. Pages 19-97 of this collection contain a convenient summary of the multifarious agrarian legislation. This chapter has drawn upon both of the above named codifications, but particularly on Bolaños.

become the target of venomous hatred and attack by those whose past heritage is at stake; while the humble Indians, who see their future fortunes and security—their *ejidos*—subject to the decisions of the National Agrarian Commission, have made it the object of all their aspirations and hopes, their dreams of a peaceful fireside. Its great powers reach into every nook and corner of the Republic, and its activities have a political and social influence greater perhaps than that of any other single department of government, always excepting, of course, the executive powers of the President of the Republic.

The National Agrarian Commission is composed of nine members. Of these, three must always be agricultural engineers and two civil engineers. The other four members must, during their period of office, have no properties liable to be affected by the laws in question. The Secretary of Agriculture is the presiding head and nominates the members of the National Agrarian Commission, while each of the members takes his turn in rotation as secretary for a month at a time. This Commission has a large subordinate personnel and an elaborate organization. Its powers, though broad, may be briefly summarized.

The Commission acts as the final link in the process of turning lands over to the villages. As such, it receives the records from the local agrarian commissions, makes a detailed study of them, approves or disapproves of the decision already taken by the state authorities, modifies, enlarges, or reduces the area already allowed in temporary possession, presents its recommendation to the President of the Republic for final judgment, and then passes this judgment back to the local authorities for execution. It has powers especially to order the giving of lands to cities and towns that have lost in population and means of subsistence. It has powers to fix the dates for the removal of the crops from lands that are going to be handed over to villages. It can also take over the records of the proceedings, requesting lands from those governors who do not give their provisional judgment within the time allowed by law. It has wide executive powers in organizing and supervising the use of the *ejidos,* in organizing the rural communities benefited by the law, in passing upon the decisions of the local executive committees, in establishing co-operatives, federating them in regional zones, and finally in establishing a national co-operative organization.

In addition, it has powers to consider the arguments of the landowners who have complaints to make, to discipline and remove the members of the local (state) agrarian commissions, as well as a multitude of other powers, the more important of which will become clear when we consider the activities of the subordinate agencies operating under the general supervision of the National Agrarian Commission.

Subordinate to the National Agrarian Commis-

sion, but next in order of importance, are the local agrarian commissions. There is one in each state or territory of the Republic. These commissions are composed of five members each—one agricultural and one civil engineer, and three members who may not possess lands subject to the laws under consideration. They are appointed by the governors with the authorization of the executive of the Republic, and occupy in the states the place that is occupied in the federal government by the National Agrarian Commission. It is their function to make the first study and revision of the demands for land by villages, to make recommendations to the governor, instruct the local executive committee to give provisional possession of the lands to the villages—in short, to act as the central state agency for the carrying out the federal agrarian legislation concerned with the grant of land to villages. The relations of the local agrarian commission with the National Agrarian Commission are carried out through the delegates of the National Commission.

There is a state executive committee subordinate to the state agrarian commission and acting as agent for it. This executive committee is composed of three members named by the governor. It assumes responsibility for supervising the surveying of the lands, and within the month that the lands are assigned it gives possession of them, with the prescribed solemnities, to the village administrative committee.

Each state and territory also has a delegate and a solicitor from the National Commission. The delegate is the direct and immediate representative of the national organization, and acts under its instruction. He is the federal agent in agrarian matters, and represents the national as against the state authority. More specifically, he is a technical expert, who with his subordinates and with the co-operation of the state executive committee, surveys the lands allotted to villages, acts as a member of the village administrative committees with the powers of veto, and supplies the National Agrarian Commission with the detailed information required for an intelligent policy of land distribution. The delegate also makes a careful study of the land distribution in the district—the relations between large, small, communal, and private holdings. He transmits the legal documents from the local to the National Agrarian Commission, and submits a critical study of the same with such recommendations as he thinks necessary. He is empowered to see to it that the villages are given provisional possession after the decision of the governor has been given, and to act as the technical advisor of the local commissions, helping to solve the problems that arise. These varied powers and influence are sufficiently great to make him an important link in the chain between the federal executive and the local villages in each state of the Republic.

The solicitor of the National Agrarian Commission

(*procurador de pueblos*) is maintained by the Commission, but his energies are devoted without charge to looking after the interests of the villages that have pending agrarian problems. He acts as the representative of the villages, as their advisor, as their legal counsel. It is his business to see to it that the demands of the villages are expedited, that the legal forms are observed, that there are no unnecessary delays in the procedure. He answers the arguments of the landowners, searches for the titles of the villages asking for restitution, urges the governor to give provisional possession to the village that has applied for land, and if the governor delays or denies the request he can forward the demands of the village to the National Agrarian Commission for study and action. In short, he is the free and active counsel provided for the villages and available for their needs.

Last in the chain of administrative organizations that have grown up about the attempt to distribute land among the villages is the local administrative committee. This committee consists of at least three members from among the villagers themselves. The delegate of the National Agrarian Commission is also a member of the committee and has veto powers, but with appeal to the National Agrarian Commission itself if the local village committee is not in agreement with the delegate of the national organization. This local administrative committee is for the time being (until final division of the lands among the villages is arranged by law) the judicial representative of the village. The committee is organized at the time the lands are given over to the village, and becomes the responsible administrative agency for the village and for the relations of the village with the National Agrarian Commission. It separates the lands received into its various kinds—cultivatable, pasture, forest, mountain—and determines the use of the different lands; sets aside five hectares of the cultivatable lands for a school where the children can receive agricultural education; regulates the proper use of the water; supervises the cultivation; looks after improvements; agrees with the local villagers upon all things essential to the welfare of the village. If 20 per cent of the villagers are dissatisfied with their management, a new election may be held within six months. The administrative committee receives 15 per cent of the crop, of which 10 per cent goes to a fund for the co-operative purchase of machinery, tools, and animals, and 5 per cent to satisfy the needs of the community as such.[2] The committee also becomes the active agent for the development of co-operatives, which must be constructed upon the basis of one member, one vote. The committee, then, is the local institution for the fulfillment of the general program of the National Agrarian Commission.

[2] Under recent amendments these powers of the local committee have been considerably reduced. See p. 256.

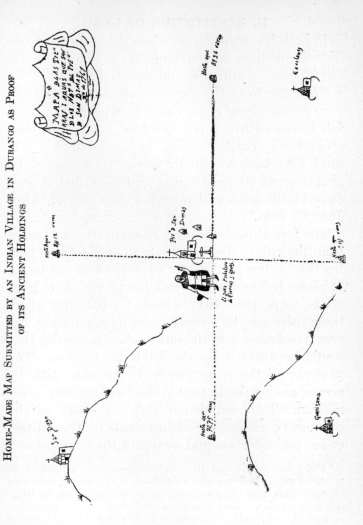

HOME-MADE MAP SUBMITTED BY AN INDIAN VILLAGE IN DURANGO AS PROOF
OF ITS ANCIENT HOLDINGS

II. RESTITUTION OF LAND

In both law and practice there are at present two distinct methods of providing lands and water for the villages—restitution and donation.

The right to restitution is conditioned by certain very definite legal requirements. The village must fall in one of five types—*pueblas, rancherías, congregaciones, condueñazgos,* or *comunidades.* It must have been known by one of these names, be able to prove its legal status, and show that it once owned lands and was deprived of them illegally after June 25, 1856.[3]

The formal initiation of a demand for land comes from the village itself in the form of a petition asking that justice be done by a return of its old lands. It places before the governor the proofs of its legal status, its previous title to lands (or indicates where these titles may be found), gives its population, the area it embraces, and the surrounding properties that would be affected by the land distribution. The governor of the state passes the petition with its accompanying documents to the local agrarian commission. The commission makes a study of the documents, verifies the claims made by the village, orders an inspection and survey of the land, takes a

---

[3] Cities and towns that have lost in population as well as in means of subsistence are also mentioned in the law as claimants for restitution, and likewise groups of population living on abandoned haciendas. The difficulties that have arisen from this enumeration of specific communities is discussed in a later section of this chapter. See p. 248.

census of the community, informs the owners of the adjoining lands of the proceedings under way, and awaits their objections, criticisms, and legal defense against the proceedings. After the lapse of the time allowed by law, the solicitor for the villages, satisfied that all of the necessary steps have been taken and that the arguments of the owners have been answered, advises the local agrarian commission to complete its study and formulate its recommendation to the governor for provisional decision. The commission is required to complete its study within four months. The governor is required to give his judgment of the pending request within a month of the time that he receives the recommendations of the local agrarian commission. Failing to do so, the solicitor may request the delegate of the national commission to send the request to the national office. If the action of the governor is favorable, immediate provisional possession is given to the village through the local executive committee—the owners being allowed the necessary time to harvest the crops that have been planted on the lands in question. However, the governor's provisional return of land to a city or town is dependent upon the National Agrarian Commission's confirmation.

After the decision of the governor, whether favorable or unfavorable, the local agrarian commission passes the petition over to the delegate from the national commission, who, after making his comments and recommendations, sends it on to the central office. There the request for land and the action taken by the governor are reviewed, and with such necessary changes as seem essential a recommendation for final action is presented to the President of the Republic. His decision is in turn passed back for enforcement. Until such time as the law finally determines the distribution of the lands to the villages, the President's decision confers upon the village the legal title to ownership of the land.

Under restitution the community receives its old lands, regardless of their extent, even if they appear excessive. In the absence of expressed limits, the village is given what it can prove to have been its previous possessions, and if these are not sufficient may ask for an additional area as donation. All properties of less than 50 hectares contained within the returned communal lands remain unaffected by the restitution, provided that the owner can prove that his lands were given him in conformity with all the legal requirements of the law of 1856, or that they have been held by him for at least ten years.

III. DONATION OF LANDS

The right to donation of lands is limited to villages that have the same legal status as those required for restitution, that is, that they belong to one of the five named groups and that they have an independent legal existence. They must also be villages that need the lands for their means of existence. Furthermore, lands cannot be given to villages that are of a temporary or permanent industrial, mining, or commercial character, or are situated within haciendas. Donation is confined also to those villages that had no lands previously, or have lost their titles, or find the lands returned as restitution inadequate for their immediate needs. The federal government is authorized to exert its powers of "expropriation" for the satisfaction of these needs. Individuals among the groups excluded from the right to benefit by a donation of land may secure the same from the national government by establishing colonies on national lands, but for each such colony there must be at least 20 petitioners.

Like restitution, donation is carried through under the auspices of the National Agrarian Commission. Nor is there much difference in the procedure followed, except that it is not necessary to prove previous title and illegal deprivation of its lands. There is a little greater emphasis upon the character of the village and its possible needs.

The information that is required by the local agrarian commission both for its own use and for submission to the National Agrarian Commission is as follows: a population census of the village, a census of those who are entitled to land—the so-called agrarian census—the character of the land that is under consideration, and the amount required by each family, the climate and rainfall, the character of the cultivation of the crops, the distance to the nearest towns, the owners who will be affected by the donation, the wages, the means of transport, fiscal value of the property, and all other information that it is possible to secure and that would be useful in arriving at a decision in the case.

The law also specifies the amount that may be donated to each of those inhabitants of the village entitled to receive land. Each member of the community counted in the agrarian census is entitled to from three to five hectares of irrigated or humid lands, from four to six hectares of subhumid lands receiving a sufficient amount of rain, or from six to eight hectares of other forms of non-irrigated land. In arid and mountain regions six times this amount may be allowed. The minimum of these areas must be granted in villages that find themselves not more than eight kilometres from a large city or from a railroad, while no more than half of the maximum is allowed when other communities in the same neighborhood have similar rights to land but have no access to other and more available sources of tillable soil. To determine the exact area within the allowed limits the engineers representing the National Agrarian Commission are required to make a careful study of the yield of the lands in question. They must also estimate the standard of living and provide for sufficient lands to maintain it.

In the case of donation the law is more generous in exempting privately-owned lands than in the process of restitution. Exempted from donation proceedings are those properties that have less than

150 hectares of irrigated or humid lands, those that have no more than 250 hectares of dry farming lands with sufficient rainfall, those that have no more than 500 hectares of other dry farming land, those that are in actual use as parts of agricultural manufacturing enterprises (but in this case the owners must cede an area equal to that which would ordinarily have been taken from them at the nearest possible point), and those that are under colonization contracts with the federal government. Exempted also are orchards, buildings, plantations under coffee, cocoa, rubber, vanilla, and similar crops, as well as water reservoirs and irrigation canals. There are, in addition, two other types of land for which exemptions are provided. The house of the hacienda must be protected by 50 hectares of land surrounding it and allowed the necessary roads for passage, while lands upon which *ciclico* (perennial) crops are grown may be replaced by the owners with other land not more than five kilometres from the village. If, however, the village is solely surrounded by small properties that would under ordinary circumstances be respected, their holdings may be reduced to half. Properties under 50 hectares must always be left intact.

The grant of lands to the villages is temporarily in communal form.[4] The process of converting the

[4] "The donation of *ejidos* in accordance with the rights derived from the revolution has nothing in common with the colonial grants of *ejidos* excepting the name.

"The capital difference that separates the colonial from the

present private property of the large owners into the small privately-owned parcels of the villagers goes through three stages. There is, first, the provisional ownership granted by the governor and enjoyed in communal form; second, the definite ownership derived from the final grant by the President of the Republic and enjoyed in common; and, finally, the definite private ownership that is to be derived from the application of Article 11 of the law of January

present dispositions resides in the ends sought by donation of *ejidos* in the two periods. In the colonial period it was a means of establishing inhabited communities. It was a means of creating communities where the Indians could definitely collect and settle. It was concerned with the achievements of a definite aim, the elimination of the difficulties resulting from a wandering indigenous population, to that extent free from control and incapable of receiving the benefits from permanent settlements. It was in fact a donation of land antecedent to permanent villages and sought to create them.

"The contemporary donation, on the other hand, is not made with the purpose of tying down a floating and unstable population, but rather it seeks to provide groups of individuals who already have a definite place, the land needed for their subsistence. It is for the purpose of correcting the observed economic evils. It is not an act accompanying the establishment of communities, but a procedure securing a better distribution of the land.

"Still another difference is the fact that essentially communal character of the primitive *ejido* imposed upon the community a series of characteristics also of a communal nature. The *ejido* was given in common to a communal group." Lic. Narciso Basols, *Consideraciones Generales;* unpublished manuscript copy, 79 pages; prepared for the National Agrarian Commission, and constituting an analysis and criticism of the agrarian legislation and its enforcement and a summation of the reasons which led to the modifications in the law under the present administration. With some change and amplifications this study has since been published as "La Nueva Ley Agraria," Mexico, 1927.

6, 1915,[5] which determines the private ownership of the individual holdings. There is, however, under all of these different forms of ownership a common basis—the nation retains at all times *dominio directo,* while the villagers either in common, or later as individuals, enjoy *dominio útil.* Under no conditions can the lands derived under this legislation be alienated. The lands therefore are not turned over to the village government—that is, the *ayuntamiento*—but to the villagers as such, organized and temporarily represented by the local administrative committee. The lands are given to the committee representing the individuals temporarily organized for the purpose of common use of the lands, and these individuals are only those who under the law have a right to benefit from the land distribution. It is important to see clearly that the legislation looks forward to individual use and enjoyment of the tillable soil and resorts temporarily to common possession and use for purposes of convenience and as a means of discipline and training for future individual ownership.[6]

---

[5] This law reads as follows: "A regulatory law shall determine the condition in which the lands restored or adjudged in behalf of the townships shall remain and the manner and time in which they shall be distributed among the neighbors, who, in the meantime, shall enjoy their possession in common." Bolaños, pp. 142-143.

[6] "We must sustain the institution of *ejidos* as the first mortal blow against large landholding and as the first step in the conversion of the *campesinos* into a factor of agricultural production. The *ejidos* are the schools where the villages learn their first

As we have already noted, a special census is taken of the community asking for land. This census serves as the basis for determining the number of people that are entitled to benefit by the law, and thus provides the means of calculating the area that will satisfy the needs of the inhabitants of the village. This census is taken by the local agrarian commission with the aid of both the local village government and one other person representing the group directly interested in the land distribution. A copy of the census is then sent to the property-owners subject to the proceedings, so that they may make their comments and criticisms of the census. The census includes two distinct classifications: a general count of all the inhabitants of the village, and a special count of those who are entitled to benefit by the law. The agrarian census, that is, the count of those who are entitled to land, includes all agriculturists in the village who lack the means of subsistence. Under this general classification are specified heads of families, boys over 18 years of age, and widows with children to support. All must be actual inhabitants of the village. Excluded specifically from the agrarian census are *profesionales,* those who own land equal to what they would be entitled to under the donation, those who can be shown to have a capital of 1,000 pesos, the employees of the federal, state, or village govern-

lessons in independence." *Sindicato de Campesinos Agraristas del Estado de Durango,* January 1, 1925, p. 43.

ment, and finally those who are privately employed and who have salaries equal to 75 pesos per month. Upon the basis of the above information—which must be given in specific form in each case—giving the names of every person living in the village, their professions, their possessions (enumerating the number of each kind of animal they possess) and telling which of them are or are not in need of land, the extent of the area to be ceded to the village is determined. The law also provides for increase of the area originally received; but by a decree of the 23rd of April, 1925, this amplification even provisionally can only be given with the previous consent of the National Agrarian Commission.

Finally, the laws reserve certain rights and prerogatives to the landowners whose properties are subject to the effects of the agrarian laws. They must be notified of the proceedings against them, must be given copies of the agrarian census, permitted to make their arguments against the proceedings, allowed to inspect and secure copies of the records of the proceedings, informed of the decisions of the local and national commissions, allowed to keep 50 hectares under restitution proceedings if they have been in possession for a period of ten years or more, allowed to keep 150 hectares of irrigated and from 250 to 500 hectares of non-irrigated land under donation proceedings, allowed to substitute other land for that under perennial crops, allowed one year after final action is taken in which to appeal to the courts, allowed time to harvest the crops that have been planted. Furthermore, they are freed from the tax upon the lands even provisionally given over to villages, and are entitled to payment for the lands taken.

CHAPTER X

CRITICISM AND AMENDMENT OF THE LAND GRANT LEGISLATION

The legislation which we have just described does not, of course, represent the final stage of Mexican revolutionary thought with regard to the problem of land distribution. Criticism both of opponents and of friends, and administrative experience obtained in attempting to apply the law, have from the beginning produced a series of amendments, interpretations, regulations, judicial opinions, and other modifying influences. Before considering these reforms, however, we shall summarize the criticisms to which it has been subjected.

I. CRITICISM OF THE EJIDO LEGISLATION

The legislation just described has from the beginning been the subject of severe and unremitting criticism. It has been argued that the legislation and the Constitution of 1917, from which this legislation is derived, are in fact unconstitutional. The Constitution, we are told, was drawn up under illegal auspices, was and is not representative of the wishes of the people of Mexico, was merely an imposition by a small and non-representative military clique, and must ultimately give place to a new and constitutional procedure.[1] Of a somewhat different order is the claim that the legislation is self-contradictory, incapable of application because of its confusing character, badly defined, drawn in a clumsy and extravagant fashion, dominated by a spirit of vindictiveness, and that legally it sustains robbery and spoliation.[2]

These criticisms are followed by others of a more specific and realistic character. It is argued that the distribution of land is economically impossible and useless; that the large landholding system of Mexico is responsive to natural forces which no mere agrarian legislation can overcome; that the small property has always given way to the large one; that the Mexican rural population—illiterate and lazy, untrained in self-direction—cannot receive the benefits of land distribution; that the agrarian legislation is merely a political matter and in reality does not reflect the needs of Mexico, since in a country where there is so much land and so few people there can exist no agrarian problem; that the agrarian legislation is impossible of application because the individual receiving the land has not the means of cultivating it, and that the Mexican government has not the resources to supply the individuals with

[1] Jorge Vera Estañol, *Al Margen de la Constitución de 1917,* Los Angeles, 1920, pp. 3-23.

[2] *ibid.,* pp. 86-98; Rafael Martínez Carrilo, *Ayuntamientos Sobre las Leyes Agrarias de México,* Mexico, 1923, p. 182.

capital and the aid that is absolutely essential in the successful carrying out of the legislation.

The administrative machinery used in carrying the laws into effect has also been subjected to severe criticism. It is argued that the system of payment by bonds is tantamount to expropriation without compensation; that the system of evaluation is unfair, and that it is robbing the landowners of their lands without sufficient compensation; that the method of paying after the expropriation, rather than previous to or during the expropriation proceedings, is merely an excuse for no payment at all. As has already been suggested, the methods developed by the National Agrarian Commission and all of its agents have been subject to merciless criticism. It has been charged that its members and employees are corrupt politicians; that they violate the laws which they are supposed to enforce, sell their favors, and abuse their power; that the village censuses are unfair; that dead men and children have been counted in the censuses so as to enlarge the area given to the villages; that the local administrative committees have been manipulated by outside interests; that the giving of the land to villages has merely served to enrich the local politicians; that the Indians who received the land did not work it, but left it untilled or rented it to others; that the area under cultivation has been reduced as a result of the insecurity of both the landowner and the individual recipient of land; and as a sum of all that

it is well known to everyone but the interested
politicians that the distribution of lands has been
and is a complete failure.[3]

[3] He who would study the criticism of the agrarian legislation
must turn to the thousands of *amparos* (injunctions) that have
been issued against the activities of the local and national
agrarian commissions. There he will find every possible legal
and administrative objection and criticism of the laws repeated
and elaborated in a thousand different ways. Another source for
the literature of criticism is the editorials and special articles in
Excelsior and *El Universal,* the two leading dailies of Mexico City.

The following references are but a few of the multitude that
could be cited. The criticisms are generally of the same type
and cover the same arguments over again, so that an exhaustive
citation would merely add cumulatively in repetition to the first
arguments. A bibliography that would list all of the articles,
pamphlets, and injunctions containing criticisms of the legislation
under discussion would fill a large volume.

En Defensa de la Agricultura Nacional, a compilation of the
editorials of *El Informador* from April 21, 1918, to July 14, 1921.
Edición del Sindicato de Agricultores de Jalisco, Guadalajara,
1921, 256 pages.

*Informe que el Señor Francisco Lozano Cardoso, Director del
Sindicato de Agricultores de Puebla Leyó en la Sesión Inaugural,*
Puebla, 1922, 37 pages.

Rafael Martínez Carillo, *Ayuntamientos Sobre las Leyes
Agrarias de México,* Mexico, 1923, 183 pages.

*Dos Escritos dirigidos a las autoridades por los Hacendados de
Morelos,* Mexico, 1921, 52 pages.

Jorge Vera Estañol, *Al Márgen de la Constitución de 1917,* Los
Angeles, 1920, 251 pages.

Ensayo Sobre la Reconstrucción de México por Manuel Calero,
Francisco S. Carvajal, Juan B. Castelazo, Toribio Esquivel
Obregón, Jesús Flores Magón, Tomás Macmanus, Rafael Martínez Carrillo, Miguel Ruelas y Jorge Vera Estañol, New York,
1920, 118 pages.

Francisco G. Palacio, *Un Llamamiento a la Opinión Pública
con motivo de la injusta Resolución de la Comisión Nacional
Agraria, que declaró propiedad de los habitantes del Pasaje, las
Tierras de que son legítimos dueños los Señores Martínez del Rio,*
Mexico, 1921, 80 pages.

The severe criticisms made by the opponents of agrarian legislation have been in part echoed by its friends. They agree that the movement has suffered from too much political manipulation, that the villages receiving land have at times been prevented from securing the expected benefits through the domination of the local *caciques,* and that the poverty of the village communities has made it difficult for them to exploit fully the lands given them. Instead of being looked upon as a cause of failure, these shortcomings are looked upon as justifying further legislative and administrative attention.[4]

Friends of the agrarian legislation have centered their criticism on its narrow scope and the specific legal qualifications demanded of communities asking for land. The objection to the legislation

El Artículo 27 Constitucional (Constitución de 1917), Dictámen de la Comisión nombrada por el Primer Congreso Nacional de Industriales, Mexico, 1917, 123 pages.

La Cuestion Agraria, Memorial de Los Agricultores Epañoles al Sr. Presidente de la República, Comisión de Agricultura, Mexico, November 15, 1921. (Manuscript copy.)

[4] *Sindicato de Campesinos Agraristas del Estado de Durango,* January, 1925, pp. 45-46.

"Exposicion de Motivos," Proyecto de Ley Reglamentaria Sobre Reparticion de Tierras Ejidales y Constitucion del Patrimonio Parcelario Ejidal, Mexico, 1925. *Imprenta de la Cámara de Diputados,* pp. 7-8.

A very full discussion of the shortcomings and failings of the agrarian legislation may be found in the debate of the House of Deputies and of the Senate which were developed in connection with the passage of the above law. The whole discussion has been reprinted in *Principales Leyes de la Secretaría de Agricultura y Fomento,* December, 1924, to January, 1927, Mexico, 1927, pp. 33-357.

as applied up to the end of April, 1927, was that it arbitrarily limited the number of communities that might benefit by land distribution. Instead of legally enabling every rural community that needed land to request it, the law specifically mentioned certain communities and excluded all the rest. But the communities mentioned by name were not representative of all the inhabited rural places.[5] Nor, for that matter, were the individuals named capable of legal identification.[6]

The law in force until April, 1927, thus erected an artificial barrier, a barrier representing a specific name and legal personality. The community had to be an incorporated one.[7] This led to many political and judicial conflicts. Communities that found themselves deprived of lands because of the fact that they lacked the required name asked the state legislatures that their names be changed, and some states undertook arbitrarily to do so, while in other cases

[5] Bassols, *Consideraciones Generales.*

[6] Rafael Martínez Carrillo, *Ayuntamientos Sobre las Leyes Agrarias de México,* Mexico, 1923, pp. 34-38.

"In none of the [civil legislation of the Republic] is there a single proviso that can regulate the existence, the functioning, or the development of the innumerable (*todo ese mundo*) communities that throb at the source of our social structure; the laws ignore the fact that there are *condueñazgos, rancherías, pueblos, congregaciones, tribus,* and so forth. It is truly shameful that when a matter referring to one of these mentioned communities comes up for consideration, one has to search for the relevant laws in the compilations of the colonial period. And there are not five lawyers in the whole republic that know these compilations well." *Diario de los Debatos del Congreso Constituyente,* Appendix, p. 32.

[7] Bolaños, *Reglamento Agrario,* April 10, 1922, pp. 177-178.

confusion arose from the attempt to prevent a change in the name of the communities through court procedure.[8]

II. REFORM OF THE EJIDO LEGISLATION

Under the present Mexican administration an attempt has been made to smooth out these conflicts and to introduce some general uniformity into the administration of the national agrarian legislation.[9]

[8] Bassols, *Consideraciones Generales,* citing the laws of Zacatecas and Nayarit.

[9] The more important decrees and laws dealing with agrarian matters that have been placed upon the statute books under the present administration are as follows:

Ley Federal de Colonización, Diario Oficial, Alcance el Número 7 del Tomo XXXVI, correspondiente al Martes 11 de mayo de 1926.

Decreto de 23 de Abril de 1925, Diario Oficial, 1925.

Ley Reglamentaria Sobre Repartición de Tierras Ejidales y Constitución del Patrimonio Parcelario Ejidal, Diario Oficial, December 31, 1925.

Ley de Crédito Agrícola, Diario Oficial, March 4, 1926.

Reglamento de la Expedición y Amortizacion de los Bonos de la Deuda Pública Agraria, Diario Oficial, March 9, 1926.

Reglamento de Ley Sobre Repartición de Tierras y Constitución del Patrimonio Parcelario Ejidal, Diario Oficial, April 5, 1926.

Ley de Bancos Agrícolas Ejidales, Diario Oficial, April 9, 1926.

Reglamento que normará la Constitucion y Funcionamiento de las Sociedades Cooperatives Agrícolas Locales y de las Uniones de Sociedades Locales que se creen con Capital Particular, Diario Oficial, May 6, 1926.

Reglamento de la Ley de Bancos Agrícolas Ejidales, Diario Oficial, April 22, 1926.

Ley de Bancos Agrícolas Ejidales, Diario Oficial, April 9, 1926.

Decreto Declarando en Suspenso la Aplicación de la Ley de Tierra Libre del 2 de Agosto de 1923, Diario Oficial, July 3, 1926.

Decreto Refundiendo, Adicionando y Modificando las Prevenciones de los Distintos Ordenamientos Vigentes Relacionados con el Uso y Aprovechamiento de Aguas de Propiedad Nacional, Diario Oficial, July 19, 1926.

In new legislation the attempt has been made both to meet criticisms and to embody the lessons derived from administrative experience. While the laws remain in a general way what they were, the changes in detail are of a sufficiently fundamental character to give the principle of land distribution a fundamentally broader objective and ultimately a greater influence. These changes have three general aims: (a) the universalization of the right to land among practically all of the Mexican communities, (b) giving the expropriated landowner a greater measure of security and protection, and (c) meeting the specific declaration of Article 27 that the lands given

Reglamento de la Ley de Colonización de 5 de abril de 1926, Diario Oficial, January 27, 1927.

Ley de Dotaciones y Restituciones de Tierras y Aguas, Reglamentaria del Artículo 27 de la Constitución, Diario Oficial, April 27, 1927.

Decreto que Reforma los Artículos 193 y 194 de la Ley Sobre Dotaciones y Restituciones de Tierras y Aguas de 23 de abril de 1927, Diario Oficial.

Decreto Facultando a los Gobiernos de los Estados de la República, para crear su Deuda Agraria, January 24, 1926.

Ley Sobre Irrigación con Aguas Federales, Diario Oficial, January 9, 1926.

Decreto Autorizando a la Comisión Nacional de Irrigación para Adquirir y Administrar las Obras del Ramo que estimo necessarias, Diario Oficial, February 19, 1926.

Decreto Declarando de Utilidad Pública la Construcción de Obras Complementarias de Irrigación, Diario Oficial, July 5, 1926.

Decreto Determinando que no se otorguen Concesiones para la explotación del suelo y del subsuelo, en las Zonas sometidas al estudio de la Comision Nacional de Irrigación, July 16, 1926.

Ley que reforma la de Dotaciones y Restituciones de Tierras y Aguas, Reglamentaria del Artículo 27 Constitución de 23 de abril 1927, Diario Oficial, August 18, 1927.

to the villages would ultimately be broken up, reinforced as it apparently was by the lessons of experience that communal holding generated a series of evils that endangered the ultimate aims of the land distribution itself.

Most important among the changes in the agrarian legislation under the present administration is the practical universalization of the right to land. It is true, of course, that the law [10] makes some few exceptions. It may be said, however, that for the first time since the revolution began in 1910 all the rural communities, without regard to name or legal status, have a right to ask for and receive land and water essential to their existence. The first article of this law reads as follows:

Every inhabited place which lacks lands and waters or has not enough of both of these elements for the agricultural needs of its population has a right to a donation of them in the amount and under the conditions determined by this law.[11]

Inhabited places excluded from this right to land are the capitals of the federal and state governments, cities of 10,000 people or over that contain less than

[10] *Ley de Dotaciones y Restituciones de Tierras y Aguas, Reglamentaria del Artículo 27 de la Constitución, Diario Oficial,* April 27, 1927; *Decreto que Reforma los Artículos 193 y 194 de la Ley sobre Dotaciones y Restituciones de Tierras y Aguas de 27 de abril 1927. Diario Oficial,* May 25, 1927.

[11] *Ley que reforma la de Dotaciones y Restituciones de Tierras y Aguas, Reglamentaria del Artículo 27 Constitución de 23 de abril 1927, Diario Oficial,* August 18, 1927, Art. 13.

200 individuals who would qualify as entitled to
land, the ports that have less than 25 individuals
entitled under the law to be counted in the agrarian
census, communities formed upon property under
colonization contracts, and the resident workers upon
agricultural lands under exploitation.[12]

The demand for access to land and water which
has played so important a part in the history of
Mexico during the last 18 years has finally been
given a legal basis sufficiently inclusive to satisfy a
large part of all total rural population of the country. In another way this definition of right to land
is significant. Article 3 repeats the right to restitution in the same general form that it is to be found
in the older law. But it is clear from the context
of the law itself that restitution has been relegated
to a subordinate place.[13] If restitution proves difficult, the request is immediately converted into one
for donation.

At the first initiation of land distribution under
the law of January 6, 1915, restitution occupied the
most prominent place both in the law and in the
reasons given for the legislation.[14] In Article 27
restitution and donation were more nearly on a
parity with each other, with restitution still occupy-

[12] This at least was the general plan upon which the law was
drawn. See Bassols, *Consideraciones Generales*.

Ley de Dotaciones y Restituciones, Art. 25, *Diario Oficial*,
April 27, 1927.

[13] *Ley de Dotaciones y Restituciones*, Art. 25, *Diario Oficial*,
April 27, 1927.

[14] Bassols, *Consideraciones Generales*.

ing first place. That also was true of the *reglamento* of April 10, 1922.[15] But now donation comes first and restitution is subordinate. That is, the law has moved from an attempt to undo an injustice by returning lands to communities that had illegally been deprived of them—an attempt that was beset with innumerable and almost insurmountable legal difficulties—to a clear recognition of the equal right of all communities to land. This is the basic change that has taken place. There are others, but they must be considered subordinate to this broad expansion of the reach of the new agrarian legislation.

The second undertaking of the reformed legislation is to meet some of the complaints of the landowners. These criticisms and complaints, as we have already seen, challenged the whole scheme of agrarian legislation. The government in meeting the opposition of the owners has tried to lessen at least four sources of discontent: to prevent the padding of the agrarian census, to prevent favoritism as between owners, to protect the landowner in his remaining properties, and to give some immediate value to the bonds issued in payment for the lands taken.

To avoid the padding of the agrarian census, the new law gives the proprietors the means of participating in its formation. This participation is a contributory judgment upon the area to be granted to the village—as the acreage is determined by the

[15] *ibid.*

number of people who under the law are specifically enumerated in the agrarian census as entitled to receive land. In each action the proprietors who may be affected are called into session and asked to appoint some one who will form part of the committee that is to make the census. If they fail to do so, a member of the committee whose expenses are chargeable to the proprietors' account is named by the agrarian authorities.[16] As a further restriction against the possibility of fraud, no one may be counted in the agrarian census who has not lived in the specific village for a period of at least a year.[17] To meet the charges of favoritism and unscrupulous disregard of the rights of the landowners, the law provides that all properties surrounding the village having an area of over 150 hectares—which is the legal exemption—must be affected proportionately according to the extent and character of their holding.[18] But in all cases the proprietor must be left an area not less than the sum of 50 parcels being given to the community.[19]

The law also establishes a period of ten years between the final donation and any request for amplification.[20] This is a positive change in the law toward a greater protection of the landowners.

[16] *Ley de Dotaciones y Restituciones,* Arts. 58 and 59, *Diario Oficial,* April 27, 1927.

[17] *ibid.,* Art. 97.

[18] The law also allows the owner to retain 2,000 hectares of pasture land.

[19] *Ley de Dotaciones y Restituciones,* Arts. 105, 134, and 135, *Diario Oficial,* April 27, 1927.

[20] *ibid.,* Art. 191.

In addition, any amplification of a grant must go for the establishment of new holdings and not for the enlargement of old parcels, the original beneficiaries or their heirs being excluded from the right to receive a further grant of land.[21] Finally, no amplification of any sort can be initiated by any village for a period of five years from the date of the publication of this law (April 27, 1927), regardless of the time that may have elapsed since it received its previous donation.[22]

In attempting to meet the problem of compensating the expropriated landowners, the present administration has sought to give the agrarian bonds immediate value. There has been no fundamental change in the law.[23] Compensation is still, as required by the constitution, to be based upon tax valuation plus 10 per cent. The bonds are as before to be amortized within 20 years and are to carry 5 per cent interest. But under special decree [24] these bonds are receivable for all governmental taxes excepting those hypothecated for the foreign debt. In addition, they are accepted as collateral by the National Agricultural Credit Bank at 66 per cent of their value.[25]

[21] *ibid.*, Art. 192.

[22] *ibid.*, Art. 195.

[23] *Reglamento de la Expedición y Amortización de los Bonos de la Deuda Pública Agraria, Diario Oficial,* March 9, 1926.

[24] *Decreto de 18 de junio 1926, Diario Oficial,* July 28, 1926; including the Decree of June 10, 1925, and the *Ley de Credito Agrícola de 10 de febrero de 1926*.

[25] Ing. Javier Hoyo, *Oficial Mayor* of the National Agrarian Commission, in a letter dated April 28, 1927, makes the following

These are the most important changes that the new law has made in the basis and method of land distribution now taking place in Mexico. They make the right to land much more inclusive—opening opportunities for at least the greater proportion of the rural villages. At the same time, a certain amount of protection and security previously lacking is now provided for the landowner. We have lastly to consider the changes in the holding and distribution of the lands among the villagers who have benefited from the land grants.

A third step in the reform of the ejido legislation was the partial subdivision of the communal lands among the inhabitants of the villages.[26] One of the

explanation of the present status of the indemnification proceedings.

The changes in the law giving the agrarian bonds immediate acceptability for purposes of taxation and as collateral in the National Agricultural Credit Bank led to the following results: Whereas up to the middle of 1925 only 60 demands for indemnification had been filed, these have now grown to the number of 670, and 120 of these represent foreigners whose properties were affected in the land grants to villages. The first drawing of bonds for immediate liquidation took place on January 3, 1927. Up to March 15 these liquidations have covered 61 demands, and amounted to $6,850,000. Of the 120 foreign claims filed, so far, 72 are Spanish, 9 American, 12 German, and the rest represent French, English, Cuban, and Dutch nationalities. Of the 61 claims liquidated, 19 were those of foreign nationals amounting to $5,063,600, and 42 were Mexican with a value of $1,786,400. (See Appendix C.)

[26] *Ley Reglamentaria sobre Repartición de Tierras Ejidales y Constitución del Patrimonio Parcelario Ejidal, Diario Oficial,* December 31, 1925; *Reglamento de la Ley sobre Repartición de Tierras y Constitución del Patrimonio Parcelario Ejidal, Diario Oficial,* April 5, 1926.

persistent criticisms against the whole scheme of land distribution has been directed at the communal character of the landholding. It has been repeatedly asserted that excessive powers of the administrative committees and the insecurity of the individual cultivator combined both to create internal friction in the communal group and to keep down productivity.

In addition to meeting the recognized shortcomings of the communal holding, this law also tries to meet the obligation imposed by Article 27 of the Federal Constitution, which, following the spirit of Article 11 of the decree of January 6, 1915,[27] says that: "these communal lands shall be so held until such time as the manner of making the division of the lands shall be determined upon." [28]

The main objective of this new legislation is to give security to an individual recipient of a parcel of land. It is to secure him in his possession, in his crop, in his improvements, and to secure his right to pass the fruits of his work on to his children. But to establish such security for an individual who has never enjoyed private ownership, whose habits of personal direction are limited, whose provision for tomorrow is notoriously childlike, and whose immediate economic needs are pressing, is a matter of

[27] *Proyecto de Ley Reglamentaria sobre Repartición de Tierras Ejidales y Constitución del Patrimonio Parcelario Ejidal, 1925, Exposición de Motivos,* p. 4.

[28] "The Mexican Constitution of 1917," Supplement to the *Annals* of the American Academy of Political and Social Science, May, 1917, p. 23.

great difficulty. It was to overcome some of these difficulties that the legislation was drawn in a compromise form—a compromise between private and communal ownership.[29] The form has among its ends not merely to protect the individual from the political manipulations within the village, but to protect him from his own weaknesses and from the possible ambitions of the neighboring landowner.[30] It is this that explains the fact that as long as the man works his parcel of land he cannot be deprived of it.[31] No legal force may take the land from him, not even the federal government unless it replaces it. To protect him from the ambitious landowner, he may neither sell the land, mortgage, or rent—in fact, no source of outside control over either the land or its usufruct is permitted.[32] Neglect of tillage, or death without heirs, are the only conditions under which the property once allotted can return to the village commune, and then only until it is again given to some landless villager.[33] The pasture lands, the forests, and the water are retained in communal ownership, but under strict supervision of an elected

[29] *Principales Leyes de la Secretaría de Agricultura y Fomento*, December, 1924, to January, 1927, p. 205.

[30] This law gave rise to a long and heated debate revolving around the nature of the ownership that is best suited to the Indian laborer for whose benefit the *ejidos* are being provided. *ibid.*, pp. 31-359.

[31] *Ley Reglamentaria Sobre Repartición de Tierras Ejidales*, *Diario Oficial*, December 31, 1925, Art. 15.

[32] *ibid.*, Art. 16.

[33] *ibid.*, Art. 15.

committee that may be removed at will by the local community.[34]

The assumption is that with security will come greater production and greater interest in building up the resources of the plot of land. We find thus definitely established a mixed form of ownership for millions of Mexican tillers of the soil. This mixed form of ownership may be summarized as follows. It gives permanent possession and usufruct of the soil and its improvements with all rights of heritage. This benefit is conditioned only by the necessity for tillage and exploitation. On the other hand, private property is limited by the fact that the possessor has no right of alienation in any form whatsoever of either the soil or its products, not even under rental or mortgage. At the same time that the individual has full private use of a parcel of land without right of alienation, he is also a possessor of rights in a community that enjoys as a commune the usufruct in village pasturage, water, and forests. But here again, the village has no right of sale, transfer, or alienation. Thus both the individual and the village have use in perpetuity.

[34] *ibid.,* Arts. 3 and 6.

CHAPTER XI

AGRARIAN LEGISLATION

While the provision of lands for villages is the central influence in the agrarian history of present-day Mexico, this grant of land to the villages is nevertheless only one of the aspects of the agrarian revolution. The "integral solution" of the agrarian problem has called for a number of other undertakings, each a part of the general scheme and each an important project in itself.

The whole agrarian program draws its inspiration from and rests its legal justification upon Article 27 of the Constitution of 1917. This article enables the government to expropriate "by means of" payment, and to put limitations upon private property without compensation.[1] The possible extent and range of these limitations upon present ownership have as yet not been defined by juridical interpretation.

The constitutional program has, however, been supplemented by numerous statutes. Their more important features call for comment. First is the insistence in the law that possession is contingent on use. Over and over again the law says in effect,

[1] Roa, *Las Cuestiones Fundamentales de Actualidad en México*, p. 175.

260

"If you do not exploit your property, the state will do so, and may do so without special compensation to you." The law undertakes to save the actual value possessed by the owner, but it reserves for itself the right to appropriate all the increment that the activities of the government may add to the property in question.

Second, and corollary to the first, is the tendency to emphasize the collective interest of the community as against the individual right of the owner. Not only is this evidenced in the expropriation of property and in the limitations upon the possession and use of property under the principle of public interest, but it is also clear in the administrative activities which the government carries on in connection with the use and exploitation of private property.

Third, and strikingly characteristic of all the contemporary legislation, is the attempted limitation upon the powers of acquisition of lands by foreigners. This takes the form of limiting the right of sale even of properties clearly and privately owned; and it takes the form of limitations of rights and obligation under contract with foreign companies. There is, fourth, the effort to stimulate group activity. Thus emphasis upon social organization is made prominent in the colonization, co-operative credit, and labor legislation. The fifth underlying motivation is the desire to reduce the large estates to smaller holdings. This is in addition to the land grants to villages. And here again, the resort for legal justification is the right to put "limitations" upon private ownership. The irrigation and colonization legislation is clearly drawn with that objective in view. In fact, as is pointed out further on in this chapter, the irrigation legislation is primarily aimed at the breakup of the large estates and the setting of small cultivators upon individually-owned properties. With these introductory remarks we turn to a consideration of the laws under discussion.

I. THE UTILIZATION OF IDLE LANDS

In the attempt to provide lands to needy villages the federal government and various states passed laws for the placing of untilled lands under cultivation. In part this legislation resulted directly from the difficulties in the way of immediately applying the *ejido* legislation. It was a short cut for placing lands, at least temporarily, at the disposal of villages that had no lands of their own.[2] It was also an attempt to increase the area under cultivation,[3] as the large areas left untilled by the haciendas[4] were

[2] Puebla: *Periódico Oficial del Gobierno del Estado,* March 17, 1925, p. 37, indicates that the idle lands law had for its purpose "the providing of lands to villages to which there had not been either returned or given *ejidos.*"

[3] Puebla: *Ley de Tierras Ociosas,* June 25, 1921. Reprinted in *Catecismo Agrario,* Julio Cuadros Caldas, Mexico, 1924, pp. 30-33; *Sindicato de Compensonos de Agraristas del Estado de Durango,* January 1, 1925, p. 38.

[4] Humbolt, Alexander, *Political Essay on the Kingdom of New Spain,* New York, 1811, Vol. I, p. 148.

Memoria, Ministerio de Fomento, Mexico, 1865, *Documento Número* 65, May 6, 1861, p. 506.

still further increased as a result of the violence or
fear of violence that resulted from the revolution.
The legislation therefore was both an outcome of
the revolution, and an effort to correct a long-stand-
ing evil in Mexican agriculture, the insufficient utilization of the arable lands of the haciendas. This
legislation takes its character and derives its powers
from Article 27 of the Constitution of 1917 and is
promulgated under the provision that: "The nation
shall have at all times the right to impose on private
property such limitations as the public interest may
demand. . . ." [5] The idle lands legislation made its
appearance early in the revolution and there are
laws dealing with that subject dating back to 1916.[6]
There is close similarity between the federal and

[5] The Mexican Constitution of 1917, Article 27, *Annals,* May,
1917, p. 16.

[6] *The Mexican Review,* Vol. I, No. 1, October, 1916, p. 6, indices
a national order to place untilled lands in the hands of cultivators.

Sonora: Decreto Número 27 issued by Gen. P. Elías Calles,
now president of Mexico, then (Jan. 15, 1916) Military Governor
of the State. *Decreto que Declara Causa de Utilidad Pública el
Cultivo Immediato de los Campos*.

Coahuila: La XXIII *Legislatura Constitucional del Estado
Libre, Independiente y Soberano de Coahuila de Zaragoza, Decreto*
(not numbered), November 26, 1917. *El* XXIII *Congreso Constitucional del Estado Independiente, Libre y Soberano de Coahuila de Zaragoza, Decreto Número* 208, *Artículo Unico,* November 19, 1918.

*Durango: Artículos de la Ley de Tierras Ociosas del Estado de
Durango, promulgado el 18 de Junio de 1918.*

*México: Ley Agraria para el Aprovechamiento de las Tierras
Laborables no Cultivadas, Decreto Número* 45, April 13, 1918.

*Tlaxcala: Ley Para la Utilización de Tierras Ociosas en el
Estado de Tlaxcala, Número* 63, June 28, 1919.

Zacatecas: Ley Para el Cultivo de Tierras Ociosas, December
15, 1919.

state legislation dealing with idle lands. The Federal Idle Lands Law (1920) follows these earlier models and is in turn followed by the state laws that have been adopted since.[7] This similarity is most clearly expressed in the definition of the objectives of the law. Like the federal law, most of the state laws begin by declaring that the cultivation of the soil is a matter of public utility. That being so, it follows within the logic of the legislation that "the state can dispose temporarily of tillable soil left untilled." [8]

[7] *Ley de Tierras Ociosas, de los Estados Unidos, Mexicanos,* June 23, 1920.

Guanajuato: Decreto Número 244, Ley que reglamenta la de Tierras Ociosas en el Estado de Guanajuato, May 18, 1925.

Puebla: Ley de Tierras Ociosas, June 25, 1921.

Veracruz: Ley de Tierras Ociosas, Jalapa-Enriquez, Oficina Tipográfica del Gobierno del Estado, 1923.

Chihuahua: Ley de Tierras Ociosas, Expedida por el C. Presidente de la República y Decreto Expedido por la XXIX Legislatura del Estado, 1923.

Querétaro: Número 37, Ley Agraria del Estado de Querétaro, Capítulo XII, De las Tierras Ociosas, Art. 99.

Campeche: Decreto Número 55, Reglamento de la Ley Federal de 23 de Junio de 1920, Art. 5.

Yucatán: Decreto Número 127, Reglamento de la Ley de Tierras Ociosas, December 26, 1920.

Chihuahua: Ley de Tierras Ociosas, Art. 3.

Sinaloa: Decreto Número 113, Ley que Declara de Utilidad Pública el Cultivo de las Tierras de Labor, December 26, 1919.

Guerrero: Decreto Número 12, Reglamentacion de la Ley Federal de Tierras Ociosas, June 4, 1923.

Morelos: Decreto Número 43, Ley de Tierras Ociosas, February 1, 1921.

[8] Tlaxcala, *Tierras Ociosas,* Art. 1. (All further references to the idle land laws will be given as follows: name of state, *T. O.,* and Article number.)

An additional and rather different attack upon the problem of

Definition of idle lands. Tillable land is defined as "lands capable of yielding an agricultural produce through the exertion of man with or without the aid of machinery." [9] Such lands, if left untilled, become subject to temporary disposal for the purpose of cultivation. This arable land may, as in the case of Mexico [10] and Querétaro, [11] have been untilled for two years in succession or, as it is in most cases, not planted by a certain date. They may also be lands capable of cultivation "denounced" as tillable by the neighbors. In Campeche, where the customs (as in other states, especially Chiapas and Guerrero) of felling and burning forests is still a fairly common method of preparing land for tillage, the law specifies that "the procedure of *tumba y quema* (felling and burning) may be followed in the same form in which on similar mountains it has been employed by the owners and possessors of the land." [12]

Pasture lands, forests, orchards, and lands given over to horticulture are generally exempt from the operation of the law. Coahuila specifically warns the cultivators that under this law they must not

idle lands was made by the state of Aguascalientes in 1925 by providing that all landowners who neglected to put to use their irrigated lands were to be taxed, in addition to the regular tax, 8 *pesos* for each *hectare*. Aguascalientes, *Decreto* No. 27, *Supplemento al Número 10 de Labor Libertaria,* March 8, 1925.

[9] Campeche, *T. O.,* Art. 2.
[10] Mexico, *T. O.,* Art. 3.
[11] Querétaro, *T. O.,* Art. 99.
[12] Campeche, *T. O.,* Art. 3.

exploit the forests or industrial fibres, their rights being limited to land and water for agricultural purposes.[13]   Two states (Campeche and Yucatan),[14] on the other hand, include the use of the mountains and the making of charcoal in the definition of the rights of cultivators of abandoned lands.

Crops and cultivation dates.   Before turning to a consideration of the special contractual conditions which the federal law and various state laws enable the county governments to establish for the use of the idle lands, we shall consider the time limits allowed for the different crops in determining whether or not the owner is tilling the soil.

Of the 18 laws under discussion, eight make no reference to crops.   They either set one date for the whole state or leave the local governments to establish the time limits.   The ten that do set a definite time limit for specific crops show great divergence not only merely in dates but in the crops selected for mention in the law.   All of them mention maize, eight enumerate wheat, while beans are mentioned by five, cotton and chile by two, rice and sesame by two, and sugar cane and tobacco by one.   The great diversity of the climate not merely in the Republic but in most of the individual states makes it very difficult to set a definite date for each crop mentioned and for every type of climate.   This fact is clearly evidenced by the provision for a change of

[13] Coahuila, *T. O.,* Art. 4.
[14] Campeche, *T. O.,* Art. 16; Yucatan, *T. O.,* Art. 12.

the time set if the local conditions make such a change necessary,[15] and by the specification that the local village governments shall set the dates.[16] This procedure, however, is not always followed. The central government and the State of Aguacalientes set separate dates for maize and wheat. Guanajuato specifies a different date for preparing and planting each of 14 crops.[17] Morelos sets dates for each of nine crops, and for maize, beans, and rice sets separate dates for irrigable and non-irrigable lands. Guerrero distinguishes between the hot and warm climates and marks the seasons accordingly for each of four different crops,[18] while Durango groups the counties into three different zones and sets a legal limit to the planting season for each of four crops.[19] But the greatest diversity and minuteness is established under the law of Oaxaca.[20] This law divides the state into 18 different zones and sets separate dates for each of the zones. As the number of crops enumerated is seven, the complexity of the law is an illuminating comment upon the agricultural structure not merely of the state of Oaxaca but of Mexico as a whole. For some of the zones the law distinguishes four different climatological conditions for the growing of maize: Non-irrigated, humid

---

[15] Chihuahua, *T. O.*, Art. 3.
[16] Sinaloa, *T. O.*, Art. 5.
[17] Guanajuato, *T. O.*, Arts. 1-7.
[18] Guerrero, *T. O.*, Arts. 1 and 2.
[19] Durango, *T. O.*, Art. 4.
[20] Oaxaca, *T. O.*, Art. 1.

ground, spring maize (*temprano* after the spring rains), and irrigated. In some of these districts three different plantings of the same crop may be grown during one year. This complexity is still further illuminated when we glance at some of the dates for the preparation of the soil for maize. These dates are as follows: February 10, February 15, March 15, March 30, April 20, April 30, May 15, May 20, June 10, June 15, June 30, September 15, November 30, January 20, and January 31. As this is only for one crop and only for one state, we have here a glimpse of the variety of Mexico's agricultural seasons.

Contracts for the cultivation of idle lands. Contracts for the cultivation of idle lands are made with the local government and are generally confined to the agricultural year. The lands must then be returned to their owners. But there are some exceptions. Querétaro provides that the cultivator may have the lands for two years in succession, and beyond that until reclaimed for the coming planting.[21] Other qualifications are found in exceptions for lands neglected for four years, or unbroken. In such cases the cultivator has a right to continued use for from two to five years: Sinaloa for two years, Yucatan and Campeche for three years each, Tlaxcala four, and Mexico five.[22]

[21] Querétaro, *T. O.*, Arts. 99 to 106.

[22] Sinaloa, *T. O.*, Art. 10; Yucatan, *T. O.*, Art. 9; Campeche, *T. O.*, Art. 10; Tlaxcala, *T. O.*, Art. 7; México, *T. O.*, Art. 8.

It is interesting to observe in this connection that these provi-

Payment for the cultivation of idle lands. Of the laws under consideration only nine make provision for payment. The others allow the local governments to let the lands, without specifying financial obligation. Three of the nine make the local government the exclusive beneficiary of the rental. One [23] specifically prescribes that the owner must not receive payment for the use of his neglected lands. Two—Campeche and Yucatan—[24] prescribe a rental equal to 5 per cent of the value of the crop, while Morelos [25] places it between 3 and 10 per cent of the crop. Zacatecas [26] gives 5 per cent to the owner and 2 per cent to the local community, while Sinaloa [27] sets the rental at 5 per cent for the village administration and 5 or 10 per cent to the owner of the land, depending upon whether or not it is fenced. For the territories the federal law gives to local governments between 5 and 10 per cent of the value of the crop, depending upon whether or not the tiller is given seed and implements in addition to the land, and 2 per cent to the owner if the land turned over to cultivators had already been

sions are not inconsistent with the time-honored practice of the *haciendas* even before the revolution. It was customary then for *haciendas*—and it still is—to break new lands by this system of giving the use of the land to new cultivators for a stipulated number of years. Santisteban, J. B., *Indicador,* p. 177. But see Chapter V of this book.

[23] Campeche, *T. O.,* Arts. 13 and 14.
[24] *ibid.,* Art. 13; Yucatán, *T. O.,* Art. 10.
[25] Morelos, *T. O.,* Art. 2.
[26] Zacatecas, *T. O.,* Art. 10.
[27] Sinaloa, *T. O.,* Art. 10.

ploughed. Querétaro is the only state that makes the tiller responsible for the tax as well as a 5 per cent rental to the owner.[28] The two remaining states [29] have a very complicated system of determining the rental that is to be paid, developing the principle that the longer the lands are held by the cultivator the greater the rental to the owner, running as high as 20 to 25 per cent in the fourth and fifth years.

Area that can be acquired under the law. When we come to consider the area that any one individual may acquire under these laws, it is evident that the legislators were fairly generous in the amount allowed when compared with the area available for purchase under state legislation or the extent given as *ejidos.*[30] Perhaps the facts that this land is not taken from the owners except for temporary use, and that neither the user nor the state assumes the obligation of long-time payments as they do under the other agrarian legislation, made it possible to open comparatively larger parcels to users. Of the laws under discussion, Querétaro enables the user to acquire what he can cultivate. The federal law makes it possible to acquire 20 hectares in the Federal District and 100 in Lower California and Quintana Roo. Chihuahua and Durango vary the amount that one may secure, depending upon whether it is irrigated or dry farming; in the case of Chihuahua one may

[28] Querétaro, *T. O.*, Art. 101.
[29] Tlaxcala, *T. O.*, Art. 7; México, *T. O.*, Art. 8.
[30] See below, pp. 320-334.

have three hectares of irrigated and fifteen of temporal, while in Durango it may be from one to seven hectares of irrigated and from one to twenty-five hectares of non-irrigated.[31] The other six states all provide a fixed area, going from seven in Yucatan to thirteen in Mexico.

The law of Oaxaca, in dividing the state into 18 districts, sets different areas that may be allotted to the would-be cultivators in the various localities. The areas are as follows: in four districts the tillers are allowed five hectares each; in one district, eight; in five, ten; in seven, fifteen; and in one, twenty.

General features of the law. We can draw to a close this discussion of the character of the idle land legislation by pointing to the fact that the states have followed the federal law in its general provision for the immediate compliance with the request for land, as well as in protecting the owner against abuse. There is provision for the maintenance of fencing in at least two states. Campeche provides that solicitants must be spread over the available untilled soil so as not to concentrate upon any one property to the exclusion of others. Also that cultivators who despoil the forests become liable to criminal action under the charge of destroying other people's property.[32] There is in addition a feeble attempt to encourage the use of modern methods.

[31] Querétaro, *T. O.*, Art. 104; Ley Federal, *T. O.*, Art. 11; Chihuahua, *T. O.*, Art. 4; Durango, *T. O.*, Art. 7.

[32] *Decreto Número 55, Reglamento de la Ley Federal de 23 de Junio de* 1923, January 27, 1921, Art. 17.

Both Yucatan and Campeche encourage tillers to use modern machinery and, if they do, exempt them from the necessity of paying the rental required by the law.[33]

It has been impossible to date to estimate the extent to which the laws dealing with idle lands have been applied. That they have been a factor in the recent development of agricultural and agrarian policies in Mexico is clear enough. The fact that the laws have been passed over a period of ten years—between 1916 and 1925—shows that the legislative process has been continuous. But better evidence of the use of the law comes from other sources. For the State of Durango we have the testimony that "the idle lands have acted as a means of escape, for a momentary solution, if you will, but effective, of the problems of some cultivators (*campesinos*) and groups of cultivators who were obstructed in the matter of securing *ejidos* or national lands."[34]   In issuing a decree abrogating the idle lands law, the governor of Puebla makes the following declaration: "That the spirit of the law of idle lands promulgated on the 23rd of June, 1920, had for its object the providing of lands to the villages to whom there had not been either restored or given *ejidos* so that they could achieve their economic independence . . .

[33] Yucatan: *Decreto Número* 127, *Reglamento de la Ley de Tierras Ociosas,* December 26, 1920, Art. 16; Campeche: *Decreto Número 55, Reglamento de la Ley Federal de 23 de Junio de* 1923, January 27, 1921, Art. 19.

[34] *Sindicato de Campesinos Agraristas del Estado de Durango,* January 1, 1925, p. 38.

and in view of the fact that those villages that have received lands under the law of January 6, 1915, no longer need the lands given them under the idle lands law, therefore all communities that are now in possession of their *ejidos* must, after taking down their crops, return to their owners those lands which they have been cultivating as idle lands." [35] And, finally, we have the testimony of the large landowner of the State of Morelos who, in a memorandum to the Department of Agriculture, said: "As the landowner cannot himself with his own hands cultivate his lands, it is sufficient that those from the neighboring villages and *rancherías,* who generally work them, should agree among themselves not to work before the day set by the law for the lands to be declared idle, for them (the lands) to be conceded to the same who previously worked them at the cost of the hacienda or under renting contracts. There is one hacienda that announced through the press its willingness to give its lands under the renting conditions prescribed by the law, but the agitators influenced the workers so that there was no one who would take them, and they were later ceded as idle lands to those who had from time immemorial worked them under renting contracts." [36] This varied testimony is evidence of the fact that the law was actually used for the purposes of putting land

[35] Puebla: *Decreto de 14 de Marzo de 1925, Periódico Oficial del Gobierno Constitucional del Estado L. y S. de Puebla,* March, 17, 1925, p. 37.

[36] *Dos Escritos Dirigidos a las Autoridades por los Hacendados de Morelos,* Mexico, 1921, pp. 10-11.

to tillage, even if under conditions that were not originally prescribed in the law.

II. IRRIGATION LEGISLATION

The irrigation law [37] is considered part of the undertaking to break up the large estates.[38] The break-up of the large estates and the settling of landless cultivators upon parcels of personally-owned tillable soil is the reason given as justifying the governmental expenditure.[39] The law aims to meet the needs of the better class of landless cultivators—those who have risen to the position of share croppers and renters, who have some animals and work tools and who would not be content with the small parcel provided by the *ejidos*.[40] The law also tries to overcome the lack of resources that has prevented the *hacendados* from developing irrigation in the past [41] and at the same time to keep them from absorbing any unearned increment arising from the increased value due to irrigation at government expense and through government initiative.[42]

Sources of the legislation. In spite of the fact

[37] *Recopilación de las Principales Leyes Expedidas por Conducto de la Secretaría de Agricultura y Fomento, Período del 1 de Diciembre de* 1924, *A 6 de Enero de* 1927, Tacubaya. This volume contains the projects of the legislation, the debates in the Senate and House of Deputies. All references, unless otherwise noted, will be to this volume.

[38] *ibid.*, p. 430.

[39] *ibid.*, p. 443.

[40] *ibid.*, p. 431.

[41] *ibid.*, p. 433.

[42] *ibid.*, p. 447.

that it is part of the agrarian legislation the law has such distinct features that it is interesting to inquire into the background of experience and ideas that led to its peculiar form. It is considered a revolutionary step in the application of the collective right embodied in the Constitution.[43] The legislators in the discussion of the law drew their inspiration from three main sources: Mexican experience, Article 27 of the federal constitution, and the theories of Henry George. It was pointed out that 80 per cent of the actual irrigation works of Mexico date back to the colonial period, that very little successful irrigation work was carried through in the last hundred years,[44] that even during the 30 years of peace under the Diaz regime, when Mexico enjoyed both tranquillity and credit, there was no development of irrigation, and that the 50 million pesos set aside for that purpose by the Diaz government were squandered upon some 90 landowners with no increase in the area under irrigation.[45] Further, the discussion showed that there are some 35,000 concessions for one or another sort of irrigation project, but that most of these have been fruitless and empty gestures.[46] In the face of these facts, and in face of the fact that only some 15 per cent of the available irrigable area is under exploitation,[47]

[43] ibid., pp. 468-472.
[44] ibid., p. 442.
[45] ibid., p. 446.
[46] ibid., p. 490.
[47] ibid., pp. 455-456.

the government was declared justified in taking energetic measures to overcome the apathy of the landowners and to provide the resources for the development of irrigation works.

As the law aims both to increase the irrigated area and to contribute to the solution of the agrarian problem, it is made to depend upon Article 27 of the federal constitution. The source of the law is again, as in so much of the contemporary legislation, the notion of the right of the nation to put "limitations" upon private property and to "regulate the development of natural resources." [48] It is of interest to note here that expropriation is rejected. [49] In fact, the law aims at leaving the owner in possession of the same value that he had before, even if he retains a smaller area. [50] It is here that the legislators seek justification from Henry George. [51]

If the government can appropriate to itself the unearned increment derived from irrigation at public expense, it can reimburse itself, secure land for distribution by sale in small parcels, increase the area under cultivation, and leave the landowner as rich as he was before. The law may, as was argued

[48] *ibid.*, p. 447.

[49] *ibid.*, p. 444. Expropriation was rejected because it led to the possibilities of long drawn-out litigation, and to the need for compensation which under the circumstances might absorb the funds that could otherwise be used for irrigation.

[50] *ibid.*, p. 509.

[51] *ibid.*, p. 445. "The government . . . frankly laid before you for consideration the project of a law eminently inspired by the theories of Henry George." Speech by Louis L. León, Secretary of Agriculture in the House of Deputies.

by the Secretary of Agriculture, be radical in appearance, but in fact it takes no value from the owner. It leaves him as rich as before and is consistent with the underlying principle of the constitution, that the exploitation of natural resources is a condition of their possession and enjoyment.[52]

The irrigation law.[53] The law enacted in 1926 declares that privately-owned properties and the rights of the users of waters under federal jurisdiction become subject to the limitations which this law prescribes for the purpose of constructing, conserving, and paying for irrigation works.

The irrigation of all private property, regardless of size or the character of its cultivation, is declared a matter of "public utility," provided it can be made to utilize water under federal jurisdiction.[54] The law creates an irrigation commission [55] to study and select the most available irrigation projects, declare

[52] ibid., p. 509. "The procedure appears radical, but it is not unjust, for it leaves the landowner with a value mathematically equal to that which he had before his lands were put under irrigation." Louis L. León, Secretary of Agriculture.

[53] *Ley Sobre Irrigación con Aguas Federales, Diario Oficial,* January 9, 1926.

Decreto Autorizando a la Comision Nacional de Irrigación para Adquirir y Administrar las Obras del Ramo que Estime Necasarias, Diario Oficial, February 19, 1926.

Decreto Declarando de Utilidad Pública la Construcción de Obras Complementarias de Irrigación, Diario Oficial, July 5, 1926.

Decreto Determinando que no se Otorguen Concesiones para la Explotación del Suelo y del Subsuelo en las Zonas Sometidas al Estudio de la Comision Nacional de Irrigación, Diario Oficial, July 16, 1926.

[54] *Ley de Irrigación, Diario Oficial,* January 9, 1926.

[55] *ibid.,* Art. 3.

the specified areas as irrigation zones, formulate the irrigation plans, calculate the budgets, and after the plans are all worked out notify the owners of the properties affected, and give them an opportunity either to carry the project through themselves or to participate with the government in the undertaking. If the owners fail to agree or cannot raise 75 per cent of the cost of the undertaking, then the Commission takes the project under its own supervision, admitting as partners those owners who are willing to participate.[56]

In each case where the government contributes to the cost, it compensates itself by taking part of the lands irrigated. This division is so calculated that the owner retains an area, the value of which under irrigation will be equal to the value of his total area before irrigation.[57] Lack of conformity on the party of the owner enables renters or other possessors, if there are any, to contribute to the undertaking and be compensated in the same manner as the government compensates itself.[58] The allotment of the irrigated area is worked out before the construction is undertaken, and the owner may appeal either to the administrative or judicial agencies of the government if he is dissatisfied with the acreage allotted to him.[59]

The irrigated lands thus acquired by the government are to be divided into lots,[60] sold to individuals

[56] *ibid.*, Art. 4.
[57] *ibid.*, Art. 5.
[58] *ibid.*, Art 6.
[59] *ibid.*, Art. 7.
[60] The size of these lots is to be determined in each case. This

at a price based upon the cost of the irrigation, and paid for over a period of not less than ten years. These provisions of payment and division apply even if the particular project is carried through under contract by a private company.[61] Private landowners may develop irrigation projects within the limitations of this law.[62] Finally, under special decree it was later added that the irrigation commission could, for purposes of "public utility," purchase irrigation works already in existence and use them to further such general irrigation schemes as they had projected; [63] and that all subsidiary activities connected with irrigation—canal building, protecting water sheds, developing electrical power, draining, and other related activities—were to be considered as part of the irrigation program and therefore came under the control of the irrigation commission as matters of "public utility." [64]

III. COLONIZATION

The provision by law for colonization, like irrigation, is essentially a part of the agrarian and agricultural program of Mexico. That this is true may be seen from the fact that practically every government

provision was put in so as to make it possible to conform to the state laws governing area that may be held by one person.

[61] *Ley de Irrigación*, Art. 10.

[62] *ibid.*, Art. 17.

[63] *Decreto Autorizando a la Comision Nacional de Irrigación para Adquirir y Administrar las Obras del Ramo que Estime Necesarias*, Art. 1.

[64] *Decreto Declarando de Utilidad Pública la Construcción de Obras Complementarias de Irrigación*, Art. 1.

in Mexico, since the first days of the Republic, has attempted to provide for colonization, and generally without success. The present colonization law must therefore be read in the light of Mexico's colonization experience. And that experience shows clearly enough that colonization projects may become instruments for alienations into foreign hands of large tracts of national territory to be held for speculative purposes, that it may increase, rather than decrease, the system of large landholding, and that it may lead to the exploitation and discouragement of would-be colonizers. Examining the present law in terms of this past experience, and in connection with the contemporary undertaking to provide a solution for the agrarian problem, it becomes immediately obvious that it is a part of the general program to break up the large estates and to settle the landless cultivator upon a piece of personally-owned and tillable soil.

Subject to the conditions laid down in this law are national lands, those acquired by the federal government, by the agricultural credit bank, and by the Irrigation Commission, and, under certain conditions, private properties.[65] Drawing its authority from Article 27 of the federal constitution, the colonization of private properties is declared a matter of public utility when coming within the terms of the law.[66]

[65] *Ley Federal de Colonización*, Art. 2, *Diario Oficial, Alcance el Número 7 del Tomo XXXVI correspondiente al martes* 11 *de Mayo de* 1926.
[66] *ibid.*

Private properties cultivated either directly or by means of croppers and renters up to 66 per cent of their cultivatable area for all types of crops are exempt from the operation of this law. So also are properties organized as agricultural-industrial units and under tillage up to 66 per cent of their available area, and properties directly cultivated without croppers or renters up to 50 per cent of their arable land.[67] Private properties, moreover, only come within the purview of the law if there are no national lands or lands acquired by the agricultural credit bank within zones set aside for purposes of colonization.[68] Colonization projects on national lands may be carried out directly by the federal government or by the National Agricultural Credit Bank, or through contracts with private corporations. If the owner of a property that has come under a colonization project wishes to conform, he must within 60 days elect either to colonize the property himself or to join with the government, the National Agricultural Credit Bank, or a private company in the carrying out of the colonization scheme.[69] Failure of the owner to conform leads to expropriation of the property at the taxable value plus 10 per cent. Payment for the property is made either directly by the National Agricultural Credit Bank or from the

[67] *ibid.*, Art. 4; *Reglamento de la Ley de Colonización*, April 5, 1926, *Diario Oficial*, January 27, 1927, Art. 56.

[68] *Ley Federal de Colonización*, Art. 4, *Diario Oficial*, January 27, 1927.

[69] *ibid.*, Art. 5.

yearly instalments covering the purchase price of the
parcels sold to colonizers. The bonds carry a 6 per
cent interest.[70] The owner, who applies for and receives permission to colonize, if the property is mortgaged must show that his directors are willing to
accept a lien on the proceeds of the sale of the lots
and not on the property itself. He must also show
a certificate from the National Agrarian Commission to the effect that his property is not at the time,
and will not be in the future, subject to a demand
for *ejidos*. In addition, he must satisfy the Department of Agriculture upon the valuation of his property and the price of the parcels to be sold, as well as
the conditions of the sale. The Department of Agriculture then inspects the lands and determines
whether they are fit for colonization. If all these
requirements are satisfactorily met, the government
declares the colonization of the particular property
a matter of public utility and grants the owner the
required permission to carry out the undertaking
that has already been approved.[71]

Before any colonization scheme can be undertaken by any company or individual, the Department of Agriculture, as a preliminary and indispensable condition, must satisfy itself that the property under consideration is fit for colonization,[72] and

[70] *ibid.*, Art. 6; *Reglamento de la Ley de Colonización*, April 6,
1926, *Diario Oficial*, January 27, 1927, Arts. 61, 63, and 14.

[71] *Reglamento de la Ley de Colonización*, Articles 48 and
49.

[72] *ibid.*, Art. 1.

approve the detailed plans of the project. Before undertaking the project the company or individual must first deposit 30 per cent of the prospective cost of the colonization scheme with the National Agricultural Credit Bank. This money is placed at his disposal after he has satisfied the Department under its own auditors that the other 70 per cent of the estimated cost of the project has been invested.[73] The project must be so planned and developed as to give direct access to the road to each and every parcel sold, and if the land under sale is irrigated the irrigation canals must reach each parcel. No single lot can be sold until the undertaking is completed and ready for settlement in accordance with the approved plans.[74]

The colony is opened for settling only after it is fully prepared and ready for occupancy and after at least 50 per cent of the required number of colonists have been secured.[75] The area allowed each individual is strictly limited, but is decidedly liberal when compared with the limitations imposed by other agrarian laws. Any one individual may acquire from 5 to 50 hectares of irrigated land, from 15 to 250 hectares of good non-irrigated land, from 200 to 500 hectares of poor land, and from 50 to 5,000 hectares of pasture lands.[76]

In addition to fixing the area, the law very care-

[73] *Ley Federal de Colonización*, Art. 7.
[74] *Reglamento de Ley de Colonización*, Arts. 2, 3 and 4.
[75] *ibid.*, Art. 21.
[76] *Ley Federal de Colonización*, Art. 8.

fully guards the conditions of admittance to the colony. Preference is given to croppers and renters of the property, to neighbors, to Mexican agriculturists, including those living in foreign countries but desiring to return to Mexico.[77] Every colonist must prove his ability to undertake the financial burden of the first year's cultivation and living expenses.[78] In the case of foreigners, this involves the placing of 1,000 pesos with the National Agricultural Credit Bank to be used by him during the first year towards his work and keep.[79] For each colony the government will especially determine both the number and kind of foreigners who are to be admitted. This judgment is aimed towards selecting those colonists that best fit into the differing climates of the Republic and who show the greatest adaptability to the special racial and cultural conditions. The foreigners must also have a sufficiently high standard of culture to be useful as an educational influence in the colony.[80]

The colonists must undertake to pay 5 per cent of the value of the lot after the first crop and the rest over a period of from 10 to 25 years. In case of failure to cover instalments due to a justifiable cause, payment will be extended for one year. But if payment is not made for two years in succession, or if the land is left untilled, the contract becomes sub-

[77] *ibid.*, Art. 10.
[78] *Reglamento de Ley de Colonización*, Art. 16.
[79] *ibid.*, Art. 16.
[80] *ibid.*, Arts. 17 and 18.

ject to cancellation, the property being sold to the
highest available bidder, the previous owner being
allowed 80 per cent of the purchase price received
under this sale.[81]   The price of government lands
put under colonization will be computed at their
value before improvements plus 5 per cent for the
technical work and facilities granted to colonists.
The concessionaire who prepares national lands for
colonization does not acquire title to the lands.   The
titles to the colonists are issued by the Department
of Agriculture, the concessionaire acting merely as
an agent of the government.[82]   Until all payments
have been completed, the purchaser has no rights of
mortgage or alienation.   He has a right of sale after
the completion of the payments upon the lots, but
that right is limited by making the transfer of title
possible only to those who satisfy the requirements
of becoming actual settlers in the colony.   An heir
who does not fulfill the requirements for becoming
a settler within the colony must sell his land to the
highest bidder from amongst those who satisfy the
requirements for being admitted as members.

The colony will be administered by the government.   As soon, however, as 10 per cent of the purchase price has been covered by the colonists, they
will be permitted to participate in its management,
and when the payments have reached 50 per cent of
the purchase price, the control of the colony will be

[81] *Ley Federal de Colonización*, Art. 11; *Reglamento de Ley de
Colonización*, Art. 5.

[82] *Reglamento de Ley de Colonización*, Art. 45.

surrendered to its members.[83] The government will admit free of import duties special articles needed in connection with the colonization projects and may help the colonists to cover their traveling expenses in Mexico.[84]

IV. HOMESTEAD LEGISLATION

Another important, though little discussed, part of the current agrarian legislation was the law of August 2, 1923,[85] which was suspended in connection with the passage of the colonization law in 1926.[86] This law was a distinct contribution to the legislation itself and had an important influence upon the extent of the area that has passed into the possession of small cultivators as a result of the revolution.[87] It had much in common with our own homestead legislation in that land was free, that title was acquired by occupancy and cultivation, and that possession became permanent with right of sale and transfer. It also differed markedly from land distribution for communities in that the area allowed was considerably larger and that the means of ac-

[83] *Ley Federal de Colonización,* Art. 14; *Reglamento de Ley de Colonización,* Art. 23.

[84] *Ley Federal de Colonización,* Art. 15.

[85] *Ley de Tierras Libres, Agosto* 2, 1923, *Catecismo Agrario, por Julio Cuadras Caldas, Segunda Edición,* Mexico, 1924, pp. 38-44.

[86] *Decreto Declarando en Suspenso la Aplicación de la Ley de Tierras Libres del 2 de Agosto de* 1923, *Junio* 10 *de* 1926, *Diario Oficial,* July 3, 1926; *Reglamento de la Ley Federal de Colonización,* Art. 79, *de 5 de Abril de* 1926, *Diario Oficial,* January 27, 1927.

[87] See p. 331 for area and number of individuals that have benefited from this law.

quisition were relatively simple and free from the burdening supervision of the National Agrarian Commission. The administration of the law was entrusted to the land section of the Department of Agriculture, which confined its supervision to verifying the claim that the land occupied was national and seeing that the conditions of actual occupation and cultivation were complied with.

This law opened the national lands [88] to any Mexican citizen,[89] and passed definite title after two years of occupancy and tillage.[90] It differed sharply from the legislation providing lands to the villages in that it was free from legal difficulties, and in that it emphasized the individual rather than the family or community. It also gave the occupant a relatively larger hold upon his possession than that provided by the other contemporary agrarian legislation. The occupant after receiving title had the right of sale and transfer, limited by the laws which prevent under any conditions the passing of the property to a foreigner or to a Mexican having an area equal or greater than that which could be taken up under the law.[91] Conforming to the present legislative tendency in Mexico, the nation reserved the subsoil for itself.[92] The suspension of this law—

[88] See p. 319 for extent of national lands claimed by the federal government.

[89] *Ley de Tierras Libres,* Art. 1.

[90] *ibid.,* Arts. 2 and 4.

[91] *ibid.,* Art. 12.

[92] *ibid.,* Art. 13.

unless other legislation involving the general principle of the easy transfer of the national lands to private individuals is substituted—will visibly retard the movement of developing small individual cultivators.[93]

[93] In addition to the legislation which we have just described, a number of states, in compliance with the mandate in Article 27, have passed laws for the reduction of the large estates. This state agrarian legislation is of a very diverse and complex character and, as can be seen from the following quotations from official letters of four state governors, has generally remained unenforced.

"The agrarian law and its *reglamentación* has to date had no application in this state, as the agricultural groups have chosen to resort to the benefits provided by the federal legislation." (Letter No. 3,227, Aguascalientes, June 10, 1927.)

"This office has not divided any *latifundia* in accord with the law previously cited (and still in force)." (Letter No. 1,952, Saltillo, Coahuila, June 29, 1927.)

"Up to date no *latifundia* in this state has been divided in accord with the laws of the state. The only donations have been those in accord with the federal law of January 6, 1915." (Letter No. 4,273, Pachuca, Hidalgo, June 24, 1927.)

"I wish to state that the agrarian law of the state relative to the division of the *latifundias* and the creation of small properties has as yet not been applied in any single case, because the necessary legislation making it possible is lacking, as well as because up to date the state agrarian debt has not been created." (Letter No. 9,503, Hermosillo, Sonora, June 16, 1927.)

In view of this lack of enforcement, we have transferred to Appendix A a discussion of the broader features of this state legislation.

CHAPTER XII

AGRICULTURAL LABOR LEGISLATION

The growth of the power and influence of organized labor in both agricultural and industrial Mexico is one of the most obvious and significant consequences of the Mexican revolution. Before the revolution there were practically no labor organizations. There was little if any class consciousness among the workers, and the revolution originally embodied few if any labor ideals. Mexico is after all largely an agricultural country. And yet, as a result of the revolution, Mexican workers have achieved a degree of organization which gives them a powerful, perhaps a preponderant, place in the determination of contemporary political policies. While many factors have contributed to shaping this tendency to organization, among which the very able leadership developed by the movement must be considered, the largest measure of its success is no doubt due to the legal position of Mexican labor.

The Mexican workers secured the embodiment of an elaborate labor code in the Constitution of 1917.[1] This code included some of the more important labor legislation developed in the industrial nations of

[1] See p. 203.

Europe and America during a century of experiment and strife. Mexican workers thus achieved at one time what the workers of the industrial nations of the world took a hundred years to acquire.

The result has been to give the Mexican working population both on the farm and in industry what is perhaps a unique constitutional position in the history of modern labor. The demands which the workers in other countries have had to contend and bargain for are here embodied in law and only need enforcement. It can therefore be said that the workers in Mexico have organized to enforce the law. It is this that has given them the basis of such rapid organization. Their objectives were definite, were part of the law of the land, were immediately within reach, and needed only to be demanded effectively to be secured.

There are two other considerations to be taken into account. The first is the fact that the government rests upon the same Constitution which contains the labor program. Since 1917, it has been closely identified with the groups that wrote the Constitution and needed their support to maintain itself in power. The government therefore was both in law and in fact committed to aid the workers in securing the enforcement of the labor program contained in the Constitution. Second, a predominant part of the industrial wealth of the country is foreign. In almost every labor conflict that developed the issue presented itself not merely as one between capital and labor, but as one between foreign capital and native labor. Every conflict raised the issue of nationalism as well as the issue of social and industrial relations. Under the circumstances every Mexican government has been compelled more or less tacitly to side with labor, not only because it needed its support but also because it could not consistently take the side of the foreigner against its own people. These factors have contributed powerfully toward giving Mexican labor its peculiar position. In a later chapter we shall discuss more in detail the organizations; here we confine ourselves to a description of the agricultural labor legislation.

All Mexican labor legislation derives its source from Article 123 of the Constitution of 1917. This article was made mandatory upon both the states and the federal territories until such time as the necessary regulatory laws were passed by the states and the federal government.[2]

[2] Because of the failure on the part of the federal congress to pass a labor law, Article 123 is still the only legal basis for the adjustment of labor relations in the Federal District and the two territories of Baja California and Quintana Roo. Article 11 of the transitory articles of the Constitution of 1917 reads as follows:

"Until such time as the Congress of the Union and the state legislatures shall legislate on the agrarian and labor problems, the basis established by this constitution for the said laws shall be put into force throughout the republic." The *Annals* of the American Academy of Political and Social Science, p. 112. See also Toledano, Vicente Lombardo, *La Libertad Sindical en México*, pp. 76-77.

There has recently developed an agitation that the federal constitution be reformed so as to make labor like agrarian legislation a matter of federal jurisdiction. C. R. O. M., *Organo de*

To date no federal labor law has been adopted, each bill being successively held up by the Senate, while only 25 out of the 28 states have passed labor laws.[3] These laws of the states are of a very diverse nature. Only one state—Guanajuato—has passed a specific agricultural labor law.[4] Thirteen have included special sections dealing with agricultural labor in their general labor laws. The others, excepting Yucatan and Durango, have merely issued regulatory laws for special provisions of Article 123, such as accident and sickness compensation, or for the establishment of boards of conciliation and arbitration.[5]

The state of Guanajuato and those that have embodied a section devoted to the agricultural laborer in their general labor laws set out in detail the classes of workers subject to the law. This is always done in the first article of each of the laws under discussion. There is no uniformity in the enumeration of the groups of workers, nor is the definition of the different types as given by various states always alike. There is confusion especially in distinctions drawn between the worker who is also a cropper or renter and the cropper who has no obligations as a laborer upon the same property. In the body of the

la *Confederación Regional Obrera Mexicana,* November 1, 1927, Mexico, *Ano. III, Numero* 65, p. 17.

   [3] Toledano, note, p. 144.

   [4] Guanajuato: *Ley del Trabajo Agrícola,* March 13, 1923, *Imprenta del Estado.*

   [5] See Toledano for comprehensive discussion of Mexican labor legislation.

laws themselves, however, these distinctions are sufficiently clear, and the provisions for the different classes of labor sufficiently concrete to make it possible for us to differentiate the following groups:

The resident worker (*acasillado*)
The temporary free worker
The casual worker
The worker-cropper
The worker-renter
The crop sharer
The renter
The employee
The domestic farm servant
And three classes of employers:
The proprietor
The small middle-man agriculturist
The cropper or renter who employs less than five workers

The terminology used in distinguishing the different classes of labor is in a measure itself sufficient to indicate their relative character and position on the hacienda and to define them for the purpose of the discussion which follows. It is essential to have this classification clearly in mind, as each of the classes has its well-defined prerogatives and rights, and its well-defined place in the scheme of the agricultural community of contemporary Mexico. A comparison of this classification with that given in Chapter V (page 110) will indicate how very similar the labor group is to that described as characteristic of Mexico before the revolution.

It is important to remember that the legislation discussed in the following pages sums up in one way the actual results of the revolution, even if in many sections of the country (see Chapter XVII) the law remains unenforced. The mere fact that such a body of legislation has been contrived and worked out, that it exists in fact upon the statute books, has contributed powerfully to a rapid movement for organization, the main purpose of which to date seems to have been the enforcement of the laws.

As has already been indicated, the state of Guanajuato has passed the most comprehensive code of law dealing with agricultural labor. In part, this is due to the fact that it has repeated in the agricultural labor law the general labor provisions contained in the Federal Constitution, which in the other states are embodied in separate sections of their general labor law, and also to the fact that it has a more detailed body of regulations than any one of the other states.[6]

I. GENERAL PROVISIONS

The law of Guanajuato prescribes that each *hacendado* must keep open the road between his property and the public highway "when it does not

[6] There may be some relation between the fact that Guanajuato has the greatest proportion of its rural population living upon *haciendas* and the fact that it is the only state that has detailed agricultural labor laws.

affect the security" of the property.[7] With the exception of house and offices, the owner may not prevent the free entrance of political "propagandists" or trade union organizers and representatives, providing, of course, that they come peacefully and sober and do not interfere with the regular work of the farm.[8] He cannot, without a justifiable cause, prohibit the titular fiestas in the accustomed places,[9] nor may he prevent a weekly market, giving free access to all hucksters and retailers having a municipal license. He must provide adequate space for the market within the inhabited place,[10] nor can he maintain a *tienda de raya* (truck store)[11] or permit gambling and the sale of intoxicating liquors,[12] while he must expel all vagrants and immoral people from the hacienda and report them to the authorities.

On supplying adequate and sanitary dwellings, or upon constructing such dwellings, the owner may, after inspection and authorization by the *presidente municipal*, charge a yearly rental of 6 per cent of the value of the houses.[13]

[7] Guanajuato: *Ley del Trabajo Agrícola*, 1923, Art. II.
[8] *ibid.*, Art. V.
[9] *ibid.*, Art. IV.
[10] *ibid.*, Art. IX.
[11] *ibid.*, Art. IX
[12] *ibid.*, Art. X.
[13] *ibid.*, Art. VI. It must be noted here that *peons* must be given free housing, water, firewood, and a little piece of land. Only croppers and renters can be charged the above rental, or they must be provided with land and material to construct same free of charge, as well as given a piece of land varying in some states from 200 to 1,000 square metres for a yard.

Subject to strict punishment under the penal code, the law prohibits the practice known as *dar faenas* (give tasks). That is a system of unpaid labor done outside of the regular working hours by the people employed or living on the hacienda, and includes not merely the working men but their families as well. In addition to the customary tasks that go under the title of *dar faenas*, the law describes under this title a wage less than the minimum customary in the neighborhood. The inadequate compensation to the worker for the tools and animals supplied by him for the use of the hacienda is similarly classed. Duress is assumed in these cases.[14]

Each rural property which has 50 children of school age must provide a school at the expense of the owner or renter. If less than 50 children are found on any one property, the neighboring properties which are at a distance of less than two kilometers must combine for the purpose of establishing a school. All financial obligations for school purposes are to be carried out through the local tax office and in co-operation with the State Department of Education.[15]

II. THE AGRICULTURAL LABORER

The labor contract of the agricultural worker may be for either piece or day work and need not be in

[14] Guanajuato: *Decreto* 227, May 29, 1923, Art. VII.

[15] *ibid.*, Art. XI as amended by *Ley Reglamentaria de los Artículos* 11 *Reformado y* 2 *Transitorios de la Ley del Trabajo Agrícola,* June 16, 1926, and August 4, 1926.

writing.[16] All work undertaken on the hacienda is understood to be under contract, and the proprietor may not bring "outsiders" if there are unemployed permanent laborers on the hacienda capable of doing the work. Laborers engaged without a specified time limit for the general work of the hacienda, who have resided on the place for three months, are considered permanent. The rights and the obligations of the housed worker expire with him who entered into the contract.[17] No contract may be entered into for more than a year. It may, however, be renewed indefinitely.[18] In case of the owner's death or change of proprietors, the contracted obligations towards the workers are assumed by the new *hacendado*.[19] Mutual agreement, expiration of the legal time limit, death, or incapacity of the peon terminate the contract.[20]

The federal provision for a minimum wage is incorporated in the law. Wages may not be less than the minimum prescribed by the local board of conciliation and arbitration. In the absence of specified wage terms, the current wage is understood, providing it does not fall below the minimum set for that municipality by the local board. Payment is to be made weekly[21] in legal tender and within the

[16] *ibid.*, Art. XII.

[17] *ibid.*, Art. XIII.

[18] *ibid.*, Arts. XIV and LXXVII. For domestic farm servants the law provides that a contract binds the employer but that the servant may leave with one week's notice.

[19] *ibid.*, Art. XXVII.

[20] *ibid.*, Art. XXVI.

[21] *ibid.*, Art. LXXXIII. The law permits an employee to be paid in periods of one month.

boundary of the property where the work is done.[22] Until the establishment of local boards of conciliation and arbitration has taken place, the "housed workers" (*acasillados*) are to receive 3 per cent of the total crop product of the hacienda as their share of the profits.[23]

This share of the products of the hacienda is to be turned over to the representatives of the "housed workers" to be sold with the aid of the local municipal authorities and the money deposited for the use of the group, the individual worker having no right to dispose of the share that accrues to him without the consent of the government, and then only in case of dire need, that is, sickness or death.[24]   This provision has been amended [25] to make the share accruing to the "housed workers" available only for use in the organization of co-operatives.[26]

The difficulties involved in working out an acceptable formula for the sharing of profits has not entirely escaped the legislators of the different states. Most of the state laws have tried to avoid the pit-

[22] *ibid.*, Art. XV.

[23] Guanajuato: *Ley del Trabajo Agrícola,* 1923.

[24] *ibid.*, Art. XX.

[25] Guanajuato: *Decreto Número* 421, December 4, 1925, *Periódico Oficial,* January 3, 1926.

[26] Reporting in 1926, the governor of the State of Guanajuato makes the following remarks on the working of this law to date: "The fund which belongs to the *campesinos* as their share of the profits is only $12,753.69, which has been collected in the state treasury. In view of the small amount involved, it is essential to study the best possible investment for this sum, as individual division between the workers would be of almost no use." Lic. Enrique Colunga C., *Gobernador Constitucional del Estado, Informe,* Guanajuato, 1926, *Imprenta del Estado,* p. 7.

falls of a percentage profit basis and have adopted flat rates in addition to the actual wage. Sinaloa, Sonora, and Veracruz have chosen one month's wages at the end of the year, providing the worker has remained on the hacienda during the year, and providing further that there has been no crop failure. Other states, like Tamaulipas and Chihuahua, have set a half month's pay every six months, repeating the above conditions of no crop loss and permanence of the worker during the period involved. The state of Nayarit has defined neither the share nor the method of distribution, and Jalisco merely indicates that the division is to be according to salary received. But even such obvious attempts to escape the difficulties involved in computing a possible basis for profit-sharing are felt to need a defense, and the one provided by the governor of the State of Veracruz in his message submitting the labor law is interesting. He writes:

"We are not unconscious of the great difficulties which arise from the attempt to apply these provisions . . . to determine exactly what are profits, to determine justly what may belong to the workers. . . . It involves an audit of the books, an examination of the contracts of raw materials, as well as of sales, the amount of money invested, the age of the establishment, the gains and losses of previous years, and many other factors. There is also the difficulty of determining the share the worker had in producing the gains."

He goes on to approve the imposition of a month's extra wage by the statement that "wages are in general terms proportional to other expenses and (contemplated) profits, and therefore the outlay of an extra month's wages is a justifiable participation," apparently on the ground that it may be calculated in advance as a definite [27] part of the cost.

In case of accident or disease not "imputable" to the peon, he is given medicine and medical treatment, if there is a doctor within four kilometers. He is to be given his full wage during the period of incapacity up to six months.[28] This provision for sickness is exceeded in the States of Nayarit [29] and Campeche. The first sets up no time limit, while Campeche provides six months' full pay and half pay after that. Campeche also provides for aid amounting to 25 per cent of the cost involved in the case of sickness on the part of any member of the worker's family.[30] The other states generally require half pay for two months and medical aid. Some, like Veracruz, prescribe aid for the family in case of sickness without defining the degree of responsibility.[31] For permanent disability, Guanajuato provides that the worker is entitled to such work as his "faculties" will permit and one payment equal to 300 days' wages.

As in the provision for sickness, the state of Guan-

[27] Veracruz: *Exposición de Motivos de la Ley del Trabajo*, 1925, p. 23.

[28] Guanajuato: The employee receives a full wage for only eight days and half pay for the rest of the time. In case of death, the employee's family receives one month's wage.

[29] Nayarit: *Ley del Trabajo*, 1925, Art. XLIX.

[30] Campeche: *Ley del Trabajo*, 1926, Art. LIX.

[31] Veracruz: *Ley del Trabajo*, 1925, Art. XLIX.

ajuato makes very liberal provision for the worker's family in case of death. Death not "imputable" to the peon entitles his family to 300 days' wages.[32] The state next most generous is that of Campeche, which provides that on account of a death for which there is no legal indemnity, and if the worker has no outstanding debts, the family is entitled to three months' pay and the cost of the funeral; and in case of a death in the worker's family, he is entitled to 50 per cent of the cost of the funeral.[33] The other states provide for one month's pay for the family and help with the funeral expenses.

To workers who are not permanently living on the hacienda, but who settle there during the period of the crop season, the employer is under obligation to fulfill all the provisions of the labor contract with the exception of that referring to the sharing of profits, and the contract is understood to terminate with the completion of the work upon the crop.[34] To the transitory workers or, as described in the law, "the casual workers," the employer is under obligation only in so far as the law refers to minimum wage and the accidental provisions.

The employer is under obligation to provide housing free of charge to all his workers,[35] as well as

[32] Guanajuato: *Ley del Trabajo Agrícola*, 1923, Art. LXXXIII.
[33] Campeche: *Ley del Trabajo*, 1926, Art. XLIX.
[34] Guanajuato: *Ley del Trabajo Agrícola*, 1923, Art. XXXIV.
[35] *ibid.*, Art. XXXVI. Compare Article VI above, page 295. There it says that he *"may* charge" 6 per cent of the value of the house, and here, that he is *"obliged* to provide free" housing to all his workers. The above refers to croppers or renters.

water in sufficient quantity, and within the custom of the hacienda to provide them with firewood (*leña*), or to permit them to cut the same in assigned places. In cases where the work contract is only for periods (crop seasons) and where the worker has built his own shelter from his own materials, he may, after the work period is over, carry the materials away with him if the proprietor does not pay for them.[36] The owner may not expel a worker who is living on his property. He may, through judicial process, demand the evacuation of the house after the work contract has terminated.[37] Nor can he deprive a man of work as a means of securing his departure from the property.[38] The workers may not be prohibited from raising hogs and fowls within the place assigned to them for purposes of habitation, the workers being responsible for damage done by the animals.[39] For the "housed workers" the employer cannot raise the quota of the pasturage (*estalaje*) or diminish the number of animals which they had when the contract was entered into, except annually or at the termination of the contract.[40]

III. SETTLEMENT OF DISPUTES

In January of each year the "housed workers" of the hacienda elect amongst themselves one, two or

[36] *ibid.*, Art. XXXII.
[37] *ibid.*, Art. XXXIX.
[38] *ibid.*, Art. XL.
[39] *ibid.*, Art. XXXVIII.
[40] *ibid.*, Art. XXXVII.

three representatives, whose names they communicate to the owner through the office of the *presidente municipal*.[41] Any difficulties between the workers and their representatives are adjusted by the local municipal authority.[42] Difficulties between the employer and the peon are settled by the local board of arbitration and conciliation. Refusal on the part of the owner to submit a dispute to adjudication makes him liable to three months' wages. The same penalty is imposed if he refuses to accept the decision of the board.[43]

The owner may break the contract with the peon before its legal expiration if the worker refuses to obey orders in regard to his work, if he does not work the regular hours, if without proper justification he fails to appear at work for two days in succession, if through negligence the animals and tools in his charge deteriorate, if he becomes drunk during his work or presents himself for work in an "inebriate" condition, if he is condemned to prison for crime, if through repeated intoxication he causes scandals and upsets the tranquillity of his neighbors, and finally if he goes to work on another farm while there is work on the place he is residing,[44] or fails to treat the employer with just consideration.[45]

[41] *ibid.*, Art. XIX.
[42] *ibid.*, Art. XXI.
[43] *ibid.*, Art. XXV. Compare the provisions in Article 123 of the federal constitution and note the close similarity.
[44] *ibid.*, Art. XIII.
[45] *ibid.*, Art. XXVIII.

On the other hand, if the employer discharges a worker without just cause, or because he has joined a union, or because he has taken part in a legal strike,[46] or if the worker abandons the place because of mistreatment, either of himself or his family at the hands of the employer or his representatives, the employer becomes liable for three months' wage payment. However, lack of sufficient work on the hacienda is recognized cause for discharge. It is a sufficient cause for the worker to break contract if the employer hires strange workers and leaves the "housed workers" idle, providing they are equally able; if he does not pay the agreed wage; if he fails to pay in legal currency; if he pays in periods longer than a week apart; if he pays in places other than the property where the work was done; if he tries to evade the provisions for the sharing of profits; if he infringes the laws relating to hours of labor and weekly rest; if he does not provide medicine in case of sickness or the stipulated wage during the same period; if he interferes with the raising of hogs and fowls within the workers' places of habitation; if he tries to expel people from the *finca* on his own initiative; if he tries to deprive the peon of work as a means of forcing him off the *finca;* and if he interferes with his personal liberty.[47]

The regulation of strikes of agricultural laborers is not very explicit. Apart from stating that workers

[46] *ibid.*, Art. XXIX.
[47] *ibid.*, Art. XXX.

have the right to organize and to strike, the laws generally lay down no further rules. In Campeche [48] the law specifies that a strike is merely a suspension of the contract and does not abrogate the prerogatives guaranteed by the contract; while Jalisco provides that if the crops are endangered by a strike the employer may, with the consent of the commission of conciliation and arbitration, hire a limited number of workers not subject to the dispute for the purpose of saving the crop.

Should an employer abandon his lands and refuse to till them, the local commission of conciliation and arbitration may, at the request of the workers, place the abandoned lands at their disposal under the general rules applied to *tierras ociosas* (idle lands).[49]

The provisions of the law relating to the agricultural peon end with the general statement that an attempt to deprive the worker of his personal liberty is a penal offense in that the provisions of the law are of public interest and are therefore not alienable. The law then takes up the share cropper. It is here that some of the most interesting provisions of the contemporary agricultural labor legislation are to be found, and the degree of detail with which the law deals is in itself an interesting commentary upon the social organization of the rural community as well as an insight into its economic relations.

[48] Campeche: *Ley del Trabajo,* 1926, Art. CCIX.
[49] See Chapter XI.

IV. THE CROPPER

There must be a written contract for crop sharing.[50] If, however, the contract is consummated by the crop sharers receiving land, it carries all the legal obligations of a written contract.[51] The states of Querétaro and Michoacán have established a legal right to demand land on shares. Every worker having oxen or other work animals has a right to land, providing that there is untilled land available,[52] and having received the land he becomes entitled to an advance of seed.[53]

A somewhat similar provision is to be found in the law of Oaxaca. A worker who has lived on a hacienda for one year becomes entitled to a piece of land which he can work with his family. He is also to be given his seed and work tools. The share of the owner is limited to one-third. This is, however, in addition to the worker's contract as a peon and is not a simple crop-sharing contract.[54] The employer is under obligation to provide the land at the proper time with implements, water, and all that is either involved in the contract or that is required by law. He also assumes responsibility for losses due to his fault and for injuries for which his family or employees are responsible.[55] Once the land has been

[50] Guanajuato: Ley del Trabajo, Art. XLIV.

[51] ibid., Art. XLV.

[52] Querétaro: Ley del Trabajo, 1922, Art. CXXXVIII; Michoacán: Ley del Trabajo, Art. 90.

[53] Querétaro: Ley del Trabajo, 1922, Art. CXXXIX.

[54] Oaxaca: Ley del Trabajo, 1926, Art. CXIV.

[55] ibid., Art. LVII.

given over to the crop sharer it may not be taken
from him, nor may he be assigned another piece of
land in its stead without his consent. Nor can the
crop sharer abandon it. The contract comes to an
end with the harvesting of the crop, and any change
before that time must be made by mutual consent.[56]
Unless otherwise provided, the employer is responsible for directing the operation of cultivation and
harvesting,[57] while the share cropper is responsible
for the damage to animals and tools entrusted to his
care. He must cultivate the land under the direction of the employer or within the custom of the
place.[58] In case of death of the owner or transfer,
the new owner assumes the obligations of the contract.[59] In case of the death of the share cropper, his
heirs may finish the contract or surrender it, having
a right to a return of the value of the work put into
the land or, if that is not possible, to a payment for
the labor expended.[60] The contract for the crop
sharing cannot invade any of the rights of the
worker if he is also a laborer on the place.[61]

The share cropper who lives on the property without being a laborer has the same rights which the
law establishes for the agricultural laborer as to
housing, use of water, firewood, raising of hogs, fowl,

[56] *ibid.*, Art. LI.
[57] *ibid.*, Art. XLIX.
[58] *ibid.*, Art. XLVIII.
[59] *ibid.*, Art. LII.
[60] *ibid.*, Art. LIII.
[61] *ibid.*, Arts. LIII and LIV.

and so forth.[62] The proprietor may break the contract if for sufficient reasons he has broken the contract of the same man as laborer, if he lived on the place temporarily during the crop-raising period and incurred the consequences of drunkenness and trouble-making; [63] and if he neglected his work so as seriously to endanger the crop.[64] The cropper, however, if the crop is certain of fruition, is entitled to one-half of the share that he would have received ordinarily, the other half going to the owner as indemnification. The cropper also is responsible for costs.[64]

The share cropper may break the contract with the employer if he has broken his contract as day laborer, if the employer has denied him the rights accruing to one living upon the property, or if he has not complied with the conditions of the contract as to land, implements, and other conditions.[65] In this case, the cropper, if the crop is assured, is entitled in addition to his own share of the crop to half of the share that would ordinarily accrue to the owner; in all other cases, wages for the work he has put into the land, or indemnification after evaluation by experts. In cases where a renter or share cropper employs on his land permanent "housed workers," he has towards them the same obligations that are incurred by the proprietor of the hacienda.[66]

[62] *ibid.*, Art. XXVIII.
[63] *ibid.*, Art. LXIV.
[64] *ibid.*, Art. LXIV.
[65] *ibid.*, Art. LIX.
[66] *ibid.*, Art. LXX.

The problems that arise out of sharing the crop between the cropper and the landlord are varied and difficult to settle. There are always so many unforeseen items in the situation that any rule is subject to criticism and easy to abuse. The different fertility of every piece of land, its more or less desirable location, the crops for which it is best suited, the work and time demanded by each separate crop, the uncertainties of rain and drought, the choice of seed and of work animals, the necessity of maintenance during the crop-growing season,—all of these and other problems make it difficult to adjust the distribution of the crop between the owner of the land and the cropper. Tradition has shaped the rules of distribution and varied them for almost every hacienda and every crop. The revolution has, however, made some important changes in the relationship between these participants in the crop and, as a whole, has worked to the advantage of the cropper. It may be questioned whether a satisfactory law can be devised for such a complicated and many-sided problem of human judgment and evaluation. The fact remains, however, that such a body of law has been devised, and that what it attempts to do becomes a matter of great importance to one who would understand the workings of the present-day Mexican community.

The state of Guanajuato [67] has by law provided a legal formula for the division of the crop between

Decreto Número 381, *Periódico Oficial del Estado*, Dec. 13, 1925
[67] Guanajuato: *Ley del Trabajo*, Art. XLVI, as amended by

the cropper and the owner. This law applies, however, only to non-irrigated land (*temporal*), and does not exclude adjustments and variations of the bargain providing that they do not violate the law itself. The distribution provided is on the basis of a legal valuation of the different factors which enter into the production of the crop. These values are as follows:

Factor	Value (per cent)
The land	30
Animals and tools	10
The seed	5
The work	50
The keep (*habilitación*)	5

The crop is to be divided in proportion to the value of the different factors contributed by each party. The keep (*habilitación*) is defined in the law as 300 kilos of maize for every five hectares of land under cultivation. The worker who agrees not to receive this keep during the crop-growing season becomes entitled to an extra 5 per cent in his share of the crop. This gives the owner, if he provides the land, work animals, tools, seed, and *habilitación,* 50 per cent, and the cropper 50 per cent. The forage is divided on the same basis. Where the owner does not provide work animals and they have to be hired, the price may not exceed that set by the local committee.[68] This committee is composed of one *hacendado,* one peon, and one representative of the local

[68] Guanajuato: *Ley del Trabajo,* 1923, Art. XCVIII.

municipal government. It is also its duty to determine the annual fee for pasture for the animals not used on the land; no limit is set as to the number.[69] The rental for the work animals may not be more than 10 per cent of the crop. The imposition of a smaller share of the crop for any cause is null and void. The owner may not, even in payment for debt, keep back a part of the crop that belongs to the cropper without the latter's consent. There is, however, a preferential right to payment for what has been advanced as keep. In case of total loss of crop for three years in succession, or of loss so great as not to leave enough to cover the cost of the work, the cropper is exempted from returning the amount advanced as keep.[70] The cropper is exempt from responsibility in case of *fuerza mayor* (superior force),[71] and in any case is only responsible for his share of the common expenses.[72] For any advancement made in specie, payment must be in the same.[73] Finally, differences between owners and

[69] There is wide variation in the different state laws as to the number of animals a cropper may pasture. In Puebla three heads of *ganado mayor* (large cattle) and as many as fifteen *ganado menor* (small cattle—sheep, goats, and so forth). Sinaloa and Tamaulipas provide for free grazing of the indispensable animals. Veracruz provides for free grazing of five *ganado mayor* and a moderate rental above that. Querétaro makes five *ganado menor* and three *ganado mayor* the legal maximum.

[70] Guanajuato: *Ley del Trabajo*, 1923, Art. LIX, as amended by *Decreto Número 227, Periódico Oficial del Estado*, June 7, 1923.

[71] *ibid.*, Art. LXI.

[72] *ibid.*, Art. LXII.

[73] *ibid.*, Art. LX.

croppers are to be submitted to the board of conciliation and arbitration and are subject to the conditions that govern disputes between workers and employers.[74] It is of interest to note that there is no special provision here for the renter as apart from the cropper. That group will therefore be treated in detail for the state of Tamaulipas.

V. THE RENTER

The provisions of the different laws that deal with the small agricultural renter are very similar to those that are provided for the share cropper. A general distinction between the renter and the other groups is that the owner is solely under obligation to provide space and materials for a house and yard, the renter doing his own construction. His right to grazing, and the conditions that govern distribution of burden in case of loss of crop, are generally similar for the renter to those described for the cropper. If there is any loan, it can bear no interest, as is the rule for other agricultural workers. The time limit on contracts is either the year or the crop season, and rentals are to be paid at the end of the crop season. The amount of rent is specifically regulated only in the case of Tamaulipas, which specifies 20 per cent of the crop measured by past yields.[75] Rentals on pasture lands are not to exceed 10 per cent of their value, and mountain lands can pay only 10 per cent of their net yield.

[74] *ibid.*, Art. LXIX.　See above, Art. XXXV.
[75] Tamaulipas: *Ley del Trabajo,* 1925, Art. LXVI.

All permanent improvements are hedged about so as to protect the renter. They cannot be made without the written consent of the owner. The renter is entitled to indemnification, nor can he have his rent increased unless he has first been compensated for his improvements.[76] The provision for unopened land is very specific in all of the states, although it varies considerably. Thus Tamaulipas provides that the charge may not be more than one-fifth of what it would be for similar land already in cultivation, and that contracts must be for three years.[77] Zacatecas provides for two years' free contract on unopened *temporal* land and three years for mountain land.[78]

Puebla and Michoacán provide two years of freedom from rent for unopened land, Veracruz one year, and Sonora assigns to the renter the accrued value of the land. Chihuahua prescribes the rule of the customary arrangement in the locality. There is also the general provision for the right to renewal under the same conditions, as a means of "gradually forming his patrimony"; [79] while Zacatecas provides that in case of a break-up of the hacienda, the renter has the first right to purchase the parcels he has been cultivating.[80]

These, then, are the general rules and regulations that the contemporary legislation has provided for

[76] *ibid.*, Arts. LXXII and LXXIII.
[77] *ibid.*, Art. LXXVI.
[78] Zacatecas: *Ley Reglamentaria del Artículo* 123, Art. XCIII.
[79] *Exposición de Motivos de la Ley del Trabajo,* 1925, p. 24.
[80] Zacatecas: *Ley Reglamentaria del Artículo* 123, Art. XCII.

the rural community. They are numerous and detailed—more detailed than it was possible to indicate in this chapter. Taken as a whole, especially in their political and social aspects, they constitute important and striking innovations in the organization of the Mexican rural community. Their purely economic stipulations—division of crop, system of rentals, relations between employer and employee—are not entirely innovations. They specify in law what has been the rule in the past. More definitely even, they extend and standardize the better regulations that prevailed in the older community. The organizations that have sprung up in the rural community as instruments of enforcement for these provisions are perhaps the most important contributions to the life of rural Mexico that the laws have made; and as the organizations are fostered and protected by the laws, they must be considered at least in part a by-product of the legislation of contemporary Mexico. Taken all in all, this body of law presents an impressive contribution to the life of the Mexican rural community.

CHAPTER XIII

INFLUENCE OF THE REVOLUTION UPON LAND DISTRIBUTION, 1915-1926

The revolution was, as we have seen, in great part motivated by agrarian difficulties, and the immediate future of Mexico will largely be determined by the changes which it brings about in the country's agrarian structure. Unfortunately, it is possible only approximately to measure the changes in landholding that have resulted from the revolution. No available material gives with exactitude the extent of private landholding in Mexico before the revolution, or its distribution by area among the total holders.[1] Considerable light, however, is thrown upon the situation in detail by a presentation of the material available on contemporary landholding in Mexico. The present picture illuminates the past.

No description of landholding in Mexico made at this time can be more than a picture of a system in the process of change. It is true that the changes to date have been comparatively slight, though in-

[1] The best and most comprehensive picture available in English of Mexican landholding before the revolution is to be found in "The Land Systems of Mexico," by George McCutchen McBride, published in *American Geographical Society Research Series* No. 12, 1923.

creasing progressively since 1915. It is probably also true that the modification taking place will prove a slow process requiring many years to affect materially the present situation. The fact remains, however, that significant changes are taking place, and we must view any description of Mexican landholding at this time with that in mind.

The increase of government-owned lands has been the greatest single change in land ownership. During the Diaz regime the government had, by one or another form of contract, concession, and sale, alienated great expanses of land into comparatively few hands.[2] The movement was so rapid that at the end of the period Mexico had but little government-owned land left—some 22,000,000 hectares, or approximately 11.6 per cent of the total area of the Republic, according to figures published in 1912.[3] The amount actually alienated during the Diaz regime cannot be given with certainty. It is easier to describe in detail the area recovered by the federal government since 1915.

The Mexican Constitution of 1917 declared: "all contracts and concessions made by former governments from and after the year 1876 which shall have resulted in the monopoly of lands, waters, and natural resources of the nation by a single individual or corporation are declared subject to revision, and the executive is authorized to declare those null and void

[2] See Chapter I.
[3] *Memoria de la Secretaría de Fomento,* 1912-13, pp. 475-477.

which seriously prejudice the public interest." Under this general mandate, the successive governments have cancelled some 200 concessions for survey, purchase, or colonization that had been made by the Mexican government between 1876 and 1910.[4] Most of these cancellations have not involved any transference of lands. Many of the concessions had apparently been held for speculative purposes or had been transferred to foreigners who failed to comply with the stipulations of the original contracts. On the other hand, a number of the cancellations did involve the recapture of enormous areas of land that had passed into the hands of a few owners, mainly foreigners. It is in this phase of the agrarian program that Carranza was most zealous. "The policy followed by the constitutional government in agrarian matters has been to recover the larger part of the national lands that the former governments had without any study or provision ceded to a few favorites. . . ."[5] In following out this policy the Carranza administration reclaimed over 13,000,000 hectares from nine owners.[6]

[4] *Lista de Las Concesiones Declarandas Caducas por la Sria. de Agricultura y Fomento. Arreglada por orden alfabético de contratantes.* September 18, 1925. (Manuscript copy.) This, however, is an incomplete list. There have been additional cancellations of contracts and concessions since 1925. The only way to secure a complete record of contracts cancelled is to compile it from the *Diario Oficial* from 1912 to date.

[5] *Informe del C. Venustiano Carranza Primer Jefe del Ejército Constitucionalista encargado del poder Ejecutivo de la República,* April 15, 1917. *Imprenta del Gobierno,* Mexico, 1917, p. 112.

[6] *Informe rendido al H. Congreso de la Unión por el Presidente Constitutional de la República C. Venustiano Carranza,* May 1, 1917, p. 38.

This process of cancellation of contracts and re-assertion of government ownership over lands that had been alienated under Diaz has continued with the succeeding administration.[7] President Calles reported a recapture of 4,604,573 hectares in 1925,[8] while in 1924 the Department of Agriculture had announced the fact that from one company alone, the Mexican Land Colonization Company, the government had regained 7,500,000 hectares in the states of Lower California and Chiapas.[9] The government agreed to pay 16,000,000 *pesos* [10] for the losses suffered by this company in the return of the lands. This indicates that not all of the lands were recaptured without some legal claims on the part of the companies whose lands were taken from them. As a whole, however, the cancellation of the contracts and the recapture of the lands has involved comparatively little friction. It is especially important to remember that most of these lands had found their way into the hands of aliens, and the transfer

[7] *Informe Rendido por el C. Adolfo de la Huerta,* September 1, 1920, p. 33. *Informe Rendido por el C. Alvaro Obregon, Presidente Constitucional de la República,* September 1, 1921, p. 49; *ibid.,* 1922, p. 56; *Informes Rendidos por el C. Gral. Plutarco Elías Calles, Presidente Constitucional de los Estados Unidos Mexicanos,* Sept. 1, 1925 and Sept. 1, 1926. Two reports in one volume; 1925 report, p. 65, and 1926 report, p. 32.

[8] *ibid.,* Report of 1925, p. 65.

[9] *Boletín Oficial de la Secretaría de Agricultura y Fomento,* Vol. 8, *Epoc.* 6-a. Numbers 1, 2, 3, and 4, p. 222, 1924. *Talleres Gráficos de la Nación.*

[10] *ibid.*

of the extensive sections of land from large land-owners to the government involved at the same time a diminution of the area held by foreigners in Mexico.

GOVERNMENT-OWNED LANDS, 1912 AND 1925, BY STATES
(In hectares)

State	1912 [a]	1925 [b]
Baja California	1,500,000	7,661,412 [c]
Campeche	1,544,000	1,460,482
Chiapas	281,400	524,283
Chihuahua	3,103,000	4,752,161
Coahuila	995,000	1,462,208
Durango	1,164,854	1,076,000
Guanajuato	....	1,113
Guerrero	1,100,000	957,692
Hidalgo	1,800	....
Jalisco	....	109,338
Quintana Roo	3,820,000	3,820,000 [d]
San Luis Potosí	92,476	93,632
Sinaloa	168,000	478,195
Sonora	5,350,000	10,981,049 [e]
Tabasco	365,580	756,532
Tamaulipas	....	390,725
Tepic (Nayarit)	1,600,000	1,552,100
Veracruz	1,409,682	52,283
Yucatán	185,041	390,846
Zacatecas	140,845	103,146
Total	22,821,678	36,623,197

[a] *Memoria de la Secretaría de Fomento*, 1912-1913, pp. 475-577.
[b] *Lista del Numero de los Terrenos Nacionales de Cada Estado que se Tiene Conocimiento en la Secretaría de Agricultura y Fomento con Indicacion de Superficies.* September 12, 1925. (Manuscript copy.)
[c] Computed by subtracting from total area of state the area for which private individuals pay taxes. This figure is an overstatement as there are 419 properties for which data with regard to area are not available. The figures for private ownership are in this case taken from table of landholdings, 1925. (Manuscript copy.)
[d] Same figures as in 1912 list.
[e] Figures as given by state government in *oficio* (letter) *Número* 20502, *Sección de Fomento y Industria*, December 12, 1927 (including roads and towns). (Manuscript.)

The Mexican government has thus regained since 1912 an area of 13,801,519 hectares, and increased the total of publicly owned lands by more than 60 per cent. The governmental-owned lands constitute at present 18.6 per cent of the total area of the Republic as against 11.6 per cent in 1912. The largest gains have been in the states of Lower California, Sonora, and Chihuahua, where some 6, 5, and 1½ million hectares of land were regained respectively. These changes have been the largest transfer in title to lands that has to date resulted from the revolution. It should be noted, however, that the largest gains by the government, as well as the greater portion of the lands now in government hands, are located in the three states of Lower California, Sonora, and Chihuahua, where the population is very sparse and where large portions of the area is more or less of desert type. The gains by the government have thus had but little bearing upon the problem of landholding and land distribution among the rural population in Mexico and can for the time being have but little influence in that direction.

More significant than the increased areas now held by the government has been the distribution of lands to the villages. The demand for *ejidos,* as we have seen, played an important part in shaping the course of the revolution and in determining its program. The distribution of the lands to the villages that has taken place must therefore be looked upon as a fulfillment of a promise embodied in the revolution. The persistence of the internal conflict and international controversy has, however, tended to interrupt the process of land distribution. It is perfectly clear that, if it had not been for objections from foreign governments on the one hand and internal military rebellion on the other, the program of land distribution would have proceeded at a faster rate. As we indicated above, the process of giving lands—*ejidos*—to villages is a highly complicated and long drawn-out process. The legislation converting the original battle cry into an effective legal deed to land has proven to be a slow and laborious undertaking.[11]

The law excludes approximately one-half of the rural population from the right to benefit by the distribution of *ejidos*.[12] All agricultural workers located upon haciendas are denied the benefit of the land grants to villages. In both 1910 and 1921 well over a third of the total rural population was located on haciendas—46.8 per cent in 1910, and 37.1 per cent in 1921. This arbitrary legal discrimination between those agricultural workers who have and those who have not a right to land tends to concentrate the rural population denied a right to land in certain states. As we have seen, differences in the proportion living upon haciendas and in villages are sharp between states. In Guanajuato, for instance, in 1921 79.1 per cent of the population was located

[11] See Chapters IX and X.
[12] See Chapters II, IX, and X.

upon haciendas, while in Oaxaca only 10.5 per cent
were so located. A still more serious discrepancy
created by the law is the fact that land can only be
given to those agricultural workers who inhabit
communities located off haciendas. The haciendas
have less than one-half of the total population located upon them, but they contain approximately
75 per cent of the communities in the Republic. In
some states as many as 95 per cent of the inhabited
places are located upon haciendas and are thus denied the benefit of the law. Of the 62,006 inhabited
places in Mexico, only 13,388 are agricultural villages under the law entitled to land. That fact has,
as we have seen, raised a great many political difficulties.[13] As it stands, it has meant that the population has more easily benefited from the land distribution in those states where it has retained its
villages and has continued living in them.

*Approximately 17 per cent of the villages entitled
to benefit under the law have to date received land.*
Of the 13,388 villages that have a right to land, there
have to date been provisionally granted lands to
2,246,[14] or 16.9 per cent, and of these, 1,650, or 12.3
per cent, have been definitely confirmed. It is interesting to observe that it is in those states where
the smallest proportion of the population lives in
haciendas that the greatest number of villages have

[13] See Chapters IX and X.
[14] Information supplied by the National Agrarian Commission.
(Manuscript copy.)

been granted land. That is, those states where the villages have best preserved themselves have been those most benefited by the legislation governing land distribution. A better picture of the importance of the land distribution that has taken place to date can be secured by viewing the country as a whole and seeing the number of people, as well as the proportion of the areas, of the states that have been affected by the process of land distribution since 1915.

PREPONDERANCE OF VILLAGE POPULATION IN STATES WHERE 100 OR MORE VILLAGES RECEIVED LAND GRANTS

State	Number of Villages Receiving *Ejidos*	Percentage of Total Rural Population Living in Villages, 1921
Yucatán	104	68.2
Hidalgo	114	77.1
México	190	80.2
Puebla	217	78.3
Veracruz	158	89.4

Less than 5 per cent of the rural population has to date received less than 3 per cent of the total area of the Republic. This is taking the provisional grants that have been made since 1915. Under these grants less than one-half million of agricultural laborers have received a little over 5 million hectares of land. The specific figures reported are 452,829 agricultural workers and 5,046,041 hectares, or an average of 11.14 hectares per person. These provisional grants include all who have been given the

right to use and occupy, even if temporarily, the
lands made available under the law. To date these
provisional grants have been converted into definite
holdings to the extent of 61.4 per cent, involving
344,020 persons and an area of 3,099,064 hectares.
It is interesting to note that the definite grants have
tended to be slightly smaller than the provisional
ones, allowing each recipient on the average 9 hectares, or 2.14 less than the average amount granted
under the provisional holdings. It should, however,
be remembered that the tendency is to give the better rather than the poorer lands to the villages. Of
1,648,093 hectares given as *ejidos* to 686 villages, 3.6
per cent were irrigated, 25.0 per cent unirrigated but
arable, and 68.3 per cent pasture and mountain.[15]

In a few states the changes in landholdings
wrought by the revolution are striking. The state
in which the greatest portion of the area and the
largest number of individuals have been affected is
the state of Morelos, which was the center of the
Zapata revolution. In this state over 25 per cent of
the population have received nearly 33 per cent of
the total area of the state.

While two other states approximate Morelos in
the proportion of the population that have received
land, Yucatan 22 per cent and Campeche 14 per
cent, no state anywhere approaches Morelos in the

---

[15] From statistics compiled by *Departamento de Aprovechamiento de Ejidos, Sección de Estadística,* 1926.   (Manuscript
copy.)

area that has been given away as a result of the revolution. The next nearest approach in the area given away are the states of Puebla and San Luis Potosí, where between 9 and 10 per cent of the total area of each state has passed to villages.[16] A summary statement of the area and population affected

EFFECT OF THE REVOLUTION ON LAND HOLDINGS IN MORELOS *

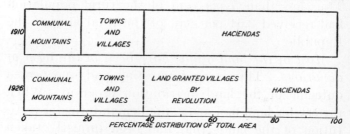

* Source: Material furnished by Morelos State Agrarian Commission.

by the land distribution from 1915 to 1926 is given in the following two tables.[17]

Percentage of rural population
(of each state)   Number of
provisionally in receipt of land   states
        20 to 30 2
        10 to 20 1
        5 to 10 9
        1 to 5 15
        Less than 1 4

Taking all of Mexico together, less than 5 per cent —the exact figure is 4.30 per cent—of the total rural

[16] For detailed table, see Appendix C.
[17] Compiled from information supplied by *Comision Nacional Agraria*. (Manuscript copy.)

population had been given *ejidos* by the end of 1926.

Percentage of state area provisionally distributed	Number of states
32 to 33	1
5 to 10	5
1 to 5	15
Less than 1	10

Thus less than 5 per cent of the rural population had received 2.64 per cent of the total area of the Republic.

Most of the land grants have been in the form of donations. This is an interesting and unexpected outcome of the land distribution program. When the cry for land first arose, the demand was for restitution of the lands that had been unjustly taken from the Indian villages. Following this general attitude, the original policy of the early revolutionary governments emphasized the restitution of lands previously possessed. It soon became apparent, however, that the original emphasis upon restitution was inadequate. The legal difficulties in the way of restitution were very great, and in many cases proved insurmountable. Many villages that claimed to have had lands could not produce titles, or the titles to the lands they had were inadequate both in legal form and in the area that they could receive under restitution. In many instances villages had lost their deeds or had occupied lands without written deeds. All of these difficulties led finally to a change in the emphasis in the agrarian program from restitution to direct donation of the lands.

PROVISIONAL LAND GRANTS 1915-1926, INCLUSIVE, BY TYPE OF GRANT

Type of Grant [a]	Villages Receiving *Ejidos*		Persons Receiving *Ejidos*		Distributed Area	
	Number	As Percentage of Total	Number	As Percentage of Total	In Hectares	As Percentage of Total
Donation............	2,068	92.1	413,624	91.3	3,579,386	70.9
Restitution..........	126	5.6	34,329	7.6	957,588	19.0
Confirmation........	17	.8	2,761	.6	460,406	9.1
Amplification.......	35	1.5	2,115	.5	48,661	1.0
Total............	2,246	100.0	452,829	100.0	5,046,041	100.0

[a] It ought perhaps to be recalled that restitution means the attempt to restore the original land formerly held by the village; donation a direct gift from the government to villages having neither title to land nor lands without title; confirmation the confirming of lands now held by communities with or without title and giving them the sanction of the present legislation; and amplification the enlargement of area for villages that had in the original grant received insufficient lands.

Donation has accounted for 70.9 per cent of the total area that has been distributed to villages, and for over 90 per cent of the total number of villages and individuals that have benefited from the distribution. Under the four types of distribution, confirmation has involved the largest average area, donation the smallest.

AVERAGE AREA OF HOLDINGS GIVEN UNDER EACH TYPE OF GRANT
(In hectares)

Type of Grant	Provisional	Permanent
Donation.............................	8.65	7.14
Restitution...........................	27.89	30.43
Confirmation.:........................	166.75	97.36
Amplification.........................	23.01	.....
Average for all types...............	11.14	9.00

The greatest changes in the final allotments have taken place in the area of the lands confirmed. The average has in this case gone from 166.75 hectares under provisional to 97.36 hectares under final grant, a reduction in average size of 42 per cent.

The rate of land distribution has been accelerating since 1915. The movement of land distribution was officially initiated with the decree issued by Carranza on January 6, 1915.[17] But the continuing struggles and conflicts in Mexico, the persistent opposition to land distribution, and the indifference of Carranza to this phase of the agrarian program

[17] See Chapter VII.

tended to retard the movement.[18] The turbulence
under Carranza, as well as the ease with which Obregon quieted the country, are explained by the fact
that the Obregon government immediately initiated
a rapid process of land distribution.[19] As we have
seen, the overthrow of Carranza was in part due to
his dilatory handling of the agrarian problem. This
is brought out by a glance at the table on this page.

LAND DISTRIBUTION, 1915-1926

Year	Provisional			Definitive		
	No. of Towns Receiving *Ejidos*	No. of Persons Receiving *Ejidos*	Area Distributed (In hectares)	No. of Villages Receiving *Ejidos*	No. of Persons Receiving *Ejidos*	Area Distributed (In hectares)
1915.....	2	705	1,823	...	......	....
1916.....	37	11,207	85,039	1	403	605
1917.....	24	7,292	90,715	7	2,683	5,490
1918.....	11	3,468	25,517	59	15,873	74,680
1919.....	7	946	6,183	59	16,934	42,271
1920.....	31	5,438	64,137	64	16,383	65,032
1921.....	275	66,688	701,942	121	25,130	185,700
1922.....	203	40,939	495,636	69	13,813	142,179
1923.....	442	89,145	1,261,621	127	29,931	272,987
1924.....	433	90,187	908,795	311	64,095	633,560
1925.....	514	93,921	889,368	418	81,076	824,063
1926.....	267	42,893	515,265	414	77,699	852,481
Total...	2,246	452,829	5,046,041	1,650	344,020	3,099,048

[18] See Chapter VII.

[19] "This administration succeeded in quelling such centers of
rebellion and in re-establishing peace throughout the national
territory, not so much by military force and bloodshed as by the
quick application of agrarian laws." From Secretary of Foreign
Affairs to the Charge d'Affaires of the American Embassy in
Mexico. *Proceedings* of the United States—Mexican Commission
Convened in Mexico City, May 14, 1923, p. 28.

CUMULATIVE RESULTS OF LAND DISTRIBUTION, 1916-1926 *

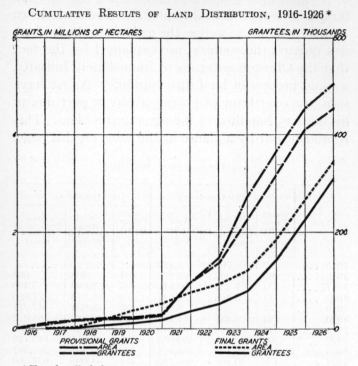

* For detailed data see p. 329.

It was only after Obregon came into power that the agrarian program was pushed ahead with vigor. In 1919, the year before Carranza was overthrown, provisional and definite land grants were made to 66 villages, while in the year following his election 396 communities were allotted *ejidos*. The movement upward has been fairly steady.

Without here discussing the future of the agrarian program, it may be said that there is apparently no reason to assume that it will come to an early end. The large mass of Mexican communities are still without land; even those that under the law are entitled to receive them have to date not been allotted their grants. Unless some very radical internal change takes place in Mexico, one sufficiently powerful to divert the forces set in motion by the last 18 years of conflict, it is to be expected that the process will continue.

In addition to the village land grants, the government has also distributed lands under a homestead law. This law was passed in August, 1923, and suspended in April, 1926. Between its initiation and the end of October, 1925, the government gave away 1,789,527 hectares of land, an area equal to 35.5 per cent of the area distributed under the *ejido* legislation. This land distribution, as we noted above,[20] took place upon an individual rather than upon a community basis. As under our own homestead laws, title was acquired through possession and use. The average area given to individuals averaged approximately 191 hectares. The number of grants was 9,385, or 2.1 per cent of the number of grants made as *ejidos*. Of the lands distributed, the largest portion—56.6 per cent—were grazing; non-irrigated 37 per cent; irrigated 7 per cent; and unclassified

[20] See Chapter VIII.

5.7 per cent. This area distributed must be added to that given away in the form of *ejidos* as one of the direct results of the revolution.

In addition to the federal government, individual state laws also made lands available to small holders. As we have seen above,[21] under Article 27 the states are empowered to break up large estates and sell small holdings to individual buyers on long-term payments. To date 17 states have passed such laws.[22] The legislation developed is a complicated and, in some instances, an unenforceable body of regulations; and most of it has remained unenforced.[23] Two of the states, however, Zacatecas and Durango, have used their state agrarian laws to increase the number of holders of small properties.

By the middle of September, 1926, Zacatecas[24] had disposed of some 299,290 hectares of land upon long-term payments to 3,000 individuals, each individual acquiring upon an average 99.8 hectares. In Durango,[25] 4,527 individuals had been enabled to purchase approximately 54,487 hectares, averaging per individual 12 hectares. These sales in the State of Durango were generally under five-year pay-

[21] See Chapter VIII.
[22] See Appendix A.
[23] *ibid.*
[24] *Informe administrative del Gobernador Constitucional de Zacatecas C. Fernando Rodarte.* September 15, 1926. Guadalupe, Zacatecas, p. 28.
[25] *Sindicato de Campesinos Agraristas del Estado de Durango. Informe que el* Lic. Alberto Terrones Benitez, *Presidente del Consejo Ejecutivo, Rinde Ante el Quinto Congreso Agrarista del Estado de Durango,* January 1, 1925, pp. 27-30.

ments, though in a few cases the period of payment extended to ten years. The prices of the land sold ranged widely, depending upon whether it was cleared or uncleared, and upon the section of the state in which it happened to be located. Some of the properties sold as low as 2 *pesos* per hectare. The highest price paid was 45 *pesos* per hectare, while the range of most frequent prices was between 20 and 40 *pesos*.

To summarize, the total net effect of land distribution has been to give some 4 per cent of the total area of the Republic to some 5 per cent of the total population. This includes all forms of federal land grants as well as sales of lands to small holders in conformity with state laws. This perhaps is not an impressive statement of the results of an agrarian revolution that has lasted over a period of some 18 years. It would, however, be an incomplete statement of the case if one did not add that, first, the social and political organization of the country is at present so shaped that a continuation of the process of land distribution on perhaps a broader scale seems certain and, second, that in at least some states the revolution has driven the landowners themselves to break up their large holdings by voluntary sale. Unfortunately, it is impossible to measure the extent of this movement in all of the states.

It is also clear that the movement has not all been one way. If we take the State of Colima, for example, the area of that state comprised in properties of over 5,000 hectares in 1910 equaled 63 per cent,[26] while in 1923 that same group of properties included 69 per cent [27] of the area. In other words, in Colima the movement has as a whole been to greater concentration rather than to a break-up of landholdings. On the other hand, if we take the state of Aguascalientes and make the same comparison of the areas embraced in properties above and below 5,000 hectares, we note a decided change in the direction from large to smaller holdings. In 1910 the properties of over 5,000 hectares embraced 67 per cent [28] of the area of the state, while in 1923 they only contained 45 per cent [29] of the area. Such comparisons are impossible for most of the states, but it is clear that in addition to the official movement for breaking up large estates, there has developed a considerable tendency for owners of the larger holdings to liquidate. This too, however, has in part at least to be counted as one of the important by-products of the revolution.

With this general summary of the changes made by the revolution in landholding, we turn to a description of the land system in Mexico in 1923.

[26] Compiled from the *Official Directory of Mines and Estates of Mexico* by John R. Southworth, F.R.G.S. Mexico, 1910, p. 185: the best, though incomplete, list of properties at present available in any printed source.

[27] See next chapter and Appendix C.

[28] Southworth, *Mines and Estates of Mexico*.

[29] See next chapter and Appendix C.

CHAPTER XIV

SIZE AND CHARACTER OF LAND OWNER-
SHIP IN CONTEMPORARY MEXICO

It is difficult to untangle the maze of landholding in contemporary Mexico. This difficulty has many sources. There is first, the discrepancy in the figures given for government-owned lands. The area claimed by the federal government as national lands is in some instances taxed as private property. More serious is the fact that among the smaller landholders there is frequently no clarity of title. The villages have varying types of rights in land distributed among their inhabitants and affecting different proportions of their members. In numerous landholding groups titles are lodged with only a few individuals, while other groups have possession, pay taxes, are recognized as owners, but hold no individual title. There is also the confusion that arises from the fact that individual owners may hold many small parcels.

Fortunately, these difficulties are somewhat relieved by the fact that we have a fairly complete record of all owners holding rural lands valued at 5,000 *pesos* or over. Knowing as we do the area and value of these properties, we can give by states the proportion held by their owners. The remaining

area of the state can then be distributed between
the small land-owners and the federal government.
Our information was derived from the original records in the federal Department of Statistics, based
in turn upon county tax records derived from decla-
rations generally made by the owners themselves.
We thus have the area and value that the owners
themselves claim and submit for purpose of taxation.
For the small owners, those that have lands valued
at less than 5,000 *pesos,* we have for all of the republic a complete record by value of the pieces of
property on which taxes were paid in 1923, and a
statement of the size of these small properties either
as given by the taxpayers or as estimated on the
basis of average value.[1]   In the state of Aguascalientes we can fortunately check these figures by the
state records for all of the rural lands by size and
value upon which taxes were paid in 1925.

We are therefore able to do the following: to show
the proportion of taxpayers upon rural property in
1923 to the total rural population; to show how
landholding is divided between those who have the
larger and those who have the smaller areas, using
5,000 *pesos* tax value as a dividing line; to show the

[1] See Appendix C for description of method employed in this
calculation.

In the state of Aguascalientes we have each owner as well as
the size and number of properties held by each owner.   This
makes it possible for us to check against each other the material
from two different sources as well as for different years; the
records in the federal Department of Statistics for 1923 and the
tax sheets of the state of Aguascalientes for 1925.

size of parcel typical in Mexico and to indicate for one state how these parcels are distributed among the individual land owners.

Approximately 20 per cent of the heads of rural families in Mexico owned land in 1923.[2]   We must take these figures with considerable caution, being only an estimate.   The total rural population in 1921 was 10,434,048,[3] and in 1923 there were 431,311 recorded owners, and approximately 4 per cent of the rural population were recorded as owners of rural lands.   Assuming an average of five members to the rural family, this would mean that 20 per cent of such families own land.   We assume, therefore, that 20 per cent of the rural families were recorded as owners in 1923.[4]

In a general way the proportion of owners among the rural families and population density seem to vary together.   The states differ widely in the proportion of owners to the rural families.   States that are located in the same general area of the republic, such as Tlaxcala and Hidalgo, both having high population density, diverge sharply in the proportion of owners to the rural families: Tlaxcala 5 and Hidalgo 40 per cent.   But generally speaking, in these states where population is comparatively dense, ownership is more widely distributed than in those where population is sparse.   Of the 15 states having popula-

[2] As we noted in the last chapter the number of owners has been increased by the distribution of *ejidos*.

[3] Excluding Quintana Roo and the Federal District.

[4] See Appendix C for detailed table.

tion densities of more than 8.7 per square kilometer, only two—Tlaxcala and Guerrero—have comparatively low ownership among the rural families: 5 and

Percentage of rural families (in each state) holding rural lands [a]	Number of states [b]
Under 10	9
10 to 20	8
20 to 30	9
30 or over	3

[a] For detailed table see Appendix C.
[b] Quintana Roo and Federal District not included.

4 per cent respectively. A summary statement of proportion of all rural families owning lands is given in the table above.

RATIO OF RURAL PROPERTY OWNERS TO ALL RURAL FAMILIES, 1923 *

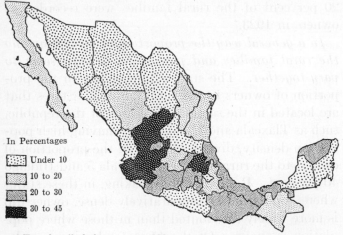

In Percentages
Under 10
10 to 20
20 to 30
30 to 45

* For detailed data see p. 338.

Approximately 4 per cent of the owning families have rural lands valued at 5,000 pesos or more. Of the 431,311 rural landowners in 1923 only 17,667 had holdings valued at 5,000 *pesos* or over ($2,500).

These 4 per cent of families that had lands valued at 5,000 *pesos* were unevenly distributed throughout the country. In some of the states, like Campeche and Tlaxcala, as many as 25 per cent of the families owning rural lands had properties valued at 5,000 pesos or more, but in others like Veracruz and Hidalgo only about 1 per cent had lands of that value. As a general rule the states with high population density had a low proportion of the larger land-holdings, though as already noted they had a high proportion of the total number of owners. The two maps on page 340 show these facts very clearly. In all but one of the states, Campeche, where the proportion of the number of owners to the number of rural families was 20 per cent or over, less than 5 per cent had lands worth 5,000 *pesos* or more.[5]

If we make comparisons between the number of larger holdings and the total number of rural families, most of these geographic differences disappear. In other words, there is considerable similarity in the several states in the proportion of owners holding properties worth 5,000 *pesos* to the number of rural families. That is an interesting fact in view of the great diversity of climate and altitude to be found in Mexico, and still more striking in view of the uneven distribution of population, and the differences in the historical conditions under which property holding developed.

[5] These conclusions, it must be remembered, are obtained by calculating the large owners (5,000 *pesos* or over) against the total number of owners among the rural families and not against the rural families themselves.

RELATIVE IMPORTANCE OF RURAL PROPERTIES VALUED AT 5000 PESOS
OR OVER, BY STATES, 1923

I. Area as a Percentage of All Private Rural Lands *

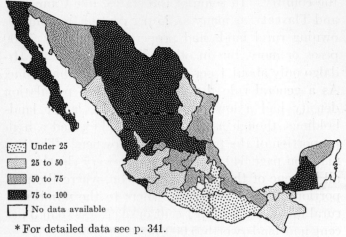

> Under 25
> 25 to 50
> 50 to 75
> 75 to 100
> No data available

* For detailed data see p. 341.

II. Number of Owners as a Percentage of All Rural Land
Owners *

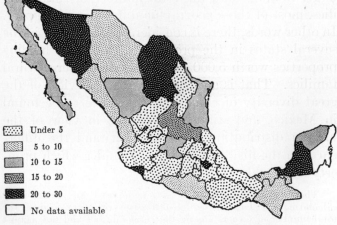

> Under 5
> 5 to 10
> 10 to 15
> 15 to 20
> 20 to 30
> No data available

* For detailed data see p. 341.

LANDHOLDINGS VALUED AT 5,000 PESOS OR MORE, BY STATES, 1923*

State	Number of Owners	Number of Owners as Percentage of all Rural Families	Area as Percentage of all Private Rural Land	Value as Percentage of all Private Rural Land
Aguascalientes.....	118	0.97	71.4	83.7
Baja California....	223	2.29	85.9	69.1
Campeche........	230	2.40	92.5	87.1
Chihuahua.......	561	0.90	83.4	....
Chiapas..........	1,199	1.70	41.4	75.1
Coahuila.........	805	1.84	93.1	79.1
Colima...........	183	1.44	99.8	88.8
Durango.........	744	1.40	81.5	85.5
Guanajuato.......	1,614	1.34	70.2	83.7
Guerrero.........	384	0.37	23.9	73.5
Hidalgo..........	513	0.46	34.2	87.6
Jalisco...........	1,744	1.03	42.3	67.2
México..........	684	0.44	69.3	85.4
Michoacán.......	1,645	1.09	33.7	78.8
Morelos..........	64	0.35	....ᵃ	54.2
Nayarit..........	128	0.63	87.5	84.6
Nuevo León......	329	0.73	48.5	61.4
Oaxaca...........	523	0.31	21.1	65.7
Puebla...........	593	0.35	20.1	83.4
Querétaro........	194	0.53	55.2	90.8
San Luis Potosí....	741	1.09	92.6	94.7
Sinaloa...........	374	0.67	48.9	73.6
Sonora...........	708	1.70	57.6	88.6
Tabasco..........	489	1.28	42.5	65.2
Tamaulipas.......	552	1.72	50.7	81.4
Tlaxcala.........	375	1.23	74.9	93.9
Veracruz.........	383	0.23	59.1	82.2
Yucatán.........	1,251	2.96	72.1	92.7
Zacatecas........	316	0.49	88.8	71.3
29 States ᵇ	17,667	0.85	63.6	84.9

* For detailed tables see Appendix C.
ᵃ Data incomplete.
ᵇ Quintana Roo and Federal District not included.

Comparison of Rural Properties of 5,000 Pesos or Over with
All Private Rural Lands, 1923 *

I. Based on Assessed Value.

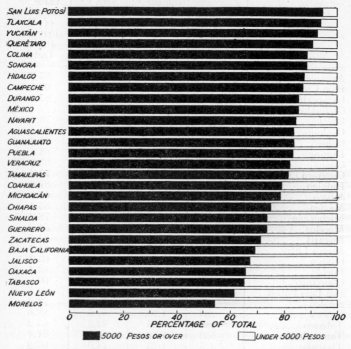

	5000 Pesos or over
	Under 5000 Pesos

* Properties of 5,000 *pesos* or over are owned by only 0.8 per
cent of the rural families. For detailed data see p. 341.

*Less than one per cent of the rural families (0.85)
have properties worth 5,000 pesos or more.* Of the
29 states here considered [6] only three have over 2 per
cent of rural families that own lands worth 5,000
pesos or over. These three states are on the fringe

[6] Excluding Quintana Roo and the Federal District.

II. Based on Area

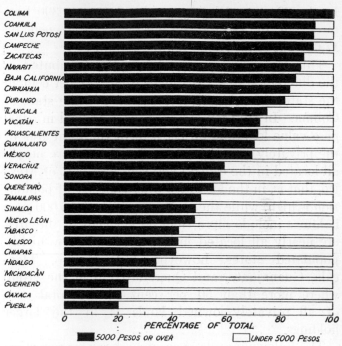

of Mexico proper, Campeche and Yucatan being located on the extreme southeastern end, while Lower California lies at the extreme northwestern end of the Republic. Of the other 26 states 14 have less than 1 per cent of their families within the 5,000 *peso* group.

Properties valued at 5,000 pesos or over constitute 64 per cent of the privately owned lands of Mexico.[7] This means that nearly two-thirds of the area is

[7] For detailed tables see Appendix C.

owned by less than 1 per cent of the rural families. In the 28 states [8] here considered 101,112,390 hectares out of 159,106,365 hectares are owned by 17,667 out of 2,104,023 families.

This ownership is very differently distributed in the different states. It ranges from 20.1 per cent in the state of Puebla to 99.8 per cent in the state of Colima. In only ten states is the area held in 5,000 *peso* value less than 50 per cent of the total area of the privately owned lands. These states are nearly all located in the central and southern part of Mexico, that is, in the localities where density of population is high, while the states in which the 5,000 *peso* holdings include more than 50 per cent of the area are nearly all located in the north. A few highly populated states, however, like Mexico, Tlaxcala, Guanajuato, and Querétaro fall in the group where more than 50 per cent of the total area of all privately owned lands is in the larger holdings.

The following table shows how large a proportion of the total area of the privately-owned land in the

Percentage of Area	Number of States
20 to 30	3
30 to 40	2
40 to 50	5
50 to 60	4
60 to 70	1
70 to 80	4
80 to 90	5
90 to 100	4

[8] Morelos not included.

several states is comprised in properties valued at 5,000 *pesos* or over.

Holdings worth 5,000 pesos or over comprise 85 per cent of the assessed value of all rural lands.[9] The value of the holdings worth more than 5,000 *pesos* is thus considerably larger in proportion to the total than is the area. The range of differences between state and state is much narrower in value than in area. For value the greatest difference is between Morelos, 54,[10] and San Luis Potosí 94.7, while in area as was shown above the range is from 20.1 in Puebla and 99.8 in Colima. As in the case of the proportion of large owners to the rural families there seems to be no systematic geographical distribution. The four states where the 5,000 *peso* group represents more than 90 per cent of the total fiscal value are widely scattered: Yucatán, Tlaxcala, Querétaro, and San Luis Potosí.

The charts on pages 342-43 indicate by states the proportions of the area and of the value of privately owned lands included in holdings with 5,000 *pesos* or more. It is to be remembered that the owners of these properties make up less than 1 per cent of the total number of rural families.

We have therefore this picture: 20 per cent of the rural families own lands, but of this 20 per cent less than 1 per cent own approximately two-thirds of the area and four-fifths of the value of the rural lands

[9] For detailed table see Appendix C.
[10] Incomplete figures.

in the Republic of Mexico. This indicates a considerable degree of concentration of both value and area in the upper owning groups. To measure more accurately the concentration of these holdings we shall next examine in greater detail the distribution of ownership within the group owning properties worth 5,000 *pesos*.

Less than 2,700 people own more than one-half of the privately owned lands in the Republic. If we take the 17,667 rural owners that have lands valued at 5,000 *pesos* and select from among them those that hold lands of 5,000 hectares or more (approximately 12,000 acres) we find that there are 2,683 such owners.[11]

These 2,683 owners own 79,762,044 hectares out of the 159,106,365 privately owned lands in the Republic. That is, 0.6 per cent of the owners (one-eighth of 1 per cent of the rural families) have 50.1 per cent of all privately held land.

As was to be expected, there is wide difference in the per cent of the area of each state held in tracts of over 5,000 hectares. In the north holdings are generally much larger than in the central and south-

[11] It should be noted that these figures involve some duplication. They were compiled by states, and an owner of properties in two or more states was counted each time he appeared in a different state. For example, the Hacienda de los Cedros overflows from Zacatecas into Durango, the Hacienda La Punta de Santo Domingo extends from Coahuila into Durango, and the Creel properties are scattered over a number of states. The actual number of owners of 5,000 hectares is therefore somewhat smaller than it appears.

ern states. In the States of Chihuahua, Coahuila, and Zacatecas over 85 per cent of the total area of the states is held in parcels of over 5,000 hectares,

OWNERSHIP, AREA, AND VALUE OF PRIVATELY-OWNED RURAL LANDS OF 5,000 HECTARES OR OVER, IN THE SEVERAL STATES, 1923

State	Number of Owners	Areas as Percentage of all Private Rural Lands	Assessed Value as Percentage of all Private Rural Lands
Aguascalientes.............	26	44.9	47.5
Baja California.........	69	77.7	51.2
Campeche..............	73	81.7	59.9
Chihuahua.............	256	86.5	41.5
Chiapas...............	72	19.9	18.9
Coahuila..............	282	88.1	57.2
Colima................	26	69.0	41.0
Durango..............	277	74.5	71.6
Guanajuato............	78	25.1	18.1
Guerrero..............	39	10.7	16.5
Hidalgo................	26	10.8	19.6
Jalisco.................	126	16.9	17.3
México................	36	20.5	22.3
Michoacán.............	76	15.9	27.8
Nayarit................	40	75.8	60.4
Nuevo León...........	123	29.5	33.6
Oaxaca................	66	10.7	33.5
Puebla................	12	3.5	12.3
Querétaro.............	24	32.0	37.2
San Luis Potosí.........	139	71.2	63.0
Sinaloa...............	133	30.9	34.7
Sonora................	149	41.7	37.9
Tabasco..............	21	19.2	10.6
Tamaulipas............	161	46.8	56.2
Tlaxcala..............	5	9.8	8.5
Veracruz..............	116	28.4	22.7
Yucatán..............	72	30.0	22.2
Zacatecas	160	93.4	68.5
28 states [a]...........	2,682	50.1	31.9

[a] Morelos, Quintana Roo, and Federal District not included.

while in Tlaxcala and Puebla less than 10 per cent
of the area of the states is so held—another illustration of the fact that low population density goes with
the larger and high population density with smaller
individual holdings.

AREA OF ALL RURAL HOLDINGS OF 5,000 HECTARES OR OVER COM-
PARED WITH AREA OF ALL PRIVATE RURAL LANDS, BY STATES, 1923 *

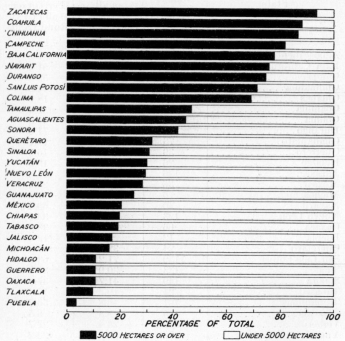

* Holdings of 5,000 Hectares or over represent 50.1 per cent of
the area of Rural Mexico and are owned by 2,682 persons, or less
than 1 per cent of all owners.

That half of the area which is held in large tracts represents only about one-third of the assessed value of the privately owned lands. An examination of the distribution by area and value of the largest properties in the Republic, those over 5,000 hectares, shows in one way the nature of the Mexican land problem. In those states where the population is sparse the large holdings represent the greater portion of the area of the state but have a lower value, per hectare, than the rest of the properties of the state. In the more densely populated sections, generally speaking, the large properties represent a smaller proportion of the area but have a greater assessed value per hectare than the rest of the lands of the state. This is well indicated by the table on page 350.

One hundred and fourteen owners own approximately one-fourth of all the privately owned lands of Mexico. We can now see more clearly how the landholding in Mexico tends to be concentrated in the upper groups. Of the 2,682 owners having lands with an area of 5,000 hectares and over, approximately one-half, 1,268 owning each from 5,000 to 10,000 hectares have among them only 5.7 per cent of the total privately owned lands of Mexico, while 114 proprietors with areas of over 100,000 hectares each owned nearly one-fourth (22.9 per cent) of all privately held lands.

AVERAGE ASSESSED VALUE PER HECTARE OF ALL PRIVATE RURAL
LANDS AND OF LARGE ESTATES

(In *pesos*)

State	All Privately Owned Lands	All Privately Owned Lands of 5,000 Hectares or over [a]
Aguascalientes	12.90	*13.65*
Baja California	8.44	5.56
Campeche	4.18	3.06
Chihuahua	....[b]	0.90
Chiapas	6.38	6.03
Coahuila	4.61	2.99
Colima	11.63	6.91
Durango	3.46	3.33
Guanajuato	36.69	26.47
Guerrero	2.60	*4.02*
Hidalgo	22.18	*39.98*
Jalisco	12.89	*13.17*
México	25.49	*27.73*
Michoacán	22.40	*39.25*
Morelos	8.88	....[b]
Nayarit	7.68	6.12
Nuevo León	1.94	*2.21*
Oaxaca	2.97	*9.28*
Puebla	14.47	*51.36*
Querétaro	21.76	*25.32*
San Luis Potosí	7.23	6.41
Sinaloa	3.47	*3.88*
Sonora	6.75	6.13
Tabasco	10.59	5.84
Tamaulipas	2.77	*3.32*
Tlaxcala	64.57	55.88
Veracruz	26.54	21.19
Yucatán	36.10	26.70
Zacatecas	2.60	1.91
29 states [c]	8.43	5.28

[a] The italicized figures show the states where the large properties have higher assessed values.
[b] Information incomplete.
[c] Quintana Roo and Federal District not included.

OWNERSHIP, AREA, AND VALUE OF 2,682 RURAL HOLDINGS OF
5,000 HECTARES OR OVER *

Size of Holdings	Owners		Total Area		Assessed Value	
	Number	As Percentage of Total	In Hectares	As Percentage of Area of All Private Rural Lands	In Thousands of Pesos	As Percentage of Value of All Private Rural Lands
5,000 to 10,000	1,268	47.3	8,761,495	5.5	109,661	8.2
10,000 to 20,000	706	26.3	9,831,263	6.2	90,874	6.8
20,000 to 30,000	233	8.7	5,541,916	3.5	46,268	3.5
30,000 to 40,000	128	4.8	4,428,500	2.8	25,155	1.9
40,000 to 50,000	71	2.6	3,232,056	2.0	20,456	1.5
50,000 to 75,000	114	4.3	7,299,097	4.6	28,844	2.1
75,000 to 100,000	48	1.7	4,224,265	2.6	22,745	1.7
100,000 or over..	114a	4.3	36,443,452	22.9	76,920	5.7
Total........	2,682	100.0	79,762,044	50.1	420,924	31.4

* Data for 28 states.
a The holdings of one company in the state of Sinaloa having approximately 500,000 hectares are not included in the above because of the deficiency of data at the time computations were completed.

This concentration is best brought out by an examination of the percentage of the area of the several states that are held by the 114 largest owners. The distribution is shown in the table on page 352. One owner out of a rural population of 101,817, in the State of Nayarit, has 10.8 per cent of the area of the state; another in Veracruz out of 840,071 rural inhabitants has nearly 3 per cent of the area of the state. Individual owners in five states have 10, 7, 3, 2, and 1 per cent of the total area of these states respectively. The table on page 352 gives the distribution of the 114 owners by state compared with the total rural population of the states and with the percentage of the total private lands in each state that these large *latifundas* embrace.

RURAL LAND HOLDINGS OF 100,000 HECTARES OR OVER
CLASSIFIED BY STATES *

State	Total Rural Population	Holdings of 100,000 Hectares or Over	
		Number of Owners	Area as a Percentage of All Private Rural Lands
Baja California.........	48,569	6	67.8
Chihuahua.............	307,839	24	60.8
Campeche.............	47,926	9	50.3
Coahuila..............	219,715	21	46.6
Zacatecas.............	344,800	11	45.8
San Luis Potosí........	350,393	6	29.5
Durango.............	266,018	16	24.4
Tamaulipas...........	165,468	5	17.9
Sonora...............	207,950	5	11.5
Nayarit..............	101,817	1	10.8
Chiapas..............	353,220	3	7.1
Tabasco..............	190,593	1	7.1
Nuevo León...........	226,719	3	5.1
Guanajuato...........	600,613	1	3.5
Veracruz.............	847,697	1	2.9
Oaxaca..............	862,007	1	1.4

* See note to table on p. 351.

If we examine the size distribution of Mexican landholdings we get a picture not merely of the size of the larger holdings but also of the smaller. For 1923 there were altogether 622,213 individual pieces of property in the Republic of Mexico,[12] and as we have seen, 431,311 owners held these pieces, making an average for each owner of 1.44 pieces. If we dis-

[12] Excluding Quintana Roo and the Federal District.

tribute these individual 622,213 pieces of property according to size we get the result shown in the table below.

ALL PIECES OF RURAL PROPERTY, BY SIZE, 1923 *

In Hectares	Number of Pieces	As Percentage of Total Number
Less than 1	151,264	24.3
1 to 5	216,152	34.7
5 to 10	65,958	10.6
10 to 50	109,936	17.7
50 to 100	25,197	4.1
100 to 200	17,720	2.8
200 to 500	15,722	2.5
500 to 1,000	7,482	1.2
1,000 to 5,000	9,506	1.5
5,000 to 10,000	1,678	0.3
10,000 and over	1,598	0.3

* For method employed in securing this distribution and for general table, see Appendix C.

It is now clear how it happens that 114 owners out of 400,000 can have one-fourth of the total area held as private property. Nearly one-fourth of all pieces of property in Mexico average less than 1 hectare apiece, and of course one single owner having a property of 100,000 hectares has an area greater than the combined holdings of 100,000 rural landowners each having less than one hectare apiece. In some states these small parcels make up one-half of all the individual pieces of property. As was noted above we have additional detail for one state, Aguascalientes. If we compare the percentage distribution of all properties by size with the size of the entire holdings of each owner in this state we get the result shown in the table below.

PROPERTIES (BY SIZE) IN 29 STATES, COMPARED WITH AGGREGATE HOLDINGS UNDER SINGLE OWNERSHIP (BY SIZE) IN AGUASCALIENTES

In Hectares a	Percentage Distribution of Pieces of Property (29 States)	Percentage Distribution of Total Area of Individual Holdings (Aguascalientes)
Less than 1	24.3	30.9
1 to 5	34.7	26.8
6 to 10	10.6	8.4
11 to 50	17.7	17.4
51 to 100	4.1	5.3
101 to 200	2.8	3.9
201 to 500	2.5	3.3
501 to 1,000	1.2	1.5
1,001 to 5,000	1.5	1.6
5,001 to 10,000	0.3	0.6
10,000 or over	0.3	0.3

a Retaining the classification used by the Mexican census.

We may now turn to an examination of the distribution of these individual parcels among the owners. We know that on the average each landowner in Mexico in 1923 had 1.44 pieces of property, but we do not know how many pieces of property each individual owner held, except for Aguascalientes. However, that the situation there is typical of all of Mexico we have every reason to believe.[13] In Aguascalientes in 1925 there were 2,992 owners having on the average 1.99 pieces of property. These holdings were distributed as shown in the table on page 355.

[13] See Chapter III.

Number of pieces of property held by each owner	Number of owners
1	1,848
2	543
3	253
4	113
5	81
6	49
7	29
8	22
9	15
10	12
11	6
12	5
13	4
14	1
15	1
17	2
18	1
19	1
21	2
29	1
35	1
36	1
56	1

While 1848 owners had one piece of property each, one owner had 56, one 36, one 35, and one 29 pieces of property; none of these owners, however, had over 200 hectares in all. We have distributed the owners in the state of Aguascalientes according to area held by each individual. The table on page 356 shows that any one of the 10 owners holding properties of over 10,000 hectares has an area greater than 10 times the area held by the 926 owners of less than 1 hectare each.

Area held by each owner (hectares)	Number of owners
Less than 1	926
1 to 5	803
6 to 10	250
11 to 20	226
21 to 30	133
31 to 40	92
41 to 50	66
51 to 75	95
76 to 100	63
101 to 200	116
201 to 500	100
501 to 1,000	45
1,001 to 5,000	49
5,001 to 10,000	18
10,000 or over	10

Mexico is predominately a country of small land-holders occupying less than 10 hectares each. It is at the same time a country where the larger part of the rural area is held in great estates by a comparatively few people.

We are now in a position to summarize the land changes that have resulted from the revolution.

The table on page 357 gives the land distribution for the years 1910 and 1927.

In 1910 the Mexican government claimed as national lands 22,821,678 hectares, or 11.6 per cent, of the Republic. The large estates, those of over 5,000 hectares, embraced 97,184,091, or 49.5 per cent of the Republic, while 38.9 per cent was left for the rural owners who held properties of less than 5,000 hectares. Most of the tracts recovered since the revolution were of over 100,000 hectares, so that the area held in the very largest pieces was considerably greater than it is at present. Since 1915 the federal government has regained 13,801,519 hectares, so that the nationally owned lands are 60 per cent larger than they were before. The government has also distributed under *ejido* and homestead legislation 6,836,486 hectares, or 3.5 per cent, of the Republic.

PERCENTAGE DISTRIBUTION OF TOTAL AREA OF MEXICO, 1910 AND 1927 *

Year	Government-Owned Lands	Holdings of 5,000 Hectares or Over	Land Given as *Ejidos* and Homesteads	All Other Holdings
1910	11.6 [a]	49.5 [b]	....	38.9
1927	18.6	40.4	3.5 [c]	37.5

* After deducting the area represented by the islands and the Federal District.

[a] Figures for 1912:

[b] The area of the 5,000 hectare group is obtained by adding to the lands now held in that group the area regained by the federal government, as practically all of those lands were in large sections. The figure is in fact an understatement, as the largest properties have decreased in size since 1910.

[c] To the end of 1926.

CHAPTER XV

FOREIGN LANDHOLDINGS IN MEXICO
IN 1923

One phase of contemporary landholding in Mexico omitted from the discussion contained in the previous chapter nevertheless is of outstanding importance in connection with the Mexican land problem. This is the question of foreign holdings. While it is impossible to ascertain the precise extent and character of foreign landholdings in Mexico, we are fortunately able to present approximate data.

Our figures have been derived from the records made available by the country tax collectors of the Republic. They are incomplete in that they omit properties of an assessed value of 5,000 *pesos* or less. This is, however, not a very serious matter, as there are comparatively few holdings of this size in the hands of foreigners, although sufficiently numerous in some of the northern states to show an appreciable effect on the figures for area. The effect on the value figures is practically negligible owing to the character of the land. For instance, in Chihuahua, where grazing land has an assessed valuation of one *peso* per hectare, a foreigner could hold 12,000 acres of land and yet fall outside our tabulation.

Even so, the percentage of error in our figures cannot be very great, as the basis of 5,000 *pesos* upon which our compilation was made includes the greatest portion of the total area of the states in question.

A second difficulty grows out of the fact that the figures for area and value were first collected in 1923, and those for nationality of the owner in 1926-1927. It is practically certain that some properties assessed at less than 5,000 *pesos* in 1923 would have been included in a count made in 1926-1927. Likewise some properties were undoubtedly omitted because of hidden nationality. This applies especially to Spanish property which in some instances passes for Mexican, as double nationality is not unknown. The nationality of the ownership of some oil lands has also been deliberately concealed.[1] In some instances it is likewise clear that companies owned by foreigners, but incorporated in Mexico, were classed as Mexican.

Subject to these qualifications and limitations, the figures show the area and value of the lands owned by foreigners as ascertained by the county tax collectors. Taken all in all, they are an understatement.[2] These figures represent only surface lands and their values, and do not include buildings, oil wells, or mines, although they do include the surface of oil and mining lands.

[1] This statement is based on personal testimony of oil men to the author.

[2] For a description of the method used in collecting the information here presented see Appendix C.

Foreigners own approximately one-fifth of the private lands of Mexico. If we divide the area of the republic between lands held by the government, lands held by Mexicans, and lands held by foreigners, we get the following result: government,[3] 19.4; Mexican, 64.4; foreign, 16.2. Foreigners own 269,-849,046 *pesos* in assessed value and 32,044,047 hectares in area, making a percentage of total assessed value[4] of privately owned lands equal to 20.1, and of 20.1 per cent of area. The area held by foreigners in Mexico is equal to the combined areas of all the New England states, New York, and New Jersey.

The proportion of foreign-owned land differs widely in the various states. While there is some foreign holding in every state of the Republic, the largest areas are in the northern and coastal states and the smallest in the central states. In Chihuahua, for example, foreign holdings amount to over 40 per cent of the total area of privately held lands, while in such central states as Aguascalientes and Jalisco they equal less than 5 per cent of this area. This is shown in the accompanying tables and maps, in which the data for population are for 1921 and the data showing area and value of foreign holdings were collected in 1923 and checked in 1925.

The map on page 361 shows the regional concentration of those states where foreigners own more

---

[3] Including the territory of Quintana Roo.
[4] See Appendix C for general table.

RELATIVE IMPORTANCE OF FOREIGN LAND HOLDINGS, 1923 *

I. In Area

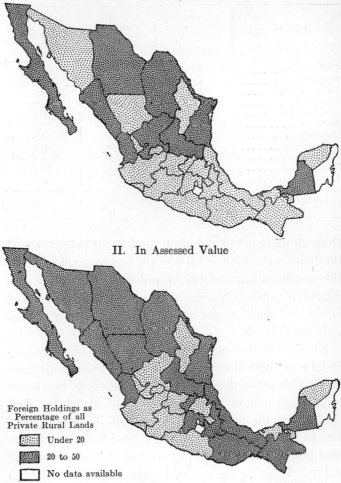

II. In Assessed Value

Foreign Holdings as
Percentage of all
Private Rural Lands

Under 20

20 to 50

No data available

* For detailed data see p. 360.

POPULATION DENSITY AND FOREIGN PROPERTY VALUES IN STATES
WITH LARGE FOREIGN HOLDINGS

State	Area Held by Foreigners as Percentage of All Private Rural Lands	Population Per Square Kilometer	Assessed Value Per Hectare (In Pesos)
Chihuahua.........	42.7	1.64	1.6
Nayarit............	41.9	6.00	5.3
Baja California.....	29.0	.44	14.4
Campeche..........	38.5	1.49	2.3
San Luis Potosí.....	27.5	7.05	6.1
Zacatecas..........	26.9	5.21	.9
Coahuila...........	22.7	2.61	4.8
Tamaulipas.........	22.0	3.60	3.1
Sinaloa............	21.3	5.83	4.8
Sonora.............	27.1	1.51	10.7
Durango...........	19.2	2.72	5.3
For the 11 states...	28.9	2.6	4.5

than 20 per cent of the total area of all private rural
lands in each state. All excepting Campeche are in
the northern part of the Republic, and in only one
northern state—Nuevo León—are foreign-owned
lands less than 20 per cent of the total area of private rural lands.

This general concentration of area is also characteristic of the value, as is shown by the map on page
360. The main difference is that whereas there are
only 11 states in which the area held by foreigners is between 20 and 43 per cent of the total, there
are 15 states in which foreign land-holdings represent between 20 and 50 per cent of the total assessed
value. It is to be noticed that 11 out of the 15
states where foreigners represent assessed values be-

POPULATION DENSITY AND FOREIGN PROPERTY VALUES IN STATES
WITH SMALL FOREIGN HOLDINGS

State	Area Held By Foreigners As Percentage of All Private Rural Lands	Population Per Square Kilometer	Assessed Value Per Hectare (In Pesos)
Veracruz	17.9	16.30	34.2
Chiapas	17.4	5.66	10.7
México	16.1	41.33	33.2
Querétaro	14.0	19.18	33.3
Colima	11.7	17.63	10.9
Tabasco	11.2	8.30	11.1
Oaxaca	8.4	10.58	14.3
Guanajuato	8.5	28.13	54.3
Tlaxcala	7.9	44.34	97.5
Puebla	5.9	30.1	51.8
Guerrero	5.6	8.79	4.2
Michoacán	5.4	15.64	70.2
Hidalgo	4.6	29.79	57.0
Jalisco	3.7	14.77	16.2
Nuevo León	3.6	5.17	4.7
Yucatán	.4	9.30	27.9
Aguascalientes	1.0	16.62	13.0
For the 17 states	8.5	14.3	26.0

tween 20 and 50 per cent are either border or coastal states.

In general, foreign holdings in Mexico tend to predominate in those states where the population is small and where lands are comparatively cheap. The states having low population density and low land values are as a rule located near the American border or along the Atlantic and Pacific seacoasts, and it is in those states that foreign property predominates. The accompanying tables group the states according to those in which foreign holdings are more than 20 per cent and those in which they are less than 20

POPULATION DENSITY AND FOREIGN PROPERTY VALUES IN STATES
WHERE FOREIGN HOLDINGS REPRESENT MORE THAN
20 PER CENT OF ASSESSED VALUES

State	Foreign Holdings as Percentage of Assessed Value of All Private Rural Lands	Population Per Square Kilometer	Assessed Value Per Hectare (In Pesos)
Baja California.....	49.4	.44	14.4
Sonora.............	42.8	1.51	10.7
Oaxaca.............	40.3	10.35	14.3
Durango...........	29.3	2.72	5.3
Sinaloa............	29.3	5.28	4.8
Chiapas............	29.2	5.66	10.7
Nayarit............	29.2	6.00	5.3
Tamaulipas........	24.3	3.60	3.1
Coahuila...........	23.5	2.61	4.8
San Luis Potosí.....	23.2	7.05	6.1
Veracruz...........	23.1	16.13	34.2
Querétaro..........	21.3	19.18	33.3
Puebla.............	21.1	30.15	51.8
Campeche..........	21.1	1.49	2.3
México.............	20.9	41.33	33.2
For the 15 states..	27.9	5.9	10.0

* Chihuahua would naturally fall in this group, but is not included because value data are incomplete.

POPULATION DENSITY AND FOREIGN PROPERTY VALUES IN STATES
WHERE FOREIGN HOLDINGS REPRESENT LESS THAN
20 PER CENT OF ASSESSED VALUES

State	Foreign Holdings as Percentage of Assessed Value of All Private Rural Lands	Population Per Square Kilometer	Assessed Value Per Hectare (In Pesos)
Michoacán........	16.9	15.64	70.2
Tlaxcala...........	12.0	44.34	97.5
Hidalgo............	11.8	29.79	57.0
Tabasco...........	11.7	8.30	11.1
Colima............	11.0	17.63	10.9
Zacatecas...	9.6	5.21	.9
Guerrero..........	9.2	8.79	4.2
Nuevo León........	8.9	5.17	4.7
Jalisco.............	4.6	14.77	16.2
Guanajuato........	1.3	28.13	54.3
Aguascalientes......	1.0	16.62	13.0
Yucatán...........	.3	9.30	27.9
For the 12 states..	9.2	12.3	15.3

per cent of the total area of all privately held lands. The two tables on page 364 bring out clearly the geographical aspect of foreign landholdings.

Americans own approximately one-half of the total rural land held by foreigners in the Republic of Mexico. As is shown in the table below, there are only five nations whose citizens own areas of considerable size. Of these, United States and Spain occupy by far the leading positions, having between them 74 per cent of the assessed value and 71 per cent of the total area held by foreigners. The British come next, with 10.3 per cent of value and 16.6 per cent of area. The German, French, and all other nationalities represent 14.2 per cent of value and 12.2 per cent of total area held by foreigners.

VALUE AND AREA OF FOREIGN-OWNED RURAL LANDS, BY NATIONALITY *

| Nationality | Value (In Thousands of *Pesos*) | Area (In Thousands of Hectares) | *Percentage of Total* | |
			Value	*Area*
Total foreign......	269,849	32,004	*100.0*	*100.0*
American (U. S.)...	112,427	16,558	*41.7*	*51.7*
Spanish..........	87,791	6,233	*32.5*	*19.5*
British...........	27,756	5,315	*10.3*	*16.6*
German..........	16,742	1,172	*6.2*	*3.7*
French...........	15,357	1,522	*5.7*	*4.7*
All other........	9,776	1,205	*3.6*	*3.8*

* Data collected in 1923 and checked in 1925.

The "All other" are distributed as follows:

Nationality	Value (In thousands of pesos)	Area (In thousands of hectares)
Italian	3,597	142.8
South American	823	409.7
Swiss	499	173.5
Dutch	485	.6
Arab	416	7.0
Japanese	406	17.6
Levantine	370	.5
Cuban	439	1.8
Guatemalan	307	13.6
"Austro-Hungarian"	221	12.6
Russian	209	8.2
Belgian	74	4.2
Miscellaneous	1,930	412.5
Total	9,776	1,204.6

As can be easily seen from an examination of the area and value figures, there are sharp differences in the value per hectare of the lands held by different nationalities. While many factors enter into determining the value of the different lands, they seem largely to be determined by the states within which they are located. The average values of the lands belonging to the people of different nationalities are as follows:

Nationality	Average value (in pesos)
German	14.3
Spanish	14.1
French	10.1
American (U. S.)	6.8
British	5.2
All other	8.1
All nationalities	8.4

American (U. S.)

Spanish

French

Data not available

* For detailed data see p. 365.

If we glance at a map showing the dominant nationality of the foreigners owning lands by states, it becomes clear that American property is of low value because it is located in the border and coastal states, while Spanish property is high because it is located in the central states where Mexico's best agricultural lands are to be found. The greatest British holdings are in the northern state of Chihuahua, and constitute 43 per cent of the total foreign-held land in the state. American property is generally located where the population is sparse and Spanish where population is dense.

Without here going into a more detailed discussion of the rural landholdings of foreigners in Mexico, it must be clear that they represent a problem of great magnitude both for the Mexican government and for the nationals holding the land. A rapid conversion of this foreign area to Mexican ownership cannot be carried through without fundamentally affecting the present agricultural organization of the country. While it is true that much of the foreign land is grazing land and lies untilled and unused, it also includes some of the best cultivated and well utilized lands of the Republic. This is true especially of the lands devoted to tropical crops. The coffee plantations of Chiapas and Oaxaca, the sugar plantations of Veracruz, Puebla, and Sinaloa, the banana plantations of Veracruz, Oaxaca, and Nayarit, and the truck lands of Sinaloa and Sonora are to a large extent in the hands of foreigners. An immediate conversion of them cannot be carried through without affecting the productivity of the lands themselves.

PERCENTAGE DISTRIBUTION OF TOTAL AREA OF MEXICO BETWEEN GOVERNMENT, FOREIGN, AND MEXICAN OWNERSHIP

Year	Government-owned Lands	Foreign-owned Lands	Mexican-owned Lands
1910	11.6	25.2 [a]	63.2
1927	19.4	16.2 [b]	64.4 [c]

[a] Secured by adding the present area of foreign-held lands valued at 5,000 *pesos* or over to total area returned to the federal government through cancellation. It is true that some of the cancelled concessions involving a return of land to the federal government were not held by foreigners, but the larger portion of it was. On the other hand, foreigners have been acquiring lands all through the revolution. From 1917 to 1924, inclusive, for example, 1,486 farmers were given permission to acquire agricultural properties. Of these, 626 were Spaniards and 432 were Americans.

[b] Value assessed at over 5,000 *pesos* in 1923 and held by foreigners in 1925-1926.

[c] For 1923.

Already the revolution has resulted (see table on page 368) in a considerable decrease of the area held by foreigners. It has increased by nearly half a million the number of small proprietors in the Republic, and generally speaking has set in motion a body of legislation and social organization to carry further the present tendency to decrease the power and influence of the foreign landholder. A somewhat detailed analysis of the problem of foreign landholding and the enforcement of legislation with reference to it will be undertaken in the chapter which follows.

CHAPTER XVI

REVOLUTIONARY LEGISLATION ON FOREIGN LANDHOLDINGS

The revolutionary legislation dealing with foreign landholdings completes and enforces the program embodied in the Constitution of 1917, which was described in Chapter VIII.[1] To understand this program, both in its constitutional and its legislative aspects, account must be taken of several circumstances. In part, the difficulties with foreigners were merely incidental, arising from the fact that many foreign holdings were large in size and thus were affected by the general effort toward redistribution of large properties, which we have already discussed.

A further cause of the legislation is the fact that the revolution has given Mexico a double system of property rights. The law governing property, especially in the subsoil, had from its Spanish antecedents persisted with little change up to 1884. Beginning in 1884 and continuing under the legislation of 1902 and 1909, the law was so modified as to place a part of the subsoil upon a different legal basis from that which it had previously occupied. This was done without changing the legal base of other property rights in Mexico which continued under the

[1] See pp. 189-203.

older legislation. The laws emanating from the revolution have tended to give the surface owners the same relation to the subsoil that existed in Mexico before 1884. So Mexico has a body of rights acquired before 1884, continued without change up to the present; a body of rights resting upon the law of 1884 and acquired between that date and 1917; and a new body of rights acquired since 1917, resting upon a legal foundation not unlike that which existed before 1884.

Without going into a discussion of the problem here raised, it must be sufficient to note that an attempt is being made to give all property rights in Mexico the same legal foundation. This is especially urged in view of the fact that under the new legal system there is developing a new body of rights that must, as time passes, become greater and greater in proportion to those acquired before the revolution. It is "therefore proper to seek the manner in which the rights acquired prior to 1917 subsist in practice within the new laws, and this cannot be done except by placing former acquired rights under the new rules under such conditions that, although the legal theory on which they are based has been changed, they are not altered or impaired." [2]

[2] "The measures that have been noted, which are those that are referred to in Articles 14 of the Petroleum Law and 4 of the Organic Law of Fraction 1 of Article 27 of the Constitution, both have the same purpose—that of adjusting pre-existing rights to the new legislation." Note in reply of the Mexican Minister for Foreign Affairs, dated October 7, 1926, press release, Department of State, November 23, 1926, p. 12.

The most significant motive, however, is undoubtedly the opposition to special privileges for foreigners in Mexico, an opposition which is only one expression of a profound sense of nationalism that has characterized the revolution.   This new nationalism, which is both political and racial, seeks the independence of Mexico from foreign economic dominion. The land laws, the banking and credit legislation,[3] the educational undertakings,[4] and the controversy over oil deposits are all but part of a general effort to make Mexico strong internally and free from external dominion.[5]

[3] President Calles, discussing the new banking legislation, said: "The bank of the republic actually does not represent a single compromise contracted with the outside nor does it contain a single cent that may shame us. It is all yours, it all belongs to the Mexicans. This undertaking places the government in a position to establish within a short time the agricultural credit bank, indispensable for the development of agriculture. . . . In this bank, as in the other, all belongs to the nation, containing not a single foreign cent; it is all yours." Calles, P. Elías, speech delivered by the President in Monterrey, and re-published from *El Democrata,* February 18, 1926, in P. Elías Calles, *México. Ante el Mundo,* 1927.

[4] *Informe Rendido por el C. Alvaro Obregon,* September 1, 1922, p. 82.

[5] *Principales Leyes de la Secretaría de Agricultura y Fomento,* December, 1924, to January, 1927; Mexico, 1927, p. 457.

"It is necessary, at the least, that the money which you spend shall not leave the country, or to purchase either food or clothing that comes from the outside. Protect your country and protect yourself, contributing to remedying the evils of the nation which are also yours." *Confederacion Nacional Agraria,* leaflet, no date.

"We appreciate the value of foreign aid, but we will prefer it when our people are sufficiently invigorated so that they can assimilate the energy that comes from the outside and not when ignorant and unprotected they may be surprised and conquered." General Salvador Alvarado, *A. Dónde Vamos.*

Although the main impulses of the current outburst of nationalism were derived from the revolution, its roots go deep into the past. Some knowledge of its historical origins is essential to an understanding of its character. Before describing in detail the legislation and the controversies to which it has given rise, we turn aside therefore to a consideration of the history of Mexico's attitude toward the foreigner.

Mexican nationalism has its roots in the antagonism between the races which followed the Spanish Conquest. The bloody conflict which preceded the Conquest, the cruelty of the Spaniards, the subjection of the Indian to forced labor in the mines and on the haciendas "degenerated into systems of fearful oppression" [6] in spite of the mitigating influences of the Spanish legislation. They have left a lingering resentment behind them,[7] and there are still places in Mexico where the words "Spaniard" and "thief" are synonymous.[8]

During the colonial period Spain manned the civil, military, and church posts with appointees from the home country, but closely restricted the immigration of Spaniards as well as foreigners from other coun-

[6] Latane, John H., *Diplomatic Relations of the United States and Spanish America,* pp. 11-12.

[7] "They hate even to have a stranger stay one night in their village. They say: 'The next town is only a little way on.'" Starr, Frederick, "The Mexican People," *Mexico and the Caribbean,* edited by George H. Blakeslee, p. 19.

[8] Toledano, Lombardo, *Problema de Educación en México,* 1924, p. 14.

tries. The completeness of this control of immigration is reflected in the remark of Baron von Humboldt that "the words 'European' and 'Spaniard' are synonymous in Mexico and Peru." [9] This indentification of European with Spaniard and Spaniard with white man contributed toward causing antagonism to the Spaniard to include also antagonism against all foreigners.

The Mexican struggle for independence in 1821 had a strong racial bias—the Indian against the white man, the *mestizo* against the *criollo*, the *criollo* against the Spaniard. It was a movement of the poorer classes against the upper ones; [10] its greatest leader was a full-blooded Indian priest. The movement attempted expulsion of Spaniards and confiscation of their property.

The general tenor of Spanish anti-foreign legislation persisted under the Republic and changed but slowly after 1821. [11] Independent Mexico, however, did prove more generous to foreigners than the Spanish colonial administration. The Constitution of the 24th of February, 1822, gave foreigners the same civil rights as Mexicans, [12] and within two years of its independence (1823) Mexico permitted for-

[9] von Humboldt, Alexander, *Political Essay on the Kingdom of New Spain*, Vol. I, New York, 1811, p. 158.

[10] Romero, Matias, *Mexico and the United States*, New York, Vol. I.

[11] Rodriguez Ricardo, *La Condición Jurídica de los Extranjeros en México*, Mexico, 1903, p. 139.

[12] Duffoo, Carlos Diaz, *México y los Capitales Extranjeros*, Mexico, 1918, p. 222.

eigners to develop mines in Mexico—something that had not been possible under Spanish law.[13]   A little later (1824), resident foreigners were permitted to acquire lands in Mexico, but not within 20 leagues, or nearly 60 miles, of the border, and 10 leagues of the sea.[14] This permission was soon (1828) modified to limit ownership of land other than mines to Mexican citizens.[15]   With one changing detail or another, the legislative prohibition of ownership by foreigners of lands within the Republic of Mexico, or an insistence that they reside within the country, or stipulation that mere acquisition of property should act as conversion to Mexican citizenship, has been a characteristic feature of nearly the whole hundred years of Mexican independence.   This Mexican legal tradition was even retained by the Maxmilian Empire.[16] The Constitution of 1857 carried on the previous legislation prohibiting foreign ownership within specified zones bordering on foreign nations or upon the sea.

The Diaz regime (1874-1911) reversed the traditional and historical foreign exclusion policy of Mexico. This reversal of the age-old policy of Mexico stands as one of the unique phases of the political

[13] Rodriguez, pp. 142-143.

[14] F. de la Maza, Francisco, *Código de Colonización y Terrenos Baldíos,* 1451-1892, Mexico, 1893, p. 191.

[15] Rodriguez, p. 144; Maza, p. 221.

[16] "Foreigners who acquire territorial property of whatever sort become Mexicans by this one act."   In other words, "no foreigner could, according to this, acquire rural property."   Duffoo, Carlos Diaz, *México y los Capitales Extranjeros,* p. 226.

policy of Diaz's rule. Nothing in the history of Mexico or in its traditions could have presaged such a reversal. The Diaz regime established peace, suppressed the internal military rebellions, opened the country to the outside world by railroads, ports, telegraphs, and telephones. To quiet the country and to develop it, Diaz as best he could attracted foreign investments.

The foreigner was not only allowed to come, but was assured of protection, which meant protection from military rebellion as well as protection from possible Indian uprisings. He had legal and political privileges thrown in his way. The law governing and defining the position of the foreigner in Mexico, passed in 1886, retained the original prohibition upon limited zones.[17] It did, however, make it possible for the government to extend a special permit to a foreigner to acquire property in the prohibited zones.[18]

The subsoil legislation was changed so as to encourage him to invest in and develop the oil industry.[19] American, English, French, German, and

[17] Rodriguez, p. 225; Decreto de 28 de Marzo de 1886, re-printed in Maza, pp. 1038-1050, Art. 31, p. 1047.

[18] As, for instance, the 28 permits conceded to foreigners to acquire property within the prohibited zones between 1878 and 1881. Memoria del Ministerio de Fomento, 1879-1882, Vol. I, Dec. 5, p. 43.

[19] Covarrubias, José, La Tracendencia Política de la Reforma Agraria, Mexico, p. 145.

"No one in Mexico, be he native or foreigner, can own a mine absolutely, or in fee, no matter what he may pay for it. He may hold it indefinitely so long as he works it, but under an old

Spanish capital poured into the country with ever-increasing speed, and the foreigner was acquiring an ever greater influence in the country. To supply labor for the developing tropical plantations, Indians and *mestizos* were forced to descend from their mountain villages against their will; [20] other villages had their lands taken from them to be given to large estates, frequently foreign ones. The Yaqui Indians were transported by the hundreds to Yucatan in consequence of a rebellion against a despoliation of their lands.[21]

As one Mexican author exclaimed, "Mexico has become a mother to the foreigner, a stepmother to her own children." The foreigner who had until that time been unknown, disliked, suspected, and feared, suddenly became a favorite of governmental

Spanish law, promulgated as far back as 1783, and still recognized, if he fails 'to work it for four consecutive months, with four operatives regularly employed and occupied in some interior or exterior work of real utility and advantage,' the title is forfeited and reverts to the state, and the mine may be 'denounced,' and shall belong under the same conditions 'to the denouncer who proves its desertion.' The denouncer, to keep the property, must, however, at once take possession and begin the prescribed work within a period of sixty days. Any person also may denounce a mine, no matter upon whose land it may be found, and also have the right to a ready access to it. This practice has one great advantage over the American mining system, and that is that litigation about original titles and conflicting claims to mining property are comparatively rare in Mexico." Wells, David A., *A Study of Mexico,* New York, 1887, p. 120. This is a good description of the mining law which up to 1884 covered all sub-soil exploitations.

[20] Starr, "The People of Mexico," *Mexico and the Caribbean,* p. 29.

[21] Turner, *Barbarous Mexico.*

policy. He became an ever-increasing force in the internal economic and political influence of the country.[22] This would not have been a serious matter if the coming of the foreigner had synchronized with an improvement of the status of the mass of the population and resulted in an obvious increase in their freedom. Just the opposite change seems to have taken place. Increasing foreign investments were in fact accompanied by increasing political domination by a small political group in Mexico, and a concomitant lowering of the standards of living of the mass of Mexican people.[23]

The craving for political freedom and social justice—the cry for "land and liberty" which arose towards the end of the Diaz regime—became a cry of rebellion not merely against the internal masters of Mexico, but against the foreigners who were so much favored by the Diaz government.[24] "Land and liberty" was thus easily transmuted into the general demand of "Mexico for the Mexicans." It stimulated both a national and regional consciousness,

[22] See Rippy, Fred, *The United States and Mexico* (Chapter XVIII, pp. 311-320), for an excellent discussion of the growing influence of foreigners under the Diaz regime.

[23] See Chapter VI.

[24] *El Constitucionalista* (December 20, 1913) reported that in answer to the foreign consuls who begged him for protection of their nationals Zapata replied that he would give them ample and full protection "with the exception of the Spaniards, who almost unanimously have taken a definite part in the internal struggles of Mexico, having always placed themselves against the people's cause which is being defended by the constitutionalists."

which became racial, political, social, and anti-foreign.

The fear of the foreigner did not disappear during the Diaz regime. In spite of the great influence of the foreigner in Mexico during the Diaz rule, and in spite of the many favors he received from the government, there remained a fear of him and his ambitions. It was this fear that lay back of the policy of the Diaz government in playing off the European against the American investors. It was this general fear that lay back of the persistence of some of the most obvious limitations upon landholding by foreigners that had continued from the early days of the Republic. Railroad and industrial expansion had been opposed because of this fear. The railway law of 1899 contained the principle that foreigners undertaking to organize, construct, or manage railways must consider themselves as Mexican citizens for the purpose of that function. The law specifically required that foreigners must make no use of their diplomatic privileges as foreigners in regard to any disputes that might arise under the railway act.[25] Even as late as 1909, one year before the revolution broke out, a mining law prohibited foreigners from acquiring mines within 80 kilometers of the border without special permission, and any transfer of the property by inheritance forced a sale of the same within one year, unless special permission to

[25] Rodriguez, reprints relative to article of the law that affects foreigners, pp. 407-412. See especially Art. 49, p. 407. Also see Powell, Fred Wilbur, *The Railroads of Mexico*, Boston, 1921.

continue the ownership of the property had been secured.[26]

Mexico feared that property-holding and industrial development by foreigners might prove the entering wedge for such a domination by outside powers as would lead to national extinction.[27] "Every individual who comes here from the United States [has in his thought] the absorption of Mexico."[28] The activities of the foreigners and their rapid accumulation of mineral resources as well as of large landholdings,[29] the persistent disregard of

[26] *Ley de Minería de los Estados Unidos Mexicanos,* November 25, 1909, Arts. 136, 141, 142. *Colección de Leyes, Decretos, Circulares Acuerdos; Refrentes a la Minería.* Secretaría de Industria, Comercio y Trabajo, pp. 34-35.

[27] See Rippy, Fred, *The United States and Mexico,* Chapter XIV, pp. 320-331, for a description of various aspects of this antiforeign feeling during the Diaz regime.

[28] *Diario de los Debates,* 1872, *Sexto Congreso,* Vol. III, quoted by Duffoo, p. 245. Similar expressions of feeling as reflected in official correspondence from American representatives in Mexico are quoted by Rippy. The American chargé in 1868 reported: "There is a feeling existing in this country towards foreigners in general. Americans do not form an exception" (p. 280). The American Minister to Mexico is quoted as having written in 1811: "Prominent persons in the country look upon the railroads which are in process of construction, as well as those which are in contemplation, as the agents of the country's destruction as a nation" (p. 322).

[29] "To these agricultural lands [having 8,500 hectares] about 1,000 individuals have rights, and they vary in a disproportionate manner. While our nationals with very few exceptions possess from one-half to 10 hectares, the foreigners possess from 50 to 300 hectares. While in the mountain and pasture lands, which embrace an area of approximately 500,000 hectares, there are rights possessed in them by about 100 individuals in a similarly disproportionate manner. While our nationals possess as a maximum 500 hectares, others, and amongst them foreigners, possess

the rights of the Indians in favor of foreigners,[30] methods of some American companies in Mexico,[31] the almost continuous propaganda in the United States for military intervention in Mexico,[32] the not infrequent utterances of responsible Americans [33] have all combined to give Mexico a definite dread that its position as a nation is in danger.[34] It is not possible fully to grasp the meaning of the recent legislation without appreciating the fact that the Mexicans feel that they are setting up a defense not merely against internal dominance by the outside investor, but that they are at the same time setting

from 75 to 100,000 hectares." *Letter from Presidente Municipal Juarez,* Chihuahua, April 23, 1926, in reply to Circular No. 2485.

[30] Beals, Carleton, *Mexico, An Interpretation,* 1923, pp. 44-45.

[31] Huasteca Petroleum Company (one of the Doheny group) vs. the Vice-President of the *"Compañia Mexicana de Combustibles,* S. A.," William H. Mealy. Mr. Mealy's vindication by the Mexican authorities and courts. Pamphlet, no date.

[32] Romero, Matias, *Mexico and the United States,* Vol. I, p. 358 (note). See Rippy, especially Chapter XVI, pp. 344-359. There is similar testimony for the whole period covered by the book.

[33] Former American Ambassador to Mexico, Henry Lane Wilson, advocated in 1921, as one of the ways to restore peace in Mexico, "the creation, organization, and recognition of a new independent republic to extend from the Rio Grande to the twenty-second parallel. This would include all of the states of Sonora, Chihuahua, Sinaloa, Durango, Coahuila, Nuevo León, and Tamaulipas, and the territory of lower California, an area more than twice that of Texas and richer in resources." "How to Restore Peace in Mexico," *Mexico and the Caribbean,* 1920, p. 151.

[34] As far back as 1877 the American Minister reported: "The conviction seems to be unanimous that it is the settled policy of the United States to promote a conflict." Quoted by Rippy, p. 304.

up a defense against their ultimate extinction as a nation.

From this brief summary of the legislation governing foreign ownership in Mexico, we see that in continuance of the Spanish colonial legislation, and in response to a multitude of causes, the Mexican governments that have come and gone in such rapid succession for over a hundred years have with singular persistence maintained a policy of restricting and sharply defining the legal prerogatives to use and ownership of real property by foreigners in Mexico.[35]

The law of December 31, 1925, is meant to enforce the foreign property provision contained in Article 27 of the Constitution of 1917.[36] Its main features are a repetition of the constitutional mandates, and its minor ones are legislative regulations of the same. Articles 1 and 2 repeat the limitation upon the right of the foreigner to hold lands within 100 kilometers

[35] In Maza, *Codigo de Colonización y Terrenos Baldios* may be found the various legal dispositions governing the rights of foreigners to acquire and use land, passed between 1821 and 1892.

[36] Organic Law of Section 1 of Article 27 of the constitution, approved by the Mexican Congress on December 31, 1925. Regulations governing the Organic Law of Section 1 of Article 27 of the general constitution. February 21, 1926, translation of the law as issued by the Mexican Embassy in the United States. For discussion of these provisions see Chapter VIII, pp. 189-203.

"The provisions contained in the legislation have already been put in practice for the last seven years in conformity with the various decrees and proclamations of the Executive, who found himself compelled from the beginning to apply fraction 1 of Article 27 of the constitution." *ibid.,* p. 12. Memorandum of Mexican Minister.

from the border and 50 from the sea, and require that foreigners agree to accept Mexican citizenship for the purpose of the property in hand [37] and not invoke diplomatic aid from their government under penalty of forfeiting the property in question to the nation.[38] Mexican companies engaged in agriculture may not pass to their foreign shareholders 50 per cent or more of their interest in the company.[39] Papers of incorporation and transfer deeds involving transfer to an alien must include a permit granted by the foreign office allowing the foreigner to acquire the property.[40] Bonds and shares must have engraved upon them the notice that the person acquiring them agrees not to invoke his government's protection in connection with the same.

These same provisions of the law must be included in the constitution and by-laws of Mexican corporations transferring participation to foreigners.[41] All new issues of stock or increases of capital must also comply with these provisions of the law.[42] A foreign person who has agricultural lands may retain them till death, but foreign corporations must dispose of

[37] Organic Law, Articles 1 and 2.

[38] It is essential to remember that these provisions have been in force since 1917 and that all titles acquired by foreigners since that date carry a specific provision that for the purpose of this property the person acquiring the property has accepted the terms of the law. There have been issued, from 1917 to 1924, 1,466 permits for rural property.

[39] *Regulations,* Article 3.

[40] *ibid.,* Article 4.

[41] *ibid.,* Article 5.

[42] *ibid.,* Article 5.

50 per cent of their shares to Mexicans within ten years.[43] This does not affect colonization contracts made by the government before the enactment of this law, and the foreigners coming into Mexico as colonists and settling within the prohibited zone may acquire up to 250 hectares of irrigated and 1,000 of non-irrigated lands upon condition of becoming Mexican citizens within six years after taking up the land.[44]   Other rights subject to the law [45] shall be conserved by their present owners till their death, while corporations of foreign origin or having foreign shareholders shall preserve their rights for the full life of the corporation.[46]   According to the Mexican Minister of Foreign Affairs, this provision does not govern rights in mining, transportation, industrial companies, and other enterprises which have no direct ownership of lands and waters located within or without the forbidden zone.[47]

Foreigners acquiring property in adjudication or as heirs, who under the law are incapable of holding it, must within five years transfer it to some one hav-

[43] ". . . which does not mean that the law is given retroactive effect in its application since it has to do with an act in the future and not with an act in the past; but if any dispute should arise on that point, that is to say, whether or not the application of the law under the terms last mentioned is retroactive, it would be for the courts to determine it in accordance with the provisions of Article 14 of the constitution." Reply of Mexican Minister, *Senate Document* No. 96, 69th *Congress,* 1st Session, p. 41.

[44] *Regulations,* Article 17.

[45] *Organic Law,* Article 5.

[46] Note of Mexican Minister, *Senate Document* No. 96, 69th *Congress,* 1st Session, p. 41.

[47] *ibid.*

ing legal capacity to hold the property.[48] If for sufficient reason title cannot be passed within the five
years, this period may be extended.[49] Foreigners
who had acquired property before the law was
adopted must make a declaration to this effect;
otherwise these properties will be considered as having been acquired after the passage of the law.[50]
Contracts made in opposition to the provisions of
this law are null and void, and violations of the law
governing the limited right of foreigners in agricultural lands make such lands subject to public auction.[51] Long-term leases are legalized "to the extent
which may be strictly necessary for the establishment of services with an industrial, mining, petroleum, or other non-agricultural object." [52]

The law just described is but a part of the legislation affecting property-holding in Mexico and, as
such, affecting the position of foreigners in Mexico.
It must be considered in connection with the legislation on such subjects as subsoil, water, mining,
labor, colonization, irrigation—legislation which has
written the principles of the revolution into the law
of real property. The effect of this varied legislation
has been succinctly described by the Spanish landowners in the following terms: "When we acquired
our rural lands in Mexico, we found property based

[48] *Organic Law,* Article 6.
[49] *Regulations,* Article 11.
[50] *ibid.,* Article 7.
[51] *ibid.,* Article 9.
[52] *ibid.,* Article 10.

upon the same rights and guarantees that exist in the rest of the world. The new constitution guarantees this property, but subjects it to limitations of the law; in one word, the nation has passed from the regime of absolute to that of relative property. The transition could not be more fundamental or more delicate." [53]

The scope of the present study does not permit of a detailed analysis and description of the controversy that has developed, but so revealing is the discussion that has taken place, so clearly does it indicate the import of the change that lies embodied in the Mexican agricultural revolution, and so obvious is the difference of approach between the United States and Mexico on the issues under discussion, that we must at least give in broad terms a description of the nature of the argument and a summary statement of what seems to be its underlying import. [54]

The American argument has run mainly upon an insistence that the legislation is confiscatory of vested interest and retroactive upon previously acquired rights. The Mexican argument, on the other hand, has been to the effect that the legislation is

[53] *El Memorial de los Agricultores Españoles al Sr. Presidente de la República. Aprobado por la Cámara Española de Comercio, ésta ha Dirigido al Sr. General Don Alvaro Obregon el importante estudio jurídico que sobre las expropiaciones de que son objeto las propiedades agrícolas de los españoles, ha formulado la Comision de Agricultura de la expresada Corporación. Dicho Memorial dice así.* (Manuscript copy.)

[54] This whole discussion should be read in connection with Chapter VIII, pp. 189-203.

neither retroactive nor confiscatory. The Mexican government insists that "the form in which a foreigner holds a right may be changed by a sovereign nation as long as the right in its essence is respected," [55] and argues that in general a change in the law affecting private property, affecting its future use and exercise, is neither retroactive nor confiscatory.[56] In fact, such changes in the legal position of property are considered to be inevitable in a growing community. "If it were otherwise, there would not have been suppressed slavery, nor rights of primogeniture, nor obligatory inheritance, nor irredeemable taxes, and so forth." [57] Any attempt to prevent a nation from making such essential adjustments, providing the rights of individuals are respected, is described as tantamount to an interference in the exercise of the sovereign rights of a nation,[58] especially when the injured individuals can

[55] Memorandum of Mexican Minister for Foreign Affairs, December 5, 1925, p. 7; *Senate Document,* No. 96, 69th *Congress,* 1st Session, p. 28.

[56] ". . . to determine the period for the future exercise of a right is not to proceed retroactively." Note in reply of the Mexican Minister of Foreign Affairs, February 12, 1926; *Senate Document,* No. 96, p. 7.

[57] Note in reply of Mexican Minister for Foreign Affairs, January 20, 1926; *Senate Document,* No. 96, p. 16.

[58] ". . . What the principles assure the foreigner is the respect of his property rights, but not respect of these rights just as they existed at the time of the acquisition, since this would be tantamount to denying to a sovereign nation the right of imposing upon all those who inhabit its territory the modifications and regulations necessary for the defense of its interests and would make impossible its subsequent development." *ibid.,* p. 9.

"The surprise of the Mexican government is legitimate, as

have recourse to the courts of law for any injury that they may have suffered.[59]

The American argument has run in distinctly opposing terms. Any intention to interfere with Mexican sovereignty is disclaimed, and the American notes have repeatedly asserted that they were motivated by "friendship" and wished to "avoid any criticism . . . of a neighboring friendly and sovereign state."[60] The American government "recognizes to the fullest extent the right of any other government by legislation to regulate the ownership of property as a purely domestic question, *unless such regulation operates to divest prior vested rights of American citizens.*"[61] We see here the different at-

would be that of any other government of a free country, including that of his Britannic Majesty, if it found that acts of interior legislation, such as the right of imposing contributions, were called into question by the diplomatic protests of the countries of subjects affected by the imposition." Reply of the Mexican government to the British Note of Protest, Mexico City, August 12, 1918. See *The Mexican Oil Question,* with documents and translations, p. 52.

[59] Note in reply of Mexican Minister for Foreign Affairs dated January 20, 1926, *Senate Document,* No. 96, 69th *Congress,* 1st Session, p. 21.

[60] *Aide memoire* of personal message from the Secretary of State, November 17, 1925, *Senate Document,* No. 96, p. 3.

[61] Author's italics.

". . . My government wished to avoid, if possible, any criticism of prospective legislation of a neighboring and sovereign state, for it recognizes to the fullest extent the right of any other government by legislation to regulate the ownership of property as a purely domestic question, unless such regulation operates to divest prior vested rights of American citizens legally acquired or held under the laws of such foreign government, and it is only because of the seeming imminence of the passage of such legisla-

titude towards the nature of private property. ". . . My government finds itself unable to acquiesce in the fundamental conception of a vested interest as evidently entertained by the Mexican government . . . as mere rights of user or enjoyment which might lawfully be interrupted or wholly be taken away by regulations affecting its future duration or imposing conditions upon future enjoyment." [62]

The argument thus stated brings the issues clearly into perspective. From the American point of view, the Mexican doctrine "strikes at the very root of the system of private property rights which lies at the bottom of all civilized society. . . . The very essence of a vested interest is that it is inviolable and cannot be impaired or taken away by the state save for a public purpose upon rendering just compensation." [63]

Attitudes toward private property differing as widely as these have their source in experiences and

tion, and because it does so affect the vested rights of American citizens." *Aide memoire,* handed by the American Ambassador to the Mexican Minister for Foreign Affairs, November 27, 1925, *Senate Document* No. 96, pp. 6-7.

[62] Note of the Secretary of State to the Mexican Minister for Foreign Affairs, July 31, 1926. Press release, Department of State, November 23, 1926, p. 2.

[63] "No title can be secure if it is to be deemed vested only in the sense that it had been enjoyed in the past and that it is therefore subject to curtailment or destruction through the enforcement of laws enacted subsequent to its acquisition." Note to the Secretary of State to the Mexican Minister for Foreign Affairs, July 31, 1926. Press Release, Department of State, November 23, 1926, p. 4.

needs that are perhaps equally divergent. The Mexican argument has undoubtedly been sharpened by a concept of the needs of Mexico as an undeveloped nation set in the midst of a dynamic industrial world. The American argument has, on the other hand, been influenced by our requirements as an expanding commercial and capital-exporting nation seeking means of protecting the nationals who venture their investments outside of the borders of the United States.[64] It is only with this background that the full significance of the two arguments can be realized. The United States has argued that "if all our foreign investments were to be transferred from the state of property, duly acquired, with guarantees of permanence, to the state of temporary concessions, requiring renewal from time to time by contracts, in the wording of which we have no share, we should

[64] "Mexico: A former Ambassador to Mexico has been insisting that Article IX of the Mexican Claims Convention is sufficiently broad to cover all disputes between the two countries, and was written in anticipation of the present difficulties. The Department of State does not so construe it. It is a mistake to test the Administration's policy in terms of international law, precedent, and so forth. There are two controlling factors in that policy, and both of them are geographical in origin. They are (a) absolute protection of the Panama Canal and (b) good behavior of the countries between the Rio Grande and Panama.

"These are objectives of national policy, not statements of international law. There is no hesitancy in the avowal of them privately, but they are not stated openly. An authority states the case bluntly for us in these words: 'We simply are not going to tolerate unfriendly governments to the south of us, and that is all there is to it.' We continue to think it quite safe to say that the Administration will not deviate from the essentials of that policy. Moreover, the Administration has assurances that a Senate majority supports its view." *Whaley-Eaton Service,* American Letter No. 438, January 22, 1927.

face an unprecedented situation. Our commercial relations, not only with Mexico but with all of Latin-America, depend upon mutual confidence." [65] Similarly, President Coolidge declared that "the person and property of a citizen are part of the general domain of the nation even when abroad." [66] In reply to this general attitude has come the Mexican insistence that "if the rights of private property over portions of the national territory are not derived from the joint rights of the nation in common, then all the nations that open their doors to foreigners will one day have to see that some of these portions acquired by some foreigners will become subject to foreign laws that escape from the sovereignty of the nation and thus destroy its sovereignty." [67]

[65] Department of Commerce, Bureau of Foreign and Domestic Commerce, Washington, No. 45, Release date October 7, 1918, Circular of the Latin-American Division. Printed in *Documents Relating to the Attempt of the Government of Mexico to Confiscate Foreign-owned Oil Properties,* compiled by the Association of Oil Producers in Mexico, February, 1919, p. 50.

"Confiscation, like conflagration, spreads. If Mexico consummates the confiscation of oil-fields contemplated in her newest constitution and decrees, other confiscatory provisions of Article 27 of the constitution will be boldly applied as against foreign and native holders of lands. It is undeniable that such consummation will encourage similar spoliation of foreign-owned interests in other new countries. The result will be commercial chaos and fatal retardation of industrial development in these new countries where development is so needed." *Memorandum Relating to the Proposed Petroleum Code of Mexico Submitted by the Executive to Congress on November 23, 1918,* printed in *The Mexican Oil Question,* with documents and translations, pp. 91-92.

[66] *United States Daily,* April 26, 1927, column 2, p. 2.

[67] *Boletín de la Secretaría de Gobernación, El Artículo 27 de la Constitución Federal,* Mexico, September, 1922, p. 2.

"The doctrine for which Secretary Kellogg is now contending

Recent changes in Mexican-American relations have brought dissension over the nature and character of private property to an end. An adjustment in the enforcement of the legislation has been worked out that seems satisfactory to both sides. And it may be that for purposes of international comity the issue has now been closed. But looked at as two theories of property and property relations, the points of view revealed by the argument retain their original interest and significance.[68]

is in effect that a right to property is an inalienable right which no government can ever impair, that it is superior under international law to the right of sovereignty, and that when the acts of the sovereign conflict with the vested rights of foreign property-holders these acts of the sovereign are null and void under international law." Lippmann, Walter, "The Kellogg Doctrine: Vested Rights and Nationalism in Latin-America," *Men of Destiny,* p. 207.

[68] It should be noted that the settlement which has been arrived at leaves the Mexican argument practically intact. The only compromise of any significance on the Mexican side has been to convert a fee simple into a perpetual concession. But in theory and in the long run, as things stand now, rights in subsoil acquired before 1917 are retained by their present owners only by accepting their conversion into a concession.

CHAPTER XVII

CHANGES IN THE RURAL COMMUNITY

No final summary of the changes that have taken place in Mexico since 1910 can be given at this time. The Mexican revolution is still on. Its future fortunes and influences may prove as varied and important as those that have already taken place. Looked at from the outside, the Mexican revolution is but one of a series of national upheavals that have taken place since 1910. It may be viewed as part of the general series of phenomena which includes the Turkish, the Chinese, and the Russian revolutions, and the broad national changes that have resulted from the Great War. Looked at more narrowly from the purely American-continental point of view, the Mexican revolution represents a new note in Latin-American politics; new not only in the ideas generated in the policies formulated, but new in the racial and economic groups which have been called to govern. Mexico is the first of Latin-American countries in which the mass of the underlying population has achieved access to political dominion in more than a purely figurative sense. Looked at internally, the Mexican revolution seems like an attempt to stem foreign imperialism and to destroy military autocracy, to resurrect an indigenous race, to bridge the gap between feudalism and democracy in one leap. Obviously, changes as basic and fundamental as these cannot be achieved in a day or evaluated at the moment of achievement. The results are far too complex and the consequences far too many-sided to provide adequate bases for immediate judgment. Without, therefore, undertaking to pass any judgment upon the revolution and its results, we will confine ourselves to a study of the actual changes that have been wrought during the past 18 years in the life of the rural community, both those that are due to the revolution and those that are due to other causes. Among these latter must be counted the decrease in the Mexican population.

Between 1910 and 1921 the Mexican population decreased by 5.8 per cent. According to the census of 1910, Mexico had 15,160,369 inhabitants.[1] This number had been reduced by 1921 to 14,280,920.[2] This change in the population cannot be entirely attributed to the internal strife. The battles of the revolution, with a few exceptions, were small and the loss of life negligible. It is probably true that the greatest loss of life during the last 18 years that may be charged to the revolution was due to petty engagements and bandit activities. In all the years

[1] *Tercer Censo de Población de los Estados Unidos Mexicanos, 1910. Oficina Impresora de la Secretaría de Hacienda. Departamento de Fomento,* 1918, Vol. I, p. 10.

[2] *Anuario Estadístico,* 1923-1924. *Departamento de la Estadística Nacional,* Vol. II. *Talleres Gráficos* de la Nación, 1926, p. 3.

of the revolution it is doubtful whether as many lives were lost as in any one of the major battles of the Great War.

The great loss of life between the census years 1910 and 1921 was apparently the result of the Spanish influenza in 1918-1919. Given the lack of sanitation, especially in the rural community, the almost complete absence of medical care, the ignorance of the population, and we have a situation where the people "died like flies" from the dread epidemic. This is testified to from many different sources. Carleton Beals found such a situation in Durango,[3] Gamio reports the same for Teotihuacán,[4] and the geographer Mondrogon reaches the same conclusion for all of Mexico.[5] The disease seems to have lingered on in the remote regions of Mexico. The author, traveling in the tropical forests of Chiapas in 1926, found the Lacandone Indians afflicted with colds, and among the few Spanish words these most primitive Indians knew was *"frio"* (cold). They stood off when we arrived and yelled, *"Frio, frio,"* and not until they were reassured that we had

[3] "The Tarahumaras in the state of Chihuahua that consisted of more than 40,000 inhabitants was seriously reduced by the so-called Spanish influenza in the winter of 1918. It can be asserted that at least 25 per cent of these people perished as a result of this disease." *Descripción de la Sierra Madre Occidental* (manuscript), Carleton Beals, Brimstone and Chili, New York, 1927, p. 227.

[4] Gamio, Manuel, *Población de Valle de Teotihuacán,* Mexico, 1922, Introduction, p. xvi.

[5] Quoted by Toledano, Lombaro, *La Libertad Sindical en México,* 1927, p. 105.

no *frio* would they come near enough to deal with us. This story illustrates the helplessness of this primitive community, and helps to explain the profound losses which this *frio* must have caused them.

The change in population was most marked in the rural communities, partly for the reason that we have given, and partly because the revolution caused a shift of the population from the rural to the urban centers—where life was more secure and individual helplessness less noticeable. In 1910 the total rural population is given as 11,779,110, or 78 per cent of the total, while in 1921 it is given as 10,563,454, or 74 per cent of the total, a decrease of the rural population by about 4 per cent.

The number of agricultural laborers has decreased in proportion to the total population. Unfortunately we can only measure this change for the years between 1910 and 1921, while it seems clear that it has been since 1921—during the regimes of Obregon and Calles—that the revolution made itself most profoundly felt in the rural community. In 1910 there were 3,109,491,[6] or approximately 21 per cent of the total population, classed as laborers, while by 1921 they had been reduced to 2,771,538,[7] or 19 per cent of the total.[8]

[6] Compiled from *Tercer Censo de Población, Departamento de Aprovisionamentos Generales. Talleres Gráficos del Gobierno Nacional*, 1918, Vol. 2, pp. 266-1340.

[7] Revista Quincenal, *Estadística Nacional*, February 15, 1927, p. 8.

[8] In the first census the laborers are classed as *"peones de campo, jornaleros."* In the 1921 census they appear under the

With the decrease in the percentage of agricultural laborers has gone an almost equal increase in the number of independent farmers. These accounted for 2.7 per cent in the 1910 census, and 4.4 per cent in the 1921 census. As we have already seen, the number of owners has been increasing slowly, since the greater proportion of the increase in owners has come through the federal land grants.[9]

But this change in the status of the agricultural laborers who have moved from the position of laborers to participants in the lands of the *ejidos* has not always been easy, nor has it always been an immediate improvement. We have already seen that approximately only one-half of the cultivatable lands given as *ejidos* have been placed under cultivation.[10] The reasons for this incomplete utilization of their newly gotten lands are to be found in the difficulties created by the process of the transition. This change in the position of the · agricultural laborer to that of owner and participant in the life and organization of the *ejidos* involves more than receiving legal title to land. It involves, in many instances, change of residence, the building of homes, and the acquisition of tools,[11] machinery, draft ani-

heading *"gananes."* The first of these classifications reflected the debt servitude that then existed. The more recent census classification reverses this and drops the debt-held worker entirely; at least implies a free wage-worker.

[9] See Chapters IX and XIII.

[10] See Chapter XIII.

[11] "The agriculturalists have almost no tools of any class. There are no draft animals, no plows; but it is impossible to ask

mals,[12] credit, and seed. It frequently involves the problem of finding the means of subsistence while the crop is growing, or of overcoming the consequence of crop failure without adequate credit or resources.

Equally serious are the persistent conflicts with the *hacendados* from whose property the lands for the *ejidos* have been taken. The *hacendados,* or their administrators, as the past 18 years show, have persisted in opposing the process of land distribution not only by legal means, especially through injunctions, but also through a great variety of petty molestations—diverting of water, the removal of fencing, the refusal to co-operate in the cleaning of irrigation canals. All of these have contributed their share to the difficulties and the disturbances of the local agrarian communities.

There have also been the political machinations of individuals and of groups, as well as the armed activities of scattered bands who have maintained themselves in various parts of Mexico. All of these have played their part in making the transition to ownership difficult, sometimes disheartening, and not infrequently impossible. In addition to all of these are inexperience, ignorance, and the lack of initiative of the rural workers. The agricultural laborer, hitherto always dependent upon a master, has at

for everything at the same time because we must not forget that these agriculturalists have just lain down their arms to pick up the plow." *Zona* 29, Morelos, February, 1923, *Municipio de Cuautla.* (Manuscript.)

[12] *Zona* 23, Mexico, April, 1923, *Municipio de Natividas.*

times found it most difficult to get along without him, and to plan his work far enough ahead to keep the agricultural work moving.[13]

Between 1910 and 1921 there was a noticeable shift in the population from resident hacienda communities to free villages. This movement undoubtedly represents one of the most significant changes that the revolution has brought into the rural communities. It represents a growth of the self-governing communities as against the communities that had no self-government. It at the same time represents a shift in the proportion of the population that live upon their own land rather than upon the private property of another and, as we have already seen, under the agrarian legislation represents a change in the total number of people who have a right to acquire land.

This shift in the rural population may be represented in various ways. The population on haciendas was reduced from 5,511,284 to 3,913,769, or a shift of from 47 to 37 per cent of the total, while the number of resident communities on haciendas was reduced from 56,825 to 46,381, or from 81.7 to 74.8 per cent of the total rural communities. These losses in population and in the number of resident communities represented an actual and relative gain by the free villages. The agricultural villages, which in 1910 contained 51 per cent of the population and represented 16 per cent of the total rural communities, in 1921 contained 58.2 per cent of the

[13] *Zona* 19, Colima, June, 1923.

population, and 21.6 per cent of the communities. The table below illustrates the points just made.

HACIENDA AND VILLAGE COMMUNITIES COMPARED, 1910 AND 1921

Community	1910			1921		
	Number	Population (in Thousands)	Average Population	Number	Population (in Thousands)	Average Population
Hacienda...	56,825	5,511	97	46,381	3,914	84
Agricultural Village...	11,117	6,011	541	13,388	6,148	459
All Other Rural....	1,607	257	160	2,237	502	224
Total...	69,549	11,779	169	62,006	10,564	170

It is interesting to observe that the changes have been accompanied by a decrease in the average population of both the hacienda and agricultural villages, the first falling from 97 to 84, and the second from 541 to 459. Only the industrial and mining villages have increased in size, going from 160 to 224. These population changes, given in percentage terms, present the following summary.

PERCENTAGE COMPARISON OF HACIENDA AND VILLAGE COMMUNITIES, 1910 AND 1921

Community	1910		1921	
	Number	Population	Number	Population
Hacienda.........	81.7	46.8	74.8	37.1
Agricultural village.	16.0	51.0	21.6	58.2
All other rural.....	2.3	2.2	3.6	4.7
Total..........	100.0	100.0	100.0	100.0

An even better understanding of the extent of this shift in the population is to be had if we examine the figures below showing the percentage increase (+) or decrease (—) in the 1921 data as compared with those for 1910.

Type of community	Number of communities	Total population
Hacienda	—18.4	—29.0
Agricultural village.....	+20.4	+ 2.3
All other rural.........	+39.2	+95.0

The haciendas have lost nearly one-fifth of their resident communities and nearly one-third of their inhabitants since 1910. While the free villages have gained one-fifth in the number of their communities and more than 2 per cent in the total of their inhabitants, the greatest change, as we have already noticed, has been in the "All other rural," both in the number of villages and in the total population—representing chiefly gains in mining communities.

We shall now present this shift of the population by states. For this purpose we shall give only the figures for the population shift of the haciendas. The reader who wishes to have a more detailed description of the whole situation may turn to Appendix B for a detailed table of all communities in each state.

In 26 out of the 31 states in Mexico the proportion of the population living upon haciendas decreased between 1910 and 1921. The movement of the rural population from the hacienda to the village is therefore a general rather than a local phenomenon.[15] If we exclude the Federal District and Quintana Roo, both of which represent very special conditions, only three states show a relative increase of the population resident upon haciendas, and in these three states the changes are comparatively unimportant, being 0.6 per cent in Tabasco, less than 3 per cent in Michoacán, and only 5 per cent in Coahuila.

The distribution, by states, given on page 403, may be summarized by grouping the states according to the percentage of the population resident in hacienda communities in 1910 and 1921.

Percentage of rural population in resident hacienda communities	Number of states 1910[a]	1921[a]
Less than 10	..	3
10 to 20	2	4
20 to 30	4	2
30 to 40	3	4
40 to 50	4	3
50 to 60	4	3
60 to 70	7	8
70 to 80	3	2
80 or over	2	..
	29	29

[a] Federal District and Quintana Roo excluded.

With these changes in population, occupational distribution, and residence have gone others of per-

[15] "In the southeastern part of the state (Chiapas) the workers have by the hundreds abandoned the haciendas and taken up lands provided by the federal government in the *municipios* of Margaritas, San Caralimpio, and La Independencia." *Edu. Púb. Exp.* 115, 1924, p. 277.

haps equal importance, but more difficult to describe, as they are not easily subject to statistical enumeration. The shifting of the population from the haci-

SHIFT IN THE PROPORTION OF THE RURAL POPULATION LIVING IN
HACIENDA COMMUNITIES, 1910 AND 1921

(All figures are in percentages)

States	1910	1921	Increase (+) or Decrease (−)
Morelos	23.7	3.5	−85.2
Guerrero	47.1	16.8	−64.3
Veracruz	24.0	9.4	−60.8
Puebla	20.1	9.9	−50.7
Tlaxcala	32.2	20.2	−37.3
Campeche	49.8	32.1	−35.5
Yucatán	45.9	31.2	−32.0
Baja California	47.3	33.3	−29.4
Chihuahua	58.2	42.0	−27.8
Oaxaca	14.5	10.5	−27.6
México	16.8	12.2	−27.4
San Luis Potosí	81.8	63.5	−22.4
Colima	57.8	44.9	−22.3
Chiapas	59.7	47.3	−20.8
Durango	66.0	53.2	−19.4
Hidalgo	20.7	16.8	−18.8
Nayarit	63.2	51.5	−18.5
Nuevo León	60.0	50.2	−16.3
Sonora	33.1	27.9	−15.7
Tamaulipas	74.6	63.4	−15.0
Sinaloa	73.4	66.5	− 9.4
Jalisco	65.5	60.8	− 7.2
Aguascalientes	65.8	61.8	− 6.1
Guanajuato	84.3	79.1	− 6.2
Zacatecas	76.1	73.8	− 3.0
Querétaro	64.8	64.2	− 0.9
Tabasco	32.3	32.5	+ 0.6
Michoacán	60.1	61.7	+ 2.7
Coahuila	57.8	60.7	+ 5.0
Distrito Federal	6.9	11.2	+62.3
Quintana Roo	9.6	16.0	+66.7
All States	46.8	37.1	−20.7

endas to the villages is evidence of a wider social change than the shift itself, and that is the freedom to leave the hacienda.

The revolution has freed approximately one-half of the rural population from serfdom. We have already seen that about 6,000,000 people were in 1910 located upon haciendas and ranchos. We have also seen that the greater portion of these occupied a position of indentured servitude or peonage. This peonage took the form of restraint on account of debt. As a result of the revolution these people, have, for the first time since the Spanish Conquest, secured freedom of movement. This liberation of approximately one-half of the rural population from serfdom was accomplished in part through legislation, but more, perhaps, through the psychological and social change brought about by the conflict itself. In no small degree these changes in the social attitude of the mass of the Mexican people is due to the influence of the United States.[16] The railroad connection with the American border established during the Diaz regime, and still more important the increasing migration to and from the United States by Mexicans who came as temporary workers to the railroads and the cotton and beet fields, as well as the forced changes of residence

[16] "Many of the villagers have been in the United States for different periods and have brought with them many good ideas and noble inspirations. The very streets of the village prove that." *Zona* 19, Chihuahua, Mayo, 1924, *C. Camargo, Congregación de Estación Oritz.*

which many Mexicans had to make on account of the revolution, all contributed to spreading new ideals of labor and social relations. It is interesting to note that a considerable number of the important leaders of Mexico, both in political and social matters, have lived for longer or shorter periods in the United States.[17] The debts of the peons were formally abolished i nthe Constitution of 1917,[18] but before that state governors and revolutionary leaders had taken steps to do the same. In Jalisco,[19] Chiapas,[20] and Yucatán [21] this was done during 1914. This wiping out of the debts went hand in hand with a number of other provisions leading in the same direction. Legal protection has been thrown about the workers; their responsibility for debts has been limited to themselves,[22] and to a specified

[17] Gamio, Manuel, *Preliminary Report on Mexican Immigration in the United States;* under the auspices of the Social Science Research Council, 1926, mimeograph copy, pp. 93-96.

[18] The Mexican Constitution of 1917 compared with the Constitution of 1857. Transitory Articles, Number 13. The *Annals* of the American Academy of Political and Social Science, May, 1917, p. 113.

[19] *Informe, C. Lic. Manuel Aguirre Berlanga, Gobernador Interino del Mismo, al C. Venustiano Carranza, Edición Oficial,* 1914, 1916, Guadalajara.

[20] *C. Jefe del Departamento de Escuelas Rurales, Secretaría de Educación Pública,* Mexico, *Foja* 47, *Exp.* 115, *Classif.* 12-3-5-2.

[21] Cárlos, *El Socialismo En Yucatán,* Havana, 1923, p. 29.

[22] ". . . it was customary among Mexicans and foreigners resident in the country to oblige their workers to contract debts so as to be able to keep them in their service. . . . If the person assuming the debt died it was passed on to his family, there have been instances in which a debt contracted by the great-grandfather served as a means of keeping his descendents in servitude."

amount of money.[23]   Equally important has been
the prohibition of the *tienda de raya* which began disappearing soon after 1910,[24] and with it has
come the legal insistence [25] upon free access to the
haciendas and upon specified market places and
days. To this is to be added the prohibition of payment in kind or in token.[26]   All of these legal provisions would perhaps have had little bearing upon
the fortunes of the Mexican rural population if the
revolution had not shifted the groups which possess
political power.

*Political power has passed from the old land-
holding aristocracy to the village, to the agricultural workers, and especially to the city laborers.*
This latter class seems to recognize that its own
position in the long run depends upon raising the
standards of the rural population and entrenching
it in its newly acquired social prerogatives. The
government, generally speaking, at least since the
day when Obregon came into power in 1920, has
striven to make effective the legislative program

Excelsior, March 18, 1928, p. 2, *Concursos Sobre Temas de Derecho
Industrial.*
    [23] See Chapters VIII and XII.
    [24] Gamio, Teotihuacán, Vol. II, p. 454.
    [25] "The Mexican *hacendados* were accustomed to pay their
workers in kind or in token money which was only accepted in
certain specified places such as a store owned by the *hacendado*
or some member of his family and which led to the store's making
a greater profit than was customary in regular commerce." *Excelsior,* March 18, 1928, p. 2, *Concursos Sobre Temas de Derecho
Industrial.*
    [26] See Chapter XII.

embodying the freedom of the rural population. That it had to do that or face grave internal difficulties—a fact which Obregon conceded—is perhaps the best indication that the program of the revolution has had actual as well as purely legal results. These changes have not made themselves equally felt in all parts of the Republic. President Calles in his report to the National Congress on September 1, 1926, said:

From the investigations of the conditions of labor over the entire country it is clear that there are still regions where they do not benefit from the constitution; where the agricultural laborers work 12 and 15 hours per day for a wage which does not permit them to live like civilized human beings, where the relations between the employers and the workers are governed by the customs of the past centuries.[27]

There are still places where payment in kind, at least in part is common, where payment in token money is practiced,[28] where the *tienda de raya* is still in vogue, and where forced labor is not entirely unknown.[29] But as a rule debt servitude has disap-

---

[27] *Informes Rendidos por el C. Gral, Plutarco Elías Calles, Presidente Constitucional de los Estados Unidos Mexicanos, ante el H. Congreso de la Unión los Dias 1, de Septiembre, de 1925 y 1 de Septiembre de 1926 y contestación de los CC. Presidentes del Citado Congreso Talleres Gráficos de la Nación, "Diario Oficial,"* Mexico, 1925.

[28] The author encountered payment in token money in one of the large industrial and agricultural enterprises in Durango in 1922.

[29] "In the Municipio of Botopilas are some families that have more than 100 *tarahumaras* each and not only do not comply

peared, payment in kind has been replaced by payment in money, the villages have been given a new stimulus, the number of small owners of rural property has increased and seems likely to increase, and political power has increasingly gone into the hands of the mass of the people.[30]

It seems fairly safe to say that whatever the fortunes of the Mexican revolution, these changes which imply the abolition of servitude have been permanently established. No change within the immediate future will return the Mexican agricul-

with the provisions of Article 123 of the constitution of the republic but they subject them and compel them to work for little or no pay and even beat them. In at least two specific cases complaints have been made before the governor of the state." Chihuahua, *Educ. Púb.* 1922, *Exp.* 55, 57-59.

"Even to this day some of the authorities when they need any service merely order that a *cuadrilla* of Indians from some of the neighboring villages be sent for, and are assigned to serve for a week without any pay." Hidalgo, *Educ. Púb., Fojas* 39, *Exp.* 382, Class. 12-1-9-170.

The author traveling in Chiapas found similar indications of forced unpaid labor by the Indians in some places and special instances of the federal army forcing the village of Amatanango to supply two hundred *cargadores* for its equipment in time of peace, and paying them five *centavos* per day. These instances are rare and seemingly getting rarer, but they exhibit an old practice which persists in spite of the law.

[30] We have pointed out in a previous chapter that Mexico has for all purposes had no party organization that is comparable to the party system that we know in the United States. Such a party system is gradually developing if one is to take the evidence available to date of parties existing under a common name for a period of years, with yearly conventions and permanent organization. But with the exception of the *Partido Laborista* which has had permanent organization since 1918 it will still be a considerable period before the political parties will take the form of definite groupings.

tural labor to the position of serf that he occupied in 1910. These changes have in part been bound up with certain accidental factors—especially the destruction of draft animals. Because of the revolution a large proportion of all the draft animals of Mexico were killed.[31] *Los Animales de los pobres* (the animals of the poor) were more generally spared. The result has been that the large estates have found themselves more dependent upon draft animals other than their own. This has led to an increase in crop-sharing and renting.[32] At least it has led to better crop-sharing and renting contracts, as the draft animals can now be more readily supplied by the crop-sharers and renters. It has given rise especially in Northern Mexico to an increasing group of agricultural operators who have no land but do have work animals. In a state like Chihuahua this movement for passing the work on to croppers and renters who work with the animals furnished by the new class of operators has been very noticeable indeed.[33]

[31] This was especially true in the northern states.

[32] Gamio, *Teotihuacán,* Vol. II, p. 109.

[33] In the reports available for the State of Chihuahua for the year 1922 practically all of the haciendas are described as doing all of their work by means of crop-sharing. As an example we may cite the following: "Distrito Judicial de Guerrero. In this region are to be found the haciendas of Babicora, Chavez, Santa Ana, Providencia, Santa Clara, San Gerónimo, San Antonio de Sáenz, La Boquilla, El Rosario, Tonachic, and San José de Albuquerque. In none of these is the agricultural exploitation carried on personally by their owners or renters. All are exploited by crop-sharers." *Boletín de Estadística del Estado de Chihuahua* No. 2, 1922, p. 46.

With the change of the position of the agricultural worker has gone a rapid increase of wages. Wages that were generally between 18 and 25 cents in 1910 are at present between 75 cents and $1.50, and in some states, especially those on the American border and in Yucatán, are considerably higher. The hours of labor which generally, though not always, have been *sol a sol* (from sun up to sun down) are now 8 or 10—and with the increasing cost of labor this reduction has developed a stimulus in the direction of agricultural machinery.[34]   But as the

[34] Without undertaking to make a comprehensive study of wage changes that have occurred in rural Mexico during the last 18 years we will give a few typical examples as reported by the *agricultural agronomist* for the different counties in some of the states:

State	Municipio	Date	Daily Wage
Chihuahua	Ciudad Camargo	April, 1923	$1.00 for permanent work. 75-80c and right to a piece of land and to pasture a cow.
Colima	Pihuamo	Feb., 1923	40-70c and ration of corn and beans.
Durango	Nayar	Oct., 1922	75c
Jalisco	Poncitlán	Nov., 1923	50c to $1.00
Jalisco	Taretán	June, 1925	75c to $1.00
Jalisco	Etzatlán	Sept., 1924	75c to $1.00
México	Calculalpan	June, 1923	80c to $1.00
Michoacán	Zamora	Feb., 1925	$1.00
Michoacán	Uruapán	June, 1924	60c
Michoacán	Testerazo	June, 1924	75c to $1.50
Michoacán	Maravatio	May, 1924	75c
Nayarit	I. del Rio	Oct., 1924	75c to $1.50
Nuevo León	Montemorelos	Oct., 1924	$1.00 to $1.25
Nuevo León	Rayones	Oct., 1925	$0.75 to $1.25
Oaxaca	Cuicatlán	Nov., 1923	$1.25 to $1.50
Zacatecas	S. Pedro Ocampo	Nov., 1924	$1.00

revolution has seriously interfered with large-scale agricultural enterprise, this movement has not gone as far as might perhaps have been expected from the greater labor costs that the revolution has forced upon agricultural enterprise.

Another series of changes of great importance for Mexico is the surprisingly rapid movement for organization of its working population. This organization is of exceptional interest, not only because it has proceeded with such great speed and apparent effectiveness, but because it has taken place in a country where the tradition of organization and collective action on the part of large masses of people has been unknown and generally believed impossible. This organization, while it wields considerable political influence, is essentially economic and social. The trade union movement, which began to take effective form about 1911,[35] now represents approximately 2,000,000 members. While largely dominated by city workers its membership is essentially agricultural. The agricultural groups that belong to it are composed, in many instances, of entire villages and of workers located upon haciendas.

The organizations of the Mexican Federation of Labor (*Confederación Regional Obrera Mexicana*) are described as follows:

[35] Lombardo Toledano, *La Libertad Sindical en México*, 1926, p. 236.

Regional and State Federations of Agricultural
    Communities and Laborers.................   50
Regional and State Federations of City Workers   35
Workers' organizations in the Federal District..   108
City Unions in entire Mexico.................   1,380
Agricultural Communities and Laborers' Unions   2,063 [a]

[a] Letter from Secretary of the *C. R. O. M.,* November, 1926.

Some of the agricultural organizations are very
large. They are said in a few instances to comprise
as many as 10,000 workers. The growth of this remarkable organization, as given in membership figures in the annual report to the convention in 1926,
is as follows: [a]

Year	Membership
1918	7,000
1919	10,000
1920	50,000
1921	150,000
1922	400,000
1923	800,000
1924	1,200,000
1925	1,500,000
1926	2,000,000

It is interesting to note that this close affiliation
between the agricultural and industrial worker in
Mexico was made possible by certain very special
conditions characteristic of Mexico and the revolution which has surged over it. The movement for
organization itself received an important stimulus
from the fact that the constitution embodied a defi-

[a] *Memoria de los Trabajos Llevados a Cabo por el Comite
Central de la C. R. O. M. Durante el Ejercicio del 23 de
Noviembre de 1924 al l. de Marzo de 1926,* Mexico, 1926, pp. 19-20.

nite legislative program for labor. But in Mexico a very large portion of the rural population occupy the position of laborers, so that the specifically industrial legislative program was applicable to a large proportion of the rural population. In other words, the rural as well as the industrial population had much to gain from common action if such action led to the enforcement of the labor program embodied in the basic law of the land.

Such joint effort would perhaps have been impossible to attain if the agricultural worker had not occupied a peculiar position in Mexican social life. From many points of view there is considerable similarity between the positions of the agricultural and the industrial worker. The agricultural worker is not an isolated farm laborer. He works with a group and is subject to a management that may control from a score up to over 1,000 peons. Like the industrial worker, he generally owns neither the instrument nor the resulting product of his labor. The Mexican agricultural laborer does not as a rule own the implements, the seed, the soil, the crop, or the work animals. He depends upon a weekly wage, upon a place to live, upon the right to water and firewood, upon a loan for food, and upon aid in case of sickness. Like the industrial laborer, he works for a large employer, frequently an absentee owner operating through a manager. Different, however, from the case of the industrial laborer is his relation to the employer. The agricultural worker lives on the

place with his family. He has in many instances
lived there for many years. In not a few cases he
was born there. He feels that it is his home. He
has rarely been off the place. The world beyond is
strange and unknown.

If the worker is not directly living on the hacienda
he comes from a nearby village. Frequently he comes
not alone as an individual but as a member of a
group—a *cuadrilla*—under the direction of some
local village official through whom the contract has
been made. The workers in this group bring their
families with them, build tiny bamboo or cornstalk
jacales on their little *milpas,* and stay there from the
day the ground is broken to the day the crop is
harvested, and then gather their few belongings and
return to the village. It is against this background
that the Mexican agricultural labor organization
must be viewed.

The Mexican agricultural laborer instead of being
an isolated individual naturally belongs to a group
and can with comparative ease act through a group.
The Mexican village tends for traditional reasons to
act with a great degree of unanimity. It has therefore been comparatively easy to organize these villages, as it has not involved the problem of organizing individuals but of groups. The growth in the
power and membership of the organized agricultural
population in Mexico is in a large measure due to
this fact. The village as such joined the organization as a means of realizing its dreams of land, of

finding aid against the local *hacendado*, of overcoming reactionary military officials, of reaching the powers of government through non-legal channels.

The same Constitution that provided for the agricultural laborer in Article 123 also provided for the agricultural village in Article 27. But the attempt to carry out the program embodied in Article 27 has raised a series of difficulties even greater than that of those embodied in Article 123. The *hacendado* has had powers of a political and economic character which were naturally greater than those of the village. He could hinder or bribe local officials, use organized force, throw innumerable obstacles in the path of granting lands to the villages. The agricultural peasants have therefore attempted to find some means of surmounting their handicaps.

The organization has served the purpose of giving the humblest village direct access to the central government in Mexico City. This works as follows: when a village has a grievance, when its demands for lands are laid aside and forgotten (sometimes it has taken five years to get action upon a demand for a land grant), when the local county or military officials take sides against the villages, when the state government does not enforce the law or winks at abuses, the little village communicates with the central committee of the Mexican Federation of Labor. This central committee, located in Mexico City and representing some two million workers, has a great deal of political influence, and the heads of the departments and the President himself are on friendly terms with the leaders of the organization. This committee immediately calls the attention of the head of the department in whose jurisdiction the problem may fall, the Secretary of Agriculture, the Secretary of Industry and Labor, or the Secretary of War, to the fact that such and such a village has this particular grievance. And because the structure of Mexican government is so highly centralized, a move taken directly at the order of the head of a department receives much readier and efficacious attention than if it had come from the local officials. This perhaps explains why the Mexican agricultural workers have organized. From the reports available it is clear that the members have converted this organization into an indirect channel of government.[36]

In addition to this most important organization there are essentially agricultural unions outside of its folds, such as the *Ligas de Resistencia* of Yucatan, Campeche, and Tabasco. These include, especially in Yucatán, all agricultural villages as well as the laborers upon the haciendas. There are also *Ligas de Comunidades Agrarias y Sindicatos Compesinos* in the states of Tamaulipas, Veracruz, the Federal District, Durango, Oaxaca, and Mexico, and other states, some of which are affiliated with the Mexican Federation of Labor. The point is that

[36] To get a picture of the varied activities in behalf of small rural communities carried on by this organization, see its official organ, *"Crom," Organo de la Confederación Regional Obrera Mexicana,* 1925 to date.

Mexico has developed new institutions of great significance; and these institutions are not only one of the outcomes of the revolution, but have proven one of the main supports of the revolutionary governments of Obregon and Calles,[37] and are looked upon as essential to a stable Mexico in the future.[38]

Village organization for the collective solution of local problems is one of the by-products of land distribution. Each new gift of land carries a new social organization taking the form of regular elections and an administrative committee empowered to deal with the important local problems that affect the community—land, water, education, credit, co-operation, and so forth. It is difficult to form an estimate of the significance of this community organization. There is a lack of detailed information, but some details may be presented.

In the state of Tamaulipas the land distribution program was delayed and did not get any effective start till 1924. In 1926 the 59 communities that had received lands held a convention, and each village

[37] When in December, 1923, the De la Huerta rebellion broke out against the Obregon administration, the *Confederación Regional Obrera* immediately stepped into the breach and placed itself at the service of the government, declaring that they accepted the challenge of the reaction with "pleasure," especially because the leading general of the rebellion had for a long time previous persecuted and killed members of the organized movement among the agriculturalists in Veracruz. *"A las Agrupaciones Obreras Confederadas del Pais," El Universal,* December 8, 1923.

[38] Saenz, Moises, and Priestley, Herbert T., *Some Mexican Problems,* p. 52.

through its elected delegates reported upon the problems, difficulties, and achievements of their special communities. We have thus a record of the organized *ejido* undertakings for one state.[39] The organizations are financed by having turned over to them 15 per cent of the crop yield from the *ejidos* and they are supposed to spend the money so gotten for the broader community needs, the purchase of machinery and animals, construction of schools, roads, and other improvements. Some of these communities have also had to use the money so accumulated to maintain their members between crops if they lacked the means of subsistence. The income of these communities was in 1926:

Maize	553,491 kls.
Sugar cane	340 tons
Cotton	72,962 kls.
Beans	43,641 kls.
Horticultural products valued at..	10,598 *pesos*
Total value was	304,278 *pesos*

Of this amount the administrative committees received 45,296 *pesos*. The recorded expenditures made by the administrative committee were as follows:

[39] *Primer Convención de la Liga de Comunidades Agrarias y Sindicatos del Estado de Tamaulipas,* 1926. This is an invaluable record of the difficulties, failures, aspirations, and achievements of the 59 villages in this state that have their *ejidos*. A large part of the book is in the form of the reports by the delegates of the different villages—and the tale they have to tell is perhaps as illuminating a picture of what is going on in contemporary Mexico, both of the good and bad, as is to be had in print.

RECEIVED AND EXPENDED BY ADMINISTRATIVE COMMITTEE, 1926

		Pesos
Receipts		45,296
Expenditures:		
Material improvements	16,736	
Purchase of implements and animals ...	12,336	
Loans	10,228	
Administration	3,231	42,531
Balance for the year		2,765
Balance from preceding year		16,671
Balance on hand		19,436

This is of course a generalized picture and some of
the villages came off very badly on account of internal difficulties or crop failures. But as a whole
the record is an interesting indication of the character and type of internal social organization that the
ejidos have brought with them. Among the material improvements are to be counted the construction
of 27 schools, so-called *escualas ejidales,* and stores
to be used for co-operative purposes. To complete
the discussion of this type of organization that is
developing in the Mexican rural community we summarize the report of one of the most successful villages among the 59 as given by the delegates to the
convention in 1926.

Condensed Report of the Delegates of the *Ejido* of
Ollama, Tamaulipas

On the 9th of August, 1924, we received provisional
possession of the *ejidos* and we gathered a regular crop.
From the 15 per cent which belonged to the administra-

tive committee there were only purchased 11 bullocks at a cost of $412.50. In May, 1925, our companion Atilano Zarala took charge as agent and suggested to the members of this *ejido* that we construct a granary in which to deposit the 15 per cent of the crop. As we did not have any funds, it was suggested that the cost be divided among the members of the *ejido*. This was approved, the granary was constructed at a cost of $400.39, which was divided among the members. In July, 1925, we collected the crop, 15 per cent of which alone produced $6,586.76, of which we put aside $3,000 for the construction of a model school for the *ejido*, bought a belt for a tractor, a disc plow for the same, 20 nail harrows, 17 cultivators, 15 planting machines, and 10 plows of the type "Universal." For the purpose of managing this machinery we sent to the agricultural school in Tamatan three young men from this *ejido* for the purpose of learning how to run the motors. These have already returned to the village. As can be seen, this benefit was solely received from 15 per cent of the spring crop. The fall crop was distributed among the members of the *ejido* of this neighborhood as a loan because they lacked the necessary seed, and for the purpose of assisting in the work of constructing the road from Estación Cruz to Villa Hidalgo. For this road the members of the *ejido* offered to complete on their own account that part which goes from Estación Cruz to Palo Alto. This work will be finished in the coming November. Among the projects which we have and which we hope to complete is the construction of a store and a credit institution. Also we have asked for an amplification of our *ejido* in order to construct a dam and thus be able to utilize the water for which we have asked. Of the crops for the present year which are now being cut we have up to date, on account of the 15 per cent, about 1,000 hectolitros of maize and expect about 400 more.

We have forgotten to add in passing that the past year we received on account of the 15 per cent about 200 *pesos* from vegetables. From the present report, which we place before this honorable assembly of delegates, it can be seen that these have been our benefits from one year of work and from the 15 per cent of our crops. Citizen delegates receive through us a strong and sincere embrace from the companions that work in the village of Ollama.[40]

Such a document is in itself an important indication of some of the forces that the revolution has set in motion.[41]

In addition to organization, there is also evident a strong educational movement in the rural community. As a part of the general constitutional mandate, all haciendas having a given number of families must establish schools.[42] This legal requirement has during the last ten years been enforced with ever greater insistence, until at present a considerable portion of the haciendas do have schools of some sort upon them.[43] In addition, each village

[40] *Primera Convención de la Liga de Communidades Agrarias y Sindicatos Campesinos del Estado de Tamaulipas,* 1926, pp. 92-94.

[41] See also *Tercera Exposición Regional, Agropecuaria Ejidal de Accionistas del Banco Agrícola Ejidal de Guanajuato, Imprenta de la Dirección de Estudios Geográficos y Climatológicos, Tacubaya,* Mexico, 1927.

[42] See Chapter IX.

[43] "When it is discovered that a school maintained by the state should be charged to the landowner he has been required to assume the obligation and the state has transferred its financial allotment for the purpose of establishing some other school." C. Lic. Enrique Colunga, *Gobernador Constitucional del Estado, Informe Guanajuato,* 1926, *Imprenta del Estado,* p. 8.

that received *ejidos* is required to set aside five hectares of land for the establishment of a school. As we have just seen, some of the villages have already complied with that requirement and actually built schools; others will with more or less regularity comply with the provision. In addition there are to be seen increased state and federal activities in the direction of rural education. The program as outlined is ample: it projects a school in each village, a central agricultural school in each agricultural zone,[44] four of which have already been opened in Guanajuato, Hidalgo, Durango, and Michoacán,[45] and a national school of agriculture for technical agricultural training. The program is under way.

It is impossible here to give more than a brief sketch of the various undertakings that the attempt to educate the Mexican rural community has called forth. The education of the Mexican people is made difficult by the great diversity of language and culture, by the lack of communication, by the great poverty of the rural community, by religious prejudice and political commotion that has been fostered as a result of the revolution, and not least by the lack of preparation and equipment on the part of the authorities who would undertake the problem. The federal educational program only began to be

[44] *Informes Rendidos por el C. Gral, Plutarco Elías Calles, Talleres Gráficos de la Nación, "Diario Oficial,"* Mexico, 1925 (1926), pp. 57-59.
[45] *ibid.*, 1926, p. 34.

developed in 1920 [46] after Obregon came into power, and has since been fostered with increasing intensity. Realizing the difficulties in the way, the government has undertaken to do what it can with the resources in hand, with poor ill-equipped one-room schools provided by the little villages, with inadequately trained teachers, and with little attention to formal pedagogical methods.[47] The educational program in Mexico is at least a triple undertaking: the work done by the counties, the work done by the states, and the work carried on by the federal government. The following data will show the progress of rural schools in Mexico during the three recent years:

Year	Schools	Teachers	Missionaries
1924	1,044	1,105	47
1925	1,926	2,382	65
1926	2,600	2,988	65

There were further initiated in 1927, 598 federal rural schools bringing the total up to 3,198 federal

[46] Saenz and Priestley, *Some Mexican Problems,* p. 64.

[47] "What kind of rural schoools we establish just now it does not matter, just so we can have schools. We are not very particular about anything. We grab a man or a woman and put them in a school if they are willing to teach it. Once he is there, we begin to ask some questions: what do you know and what are you doing; and we are trying to improve those teachers in service. We need a thousand teachers this year. Most of our teachers do not have more than a primary school education, that is, six years; some have a little more; some are normal graduates; but some of them have not even completed primary school; they have had not more than four or five years schooling." Dr. Moises Saenz, *Interviews obtained by the Alva W. Taylor Good Will Mission in the City of Mexico from July 28 to August 9, 1926,* p. 44. See also Moises Saenz, *Escuelas Federales en San Luis Potosi,* Mexico, 1928.

rural schools.[48] There were also in 1925, 4,635 rural schools maintained by the state governments.[49] If we assume that the number of rural schools did not diminish after that date, a total of 7,833 schools are now established in the rural districts, mainly in little villages of the type that we described above or located upon haciendas. There was in 1926 an enrolment of 1,049,521 students in the state and federal rural schools.[50] The total budget for education for the states amounted to approximately 40 per cent of their outgo,[51] and the federal government in 1926 appropriated 26,000,000 million *pesos* to education.[52]

But looked at from the point of view of the changes that are taking place in the rural community, the type of school being established is perhaps of even greater importance than the number of schools. It is essentially an "action" school. The rural school is socialized and as far as possible made the center of the life of the community. The school almost always has a piece of land, and there is instruction in agriculture, in the raising and care of animals, in the keeping of bees, and in raising vegetables. The teacher is expected not merely to teach the three R's, but to vaccinate the people in the community, to organize them for purposes of social activity, and in general to become the leader of the

[48] *ibid.*, p. 314.
[49] Saenz and Priestley, p. 66.
[50] *ibid.*, p. 67.
[51] *ibid.*, p. 62.
[52] *ibid.*, p. 62.

little rural community. That this is an ideal which frequently falls short of realization is recognized, but the project and the effort is bent in that direction.

In each rural village a school committee of the older and more responsible people is organized for the purpose of helping the teacher develop the program of the community. And at present an attempt is being made to utilize the crops grown by the children in the agricultural plots as a means of teaching the children organization in co-operatives, in the keeping of accounts, in the selling of their products. In fact the school aims to be an instrument for incorporating the rural community into the body of the nation.

The "Cultural Mission," sent out by the Department of Education, a sort of intensive training school for rural teachers, meets in a given village once a year for a period of three weeks. This village becomes a model with its school as a center. The rural teachers gathered in from the outlying district are put through a system of practical education in the hope that they will carry some of it back to the little village schools. These missions carry a teacher trained in rural education, a nurse, an expert agriculturist, and a teacher in physical education. This is a travelling training school that is carried to the rural districts, and it is hoped that in a period of years the regular repeated efforts will contribute to building a better personnel for rural schools.

It is clear that education for the rural community is one of the new influences that has developed in the Mexican rural community, and it is a product of the revolution.[53] It is worth noting that the education in Mexico has been influenced by the work of Professor John Dewey.[54]

An attempt is being made to organize agricultural co-operative credit institutions. Within the last few years, in connection with the new agricultural credit bank, there were established 254 of these credit institutions in four states, and representing a total membership of 25,000 people.[55]

One must not overlook the shortcomings, failures, dishonesty, bad management, and incapacity that have found a place in the attempt to reconstruct the Mexican rural community, but the result is not completely to be described in these terms. It is possible that both the significance and the probable influence of the various new forces which we have described may not prove as important as the above discussion probably assumes. It must, however, be clear that in one way or another a Mexico different from the one that existed before the revolution is being forged.

[53] Saenz and Priestley, *Some Mexican Problems,* pp. 55-84.

[54] "When John Dewey gets to Mexico he will find his ideas at work in our schools." *ibid.,* p. 78.

[55] Gómez Morin, *El Problema de Crédito Agricola en México,* Madrid, 1928.

APPENDICES

APPENDIX A

STATE AGRARIAN LEGISLATION

THE agrarian laws of the Mexican states, like the federal laws, take their origin from Article 27 of the Constitution of 1917. This article covers both the objectives to be aimed at and the methods to be employed in the process.[1] The states are to pass laws aimed at dividing the large haciendas, protecting small communities, developing individual holdings, and looking to the establishment of new centers of rural population. These general ends are to be achieved by setting limits upon the extent which any one individual or corporation may hold within the state, and by determining the time limit within which the owner must, or in the case of non-compliance the state may, forcibly expropriate and dispose of the area in excess of that established by the law. In case of state expropriation, the compensation is to be paid over a period of not less than 20 years and to carry an interest charge of not more than 5 per cent. The states are to issue agrarian bonds to cover these expropriations when authorized by the federal government. They are also to determine the character of the inalienable property which must be free from attachment and mortgage.

[1] See Chapter VIII.

It will be recalled that the attention of the federal government has been centered upon the return or grant of lands to villages, upon irrigation, colonization, and homestead legislation. These laws, broad as they are, still leave the problem of the large estates practically unsolved, for even under the irrigation and colonization laws only a small number of the properties can ultimately be affected, and that only over a long period of time. The states have more directly and immediately aimed at destroying the large properties.

I. DIVERGENCE BETWEEN STATE AND FEDERAL PROGRAMS

The state legislation differs from the federal not merely in the method of land distribution, but also in the groups of the agricultural population that are made to benefit by the laws. The federal legislation deals mainly with the community; the state legislation with the individual. The state sells the land, acting as an agent for the hacienda which is broken up, while the federal government gives the lands to the communities and indemnifies the owner with national bonds. The federal legislation has confined itself to giving each individual within the benefited community an approximately equal amount of land and one which is calculated to enable him to maintain his present standard of living. The federal government has dealt with the poorest of the rural population; in fact, a large portion of the criticism of the federal agrarian program has dealt with the inability of the poor peons to make proper use of the lands given them. The state, on the other hand, has attempted to provide an adequate area for the individual who has sufficient capital to be able to cultivate properly on his own account the land placed at his disposal.

These wide differences of policy between the state and federal programs involve a certain amount of conflict. If too much land is sold to the middle group of the agricultural population, if too many agricultural colonies are planted and developed on an individual basis, then the lands available for distribution as *ejidos* to communal groups are diminished by that much. On the other hand, if lands in excessive amount are given to communal villages and to the poorest workers, the man who has a few animals and some tools, who has shown ability to rise above poverty, is deprived of the opportunity of acquiring land sufficient for his needs. This would seriously interfere with the attempt to develop an independent and self-sufficient agricultural class,[2] a class owning small areas of tillable soil, but enough for their needs and enough to make them contented citizens of a new democracy.

Land Classification. In spite of the fact that the program for the states is clearly marked out in Article 27, the states have adopted a highly diverse body of laws. Classification of the land marks the

[2] *Fraccionamiento de Latifundios, Bases para la Ley Federal,* 1925, p. 15.

first indication of diversity in the state agrarian legislation. Ten of the eighteen states that have to date passed agrarian laws classify the lands as a basis for determining the maximum area which a single owner may hold. It is obvious that the states cannot differ so widely in the character of their soil as to make one require a system of land classification as the base for its agrarian law and another, perhaps an adjacent state, independent of any such need. The significance of this diversity is indicated by the following statement from the message of the governor of Chihuahua in submitting the agrarian law to the state legislature:

Some of the states in expressing the limits that any one individual may hold do not classify the character of the land for which a limit is set up. The result of this is to set the same limit upon the irrigated lands on the border of rivers as upon the mountain or desert lands. In the first case such a limit might consist of an intolerable *latifundia*, while in the second insufficient lands for any yield to its owner.[3]

In the first case the limit might permit a highly valuable property; in the second it might make the owner land poor—and only that.

But even where the states do have classification as a means of determining the area that any one person may hold, the types of soil defined by law are sufficiently varied to make their representative character a matter of doubt. Of the ten states that have catalogued their soil, one has two classifications, two

[3] Chihuahua: *Exposicion de Motivos, Ley Agraria*, p. 7.

three, three four, one five, and two six different
legally defined types of soil.[4]

Limits. This divergence between the states which
we noted in regard to land classification is equally
evident in the limits the different states set up for
private holding. Of the 18 states that have passed
agrarian legislation 13 set definite limitations upon
the extent that any one individual may hold. Ten
of the states, as was noted above, classify the soil and
determine the area under each classification that
may be held by one person. Chiapas, México, and
Veracruz merely set limits to the area without reference to kind.

Of the states using classification as a basis upon
which to determine the area, Chihuahua and Coahuila are the most generous in the extent they per-

---

[4] These classifications are as follows:

> Coahuila: agricultural, non-agricultural.
>
> Durango: agricultural, grazing, and forest.
>
> Sonora: irrigated, non-irrigated, and pasture.
>
> Chihuahua: irrigated, half-irrigated, dry farming, and
> pasture.
>
> Michoacán: irrigated, non-irrigated, forest, pasture, or
> mountain.
>
> Guerrero: irrigated, dry farming, mountain, anl pasture.
>
> Querétaro: irrigated, irrigated by mechanical means, dry
> farming, land capable of cultivation, and mountain.
>
> Colima: nitros lands, irrigated, non-irrigated (three classes),
> and pasture lands.
>
> Hidalgo: irrigated, half-irrigated, maguey, dry farming,
> forest, and pasture or mountain.
>
> San Luis Potosí: the state of San Luis Potosí instead of
> dividing the lands into different types divides the state
> into three zones and determines the extent that may be
> held in each zone by any one individual. San Luis
> Potosí: *Exposicion de Motivos, Ley Agraria,* Par. 2.

mit an owner to retain. Next in order are Querétaro, Durango, Sonora, San Luis Potosí, and Guerrero. The other states—Colima, Hidalgo, and Michoacán —fall far below in the area they allow. In fact, the area permitted is so small as to make the feasible operation of the law a matter of considerable doubt.

A glance at the accompanying table will show the great unevenness of the limitations set by the different states. Under irrigated lands we have Chihuahua and Guerrero setting 1,000 hectares each as against 100 by the state of Sonora. Half-irrigated lands vary from 2,000 for Chihuahua to 250 for Hidalgo, while under *temporal* we have 5,000 hectares in Durango as against 300 in Sonora.[5]

Great as these divergencies are for cultivatable lands, they are exceeded by the differences which are legalized in the various states for pasture lands. Chihuahua and Coahuila provide 40,000 and 35,000, respectively; Querétaro 12,500; Durango and Sonora 10,000 each, as against limits as low as 1,000 for Colima and 700 for Hidalgo. The large area permitted by Chihuahua (44,000 hectares) is amplified by 16 square kilometres (1,600 hectares) for the protec-

[5] "In the state of Sonora the maximum of agricultural land is from 50 to 300 hectares, according to the character of the land, while the limit in Durango is 5,000 hectares. In conformity with these laws, therefore, a *latifundia* in Durango is equal to a hundred *latifundias* in the state of Sonora. Under special conditions defined by the law the owner may have 7,500 hectares of agricultural lands in Durango, an equivalent of from 25 to 150 *latifundias* in the state of Sonora. We all know that there can be no such disproportion in the population or agricultural conditions of the states." *Fraccionamiento de Latifundios*, p. 58.

AREA, BY TYPE OF SOIL, THAT MAY BE HELD IN EACH OF TEN STATES

(IN HECTARES)

State	Nitrous	Irrigated	Half Irrigated	Non-irrigated	Pasture and Mountain	Maguey	Forest	Total
Chihuahua	....	1,000	2,000	4,000	40,000	....	No limit	44,000 [a]
Coahuila	....	....	....	2,000 [b]	35,000	....	....	35,000 [c]
Colima	200	500	....	600 to 800	1,000	....	....	1,500 [d]
Durango	....	....	....	5,000 [b]	10,000	....	20,000	20,000 [e]
Guerrero	....	1,000	....	2,000	6,000	....	....	9,000
Hidalgo	....	150	250	500	700	450	1,800	1,000 [d]
Michoacán	....	600	....	1,200	3,600	....	....	...... [e]
Querétaro	....	250	1,000 [f]	2,000 [g]	12,500	....	....	12,500 [e]
San Luis Potosí	....	100	....	2,000 to 4,000	....	....	....	9,000 [h]
Sonora	....	50	....	300	10,000	....	....	10,400

[a] Plus the 16 square kilometers surrounding the "Casco de la Hacienda."

[b] Classed as agricultural in law and included here under non-irrigated as that is the most common type of agricultural land.

[c] Apparently an owner may hold the maximum of one but not of all classes of land.

[d] In Colima and Hidalgo the owner may hold all classifications if their total does not exceed the given limit.

[e] In the case of Michoacán the total cannot be given as the law does not indicate whether one owner may hold the full limit of each class.

[f] Distinguished from irrigated land by definition as land irrigated by mechanical means.

[g] Land that can be cultivated but is not cultivated at present, 2,500 hectares.

[h] Total of land that can be held by one owner in the three zones of the state.

tion of the abode of the hacienda and the surrounding living quarters of the people employed on the place, the so-called *ejidos de la hacienda*. In justifying such a large tract the governor, in his message placing the law before the state legislature, explains that the law is so framed because of the great extent of the state, the small population, the aridity of so much of the area, and also because enough land must be provided for the development of initiative and energy of individuals who have capital to invest.[6] These reasons may also serve to explain the large area allowed in the neighboring state of Coahuila. In the case of Chihuahua it is important to note that forest lands are specifically exempted from the operations of the law, except as they may be available for grazing or agricultural purposes. Again, the reason given is that small-scale utilization of forest lands is made impossible by the large capital investment which this industry demands.

Before turning to a discussion of the states that establish no system of classification for determining area, we must note that the state of San Luis Potosí, which is included in the table above, falls into a class by itself. The law divides the state into three distinct sections. "The western arid and dry region, where cattle raising and fibres constitute the principal use, and where agriculture is reduced to a highly speculative undertaking; the central regions, typical of dry farming, with good lands, but without

[6] *Exposicion de Motivos,* pp. 8, 15.

irrigation, and therefore insecure crops; the eastern region, whose fertility is famous in the Republic, with certain crops and with natural resources that make it one of the richest spots on the Mexican soil." The owner may retain 4,000 hectares in the western part of the state, 3,000 in the central, and 2,000 in the eastern part,[7] and one owner may hold the full limit for each region, provided the lands are not contiguous.[8]

If we turn now to the three states that set up a limited area for individual ownership, but provide no system of classification, we find an equally great lack of uniformity in the extent permitted. Chiapas sets a limit of 8,000 hectares without distinction as to type. Far below in the scale come México and Veracruz with 600 and 200 hectares, respectively. These limits are obviously very low, and the law cannot be enforced literally, at least not for the state of Veracruz, where there are very large properties. That such is the case seems to be implied in the very law itself. It sets no time limit within which the owner must divide the area in his possession in conformity with the law. "The actual owners of the estates may continue in the possession of the lands marked out by their titles until such time as the state needs them for purposes of public utility."

All of the states provide that the properties shall continue in the hands of their present owners until

[7] San Luis Potosí: *Ley Agraria*, Art. II.
[8] San Luis Potosí: *Reglamento de la Ley Agraria,* Art. II.

such time as the state takes expropriation proceedings against them, and give the proprietors from six months to two years to comply voluntarily with the law. In addition, the laws call for a given number of competent purchasers before authorizing condemnation proceedings.

Apart from time and available purchasers as factors limiting the immediate applicability of the laws, there are positive encouragements to the owners to secure the right to retain an area larger than that stipulated by the law. The state of Durango offers any proprietor an opportunity to retain double the amount of land stipulated by law for all but the first type, that is, an additional 2,500 hectares of agricultural lands, 5,000 of mixed, 10,000 of grazing, and 20,000 of forest lands, providing he puts them to full use.[9]

In Veracruz those properties which need more land than is allowed by the law can retain it, and the law sets no limit upon the same,[10] while in Guerrero any owner showing that he has more livestock than the amount of pasture-land allowed can support, may secure such additional lands as he needs.[11]

Six of the states under consideration provide that any owner converting his grazing into agricultural land, or these latter into irrigated, may retain in their new form the larger original size.

Lands held by communal groups, except in the

[9] Durango: *Ley Agraria,* Arts. 2 and 3.
[10] Veracruz: *Ley Agraria,* Art. 3.
[11] Guerrero: *Ley Agraria,* Art. 14.

state of San Luis Potosí, are generally exempted from the legal limitations upon area prescribed for individually-owned properties.[12] This exemption, however, does not include properties acquired by the state; they are subdivided and sold to small holders. Exempted from the application of the law are reservoirs and essential canals for irrigation.

The discussion has so far been limited to the states that have established legal limits to the amount of land that any one individual may hold within the confines of their respective boundaries. We have seen that some of the states make classification of the soil a basis for determining the area that may be held, while others merely indicate the limited areas prescribed by law without regard to the type of soil. These definite limitations are further subject to considerable modification and extension by various provisions of the laws. It might perhaps be repeated here that altogether only 13 states have established the limitations discussed above, and that more than half of the individual states—that is, 15—have set no limit upon the area which any one individual may hold. We turn now to a discussion of another feature of the state agrarian laws—the attempt to protect the small agricultural community.

II. PROTECTING THE RURAL COMMUNITY

The freeing of the rural community from the dominance of the large hacienda has repeatedly been

[12] San Luis Potosí: *Reglamento de la Ley Agraria*, Art. 1.

described in the writings and speeches of the Mexican revolutionists as one of the main objectives of the revolution. When one turns, however, to an examination of the concrete legislation which has been developed by the states for carrying these oft-expressed purposes into effect, one is struck by the paucity of the results. It is true that all but four of the eighteen states that have legislation on agrarian matters make some mention of the rural community, but this mention in most cases carries a very narrow margin of benefit.

Of the eighteen states, six attempt to protect the small community by surrounding it with an area within which the size of the holdings will be limited. Of these, México alone has only one type of community. The others provide for three different classes of communities. The community for which protection is provided by the state of México is one having a population of 1,000 and over, and a surrounding area of four square kilometres is set apart for these communities. Single holdings within these areas are limited to 3,000 hectares. This is a state constitutional provision, and is made operative through forced division among heirs for properties above the given area.[13] The other states provide for three classes of communities, according to their size, and mark a different radius for each one. The table on page 443 indicates the size of the community and the protective zone in each of six states.

This table is in some degree misleading. It gives

[13] Mexico: *Constitucion del Estado,* Art. CXCVII.

the impression of a similiarity that does not exist. Five of the six states—Colima, Hidalgo, San Luis Potosí, México, and Zacatecas—include all inhabited places under the range of their laws, while Querétaro merely covers villages, not haciendas. Another important difference to be noted is the lower limit set by the different states: Colima, 200; San Luis Potosí, 600; Zacatecas, 500; México, 1,000. For these states, therefore, all communities below the given figure, whether villages or haciendas, are exempt from the law. Hidalgo and Querétaro, however, set no lower limit.

III. SIZE OF LOTS SOLD

When it comes to determining the amount of land that any one purchaser may acquire, there is consid-

AREA WHICH ONE PURCHASER MAY ACQUIRE
(In Hectares)

State	Irrigated	Non-irrigated	Pasture
Aguascalientes [a]	5–10	. . . .	. . . .
Coahuila	25–50	50–100	100–1,000
Chihuahua [b]	4–20	16–40	. . . .
Guerrero	10–20	. . . .	60
Michoacán [c]	50–75	. . . .	500–600
Querétaro [d]	. . . .	10–50	. . . .
San Luis Potosí [e]	10–150	. . . .	. . . .
Veracruz	1–50	. . . .	. . . .
Zacatecas [f]	. . . .	7–50	50–500

[a] All heads of families in communities of over 75 inhabitants are entitled to from 5 to 10 hectares.
[b] For colonies only.
[c] Apart from the provision for communities of 200 inhabitants, in which case the limits are the same as in Aguascalientes.
[d] In the protected community zones.
[e] Only in the protected zones and depending upon the part of the state.
[f] The original owner may retain 2,000 hectares, providing he makes available a similar area in the immediate neighborhood.

erable difference between the states. A table will best indicate the area allowed to individual purchasers. With the exception of San Luis Potosí and Zacatecas, the laws deny the rights of ownership in the zone of subdivision to people who have property in other parts of the state. The case of Zacatecas is exceptional in that it allows as much. as 2,000 hectares within the zone,[14] providing the owner makes available a similar property within the immediate neighborhood.

The purchasers are in all states placed under sharp limitation as to the obligations that the purchase of the property places upon them. The first emphasis is upon cultivation of the purchased lots. Irrigated land, or land already under cultivation, must be cultivated in full during the first year.[15] If the lands are agricultural, but were not under cultivation at the time the property was broken up, then the new purchaser must place at least 50 per cent under cultivation during the first year. Pasture lands denounced as agricultural and broken up as such must be placed under cultivation at the rate of 20 per cent of the area every year for five years. Grazing lands must have on them in Sonora at least fifteen head of livestock (ganado mayor) or thirty of sheep and hogs (ganado menor); and in Hidalgo in proportion to the area of the land. In Zacatecas the new purchaser must cultivate at least three hectares during the first

[14] Zacatecas: Ley Agraria, Art. 51.
[15] Sonora: Ley Agraria, Art. 34; Hidalgo: Ley Agraria, Art. 49; similar citations could be drawn from the other states.

PROTECTIVE ZONE PROVIDED FOR COMMUNITIES WITH GIVEN POPULATION IN EACH OF SIX STATES

State	Population of Community	Zone in Square Kilometers	Population of Community	Zone in Square Kilometers	Population of Community	Zone in Square Kilometers
Colima.........	200–500	5	1,000–5,000	10	over 5,000	20
Hidalgo........	less than 500	2	500–5,000	6	over 5,000	8
México.........	1,000 or more	4	......	......	......	......
Querétaro a....	less than 1,000	10	1,000–5,000	10	over 5,000	10
San Luis Potosí b	600–1,000	6–10	1,000–5,000	9–15	over 5,000	12–20
Zacatecas......	500–1,000	8	1,000–5,000	16	over 5,000	25

a Querétaro retains the same zone for all communities, but varies in size the lots that may be purchased and held in the neighborhood of the different communities.
b San Luis Potosí has different areas for different sections of the state.

five years.[16]   He must also work his lands himself.[17] He must, of course, cover his yearly payment. A violation of these requirements leads to dispossession and loss of the title.   During the period of payment for the lot—a period of twenty years—the owner can make no transfer of the property, give no mortgage, nor in any way place the property under lien. This general rule is not followed by the states of Colima [18] and Chihuahua,[19] where transfer is possible with consent of owner and acceptance of full responsibility by new purchaser. A violation of these provisions leads to dispossession.

There is but one other feature to be noted in the discussion of the state agrarian legislation; that is the provision for the family patrimony, the so-called *Ley de Patrimonio,* which is provided for in the Federal Constitution, and which is to be inalienable under any and all circumstances.   Under the legislation reviewed, only five of the states have made provision for this inalienable family property.   The state of Chihuahua makes the parcels purchased by the colonists subject to this regulation.[20]   Michoacán [21] and Aguascalientes [22] provide that the parcels

[16] Zacatecas: *Ley Agraria,* Art. 38.
[17] Sonora: *Ley Agraria,* Art. 34.
[18] Colima: *Ley Agraria para el Fraccionamiento de Latifundios,* Art. 9.
[19] Chihuahua: *Ley Agraria,* Art. 30.
[20] Chihuahua: *Ley Agraria,* Art. 65.
[21] Michoacán: *Decreto Numero* 47, March 4, 1919.
[22] Aguascalientes: *Ley Reglamentaria del Decreto Numero 31,* Art. 67.

of land conceded to the villagers are inalienable under any and all conditions even after the full payment upon it has been made. Querétaro [23] and San Luis Potosí [24] bring one-half of the area purchased in the zone of subdivision under this heading.

IV. GENERAL PROVISIONS

In spite of the great divergence in the character of the legislation passed by the several states, there is unexpected uniformity in the procedure developed for its enforcement. All of the states that set up limits to the amount of land an individual may retain concede the present owner the right of choice to the part of the property he wishes to retain. They all allow a time limit for such choice, ranging from six months to two years. Those states that set up classifications of soil as a means of determining the area an individual may hold enable the owner to choose within the different types of soil what he would prefer to retain. A typical illustration of this is the law of Chihuahua. A hectare of irrigated land is valued as equal to two of half-irrigated and four of non-irrigated. The proprietor may, if he so desires, retain for each hectare of irrigated, two of the first and four of the second.

The owner may, within the time allowed by the law, divide his own property. This is in accordance with the provision of the Federal Constitution. [25]

[23] Querétaro: *Ley Agraria,* Art. 45.
[24] San Luis Potosí: *Ley Agraria,* Art. 35.
[25] See p. 526.

In providing for voluntary division, the states develop different systems of evaluation. Under the federal provisions governing expropriation proceedings carried through by the states under the mandate for breaking up the large properties, the value is set at tax value plus 10 per cent, with a provision that improvements made since the last valuation shall be taken into account.[26] But when it comes to voluntary compliance with the law, no such general rule exists. Three of the states—Colima, Sonora, and Chiapas—make no mention of the valuation for the purpose of voluntary division. Six of the states provide for free agreement upon both value and payment between the seller and purchaser. There is, however, a curious limitation of this freedom in the state of Zacatecas. "Those lots that remain unsold are to be reduced in price every thirty days so that at the end of nine months their value should not be greater than the assessed value plus thirty per cent."[27]

In carrying out forced expropriation there is a general resort to a broad and comprehensive use of the concept of "public utility." In fact, it may be described as the basic legal instrument for the enforcement of the agrarian legislation. It enables the legislator to stay within the province of legal procedure without too great a restriction upon his program. "Public utility" is used as a legal instru-

[26] See p. 524.
[27] Zacatecas: *Ley Agraria* 1919, Art. 12.

ment and made to apply not merely for the purpose of breaking up the large estates, the regulation of water, the establishment of roads, but is used for other and less obvious ends. In the attempt to carry through the program of breaking up the haciendas and to overcome the difficulties presented by mortgages, debts, and liens, the laws of the states bring these financial encumbrances under "public utility" and set up provisions for the division of mortgages, the reduction of interest, and the suspension of payments during the periods of subdivision.

The laws provide that not only the owner but the mortgagee must accept bonds in payment for his property, or loan-bonds redeemable over a period of twenty years with a limited interest of 5 per cent. The mortgage must be adjusted to the parcels broken up, the interest reduced, and payments spread over twenty years. The state generally makes itself responsible for the actual delivery of the cash to redeem the bonds, and acts as an agent for the owner and the purchaser. The refusal to accept the money for a period of three years places the owner of the property in a position of having presented the sum involved to the state as a voluntary gift.[28] The owner, if he does not comply with the provisions for voluntary subdivision, continues in full possession of his property. The state only undertakes to apply the law when there is a sufficient number of

[28] Chiapas: *Ley Agraria,* Art. 14; Hidalgo: *Ley Agraria,* Art. 29; Durango: *Ley Agraria,* Art. 16.

demands for land. This number must generally be ten, although in the case of Querétaro it may be as low as three. In Sonora, if there are less than ten, they must desire to purchase in total at least fifty hectares. The state then initiates expropriation proceedings for the necessary land after giving notice to the owner and allowing him a specified time to select from his property the part he wishes to retain. The notice of the proceedings is given publicity through publication in the official periodical of the state, through public notice on the walls of the *municipios,* and in some instances through notice in the newspapers. The amount of land taken is only sufficient to cover the needs of the actual applicants.

The water goes with the land purchased, and its use is adjusted by the state. All purchasers of land are entitled to access to the water in the immediate neighborhood whether that water comes from natural springs or from reservoirs.[29]

The states set up a body of qualifications for the would-be purchasers. There is general uniformity in these standards, which illustrates the difference already mentioned between the legislation of the states and that of the federal government. The federal government tends to bring need to the front as the point of major consideration. The would-be purchaser must be 18 years of age or over, or a widow with children to support. He must be a Mexican citizen or, if a foreigner, one who has complied with

[29] Chihuahua: *Ley Agraria,* Art. 37.

the constitutional requirements determining the rights of foreigners to landholding. He must be of good character and possess the means for cultivating the soil which he is purchasing. Here there appears some divergence between the state laws. In Sonora [30] he must have at least 15 head of livestock or 30 of sheep and hogs, or show ability to purchase them. In Zacatecas he must demonstrate that he can cultivate at least three hectares of land,[31] or that he has ten head of livestock or 20 of sheep and hogs. But such specifications are not universal. Preference is given to those who are renters on the property, or croppers, or who under the law of "idle lands" are occupying the property, or neighbors living near the property.[32] Typical is also the preference of those who have served in the army, or widows of soldiers, or people who in some other fashion have served the state. The first who apply are, in equal circumstances, to have the choice of land, and in case of equal right the drawing of lots is to decide the one who is to be given the preference.

If we survey the legislation provided by the different states for the purpose of complying with the agrarian program of the revolution, we are impressed first by its great diversity, and second by its comparative ineffectiveness. Only 13 states provide for limitation of holdings; only eight for the protection

[30] Sonora: *Ley Agraria,* Art. 31.
[31] Zacatecas: *Ley Agraria,* Art. 34.
[32] Chihuahua: *Ley Agraria,* Art. 51.

of the community in any but the most general way. Fifteen states make available land for purchasers, but this is done under very diverse conditions as to the area allowed. The state legislation has to date made but little impression upon Mexico's legal system of landholding.

Limited in scope as is the legislation, it has been in a large measure unenforced. Only a very few of the states have made the state laws effective instruments either in breaking up large estates or in providing lands for individual purchasers. In most of the states the laws have remained, for one reason or another, without any effect whatsoever.

APPENDIX B

POPULATION STATISTICS

The population statistics presented in Chapters II and XIV are based upon the two most recent censuses of the Mexican Republic—those of 1910 and 1921, respectively.[1] These censuses classify the Mexican population under some one hundred different types of communities. For the sake of obtaining a clear picture of the rural population by type of community, it was necessary to re-group these figures. This was done by combining the different types of community given in such a way as to show the population resident upon haciendas, in agricultural villages, and in rural industrial villages. This undertaking was facilitated by the fact that the greater part of the rural population is found residing in communities under comparatively few census classifications, leaving the large majority of

[1] *Secretaria de Fomento, Colonizacion e Industria: Division Territorial de los Estados Unidos Mexicanos. Correspondiente al Censo de 1910*, 31 volumes. These volumes, one for each state of federal territory, appeared irregularly and under slightly differing titles between 1910 and 1918: *Censo General de Habitantes*, November 30, 1921. Of this last census there still remain (June, 1928) unpublished the census records for the states of *San Luis Potosí, Tamaulipas, Veracruz, Yucatán,* and *Zacatecas.* For these states, as well as for six others, the data presented were compiled from the original sheets.

the types given in the census with few inhabitants. The inhabited places having the larger populations generally go under the names of *pueblo, ranchería, congregación, villa, communidad, hacienda, rancho, mineral, barrio,* and so forth.

For the tables showing the distribution of the population between haciendas, villages, and all other communities (mainly mining communities) all inhabited places that are of the hacienda type (*hacienda, rancho, labor, finca, campo-agricola,* and so forth) were grouped together under the general heading of "haciendas," while the agricultural villages, regardless of name, were classed under "agricultural villages"; and the mining and other non-agricultural rural communities were classed as "all other communities." [2]

In the distribution of the rural population of 1921 by type and size of community (see Appendix B, pp. 456-465), it was found mechanically more feasible to make two instead of three groupings, combining the haciendas and ranchos, and leaving the others of this type, as well as the non-agricultural communities, to go into a general classification with the agricultural villages as "all other communities." [3] That means that we have somewhat understated the number of people living upon the hacienda type of

[2] The word hacienda as used in the tables based on the 1910 census, therefore, covers all of the rural population of Mexico except those living in villages.

[3] The expression "haciendas and ranchos" as used in tables, pp. 456-459 and 460-465, based on the 1921 census, covers only the population which the census classifies under these two heads.

community in 1921 as shown in the table on pp. 460-465, for ranchos and haciendas. But the percentage of difference is very small, as may be seen by comparing the total population on haciendas and ranchos, as shown in this table, which is 3,837,820, with the total shown under haciendas, 1921, in the table on pp. 466-473, 3,913,766 (compare note *, pp. 464-465).

All this re-grouping was done at the Institute of Economics. Copies of the basic tables are on file in the library of the Institute, and may be consulted by interested students.

I. All Communities in the Several States

STATE	Under 10	10 to 20	20 to 30	30 to 40	40 to 50	50 to 75	75 to 100	100 to 200	200 to 300	300 to 400
					Rural Communities, with Specified					
Aguascalientes............	45	39	48	42	31	57	39	67	26	16
Baja California										
{ Del Sur...............	353	291	79	32	13	19	10	13	8	5
{ Del Norte..............	123	74	29	20	8	20	24	24	4	2
Campeche	102	95	45	31	22	30	25	34	10	10
Chihuahua................	420	402	248	160	108	209	141	305	145	59
Chiapas..................	805	728	448	271	249	381	244	442	132	75
Coahuila.................	158	185	130	99	67	143	106	205	87	44
Colima...................	14	28	25	25	29	52	46	58	30	20
Durango..................	221	240	152	91	77	151	107	286	143	63
Guanajuato...............	170	267	257	241	272	524	359	881	393	183
Guerrero.................	78	97	87	73	81	158	142	481	249	153
Hidalgo..................	147	188	157	116	91	252	197	510	271	164
Jalisco..................	833	1,032	857	633	506	946	533	971	323	143
México...................	110	116	77	70	60	144	118	363	227	173
Michoacán................	587	689	478	359	275	499	362	806	334	183
Morelos..................	2	7	6	7	6	13	14	52	28	20
Nayarit..................	62	68	41	36	35	57	49	89	44	26
Nuevo León...............	767	595	276	205	136	209	113	243	65	50
Oaxaca...................	132	118	76	88	80	149	144	394	267	164
Puebla...................	50	63	62	45	47	98	108	310	282	192
Querétaro................	34	47	68	43	55	107	72	205	104	46
San Luis Potosí..........	78	127	112	95	93	181	151	331	188	99
Sinaloa..................	318	352	247	161	127	242	169	321	164	68
Sonora...................	498	439	233	148	84	123	97	172	64	39
Tabasco..................	493	492	254	159	101	144	72	131	52	33
Tamaulipas...............	469	631	325	223	139	210	112	167	55	29
Tlaxcala.................	27	34	27	13	12	31	25	65	59	23
Veracruz.................	201	331	261	208	169	337	257	590	311	223
Yucatán..................	459	274	128	80	74	99	70	154	61	38
Zacatecas................	186	249	188	151	137	227	154	378	150	84
Quintana Roo.............	25	15	8	4	4	8	1	9	2	1
Distrito Federal..........	9	22	10	6	6	10	19	32	16	23
Total.................	7,976	8,335	5,439	3,935	3,194	5,830	4,080	9,089	4,294	2,451

* Data from Federal Census of 1921. There appear in the census 766 additional communities listed as

CLASSIFIED BY NUMBER OF INHABITANTS, 1921*

| Number of Inhabitants | | | | | | Urban Communities, with Specified Number of Inhabitants | | | | | | All Communities |
400 to 500	'500 to 1,000	1,000 to 2,000'	2,000 to 3,000	3,000 to 4,000	Total 4,000 or Under	4,000 to 5,000	5,000 to 10,000	10,000 to 20,000	20,000 to 30,000	30,000 or Over	Total Urban	
9	15	3	3	..	440	..	..	..	..	1	1	441
3	6	5	..	1	838	..	1	..	..	..	1	839
3	1	1	1	..	334	..	1	..	..	..	1	335
6	9	7	2	1	429	1	1	1	..	..	3	432
50	89	34	10	4	2,384	..	3	2	..	1	6	2,390
36	90	31	8	2	3,942	4	3	2	..	..	9	3,951
32	59	25	8	4	1,352	3	4	3	..	2	12	1,364
7	7	6	6	..	353	..	..	..	1	..	1	354
42	82	25	4	4	1,688	..	1	..	1	1	3	1,691
89	141	32	10	5	3,824	4	11	5	2	1	23	3,847
80	171	63	21	3	1,937	3	4	1	..	..	8	1,945
107	201	57	16	2	2,476	2	1	1	..	1	5	2,481
86	161	84	30	14	7,152	13	13	5	..	1	32	7,184
105	282	163	42	10	2,060	5	5	1	..	1	12	2,072
101	177	78	36	8	4,972	6	12	3	..	1	22	4,994
9	34	17	5	1	221	1	1	..	..	..	2	223
16	28	13	4	1	569	1	4	1	..	..	6	575
22	49	26	4	4	2,764	1	2	..	..	1	4	2,768
129	356	145	36	15	2,293	7	7	1	1	..	16	2,309
126	334	163	36	14	1,930	6	6	..	..	1	13	1,943
29	54	18	4	2	888	..	1	..	..	1	2	890
66	105	34	11	4	1,675	..	4	1	..	1	6	1,681
43	69	23	4	4	2,312	..	3	1	1	..	5	2,317
27	58	25	7	4	2,018	3	3	2	..	..	8	2,026
26	62	23	6	2	2,050	1	..	1	..	..	2	2,052
9	21	22	3	2	2,417	..	3	3	..	1	7	2,424
27	50	28	8	3	432	1	4	..	..	..	5	437
145	311	129	21	6	3,500	5	16	1	1	2	25	3,525
23	51	41	12	4	1,568	7	2	..	..	1	10	1,578
59	90	30	9	8	2,100	1	2	1	..	..	4	2,104
1	..	2	..	..	80	..	..	..	..	..	..	80
13	34	29	9	4	242	..	4	6	..	2	12	254
1,526	3,197	1,382	376	136	61,240	75	122	42	7	20	266	61,506

without inhabitants.

II. Hacienda and Rancho Communities in the

STATE	Under 10	10 to 20	20 to 30	30 to 40	40 to 50	50 to 75	75 to 100
Aguascalientes.......	41	38	46	38	29	54	37
Baja California:							
{ Del Sur.........	352	289	78	30	12	17	7
{ Del Norte........	86	42	10	5	1	4	3
Campeche..........	96	84	38	27	18	20	22
Chihuahua..........	279	317	194	132	90	180	119
Chiapas.............	784	697	402	223	195	294	173
Coahuila............	156	175	120	87	57	133	97
Colima.............	13	21	22	23	25	41	39
Durango............	199	209	135	81	69	134	96
Guanajuato.........	166	256	247	234	267	517	355
Guerrero............	77	90	75	59	59	83	60
Hidalgo.............	101	137	106	66	46	118	79
Jalisco..............	816	1,009	833	617	485	913	512
México..............	101	103	55	53	40	80	57
Michoacán.........	584	681	474	352	269	497	355
Morelos.............	...	3	...	3	1	3	7
Nayarit.............	58	65	39	35	35	54	48
Nuevo León.........	749	583	259	184	126	188	92
Oaxaca.............	98	67	44	58	47	86	89
Puebla.............	44	56	55	36	29	72	69
Querétaro..........	32	46	64	43	54	102	72
San Luis Potosí......	73	121	109	91	92	169	138
Sinaloa[a].............	315	345	242	159	124	232	160
Sonora.............	412	379	188	120	64	75	64
Tabasco............	491	485	246	155	94	127	68
Tamaulipas.........	450	618	318	217	137	206	103
Tlaxcala............	27	33	25	13	12	26	21
Veracruz............	168	249	178	129	88	173	91
Yucatán............	362	233	108	68	65	87	58
Zacatecas...........	181	248	183	144	133	220	152
Quintana Roo.......	20	7	4	3	3	5	1
Distrito Federal.....	7	18	6	2	4	7	11
Total.............	7,338	7,704	4,903	3,487	2,770	4,917	3,255

* Data from Federal Census of 1921.

a One community of 6,649 inhabitants, reported as a hacienda, is omitted because

SEVERAL STATES CLASSIFIED BY NUMBER OF INHABITANTS, 1921*

100 to 200	200 to 300	300 to 400	400 to 500	500 to 1000	1000 to 2000	2000 to 3000	3000 to 4000	Total
57	22	10	4	10	...	...	...	386
8	2	2	...	...	...	...	...	797
2	1	...	...	...	...	...	...	154
17	5	4	2	1	...	...	...	334
243	100	35	15	15	1	...	...	1,720
298	74	32	18	17	...	...	...	3,207
185	68	39	26	36	8	1	...	1,188
44	21	11	2	6	...	...	...	268
225	108	41	29	34	1	1	...	1,362
865	373	163	73	101	8	...	...	3,625
146	55	28	9	14	6	1	...	762
155	62	31	20	18	1	...	...	940
895	260	104	49	73	16	...	...	6,582
135	60	30	16	27	9	...	...	766
778	311	157	73	93	15	1	...	4,640
6	4	1	...	...	...	...	...	28
82	32	21	8	10	1	1	...	489
198	41	30	12	14	2	...	...	2,477
144	65	25	13	15	4	1	...	756
136	75	39	18	14	1	...	...	644
187	92	39	17	35	2	...	...	785
283	158	82	43	68	13	1	...	1,441
287	134	47	27	31	5	1	...	2,109
82	23	3	5	4	...	...	...	1,419
101	25	3	...	4	...	...	...	1,800
154	40	21	4	7	1	...	...	2,276
46	37	9	9	3	...	...	...	261
112	25	8	6	6	1	...	...	1,234
117	43	19	8	6	...	...	...	1,174
370	143	74	54	69	10	...	...	1,981
2	...	...	...	...	...	...	...	45
13	1	5	2	1	...	...	...	77
6,373	2,460	1,113	562	732	105	8	0	45,727

communities of over 4,000 are defined by the Census as urban.

III. ALL RURAL COMMUNITIES OTHER THAN HACIENDAS AND RANCHOS IN

STATE	Under 10	10 to 20	20 to 30	30 to 40	40 to 50	50 to 75	75 to 100
Aguascalientes........	4	1	2	4	2	3	2
Baja California:							
{ Del Sur..........	1	2	1	2	1	2	3
{ Del Norte........	37	32	19	15	7	16	21
Campeche...........	6	11	7	4	4	10	3
Chihuahua..........	141	85	54	28	18	29	22
Chiapas............	21	31	46	48	54	87	71
Coahuila............	2	10	10	12	10	10	9
Colima.............	1	7	3	2	4	11	7
Durango............	22	31	17	10	8	17	11
Guanajuato.........	4	11	10	7	5	7	4
Guerrero............	1	7	12	14	22	75	82
Hidalgo.............	46	51	51	50	45	134	118
Jalisco.............	17	23	24	16	21	33	21
México.............	9	13	22	17	20	64	61
Michoacán..........	3	8	4	7	6	2	7
Morelos.............	2	4	6	4	5	10	7
Nayarit.............	4	3	2	1	...	3	1
Nuevo León.........	18	12	17	21	10	21	21
Oaxaca.............	34	51	32	30	33	63	55
Puebla.............	6	7	7	9	18	26	39
Querétaro...........	2	1	4	...	1	5	...
San Luis Potosí......	5	6	3	4	1	12	13
Sinaloa.............	3	7	5	2	3	10	9
Sonora.............	86	60	45	28	20	48	33
Tabasco............	2	7	8	4	7	17	4
Tamaulipas.........	19	13	7	6	2	4	9
Tlaxcala............	...	1	2	...	...	5	4
Veracruz............	33	82	83	79	81	164	166
Yucatán............	97	41	20	12	9	12	12
Zacatecas...........	5	1	5	7	4	7	2
Quintana Roo........	5	8	4	1	1	3	...
Distrito Federal......	2	4	4	4	2	3	8
Total.............	638	631	536	448	424	913	825

* Data from Federal Census of 1921.

THE SEVERAL STATES CLASSIFIED BY NUMBER OF INHABITANTS, 1921*

100 to 200	200 to 300	300 to 400	400 to 500	500 to 1000	1000 to 2000	2000 to 3000	3000 to 4000	Total
10	4	6	5	5	3	3	...	54
5	6	3	3	6	5	...	1	41
22	3	2	3	1	1	1	...	180
17	5	6	4	8	7	2	1	95
62	45	24	35	74	33	10	4	664
144	58	43	18	73	31	8	2	735
20	19	5	6	23	17	7	4	164
14	9	9	5	1	6	6	...	85
61	35	22	13	48	24	3	4	326
16	20	20	16	40	24	10	5	199
335	194	125	71	157	57	20	3	1,175
355	209	133	87	183	56	16	2	1,536
76	63	39	37	88	68	30	14	570
228	167	143	89	255	154	42	10	1,294
28	23	26	28	84	63	35	8	332
46	24	19	9	34	17	5	1	193
7	12	5	8	18	12	3	1	80
45	24	20	10	35	24	4	4	287
250	202	139	116	341	141	35	15	1,537
174	207	153	108	320	162	36	14	1,286
18	12	7	12	19	16	4	2	103
48	30	17	23	37	21	10	4	234
34	30	21	16	38	18	3	4	203
90	41	36	22	54	25	7	4	599
30	27	30	26	58	23	6	2	250
13	15	8	5	14	21	3	2	141
19	22	14	18	47	28	8	3	171
478	286	215	139	305	128	21	6	2,266
37	18	19	15	45	41	12	4	394
8	7	10	5	21	20	9	8	119
7	2	1	1	...	2	...	...	35
19	15	18	11	33	29	9	4	165
2,716	1,834	1,338	964	2,465	1,277	368	136	15,513

IV. Rural Population by State, and by

Classification	Total Population	Less Than 10	10 to 20	20 to 30	30 to 40	40 to 50
Aguascalientes, total............	60,620	241	579	1,153	1,440	1,390
On ranchos and haciendas.......	37,153	226	560	1,103	1,297	1,305
In all other communities........	23,467	15	19	50	143	85
Baja California, del Norte, total...	16,755	677	1,021	697	677	349
On ranchos and haciendas......	2,566	468	575	240	137	84
In all other communities........	14,189	209	446	457	540	265
Baja California, del Sur, total.....	31,904	2,145	3,830	1,884	1,062	562
On ranchos and haciendas.......	13,359	2,131	3,800	1,861	988	518
In all other communities........	18,545	14	30	23	74	44
Campeche, total............	47,925	550	1,309	1,055	1,052	951
On ranchos and haciendas.......	13,918	509	1,134	884	919	780
In all other communities........	34,007	41	175	171	133	171
Chihuahua, total..............	306,102	2,392	5,735	6,157	5,499	4,805
On ranchos and haciendas.......	127,947	1,629	4,615	4,649	4,531	4,094
In all other communities........	178,155	763	1,120	1,508	968	711
Chiapas, total..................	352,802	4,785	10,203	10,899	9,253	11,018
On ranchos and haciendas.......	163,020	4,646	9,587	9,731	7,580	9,086
In all other communities........	189,782	139	616	1,168	1,673	1,932
Coahuila, total.................	219,324	967	2,616	3,193	3,407	2,942
On ranchos and haciendas.......	133,072	955	2,447	3,003	2,987	2,456
In all other communities........	86,252	12	169	190	420	486
Colima, total..................	63,423	87	403	577	849	1,283
On ranchos and haciendas......	28,490	80	306	504	772	1,104
In all other communities........	34,933	7	97	73	77	179
Durango, total..................	265,686	1,363	3,326	3,666	3,106	3,399
On ranchos and haciendas.......	141,244	1,219	2,882	3,265	2,754	3,054
In all other communities........	124,442	144	444	401	352	345
Guanajuato, total...............	600,914	1,042	3,856	6,305	8,234	12,069
On ranchos and haciendas.......	475,023	1,012	3,687	6,069	7,964	11,851
In all other communities........	125,891	30	169	236	270	218
Guerrero, total.................	515,721	412	1,338	2,114	2,561	3,538
On ranchos and haciendas.......	86,355	405	1,227	1,825	2,054	2,558
In all other communities........	429,366	7	111	289	507	980
Hidalgo, total...................	552,762	793	2,674	3,761	3,664	4,097
On ranchos and haciendas.......	92,282	565	2,003	2,473	1,876	1,991
In all other communities........	460,480	228	671	1,288	1,788	2,106
Jalisco, total...................	843,666	4,954	14,681	22,720	21,560	22,473
On ranchos and haciendas.......	502,077	4,856	14,443	22,166	20,981	21,543
In all other communities........	341,589	98	238	554	579	930
México, total...................	782,525	575	1,600	1,903	2,419	2,695
On ranchos and haciendas.......	95,198	536	1,399	1,392	1,870	1,768
In all other communities........	687,327	39	201	511	549	927
Michoacán, total................	756,685	3,489	9,807	11,497	12,289	12,261
On ranchos and haciendas.......	466,301	3,478	9,734	11,401	12,080	12,037
In all other communities........	290,384	11	73	96	209	224

TYPE AND SIZE OF COMMUNITY, 1921*

50 to 75	75 to 100	100 to 200	200 to 300	300 to 400	400 to 500	500 to 1,000	1,000 to 2,000	2,000 to 3,000	3,000 to 4,000
4,621	3,333	9,611	6,039	5,636	3,935	10,491	4,154	7,997	...
4,432	3,142	8,114	5,111	3,461	1,786	6,616	......	....	...
189	191	1,497	928	2,175	2,149	3,875	4,154	7,997	...
1,195	2,052	3,216	980	723	1,325	637	1,028	2,178	...
174	276	314	298	....	......	......	......	....	...
1,021	1,776	2,902	682	723	1,325	637	1,028	2,178	...
1,201	853	1,792	1,848	1,751	1,342	4,264	6,107	....	3,263
1,201	604	1,093	504	659	....	......	......	....	...
....	249	699	1,344	1,092	1,342	4,264	6,107	....	3,263
1,814	2,159	4,947	2,537	3,612	2,610	5,927	10,578	5,024	3,800
1,206	1,886	2,599	1,233	1,359	891	518	......	....	...
608	273	2,348	1,304	2,253	1,719	5,409	10,578	5,024	3,800
12,570	12,007	42,177	35,914	19,781	22,394	53,221	45,979	23,585	13,886
10,844	10,534	33,109	24,330	12,192	7,159	9,221	1,040	....	...
1,726	1,473	9,068	11,584	7,589	15,235	44,000	44,939	23,585	13,886
23,161	20,888	61,154	30,690	25,630	15,928	62,070	42,762	17,597	6,764
17,825	14,687	41,105	17,228	10,886	7,986	12,673	......	....	...
5,336	6,201	20,049	13,462	14,744	7,942	49,397	42,762	17,597	6,764
8,787	8,782	29,541	21,001	15,039	14,214	39,745	34,496	20,280	14,314
8,240	8,451	26,768	16,482	13,312	11,555	24,063	10,089	2,264	...
547	331	2,773	4,519	1,727	2,659	15,682	24,407	18,016	14,314
3,114	4,071	7,873	7,124	6,877	3,177	4,553	7,925	15,510	...
2,448	3,467	6,062	4,976	3,842	902	4,027	......	......	...
666	604	1,811	2,148	3,035	2,275	526	7,925	15,510	...
9,521	9,085	40,871	34,436	21,543	19,019	57,755	36,910	9,379	12,307
8,491	8,224	32,378	26,190	14,311	12,970	21,455	1,101	2,950	...
1,030	861	8,493	8,246	7,232	6,049	36,300	35,809	6,429	12,307
32,221	31,208	125,462	96,919	62,256	39,037	94,193	47,253	23,811	17,048
31,921	30,857	123,199	92,163	55,894	33,841	65,111	11,454	....	...
300	351	2,263	4,756	6,362	5,196	29,082	35,799	23,811	17,048
9,850	12,011	69,251	60,916	50,348	34,913	117,816	88,988	51,491	10,174
4,900	5,245	20,518	15,572	9,660	4,008	9,140	6,956	2,287	...
4,950	6,766	48,733	45,344	40,688	30,905	108,676	82,032	49,204	10,174
15,701	16,979	74,451	66,382	55,543	48,861	137,872	77,271	37,522	7,191
7,244	6,817	21,949	14,982	11,151	8,886	11,198	1,147	....	...
8,457	10,162	52,502	51,400	44,392	39,975	126,674	76,124	37,522	7,191
57,552	45,980	134,724	77,412	48,973	37,710	113,566	119,966	73,487	47,908
55,511	44,146	123,701	61,955	35,773	21,472	53,608	21,922	....	...
2,041	1,834	11,023	15,457	13,200	16,238	59,958	98,044	73,487	47,908
9,439	10,006	51,202	55,703	58,951	47,005	192,509	219,072	96,367	33,079
5,348	4,663	18,531	14,259	10,435	7,153	16,542	11,302	....	...
4,091	5,343	32,671	41,444	48,516	39,852	175,967	207,770	96,367	33,079
30,509	31,298	112,092	80,035	61,231	44,959	124,438	108,204	87,070	27,506
30,390	30,650	108,066	76,332	53,766	32,609	64,544	19,192	2,022	...
119	648	4,026	3,703	7,465	12,350	59,894	89,012	85,048	27,506

IV. Rural Population by State, and by

Classification	Total Population	Less Than 10	10 to 20	20 to 30	30 to 40	40 to 50
Morelos, total..................	91,861	11	96	146	250	266
On ranchos and haciendas.......	3,220	....	43	....	106	47
In all other communities........	88,641	11	53	146	144	219
Nayarit, total..................	101,817	349	957	901	1,224	1,553
On ranchos and haciendas.......	52,429	323	922	855	1,188	1,553
In all other communities........	49,388	26	35	46	36	....
Nuevo León, total..............	226,585	4,403	8,308	6,628	6,970	6,003
On ranchos and haciendas......	113,685	4,294	8,123	6,211	6,248	5,573
In all other communities........	112,900	109	185	417	722	430
Oaxaca, total..................	849,384	767	1,645	1,893	3,061	3,615
On ranchos and haciendas......	88,591	593	919	1,081	2,033	2,195
In all other communities........	760,793	174	726	812	1,028	1,420
Puebla, total..................	854,368	294	923	1,526	1,553	2,056
On ranchos and haciendas.......	84,224	254	809	1,340	1,225	1,269
In all other communities........	770,144	40	114	186	328	787
Querétaro, total................	184,601	191	681	1,668	1,510	2,467
On ranchos and haciendas.......	117,623	174	671	1,568	1,510	2,420
In all other communities........	66,978	17	10	100	....	47
San Luis Potosí, total...........	341,286	451	1,647	2,673	3,116	3,960
On ranchos and haciendas.......	209,103	418	1,598	2,569	3,011	3,918
In all other communities........	132,183	33	49	104	105	42
Sinaloa, total..................	280,125	1,905	5,021	5,979	5,479	5,464
On ranchos and haciendas.......	178,915	1,893	4,923	5,859	5,407	5,327
In all other communities........	101,210	12	98	120	72	137
Sonora, total..................	207,950	2,892	5,985	5,605	5,082	3,680
On ranchos and haciendas.......	52,011	2,392	5,161	4,574	4,160	2,833
In all other communities........	155,939	500	824	1,031	922	847
Tabasco, total..................	190,532	3,063	6,961	6,055	5,415	4,435
On ranchos and haciendas.......	61,472	3,053	6,889	5,867	5,318	4,123
In all other communities........	129,060	10	72	188	97	312
Tamaulipas, total...............	160,106	2,842	8,750	7,659	7,432	5,961
On ranchos and haciendas.......	95,772	2,734	8,577	7,492	7,234	5,871
In all other communities........	64,334	108	173	167	198	90
Tlaxcala, total.*...............	151,994	168	477	661	438	528
On ranchos and haciendas.......	30,438	168	463	617	438	528
In all other communities........	121,556	....	14	44	....	....
Veracruz, total.................	840,071	1,180	4,517	5,969	6,898	6,944
On ranchos and haciendas.......	65,511	957	3,470	4,540	4,269	3,976
In all other communities........	774,560	223	1,047	1,429	2,629	2,968
Yucatán, total..................	211,451	2,333	3,617	3,013	2,668	3,191
On ranchos and haciendas.......	59,267	1,826	3,124	2,561	2,255	2,752
In all other communities........	152,184	507	493	452	413	439
Zacatecas, total................	325,103	1,091	3,342	4,377	5,120	5,933
On ranchos and haciendas.......	239,408	1,063	3,324	4,253	4,884	5,799
In all other communities........	85,695	28	18	124	236	134

Type and Size of Community, 1921*—(Continued)

50 to 75	75 to 100	100 to 200	200 to 300	300 to 400	400 to 500	500 to 1,000	1,000 to 2,000	2,000 to 3,000	3,000 to 4,000
856	1,210	7,511	6,935	6,777	3,840	23,589	24,597	12,527	3,250
173	609	876	1,028	338	....	......	....	....	...
683	601	6,635	5,907	6,439	3,840	23,589	24,597	12,527	3,250
3,378	4,269	12,536	10,911	8,667	7,115	19,302	17,371	9,523	3,761
3,200	4,194	11,220	8,202	7,036	3,571	6,955	1,110	2,100	...
178	75	1,316	2,709	1,631	3,544	12,347	16,261	7,423	3,761
12,545	9,784	33,807	15,795	16,921	9,712	34,528	37,253	9,725	14,203
11,226	7,873	27,215	9,998	10,026	5,352	8,993	2,553	....	...
1,319	1,911	6,592	5,797	6,895	4,360	25,535	34,700	9,725	14,203
9,182	12,402	56,237	64,860	55,805	57,210	247,414 ·	196,141	89,112	50,040
5,558	7,505	20,057	15,196	8,562	6,271	9,943	6,020	2,658	...
3,624	4,897	36,180	49,664	47,243	50,939	237,471	190,121	86,454	50,040
6,027	9,393	43,294	68,924	65,959	56,234	238,255	222,923	88,411	48,596
4,596	6,403	19,128	18,267	13,226	7,494	9,083	1,130	....	...
1,431	2,990	24,166	50,657	52,733	48,740	229,172	221,793	88,411	48,596
6,410	6,270	30,295	25,526	16,123	12,828	38,325	25,467	10,358	6,482
6,113	6,270	28,228	22,592	13,693	7,486	24,626	2,272	....	...
297	....	2,067	2,934	2,430	5,342	13,699	23,195	10,358	6,482
10,766	12,369	48,187	45,413	34,162	28,767	65,384	46,119	24,612	13,660
10,026	11,225	40,762	37,888	28,171	18,906	41,740	6,694	2,177	...
740	1,144	7,425	7,525	5,991	9,861	23,644	39,425	22,435	13,660
14,518	14,677	43,689	39,532	24,024	19,691	46,961	30,609	12,658	9,918
13,956	13,699	39,033	31,905	16,424	11,990	20,128	5,586	2,785	...
562	978	4,656	7,627	7,600	7,701	26,833	25,023	9,873	9,918
7,291	8,484	23,860	15,513	13,934	12,141	39,801	33,093	17,761	12,828
4,390	5,548	11,023	5,621	1,125	2,278	2,906	......	....	...
2,901	2,936	12,837	9,892	12,809	9,863	36,895	33,093	17,761	12,828
8,632	6,206	17,715	12,268	11,866	11,405	41,605	33,073	15,649	6,184
7,664	5,929	13,289	5,881	1,102	....	2,357	......	....	...
968	277	4,426	6,387	10,764	11,405	39,248	33,073	15,649	6,184
11,868	8,760	22,289	13,072	9,390	3,881	13,099	31,973	6,548	6,582
11,623	7,976	20,872	9,168	6,532	2,186	3,916	1,591	....	...
245	784	1,417	3,904	2,858	1,695	9,183	30,382	6,548	6,582
1,934	2,168	9,528	14,482	7,893	12,083	35,289	37,852	17,605	10,888
1,627	1,816	6,551	8,847	3,034	3,985	2,364	......	....	...
307	352	2,977	5,635	4,859	8,098	32,925	37,852	17,605	10,888
19,236	21,131	120,451	75,727	74,273	61,436	207,066	157,928	57,166	20,149
10,303	7,079	15,696	5,167	2,672	2,684	4,698	......	....	...
8,933	14,052	104,755	70,560	71,601	58,752	202,368	157,928	57,166	20,149
5,803	5,722	21,558	13,833	12,692	10,259	32,339	52,561	28,695	13,167
5,057	4,927	16,492	9,608	6,666	3,117	882	......	....	...
746	795	5,066	4,225	6,026	7,142	31,457	52,561	28,695	13,167
13,494	12,459	51,888	36,252	27,961	24,461	48,595	37,949	22,251	29,930
13,000	12,292	50,975	34,453	24,477	22,320	34,887	27,681	....	...
494	167	913	1,799	3,484	2,141	13,708	10,268	22,251	29,930

IV. Rural Population by State, and by

Classification	Total Population	Less Than 10	10 to 20	20 to 30	30 to 40	40 to 50
Quintana Roo, total.............	6,966	103	216	198	134	178
On ranchos and haciendas.......	1,093	77	97	100	98	134
In all other communities........	5,873	26	119	98	36	44
Distrito Federal, total............	122,440	46	319	244	198	263
On ranchos and haciendas.......	7,053	39	276	140	64	178
In all other communities........	115,387	7	43	104	134	85
Total Rural Population...........	10,563,454	46,561	116,440	132,776	133,620	140,329
On ranchos and haciendas.......	3,837,820	42,973	107,788	120,193	118,238	122,725
In all other communities........	6,725,634	3,588	8,652	12,583	15,382	17,604

* Data from Federal Census of 1921. The figures given in this table for ranchos and haciendas include census. In the table on pages 466-473 the word "hacienda" is used as a general term for all agricultural

Type and Size of Community, 1921*—(Concluded)

50 to 75	75 to 100	100 to 200	200 to 300	300 to 400	400 to 500	500 to 1,000	1,000 to 2,000	2,000 to 3,000	3,000 to 4,000
476	76	1,269	486	384	485	......	2,961	....	....
288	76	223	......	....	....	......	......	....	....
188	....	1,046	486	384	485	......	2,961	....	....
596	1,600	4,658	3,835	7,918	5,897	25,054	36,255	21,342	14,215
413	891	1,737	214	1,307	907	887	......	21,342	....
183	709	2,921	3,621	6,611	4,990	24,167	36,255	21,342	14,215
354,268	347,692	1,317,136	1,041,300	832,643	673,874	2,175,663	1,876,285	913,774	461,093
299,388	277,961	890,883	595,650	381,092	249,765	473,081	138,840	19,243	...
54,880	69,731	426,253	445,650	451,551	424,109	1,702,582	1,737,445	894,531	461,093

only the population located on agricultural properties that are classified under these names in the Mexican properties. This accounts for the apparent discrepancy in the figures given in the two tables.

V. Population on Haciendas and in Agricultural Villages, 1910 and 1921*

CLASSIFICATION	1910				1921			
	Total	Haciendas a	Agricultural Villages b	All Other Rural Communities c	Total	Haciendas	Agricultural Villages	All Other Rural Communities
Aguascalientes:								
Number of Communities.	570	506	52	12	460	385	42	33
Population.	70,507	46,411	23,657	439	60,620	37,482	22,638	500
Percentage of total Pop.	*100.0*	*65.8*	*33.6*	*0.6*	*106.0*	*61.8*	*37.3*	*0.9*
Average No. of Inhab.	.....	92	455	37	.....	97	539	15
Baja California:								
Number of Communities.	1,177	1,102	57	18	1,173	955	184	34
Population.	46,736	22,118	24,294	324	48,659	16,198	26,812	5,649
Percentage of total Pop.	*100.0*	*47.3*	*52.0*	*0.7*	*100.0*	*33.3*	*55.1*	*1.6*
Average No. of Inhab.	.....	20	426	18	.....	17	146	166
Campeche:								
Number of Communities.	406	305	95	6	429	334	87	8
Population.	63,351	31,561	31,265	525	47,925	15,393	32,438	94
Percentage of total Pop.	*100.0*	*49.8*	*49.4*	*0.8*	*100.0*	*32.1*	*67.7*	*0.2*
Average No. of Inhab.	.....	103	329	88	.....	46	373	12
Chihuahua:								
Number of Communities.	3,038	2,605	214	219	2,443	1,798	503	142
Population.	315,329	183,587	104,148	27,594	306,102	128,540	150,101	27,461
Percentage of total Pop.	*100.0*	*58.2*	*33.0*	*8.8*	*100.0*	*42.0*	*49.0*	*9.0*
Average No. of Inhab.	.....	70	487	126	.....	71	298	193

V. POPULATION ON HACIENDAS AND IN AGRICULTURAL VILLAGES, 1910 AND 1921*—(Continued)

CLASSIFICATION	1910				1921			
	Total	Haciendas a	Agricultural Villages b	All Other Rural Communities c	Total	Haciendas	Agricultural Villages	All Other Rural Communities
Chiapas								
Number of Communities.	3,288	2,915	316	57	3,963	3,238	606	119
Population..............	361,246	215,590	130,938	14,718	352,802	166,829	174,664	11,309
Percentage of total Pop...	100.0	59.7	36.2	4.1	100.0	47.3	49.5	3.2
Average No. of Inhab..	.....	74	414	258	.....	52	288	95
Coahuila:								
Number of Communities.	1,274	1,111	61	102	1,355	1,185	81	89
Population..............	239,736	138,510	73,019	28,207	219,324	133,198	54,616	31,510
Percentage of total Pop...	100.0	57.8	30.4	11.8	100.0	60.7	24.9	14.4
Average No. of Inhab..	.....	125	1,197	277	.....	112	674	354
Colima:								
Number of Communities.	357	333	20	4	354	269	81	4
Population..............	52,556	30,400	20,556	1,600	63,423	28,490	34,744	189
Percentage of total Pop...	100.0	57.8	39.1	3.1	100.0	44.9	54.8	0.3
Average No. of Inhab..	.....	91	1,028	400	.....	106	429	47
Durango:								
Number of Communities.	3,046	2,700	211	135	1,765	1,364	242	159
Population..............	407,577	268,961	120,384	18,232	265,686	141,244	101,169	23,273
Percentage of total Pop...	100.0	66.0	29.5	4.5	100.0	53.2	38.1	8.7
Average No. of Inhab..	.....	99	571	135	.....	104	418	146

V. Population on Haciendas and in Agricultural Villages, 1910 and 1921*—(Continued)

CLASSIFICATION	1910				1921			
	Total	Haciendas [a]	Agricultural Villages [b]	All Other Rural Communities [c]	Total	Haciendas	Agricultural Villages	All Other Rural Communities
Guanajuato:								
Number of Communities..	4,480	4,285	134	61	3,824	3,629	118	77
Population..	772,237	650,974	102,648	18,615	600,914	475,151	109,885	15,878
Percentage of total Pop...	*100.0*	*84.3*	*13.3*	*2.4*	*100.0*	*79.1*	*18.3*	*2.6*
Average No. of Inhab..	.....	152	766	305	.....	131	931	206
Guerrero:								
Number of Communities.	2,115	1,709	325	81	1,937	762	1,160	15
Population..	545,183	256,615	271,482	17,086	515,721	86,677	425,780	3,264
Percentage of total Pop...	*100.0*	*47.1*	*49.8*	*3.1*	*100.0*	*16.8*	*82.6*	*0.6*
Average No. of Inhab..	.....	150	835	211	.....	114	367	218
Hidalgo:								
Number of Communities.	4,490	1,662	2,675	153	2,486	938	1,361	187
Population..	590,797	122,001	462,271	6,525	552,762	93,125	426,341	33,296
Percentage of total Pop...	*100.0*	*20.7*	*78.2*	*1.1*	*100.0*	*16.8*	*77.1*	*6.1*
Average No. of Inhab..	.....	73	173	43	.....	99	313	178
Jalisco:								
Number of Communities..	8,405	7,928	405	72	7,153	6,590	489	74
Population..	932,235	610,700	311,015	10,520	843,666	513,117	313,100	17,449
Percentage of total Pop...	*100.0*	*65.5*	*33.4*	*1.1*	*100.0*	*60.8*	*37.1*	*2.1*
Average No. of Inhab..	.....	77	768	146	.....	78	640	236

V. POPULATION ON HACIENDAS AND IN AGRICULTURAL VILLAGES, 1910 AND 1921*—(Continued)

CLASSIFICATION	1910				1921			
	Total	Haciendas ᵃ	Agricultural Villages ᵇ	All Other Rural Communities ᶜ	Total	Haciendas	Agricultural Villages	All Other Rural Communities ᶜ
México:								
Number of Communities.	1,887	888	964	35	2,128	796	1,126	206
Population.	835,525	140,366	686,214	8,945	782,525	95,446	627,499	59,580
Percentage of total Pop.	*100.0*	*16.8*	*82.1*	*1.1*	*100.0*	*12.2*	*80.2*	*7.6*
Average No. of Inhab.	.....	158	712	256	.....	120	557	289
Michoacán:								
Number of Communities.	4,907	4,835	44	28	4,975	4,641	281	53
Population.	828,947	498,153	327,042	3,752	756,685	466,670	281,535	8,480
Percentage of total Pop.	*100.0*	*60.1*	*39.4*	*0.5*	*100.0*	*61.7*	*37.2*	*1.1*
Average No. of Inhab.	.....	103	7,433	134	.....	101	1,002	163
Morelos:								
Number of Communities.	284	142	125	17	228	28	178	22
Population.	139,467	33,114	103,273	3,080	91,861	3,220	86,391	2,250
Percentage of total Pop.	*100.0*	*23.7*	*74.1*	*2.2*	*100.0*	*3.5*	*94.0*	*2.5*
Average No. of Inhab.	.....	233	826	181	.....	115	485	102
Nayarit:								
Number of Communities.	1,805	1,737	59	9	1,000	907	75	18
Population.	139,273	88,028	48,335	2,910	101,817	52,429	45,535	3,853
Percentage of total Pop.	*100.0*	*63.2*	*34.7*	*2.1*	*100.0*	*51.5*	*44.7*	*3.8*
Average No. of Inhab.	.....	51	819	323	.....	58	607	214

V. POPULATION ON HACIENDAS AND IN AGRICULTURAL VILLAGES, 1910 AND 1921*—(Continued)

CLASSIFICATION	1910				1921			
	Total	Haciendas a	Agricultural Villages b	All Other Rural Communities c	Total	Haciendas	Agricultural Villages	All Other Rural Communities
Nuevo León:								
Number of Communities.	2,603	2,354	168	81	2,770	2,482	215	73
Population..........	263,603	158,263	98,180	7,160	226,585	113,835	104,890	7,860
Percentage of total Pop...	*100.0*	*60.0*	*37.3*	*2.7*	*100.0*	*50.2*	*46.3*	*3.5*
Average No. of Inhab...	.....	67	584	88	.....	46	488	108
Oaxaca:								
Number of Communities.	2,053	968	1,044	41	2,293	760	1,438	95
Population..........	901,442	130,749	765,204	5,489	849,384	89,019	751,416	8,949
Percentage of total Pop...	*100.0*	*14.5*	*84.9*	*0.6*	*100.0*	*10.5*	*88.5*	*1.0*
Average No. of Inhab...	.....	135	733	134	.....	117	523	94
Puebla:								
Number of Communities.	2,412	1,275	1,054	83	1,936	648	1,013	275
Population..........	903,273	181,293	697,636	24,344	854,368	84,400	669,266	100,702
Percentage of total Pop...	*100.0*	*20.1*	*77.2*	*2.7*	*100.0*	*9.9*	*78.3*	*11.8*
Average No. of Inhab...	.....	142	662	293	.....	130	661	366
Querétaro:								
Number of Communities.	746	642	94	10	888	784	96	8
Population..........	200,211	129,689	66,168	4,354	184,601	118,450	64,000	2,151
Percentage of total Pop...	*100.0*	*64.8*	*33.0*	*2.2*	*100.0*	*64.2*	*34.7*	*1.1*
Average No. of Inhab...	.....	202	704	435	.....	151	667	269

V. POPULATION ON HACIENDAS AND IN AGRICULTURAL VILLAGES, 1910 AND 1921*—(Continued)

CLASSIFICATION	1910				1921			
	Total	Haciendas[a]	Agricultural Villages[b]	All Other Rural Communities[c]	Total	Haciendas	Agricultural Villages	All Other Rural Communities
San Luis Potosí:								
Number of Communities.	1,817	1,747	62	8	1,675	1,434	204	37
Population.	486,160	397,576	86,433	2,151	341,286	216,639	116,793	7,854
Percentage of total Pop.	100.0	81.8	17.8	0.4	100.0	63.5	34.2	2.3
Average No. of Inhab.	.....	228	1,394	269	.....	151	573	212
Sinaloa:								
Number of Communities.	3,186	3,064	119	3	2,312	2,108	180	24
Population.	278,423	204,291	73,527	605	280,125	186,292	89,021	4,812
Percentage of total Pop.	100.0	73.4	26.4	0.2	100.0	66.5	31.8	1.7
Average No. of Inhab.	.....	67	618	202	.....	88	495	200
Sonora:								
Number of Communities.	2,415	1,694	467	254	2,046	1,449	406	191
Population.	219,563	72,628	119,516	27,419	207,950	58,061	110,607	39,282
Percentage of total Pop.	100.0	33.1	54.4	12.5	100.0	27.9	53.2	18.9
Average No. of Inhab.	.....	43	256	108	.....	40	272	206
Tabasco:								
Number of Communities.	1,857	1,608	248	1	2,050	1,800	249	1
Population.	175,247	56,565	118,662	20	190,532	61,954	128,557	21
Percentage of total Pop.	100.0	32.3	67.7	0.0	100.0	32.5	67.5	0.0
Average No. of Inhab.	.....	35	478	20	.....	34	516	21

V. POPULATION ON HACIENDAS AND IN AGRICULTURAL VILLAGES 1910, AND 1921*—(Continued)

CLASSIFICATION	1910				1921			
	Total	Haciendas[a]	Agricultural Villages[b]	All Other Rural Communities[c]	Total	Haciendas	Agricultural Villages	All Other Rural Communities
Tamaulipas:								
Number of Communities.	3,164	3,063	58	43	2,417	2,284	62	71
Population.	198,770	148,358	46,034	4,378	160,106	101,557	44,529	14,020
Percentage of total Pop.	*100.0*	*74.6*	*23.2*	*2.2*	*100.0*	*63.4*	*27.8*	*8.8*
Average No. of Inhab.	.....	48	794	102	.....	44	718	197
Tlaxcala:								
Number of Communities.	373	227	131	15	446	261	149	36
Population.	157,110	50,677	102,094	4,339	151,994	30,656	115,339	5,999
Percentage of total Pop.	*100.0*	*32.2*	*65.0*	*2.8*	*100.0*	*20.2*	*75.9*	*3.9*
Average No. of Inhab.	.....	223	779	289	.....	117	774	167
Veracruz:								
Number of Communities.	3,311	1,962	1,342	7	3,500	1,259	2,201	40
Population.	887,369	212,759	672,624	1,986	840,071	78,945	750,900	10,226
Percentage of total Pop.	*100.0*	*24.0*	*75.8*	*0.2*	*100.0*	*9.4*	*89.4*	*1.2*
Average No. of Inhab.	.....	108	501	284	.....	63	341	256
Yucatán:								
Number of Communities.	2,165	1,785	375	5	1,568	1,180	360	28
Population.	249,061	114,310	134,401	350	211,451	66,006	144,293	1,152
Percentage of total Pop.	*100.0*	*45.9*	*54.0*	*0.1*	*100.0*	*31.2*	*68.2*	*0.6*
Average No. of Inhab.	.....	64	358	70	.....	56	401	41

V. POPULATION ON HACIENDAS AND IN AGRICULTURAL VILLAGES, 1910 AND 1921*—(Concluded)

CLASSIFICATION	1910				1921			
	Total	Haciendas[a]	Agricultural Villages[b]	All Other Rural Communities[c]	Total	Haciendas	Agricultural Villages	All Other Rural Communities
Zacatecas:								
Number of Communities.	1,702	1,593	65	44	2,100	1,981	69	50
Population.	406,214	309,047	85,597	11,570	325,103	239,892	75,533	9,678
Percentage of total Pop.	*100.0*	*76.1*	*21.1*	*2.8*	*100.0*	*73.8*	*23.2*	*3.0*
Average No. of Inhab.	.....	194	1,317	263	.....	121	1,095	194
Quintana Roo:								
Number of Communities.	58	27	28	3	80	45	24	11
Population.	9,109	881	8,094	134	6,966	1,115	5,257	594
Percentage of total Pop.	*100.0*	*9.6*	*88.9*	*1.5*	*100.0*	*16.0*	*75.5*	*8.5*
Average No. of Inhab.	.....	33	289	45	.....	25	219	54
Distrito Federal:								
Number of Communities.	158	53	105	...	252	87	108	57
Population.	102,853	7,109	95,744	...	122,440	13,739	64,078	44,623
Percentage of total Pop.	*100.0*	*6.9*	*93.1*	*...*	*100.0*	*11.2*	*52.3*	*36.5*
Average No. of Inhab.	.....	134	912	...	.....	178	593	842
All Mexico:								
Number of Communities.	69,549	56,825	11,117	1,607	62,006	46,381	13,388	2,237
Population.	11,779,110	5,511,284	6,010,455	257,371	10,563,454	3,913,766	6,147,727	501,958
Percentage of total Pop.	*100.0*	*46.8*	*51.0*	*2.2*	*100.0*	*37.1*	*58.2*	*4.7*
Average No. of Inhab.	.....	97	541	160	.....	84	459	224

* Data from Federal Censuses of 1910 and 1921.
a The word "hacienda" in this table is used to cover all of the different names given to agricultural properties in the Mexican census. See note to the table on pp. 460–465.
b In Chapter II the agricultural villages are classed as free villages for the purpose of clearly indicating the difference between the political structure of the hacienda communities and that of the agricultural villages that have municipal organization.
c All communities under 4,000 inhabitants were classed as rural by 1910 population census.

VI. Rural Communities, by Size, 1921*

Population of Community	Communities		Population	
	Number	As Percentage of All Rural Communities	In Thousands	As Percentage of Total Rural Population
Under 10.........	7,976	13.0	46	.4
10–20............	8,335	13.6	116	1.1
20–30............	5,439	8.9	133	1.2
30–40............	3,935	6.4	134	1.3
40–50............	3,194	5.2	140	1.3
50–75............	5,830	9.5	354	3.3
75–100...........	4,080	6.7	348	3.3
100–200..........	9,089	14.9	1,317	12.5
200–300..........	4,294	7.0	1,041	9.9
300–400..........	2,451	4.0	833	7.9
400–500..........	1,526	2.5	674	6.4
500–1,000........	3,197	5.2	2,176	20.6
1,000–2,000.......	1,382	2.3	1,876	17.8
2,000–3,000.......	376	.6	914	8.6
3,000–4,000.......	136	.2	461	4.4
Total...........	61,240	100.0	10,563	100.0

*Data from Federal Census of 1921.

VII. Rural Population Compared with Total Population, by States, 1921*

STATE	Total Population	Rural Population	
		Number	As Percentage of Total
Aguascalientes.........	107,581	60,620	56.3
Baja California........	62,831	48,659	77.4
Campeche.............	76,419	47,925	62.7
Chihuahua............	401,622	306,102	76.2
Chiapas..............	421,744	352,802	83.7
Coahuila.............	393,480	219,324	55.7
Colima...............	91,749	63,423	69.1
Durango..............	334,037	265,686	79.5
Guanajuato...........	860,364	600,914	69.8
Guerrero.............	566,836	515,721	91.0
Hidalgo..............	622,241	552,762	88.8
Jalisco..............	1,191,957	843,666	70.8
México...............	884,617	782,525	88.5
Michoacán............	939,849	756,685	80.5
Morelos..............	103,440	91,861	88.8
Nayarit..............	146,093	101,817	69.7
Nuevo León..........	336,412	226,585	67.4
Oaxaca..............	976,005	849,384	87.0
Puebla..............	1,024,955	854,368	83.4
Querétaro............	220,231	184,601	83.8
San Luis Potosí.......	445,681	341,286	76.6
Sinaloa..............	341,265	280,125	82.1
Sonora..............	270,707	207,950	76.8
Tabasco..............	210,437	190,532	90.5
Tamaulipas...........	285,206	160,106	56.1
Tlaxcala.............	178,570	151,994	85.1
Veracruz.............	1,110,971	840,071	75.0
Yucatán.............	358,221	211,451	59.0
Zacatecas............	379,329	325,103	85.7
Distrito Federal.......	906,063	122,440	13.5
Quintana Roo.........	6,966	6,966	100.0
All Mexico..........	14,255,879	10,563,454	74.1

*Data from Federal Census of 1921.

APPENDIX C

LAND STATISTICS

The following methods were employed in the collection and compilation of the tables giving size of rural properties, ownership of rural properties, and the extent of foreign holdings in Mexico. All of these figures have as their base the land census of 1923, and the basic material upon which these tables rest was summarized in *Anuario Estadistica*, 1923–1924, Vol. II, pp. 107–108.

I. Size of Rural Properties, 1923

The original sheets of this census, on file in the *Departamento de la Estadistica Nacional*, were used as a basis for estimating the size of those properties for which the area was not given. This was done by taking the average value per hectare of the properties for each *municipio* for which both area and value were given, and calculating from the value figures the size of the properties for which no area was given. The following table shows the number of properties in each state for which a record was obtained by the Census of 1923, the number of properties for which area was not given, and the number of properties for which area was accounted for by the Institute of Economics.

After estimating the area of the properties for which only value was given in the original census sheets, these properties were distributed according to the classification by areas used by the Mexican Department of Statistics. As an example of the method we give below the data for the state of Aguascalientes. This state is one of those where a very large number of the properties were given in the Census of 1923 with value only. Of a total of 5,065 properties given in the census 4,651 had no area given. In working over the census records we found all but nine or 4,642 of these properties. The area of these 4,642 properties was then estimated on the basis of their value. The table on page 478, in which all listed properties in the state are classified by size, shows the number we found and estimated.

If we compare the size distribution of the properties from the 1923 census records and the 1925–26 tax records for the state of Aguascalientes, we find that they run fairly close together. The first two classifications, those under five hectares, contain 55.4 per cent of the total in the 1923 census and 57.7 per cent of the total in the 1925–26 tax record. This is especially striking when we note the fact that the Federal census gives the pieces of property and the tax records give the owners.

476

NUMBER OF PROPERTIES FOR WHICH AREA WAS ESTIMATED
COMPARED WITH THE TOTAL NUMBER LISTED IN THE
CENSUS OF 1923

STATE	All Properties Listed	Listed Properties with Area Not Given		Properties for Which Area Was Estimated	
		Number	As Percentage of All Properties Listed	Number	As Percentage of Those Listed With Area Not Given
Aguascalientes	5,065	4,651	91.8	4,642	99.8
Baja California	2,732	419	15.3	409	97.6
Campeche....	1,289	425	33.0	435	102.4 a
Coahuila.....	4,166	720	17.3	703	97.6
Colima.......	856	5 85	68.3	582	99.5
Chiapas......	15,839	1,550	9.8	1,413	91.2
Chihuahua....	5,957	1,675	28.1	1,546	92.3
Durango.....	7,409	71	1.0	71	100.0
Guanajuato...	19,657	2,164	11.0	1,591	73.5
Guerrero.....	5,501	828	15.1	821	99.2
Hidalgo......	63,639	61,372	96.4	66,493	108.3 a
Jalisco.......	144,523	516	0.4	468	90.7
México.......	39,610	34,706	87.6	32,685	94.2
Michoacán....	54,061	8,501	15.7	8,375	98.5
Morelos......	7,384	2,534	34.3	2,526	99.7
Nayarit......	2,595	260	10.0	259	99.6
Nuevo León...	8,218	705	8.6	697	98.9
Oaxaca.......	45,660	43,321	94.9	43,417	100.2 a
Puebla.......	42,399	41,555	98.0	41,555 b	100.0
Querétaro.....	14,481	5,525	38.2	5,366	97.1
San Luis Potosí	4,415	2,809	63.6	2,781	99.0
Sinaloa.......	9,769	3,981	40.8	3,959	99.4
Sonora.......	4,103	346	8.4	326	94.2
Tabasco......	11,741	55	0.5	71	129.1 a
Tamaulipas...	4,777	14	0.3	14	100.0
Tlaxcala......	1,622	767	47.3	764	99.6
Veracruz.....	51,290	507	1.0	167	32.9
Yucatán......	14,589	15	0.1	15	100.0
Zacatecas.....	27,783	25,844	93.0	26,198	101.4 a
29 States c..	621,130	246,421	39.7	248,349	100.8 a

a The tax records show a larger number of properties than had been listed in the Census; hence the percentages sometimes run above 100.

b Because of misplacement of records, 13,088 of the properties for which area was missing were distributed on the basis of percentage relationship of those available.

c Distrito Federal and Quintana Roo not included.

Size Distribution of Pieces of Property in the State of
Aguascalientes, 1923 *

Size of Property (In hectares)	Properties Classified by		Total
	Official Census	Institute of Economics	
Less than 1..........	22	1,026	1,048
1 to 5...........	116	1,637	1,753
6 to 10..........	31	620	651
11 to 50..........	78	986	1,064
51 to 100........	14	216	230
101 to 200........	35	76	111
201 to 500........	51	47	98
500 to 1,000........	19	14	33
1,001 to 5,000........	30	18	48
5,001 to 10,000.......	9	2	11
10,000 or over........	9	....	9
Total..............	414	4,642	5,056

*In this table the classification follows the one used by the Mexican Census.
The classification "1 to 5," we are advised, includes properties of more than five
and less than six hectares; "6 to 10" includes more than ten and less than eleven,
and so on.

II. Foreign-owned Properties

From the original sheets of the census a list of all properties of the
Republic valued at more than 5,000 pesos was copied—some 30,000.
The properties of such valuation in each *municipio* were listed upon
a separate sheet. These sheets gave the owner, property, value and,
where possible, the area of each property. A margin was left at the
left-hand side for the writing in of the nationality of the owner of
each property. The sheets were mailed, through the good offices of
the Mexican Department of Statistics, to the governor of each of
the states and territories of the Republic. In turn, they were sent
by the governors to the tax collectors in each one of the *municipios*
of the respective states, and then returned to the Department of
Statistics, and finally placed at the disposal of the Institute of
Economics. It required something over two years to prepare the
sheets, gather the material, and have the reports returned for
tabulation. These sheets are the source of our study of foreign
property in Mexico. A sample sheet with replies is reprinted on
p. 479.

Nacionalidad.	Municipio de Ometepec. Del Estado de Guerrero. Nombre del predio.	Nombre del propietario.	Valor.	Extensión
	El Limón.	Anchara de la Cruz.	3.000.	
Mexicana	Pastoría.	Antonio Landa Infte.	6.000.	80.
Id.	Masapa.	Amado G. Sandoval	5.000.	300.
Id.	V. Pie de Gente.	Angel Sandoval.	9.000.	700.
Id.	El Carrizo.	Adolfo Zapata.	10.000.	340.
Id.	Paso del Tabaco	Ignacio L. Montegreina.	120.000.	2.000.
	Libertad.	Miller y Reguera.	45.000.	15.000.
Mexicana	Talapa.	Juan Noriega Test.	8.000.	4.200.
Id.	Quetzala.	Sta. Cruz L. M.	20.000.	1.200.
Id.	La Ala.	Rafael G. Salinas.	15.000.	1.275.
Id.	Cueva de Huajuitepec.	Luz Reyna Vda. de Reyna.	7.000.	2.000.
Id.	" " "	Nicolás Vasques.	15.000.	562.
Id.	Cochopa y S. Miguel	Sostenes López.	7.000.	37.
Id.	Cañada de Ocampa.	Josefa Zambra.	6.000.	70.
Id.	Patehuilla, ahuapan y			
Id.	Conchita.	Librado López.	17.000.	380.
Id.	Zoquipalanque.	Efren Sandoval.	5.000.	80.
Id.	Boca de Jalapa.	Francisco Estrada.	5.000.	1.300.

Nota: El predio que figura bajo el nombre de "Libertad", de la Sociedad Miller y Reguera, el primero es de nacionalidad Americana (Miller) y el segundo (Reguera) mexicana.

Ometepec mayo 29 de 1926

El Recaudador

Daniel Romero

III. Size of Holdings Valued at Over 5,000 Pesos, 1926–27

In addition to serving as a base for the foreign property study, the sheets served two other purposes. The letter which accompanied the sheets contained a special request to the tax collectors in the different *municipios* asking them to fill in the size of the properties for which area was missing. As the number of properties on the sheet sent to each *municipio* was comparatively small, this request was generally complied with. This gave us a check on our previous estimate, for properties valued at over 5,000 *pesos*. It also gave us a fuller record of the area of these properties than is to be found in the original sheets of the Census of 1923, and thus made possible the estimate given in the text (pp. 335–357) for area and value of all properties in the Republic of over 5,000 *pesos*.

Finally, these records were used to consolidate the properties of owners in each state whose total holdings of properties valued at

5,000 *pesos* or over made an area of 5,000 hectares or over, and thus made possible our study (pp. 346–357) of the number of people that own one-half of the privately held lands of the country.

In addition, the tax records of eleven states were copied out. These were useful for checking the material from the census. We publish below (p. 496) the figures derived from the tax records for the state of Aguascalientes.

All of the original records used in the organization of the land statistics are on file in the library of the Institute of Economics and available to students interested in the subject.

I. NUMBER OF RURAL PROPERTIES,

STATE	Total	Less Than 1 Hectare	1 to 5 Hectares	6 to 10 Hectares	11 to 50 Hectares
Aguascalientes..........	5,056	1,048	1,753	651	1,064
Baja California........	2,722	72	232	138	461
Campeche.............	1,299	90	170	53	238
Coahuila..............	4,149	19	435	323	896
Colima................	853	1	57	50	285
Chiapas...............	15,702	1,147	5,361	1,778	3,363
Chihuahua............	5,828	34	1,389	629	1,060
Durango..............	7,409	335	2,384	1,058	1,133
Guanajuato...........	19,084	4,145	5,040	2,190	4,132
Guerrero..............	5,494	271	1,774	686	1,116
Hidalgo...............	68,760	33,688	26,600	3,084	3,860
Jalisco................	144,475	40,490	55,453	14,802	24,267
México................	37,589	6,148	24,329	2,983	2,792
Michoacán............	53,935	17,020	22,433	5,208	6,296
Morelos...............	7,376	4,099	2,654	273	276
Nayarit...............	2,594	580	622	273	506
Nuevo León...........	8,210	1,353	2,437	1,054	1,335
Oaxaca...............	45,756	6,301	15,522	11,286	9,757
Puebla...............	41,555	18,981	15,041	2,089	2,869
Querétaro............	14,322	4,630	5,518	1,321	1,867
San Luis Potosí........	4,386	103	785	343	1,302
Sinaloa...............	9,747	220	2,183	1,248	3,424
Sonora...............	4,083	78	1,195	446	786
Tabasco	11,757	253	2,317	1,654	5,097
Tamaulipas...........	4,777	104	567	406	983
Tlaxcala..............	1,619	122	536	234	322
Veracruz..............	50,950	8,541	14,730	6,208	14,030
Yucatán..............	14,589	1,165	2,561	2,360	5,108
Zacatecas.............	28,137	226	2,074	3,130	11,311
29 states [a]...........	622,213	151,264	216,152	65,958	109,936

* In this table the classification follows the one used by the Mexican Census.   The classi-
10'' includes those ranging from 6 to 11; and so on.

[a] Quintana Roo and Distrito Federal not included.

BY STATE AND SIZE OF HOLDING, 1923*

51 to 100 Hectares	101 to 200 Hectares	201 to 500 Hectares	501 to 1,000 Hectares	1,001 to 5,000 Hectares	5,001 to 10,000 Hectares	10,000 Hectares or Over
230	111	98	33	48	11	9
345	325	483	213	403	34	16
120	107	107	100	203	55	56
499	478	541	255	356	123	224
108	113	91	57	64	10	17
923	795	981	571	698	54	31
457	528	594	294	506	133	204
487	674	328	233	436	126	215
1,195	770	692	435	399	57	29
415	374	351	216	223	41	27
533	292	279	162	209	38	15
4,279	2,245	1,533	626	617	120	43
439	249	251	156	189	33	20
1,099	664	572	232	319	55	37
38	19	9	7	1	. . .	. . .
147	114	133	58	106	20	35
531	394	432	203	312	89	70
1,176	729	558	203	169	38	17
718	553	507	322	409	36	30
392	246	130	66	110	24	18
481	472	380	176	222	49	73
816	493	457	265	482	102	57
240	216	324	199	411	112	76
1,035	645	451	174	113	10	8
537	551	594	358	530	84	63
68	77	97	74	84	4	1
2,860	1,857	1,470	570	558	71	55
882	569	814	423	640	44	23
4,147	3,060	2,465	801	689	105	129
25,197	17,720	15,722	7,482	9,506	1,678	1,598

fication "1 to 5", we are advised, includes properties ranging from 1 to 6 hectares; "6 to

II. Percentage Distribution of the Number of Rural

STATE	Less Than 1 Hectare	1 to 5 Hectares	6 to 10 Hectares	11 to 50 Hectares
Aguascalientes............	20.7	34.7	12.9	21.0
Baja California..........	2.7	8.5	5.1	16.9
Campeche..............	6.9	13.1	4.1	18.4
Coahuila................	0.5	10.5	7.8	21.6
Colima.................	0.1	6.7	5.9	33.4
Chiapas................	7.3	34.2	11.3	21.4
Chihuahua..............	0.6	23.8	10.8	18.2
Durango................	4.5	32.2	14.3	15.3
Guanajuato.............	21.7	26.4	11.5	21.7
Guerrero...............	4.9	32.3	12.5	20.3
Hidalgo................	49.0	38.7	4.5	5.6
Jalisco.................	28.0	38.4	10.2	16.8
México.................	16.3	64.7	7.9	7.4
Michoacán..............	31.6	41.6	9.6	11.7
Morelos................	55.6	36.0	3.7	3.7
Nayarit................	22.4	24.0	10.5	19.5
Nuevo Léon.............	16.4	30.0	12.8	16.2
Oaxaca................	13.8	33.9	24.7	21.3
Puebla.................	45.7	36.2	5.0	6.9
Querétaro..............	32.3	38.5	9.2	13.0
San Luis Potosí.........	2.3	17.9	7.8	29.7
Sinaloa................	2.3	22.4	12.8	35.1
Sonora.................	1.9	29.3	10.9	19.3
Tabasco................	2.1	19.7	14.1	43.4
Tamaulipas.............	2.2	11.9	8.5	20.6
Tlaxcala...............	7.5	33.1	14.5	19.9
Veracruz...............	16.8	28.9	12.2	27.5
Yucatán...............	8.0	17.5	16.2	35.0
Zacatecas..............	0.8	7.4	11.1	40.2
29 states a............	24.3	34.7	10.6	17.7

* In this table the classification follows the one used by the Mexican census.   See note *
a Quintana Roo and Distrito Federal not included.

PROPERTIES, BY STATE AND BY SIZE OF HOLDING, 1923*

51 to 100 Hectares	101 to 200 Hectares	201 to 500 Hectares	501 to 1,000 Hectares	1,001 to 5,000 Hectares	5,001 to 10,000 Hectares	10,000 Hectares or Over
4.5	2.2	1.9	0.7	1.0	0.2	0.2
12.7	11.9	17.7	7.8	14.8	1.3	0.6
9.3	8.2	8.2	7.7	15.6	4.2	4.3
12.0	11.5	13.0	6.2	8.6	2.9	5.4
12.7	13.2	10.7	6.7	7.5	1.2	1.9
5.9	5.1	6.3	3.6	4.4	0.3	0.2
7.8	9.1	10.2	5.0	8.7	2.3	3.5
6.6	9.1	4.4	3.1	5.9	1.7	2.9
6.3	4.0	3.6	2.3	2.1	0.3	0.1
7.6	6.8	6.4	3.9	4.1	0.7	0.5
0.8	0.4	0.4	0.2	0.3	0.1	...
3.0	1.6	1.1	0.4	0.4	0.1	...
1.2	0.7	0.7	0.4	0.5	0.1	0.1
2.0	1.2	1.1	0.4	0.6	0.1	0.1
0.5	0.3	0.1	0.1	...	...	...
5.7	4.4	5.1	2.2	4.1	0.8	1.3
6.4	4.8	5.2	2.5	3.8	1.1	0.8
2.6	1.6	1.2	0.4	0.4	0.1	...
1.7	1.3	1.2	0.8	1.0	0.1	0.1
2.7	1.7	0.9	0.5	0.8	0.2	0.2
10.9	10.8	8.7	4.0	5.1	1.1	1.7
8.4	5.1	4.7	2.7	4.9	1.0	0.6
5.9	5.3	7.9	4.9	10.1	2.7	1.8
8.8	5.5	3.8	1.5	0.9	0.1	0.1
11.2	11.5	12.4	7.5	11.1	1.8	1.3
4.2	4.7	6.0	4.6	5.2	0.2	0.1
5.6	3.7	2.9	1.1	1.1	0.1	0.1
6.0	3.9	5.6	2.9	4.4	0.3	0.2
14.7	10.9	8.8	2.8	2.4	0.4	0.5
4.1	2.8	2.5	1.2	1.5	0.3	0.3

to preceding table.

III. Number of Rural Properties of 1,000

STATE	Total	1,000 to 2,000 Hectares	2,000 to 3,000 Hectares	3,000 to 4,000 Hectares	4,000 to 5,000 Hectares	5,000 to 10,000 Hectares
Aguascalientes.......	50	20	5	7	2	10
Baja California......	291	62	110	30	21	44
Campeche..........	258	58	46	24	20	53
Coahuila...........	567	93	62	45	33	114
Colima............	86	37	10	8	5	11
Chiapas...........	728	381	169	60	44	52
Chihuahua.........	494	57	44	40	22	106
Durango...........	622	74	78	80	58	131
Guanajuato........	442	215	77	46	25	59
Guerrero...........	250	96	42	34	21	31
Hidalgo............	163	85	27	21	7	14
Jalisco.............	709	339	111	73	48	94
México............	225	94	52	24	17	21
Michoacán.........	379	186	53	41	21	47
Nayarit............	125	40	22	9	7	18
Nuevo León........	262	34	27	30	25	77
Oaxaca............	330	161	46	31	16	44
Puebla............	150	87	14	21	7	11
Querétaro..........	120	39	31	11	7	22
Quintana Roo a.....	2	...	...	...	...	...
San Luis Potosí.....	458	166	92	33	25	56
Sinaloa............	457	114	86	37	44	114
Sonora............	577	197	121	55	32	91
Tabasco...........	126	68	22	8	11	9
Tamaulipas........	538	164	137	53	41	77
Tlaxcala...........	88	50	22	8	3	4
Veracruz...........	683	330	118	70	37	73
Yucatán...........	687	396	122	70	32	45
Zacatecas..........	259	50	35	38	20	36
29 states b........	10,126	3,693	1,781	1,007	651	1,464

* This table and the four which follow it are based on tax records of the various states.
a Data for Quintana Roo incomplete.
b Distrito Federal and Morelos not included.

HECTARES OR OVER, BY STATE AND SIZE, 1923*

10,000 to 20,000 Hectares	20,000 to 30,000 Hectares	30,000 to 40,000 Hectares	40,000 to 50,000 Hectares	50,000 to 75,000 Hectares	75,000 to 100,000 Hectares	100,000 Hectares or Over
4	. . .	2	. . .	. . .	. . .	. . .
15	3	. . .	. . .	. . .	. . .	6
37	8	2	. . .	4	1	5
89	28	29	13	28	9	24
10	3	2	. . .	. . .	. . .	. . .
10	3	4	1	1	. . .	3
74	49	31	13	18	10	30
103	29	21	11	12	16	9
16	2	. . .	. . .	. . .	2	. . .
16	7	1	. . .	1	. . .	1
9	. . .	. . .	. . .	. . .	. . .	. . .
35	3	5	. . .	1	. . .	. . .
12	3	2	. . .	. . .	. . .	. . .
21	5	3	1	1	. . .	. . .
12	7	3	2	1	4	. . .
45	11	2	3	6	. . .	2
22	3	1	1	2	1	2
6	4	. . .	. . .	. . .	. . .	. . .
5	3	2	. . .	. . .	. . .	. . .
1	. . .	1	. . .	. . .	. . .	. . .
31	24	8	7	7	. . .	9
50	7	3	1	1	. . .	. . .
44	15	7	4	5	2	4
6	2	. . .	. . .	. . .	. . .	. . .
38	11	6	2	5	1	3
1	. . .	. . .	. . .	. . .	. . .	. . .
39	7	2	1	3	2	1
19	1	. . .	. . .	. . .	. . .	1
34	13	7	2	10	4	10
804	251	145	62	106	52	110

They include only properties valued at 5,000 *pesos* or more.

IV. AGGREGATE AREA OF ALL HACIENDAS OF 1,000

(In

STATE	Total	1,000 to 2,000 Hectares	2,000 to 3,000 Hectares	3,000 to 4,000 Hectares	4,000 to 5,000 Hectares	5,000 to 10,000 Hectares
Aguascali- entes.....	281,327	27,211	12,473	25,231	8,569	75,520
Baja California.	5,681,528	91,477	272,189	103,465	95,062	288,564
Campeche...	3,044,942	91,193	111,005	83,159	88,081	380,371
Coahuila....	13,076,923	131,769	150,164	152,316	145,893	798,284
Colima.....	482,497	51,091	23,585	26,978	21,527	72,769
Chiapas.....	2,628,041	542,940	413,456	210,064	194,143	341,052
Chihuahua..	16,290,239	84,756	103,539	134,711	93,160	736,866
Durango.....	9,006,052	112,696	188,970	276,651	261,220	892,531
Guanajuato.	1,579,409	304,978	184,647	163,331	112,493	384,241
Guerrero....	1,290,432	131,624	97,618	115,099	90,137	202,993
Hidalgo.....	510,060	138,901	67,344	72,448	31,032	92,180
Jalisco......	2,612,565	488,422	267,214	251,079	212,497	629,141
México.....	852,086	131,099	127,275	83,204	76,156	146,087
Michoacán..	1,521,384	260,938	125,261	140,658	91,759	312,170
Morelos a ...	195,283	6,724	5,432	3,980	4,311	34,010
Nayarit.....	1,238,367	57,507	52,907	32,762	31,385	137,287
Nuevo León..	2,502,553	48,855	65,367	103,108	110,953	512,250
Oaxaca.....	1,713,518	225,191	110,526	104,489	72,510	311,276
Puebla......	518,367	126,772	35,669	74,386	32,696	68,295
Querétaro...	573,025	52,832	74,568	39,426	39,840	151,686
Quintana Roo a.....	44,198	......	......	......	......	......
San Luis Potosí....	5,281,520	237,395	226,743	114,954	110,632	377,646
Sinaloa......	2,530,386	164,642	217,374	126,787	196,687	787,006
Sonora......	3,917,401	286,351	294,494	184,883	140,135	634,188
Tabasco.....	406,166	95,493	51,573	26,013	48,321	56,999
Tamaulipas..	3,580,134	251,161	323,298	181,719	183,291	523,662
Tlaxcala....	201,706	66,158	55,636	27,032	13,484	29,289
Veracruz....	3,030,951	455,780	285,038	236,428	167,981	500,805
Yucatán....	1,987,472	600,937	296,601	241,530	141,882	298,924
Zacatecas...	6,067,888	75,218	90,672	130,163	90,244	254,210
30 states b.	92,646,420	5,340,111	4,330,638	3,466,054	2,906,081	10,030,302

* See note * on pp. 486-487.
a Area and value figures incomplete.
b Distrito Federal not included.

Hectares or Over, by State and Size, 1923*
hectares)

10,000 to 20,000 Hectares	20,000 to 30,000 Hectares	30,000 to 40,000 Hectares	40,000 to 50,000 Hectares	50,000 to 75,000 Hectares	75,000 to 100,000 Hectares	100,000 Hectares or Over
57,605	......	74,718	......	......	......	......
215,063	78,596	......	......	......	......	4,537,112
502,798	192,511	63,050	......	260,537	88,272	1,183,965
1,255,133	679,637	997,503	596,210	1,678,314	778,383	5,713,317
146,479	69,801	70,267	......	......	......	......
117,635	69,978	142,188	48,114	57,162	......	492,309
1,019,996	1,116,150	1,045,846	561,112	1,074,118	842,545	9,477,440
1,472,554	712,772	731,795	483,353	777,557	1,401,574	1,694,379
199,409	47,186	......	......	......	183,124	......
206,547	167,462	34,612	......	50,895	......	193,445
108,155	......	......	......	......		......
468,301	68,450	164,961	......	62,500		......
160,084	63,337	64,844	......	......		......
263,495	117,448	111,053	40,115	58,487		......
47,109	48,799	......	44,918	......		......
160,285	159,922	91,000	87,198	64,756	363,358	......
591,871	259,200	68,015	140,446	374,688	......	277,800
292,650	70,440	35,601	47,683	119,607	78,870	244,675
83,484	97,065	......	......	......	......	......
78,067	71,993	64,613	......	......	......	......
12,050	......	32,148	......	......	......	......
452,526	587,036	284,546	311,696	394,369	......	2,183,977
663,623	183,814	96,222	44,168	50,063	......	......
609,434	361,982	242,104	174,309	293,200	187,330	508,991
80,688	47,079	......	......	......	......	......
517,163	269,924	207,351	87,384	300,959	97,218	637,004
10,107	......	......	......	......	......	......
536,902	181,194	72,667	49,261	174,566	164,329	206,000
246,198	28,409	32,991	......	......	......	100,000
529,981	323,239	239,900	96,298	547,489	343,113	3,347,361
11,105,392	6,072,424	4,967,995	2,812,265	6,339,267	4,528,116	30,747,775

V. Percentage Distribution, by State and Size, of the Aggregate

(Aggregate area of each class as a

STATE	All Haciendas of 1000 Hectares or Over	1,000 to 2,000 Hectares	2,000 to 3,000 Hectares	3,000 to 4,000 Hectares	4,000 to 5,000 Hectares
Aguascalientes......	43.5	4.2	1.9	3.9	1.3
Baja California.....	84.3	1.4	4.0	1.5	1.4
Campeche..........	83.8	2.5	3.0	2.3	2.4
Coahuila...........	.93.6	0.9	1.1	1.1	1.0
Colima............	92.7	9.8	4.5	5.2	4.1
Chiapas...........	38.1	7.9	6.0	3.0	2.8
Chihuahua.........	82.2	0.4	0.5	0.7	0.5
Durango...........	79.9	1.0	1.7	2.4	2.3
Guanajuato........	51.7	10.0	6.0	5.3	3.7
Guerrero..........	23.5	2.4	1.8	2.1	1.6
Hidalgo...........	24.4	6.6	3.2	3.5	1.5
Jalisco............	32.8	6.1	3.4	3.2	2.7
México............	39.8	6.1	6.0	3.9	3.6
Michoacán.........	25.3	4.3	2.1	2.3	1.5
Morelos a..........	39.3	1.4	1.1	0.8	0.9
Nayarit...........	83.4	3.9	3.6	2.2	2.1
Nuevo León........	38.4	0.8	1.0	1.6	1.7
Oaxaca...........	18.2	2.4	1.2	1.1	0.8
Puebla............	15.2	3.7	1.0	2.2	1.0
Querétaro.........	49.9	4.6	6.5	3.4	3.5
San Luis Potosí.....	84.8	3.8	3.6	1.8	1.8
Sinaloa............	47.1	3.1	4.0	2.4	3.7
Sonora............	53.8	3.9	4.0	2.5	1.9
Tabasco...........	22.8	5.4	2.9	1.5	2.7
Tamaulipas........	47.3	3.3	4.3	2.4	2.4
Tlaxcala..........	50.1	16.4	13.8	6.7	3.4
Veracruz..........	42.5	6.4	4.0	3.3	2.4
Yucatán...........	57.4	17.4	8.6	7.0	4.1
Zacatecas.........	84.5	1.0	1.3	1.8	1.3
29 States b.........	58.2	3.4	2.7	2.2	1.8

* See note* on pp. 486, 487.
a Area and value data incomplete.
b Distrito Federal and Quintana Roo not included.

AREA OF ALL HACIENDAS OF 1,000 HECTARES OR OVER, 1923*
percentage of all private rural land)

5,000 to 10,000 Hectares	10,000 to 20,000 Hectares	20,000 to 30,000 Hectares	30,000 to 40,000 Hectares	40000 to 50,000 Hectares	50,000 to 75,000 Hectares	75,000 to 100,000 Hectares	100,000 Hectares or Over
11.7	8.9	...	11.5	...	...	...	...
4.3	3.2	1.2	...	...	...	...	67.3
10.5	13.8	5.3	1.7	...	7.2	2.4	32.6
5.7	9.0	4.9	7.1	4.3	12.0	5.6	40.9
14.0	28.1	13.4	13.5	...	...	...	...
4.9	1.7	1.0	2.1	0.7	0.8	...	7.1
3.7	5.2	5.6	5.3	2.8	5.4	4.3	47.8
7.9	13.1	6.3	6.5	4.3	6.9	12.4	15.0
12.6	6.5	1.5	...	...	...	6.0	...
3.7	3.8	3.0	0.6	...	0.9	...	3.5
4.4	5.2	...	...	...	...	...	...
7.9	5.9	0.9	2.1	...	0.8	...	...
6.8	7.5	3.0	3.0	...	...	...	...
5.2	4.4	2.0	1.8	0.7	1.0	...	...
6.9	9.5	9.8	...	9.0	...	...	...
9.2	10.8	10.8	6.1	5.9	4.4	24.4	...
7.9	9.1	4.0	1.0	2.2	5.8	...	3.5
3.3	3.1	0.8	0.4	0.5	1.3	0.8	2.6
2.0	2.5	2.9	...	...	...	...	...
13.2	6.8	6.3	5.6	...	...	...	...
6.1	7.3	9.4	4.6	5.0	6.3	...	35.0
14.6	12.4	3.4	1.8	0.8	0.9	...	...
8.7	8.4	5.0	3.3	2.4	4.0	2.6	7.0
3.2	4.5	2.6	...	...	...	...	...
6.9	6.8	3.6	2.7	1.2	4.0	1.3	8.4
7.3	2.5	...	...	...	...	...	...
7.0	7.5	2.5	1.0	0.7	2.4	2.3	2.9
8.6	7.1	0.8	1.0	...	...	...	2.9
3.5	7.4	4.5	3.3	1.4	7.6	4.8	46.6
6.3	7.0	3.8	3.1	1.8	4.0	2.8	19.3

VI. Distribution, by State and by Size, of the Aggregate

(Figures in

STATE	Total	1,000 to 2,000 Hectares	2,000 to 3,000 Hectares	3,000 to 4000 Hectares	4,000 to 5,000 Hectares
Aguascalientes......	3,855	473	191	313	151
Baja California.....	34,950	1,449	1,946	319	1,481
Campeche..........	10,941	1,252	826	635	694
Coahuila...........	47,616	4,361	4,306	1,262	1,898
Colima.............	4,097	649	266	264	466
Chiapas............	21,400	7,493	3,753	1,714	1,458
Chihuahua.........	26,937	539	367	431	513
Durango...........	33,296	1,461	1,020	1,029	1,190
Guanajuato........	43,844	5,350	7,647	6,687	4,419
Guerrero...........	6,932	1,483	729	971	514
Hidalgo............	24,009	7,502	3,778	3,127	1,698
Jalisco.............	43,282	11,013	5,198	5,615	4,502
México.............	26,557	5,550	4,933	3,062	2,222
Michoacán.........	56,085	13,952	4,473	10,223	4,526
Nayarit............	8,465	905	469	320	98
Nuevo León........	5,720	524	493	519	260
Oaxaca............	16,525	2,328	1,418	1,283	926
Puebla............	21,467	7,974	1,662	3,524	1,286
Querétaro..........	17,824	2,301	2,348	1,077	1,211
Quintana Roo......	132	....	....	....	....
San Luis Potosí.....	35,695	2,980	2,533	1,130	1,216
Sinaloa............	11,282	1,926	1,652	574	892
Sonora.............	36,571	3,459	3,002	1,635	874
Tabasco...........	3,655	1,617	582	212	388
Tamaulipas........	15,106	1,361	1,290	669	748
Tlaxcala...........	13,473	4,699	3,737	1,911	924
Veracruz...........	77,340	8,175	14,909	7,477	4,740
Yucatán...........	71,027	21,245	17,021	10,044	7,745
Zacatecas..........	10,833	447	324	379	198
29 States [a]	728,916	122,468	90,873	66,406	47,238

*See note * on pages 486, 487.
[a] Morelos and Distrito Federal not included.

Value of All Haciendas of 1,000 Hectares or Over, 1923*
thousands of *pesos*)

5,000 to 10,000 Hectares	10,000 to 20,000 Hectares	20,000 to 30,000 Hectares	30,000 to 40,000 Hectares	40,000 to 50,000 Hectares	50,000 to 75,000 Hectares	75,000 to 100,000 Hectares	100,000 Hectares or Over
1,031	665	. . .	1,031	. . . . .	. . . . .	. . . . .	. . . . .
2,378	640	720	. . . . .	. . . . .	. . . . .	. . . . .	26,017
2,061	2,202	647	310	. . . . .	625	50	1,640
10,335	4,330	3,874	1,803	932	5,193	2,157	7,164
568	1,190	305	390	. . . . .	. . . .	. . . . .	. . . . .
3,246	976	570	612	392	237	. . . . .	948
1,360	1,707	2,674	1,833	1,214	1,873	1,385	13,041
4,056	4,987	2,146	1,689	6,905	2,773	3,092	2,948
13,718	4,454	710	. . . . .	. . . . .	. . . . .	859	. . . . .
1,118	1,497	291	66	. . . . .	60	. . . . .	202
4,589	3,315	. . . . .	. . . . .	. . . . .	. . . . .	. . . . .	. . . . .
10,452	4,127	1,025	1,310	. . . . .	40	. . . . .	. . . . .
4,405	2,956	1,930	1,500	. . . . .	. . . . .	. . . . .	. . . . .
4,593	11,722	2,370	1,745	2,100	380	. . . . .	. . . . .
995	793	1,417	941	402	1,093	1,033	. . . . .
1,056	1,410	514	77	295	329	. . . . .	242
3,174	2,654	243	329	441	739	729	2,261
1,655	3,330	2,037	. . . . .	. . . . .	. . . . .	. . . . .	. . . . .
5,533	1,747	1,968	1,640	. . . . .	. . . . .	. . . . .	. . . . .
. . . . .	36	. . . . .	96	. . . . .	. . . . .	. . . . .	. . . . .
4,168	5,212	5,025	2,382	2,373	3,683	. . . . .	4,993
2,456	2,798	277	662	11	35	. . . . .	. . . . .
4,945	5,714	6,202	1,359	1,266	2,576	1,124	4,414
383	353	120	. . . . .	. . . . .	. . . . .	. . . . .	. . . . .
2,086	1,995	943	886	293	1,297	292	3,246
2,051	150	. . . . .	. . . . .	. . . . .	. . . . .	. . . . .	. . . . .
14,435	9,183	8,139	724	1,073	2,712	3,567	2,206
9,386	4,403	460	33	. . . . .	. . . . .	. . . . .	690
1,103	1,385	812	528	623	1,398	602	3,034
117,336	85,931	45,419	21,946	18,320	25,043	14,890	73,046

VII. Percentage Distribution, by State and Size, of the Aggregate
(Aggregate Value of Each Class as a Percentage

STATE	All Haciendas of 1,000 Hectares or Over	1,000 to 2,000 Hectares	2,000 to 3,000 Hectares	3,000 to 4,000 Hectares	4,000 to 5,000 Hectares
Aguascalientes......	46.2	5.7	2.3	3.8	1.8
Baja California.....	61.4	2.6	3.4	0.6	2.6
Campeche.........	72.0	8.2	5.4	4.2	4.6
Coahuila..........	73.9	6.8	6.7	2.0	2.9
Colima...........	67.7	10.7	4.4	4.4	7.7
Chiapas...........	48.6	17.0	8.5	3.9	3.3
Durango..........	85.2	3.7	2.6	2.6	3.0
Guanajuato.......	39.1	4.8	6.8	6.0	3.9
Guerrero..........	48.5	10.4	5.1	6.8	3.6
Hidalgo..........	51.8	16.2	8.2	6.8	3.7
Jalisco............	42.2	10.7	5.1	5.5	4.4
México...........	48.7	10.2	9.0	5.6	4.1
Michoacán........	41.7	10.4	3.3	7.6	3.4
Nayarit...........	74.2	7.9	4.1	2.8	0.9
Nuevo León.......	45.2	4.1	3.9	4.1	2.1
Oaxaca...........	59.1	8.3	5.1	4.6	3.3
Puebla............	43.6	16.2	3.4	7.2	2.6
Querétaro.........	71.4	9.2	9.4	4.3	4.8
San Luis Potosí.....	79.2	6.6	5.6	2.5	2.7
Sinaloa...........	60.6	10.3	8.9	3.1	4.8
Sonora...........	74.5	7.0	6.1	3.3	1.8
Tabasco..........	19.4	8.6	3.1	1.1	2.1
Tamaulipas........	72.1	6.5	6.2	3.2	3.6
Tlaxcala..........	51.8	18.1	14.4	7.4	3.6
Veracruz..........	40.8	4.3	7.9	4.0	2.5
Yucatán..........	56.9	17.0	13.6	8.0	6.2
Zacatecas.........	57.9	2.4	1.7	2.0	1.1
27 States [a].........	54.4	9.1	6.8	5.0	3.5

* See note* on pages 486, 487.
a Morelos, Distrito Federal, and Quintana Roo, not included, because of insufficiency of

VALUE OF HACIENDAS OF 1,000 HECTARES OR OVER, 1923*
OF THE VALUE OF ALL PRIVATE RURAL LANDS)

5,000 to 10,000 Hectares	10,000 to 20,000 Hectares	20,000 to 30,000 Hectares	30,000 to 40,000 Hectares	40,000 to 50,000 Hectares	50,000 to 75,000 Hectares	75,000 to 100,000 Hectares	100,000 Hectares or Over
12.3	8.0	...	12.4	...	...	...	...
4.2	1.1	1.3	...	...	...	...	45.8
13.6	14.5	4.3	2.0	...	4.1	0.3	10.8
16.0	6.7	6.0	2.8	1.4	8.1	3.4	11.1
9.4	19.7	5.0	6.4	...	...	...	...
7.4	2.2	1.3	1.4	0.9	0.5	...	2.2
10.4	12.8	5.5	4.3	17.7	7.1	7.9	7.6
12.2	4.0	0.6	...	...	...	0.8	...
7.8	10.5	2.0	0.5	...	0.4	...	1.4
9.9	7.2	...	...	...	...	...	...
10.2	4.0	1.0	1.3	...	0.1	...	...
8.1	5.4	3.5	2.8	...	...	...	...
3.4	8.7	1.8	1.3	1.6	0.3	...	...
8.7	7.0	12.4	8.2	3.5	9.6	9.1	...
8.4	11.1	4.1	0.6	2.3	2.6	...	1.9
11.4	9.5	0.9	1.2	1.6	2.6	2.6	8.1
3.4	6.8	4.1	...	...	...	...	...
22.2	7.0	7.9	6.6	...	...	...	...
9.2	11.6	11.2	5.3	5.3	8.2	...	11.1
13.2	15.0	1.5	3.6	0.1	0.2	...	...
10.1	11.6	12.6	2.8	2.6	5.2	2.3	9.0
2.0	1.9	0.6	...	...	...	...	...
10.0	9.5	4.5	4.2	1.4	6.2	1.4	15.5
7.9	0.6	...	...	...	...	...	...
7.6	4.8	4.3	0.4	0.6	1.4	1.9	1.2
7.5	3.5	0.4	0.1	...	...	...	0.6
5.9	7.4	4.3	2.8	3.3	7.5	3.2	16.2
8.8	6.4	3.4	1.6	1.4	1.9	1.1	5.4

data. Chihuahua omitted because of conflict between state and federal data.

VIII. Owners of Rural Lands in the State of Aguascalientes, by Number and Aggregate Area of Their Holdings, 1923 *

Number of Pieces of Property Owned	Total Number of Owners	Less than 1 Hectare	1 to 5	6 to 10	11 to 20	21 to 30	31 to 40	41 to 50	51 to 75	76 to 100	101 to 200	201 to 500	501 to 1,000	1,001 to 5,000	5,000 to 10,000	10,000 Hectares or Over
1	1,848	713	394	141	134	79	55	44	53	34	61	57	21	39	15	8
2	543	131	176	46	41	32	18	10	13	10	33	15	9	4	3	2
3	253	53	103	18	13	7	5	6	10	7	11	13	5	2		
4	113	20	44	10	12	5	5	1	5	1	4	3	2	1		
5	81	6	35	7	7	4	4		5	3		4	3	3		
6	49	2	17	8	5	3			3	3	3	2	3			
7	29		13	5	5		1	1	1	1		2				
8	22		6	3	1	1	1	2		2	2	2	2			
9	15	1	5	3	1		2		1	1		1				
10	12		5	1	3	1					1	1				
11	6		2	3	1		1		1							
12	5		2	3				1								
13	4		1		1				1							
14	1			1		1										
15	1				1			1								
17	2															
18	1								1		1					
19	1			1	1				1							
21	2															
29	1															
35	1															
36	1									1						
56	1															
	2,992	926	803	250	226	133	92	66	95	63	116	100	45	49	18	10

* Data from tax records.

IX. PROVISIONAL LAND GRANTS (EJIDOS), 1915 TO 1926 INCLUSIVE, BY STATES

STATE	Area of State a (In hectares)	Area in Provisional Grants		Rural Population of State b	Persons Receiving Ejidos	
		In Hectares	As Percentage of Total		Number c	As Percentage of Rural Population
Aguascalientes	647,200	35,304	5.45	60,620	3,893	6.42
Baja California	14,409,300	9,286	.06	48,659	1,219	2.51
Campeche	5,013,700	129,985	2.59	47,925	6,916	14.43
Coahuila	15,039,500	116,051	0.77	219,324	4,759	2.17
Colima	520,500	17,434	3.35	63,423	1,678	2.65
Chiapas	7,441,500	57,819	0.78	352,802	7,141	2.02
Chihuahua	24,561,200	717,072	2.92	306,102	15,563	5.08
Durango	12,352,000	418,039	3.38	265,686	12,397	4.67
Guanajuato	3,058,500	35,471	1.16	600,914	6,458	1.07
Guerrero	6,445,800	148,517	2.30	515,721	17,894	3.47
Hidalgo	2,088,400	133,008	6.37	552,762	17,557	3.18
Jalisco	8,068,300	200,284	2.48	843,666	36,157	4.29
México	2,140,000	91,197	4.26	782,525	42,217	5.39
Michoacán	6,008,300	130,481	2.17	756,685	27,665	3.66
Morelos	496,400	163,162	32.87	91,861	23,238	25.30
Nayarit	2,705,300	12,488	0.46	101,817	2,044	2.01
Nuevo León	6,510,300	24,863	0.38	226,585	1,014	0.45
Oaxaca	9,421,100	68,336	0.73	849,384	14,838	1.75
Puebla	3,399,500	333,588	9.81	854,368	56,338	6.59
Querétaro	1,148,000	24,405	2.13	184,601	3,854	2.09
San Luis Potosí	6,324,100	627,708	9.93	341,286	31,249	9.16

IX. Provisional Land Grants (Ejidos), 1915 to 1926 Inclusive, by States—*(Concluded)*

STATE	Area of State[a] (In hectares)	Area in Provisional Grants		Rural Population of State [b]	Persons Receiving Ejidos	
		In Hectares	As Percentage of Total		Number [c]	As Percentage of Rural Population
Sinaloa	5,848,800	790	.01	280,125	79	...
Sonora	18,255,300	103,027	5.60	207,950	5,867	2.82
Tabasco	2,533,700	29,132	1.15	190,532	1,031	0.54
Tamaulipas	7,960,200	78,395	0.98	160,106	9,022	5.64
Tlaxcala	402,700	12,479	3.10	151,994	7,938	5.22
Veracruz	7,189,600	162,534	2.26	840,071	25,580	3.04
Yucatán	3,850,800	864,662	2.25	211,451	45,732	21.63
Zacatecas	7,284,300	291,717	4.00	325,103	15,419	4.74
Distrito Federal	148,300	8,807	5.94	122,440	8,072	6.59
30 States [d]	191,272,600	5,046,041	2.64	10,556,488	452,829	4.29

a Source: *Estadística Nacional*, Nov. 30, 1926, p. 6.
b Compiled from Census of 1921.
c Courtesy *Comisión Nacional Agraria*.
d Quintana Roo not included.

X. Provisional Land Distribution

YEAR	Restitution			Donation			Number of Villages
	Number of Villages	Area in Hectares	Number of People Receiving Land	Number of Villages	Area in Hectares	Number of People Receiving Land	
1915....	1	68	65	1	1,755	640	..
1916....	13	45,848	5,171	24	36,011	6,036	..
1917....	7	61,394	3,511	17	24,077	3,781	..
1918....	1	3,902	442	10	21,615	3,026	..
1919....	1	1,650	165	6	4,533	781	..
1920....	2	29,560	409	28	33,509	5,029	..
1921....	25	138,972	6,426	245	519,357	59,561	2
1922....	12	20,047	2,337	184	425,408	37,865	..
1923....	29	396,177	10,714	389	700,422	76,824	9
1924....	21	176,448	2,473	408	653,609	86,767	..
1925....	8	66,582	2,144	502	720,969	91,498	2
1926....	6	16,940	472	254	438,121	41,816	4
Total...	126	957,588	34,329	2,068	3,579,386	413,624	17

*Comisión Nacional Agraria (Manuscript copy).

1915–1926, BY TYPE OF GRANT*

Confirmation		Amplification			Total		
Area in Hectares	Number of People Receiving Land	Number of Villages	Area in Hectares	Number of People Receiving Land	Number of Villages	Area in Hectares	Number of People Receiving Land
. . . . .	. . .	. .	. . . . .	. . .	2	1,823	705
3,180	. . .	. .	. . . . .	. . .	37	85,039	11,207
5,244	. . .	. .	. . . . .	. . .	24	90,715	7,292
. . . . .	. . .	. .	. . . . .	. . .	11	25,517	3,468
. . . . .	. . .	. .	. . . . .	. . . . .	7	6,183	946
564	. . .	1	504	. . .	31	64,137	5,438
40,439	470	3	3,174	231	275	701,942	66,688
38,722	. . .	7	11,459	737	203	495,636	40,939
145,031	1,407	15	19,991	200	442	1,261,621	89,145
73,654	. . .	4	5,084	947	433	908,795	90,187
96,770	279	2	5,047	. . .	514	889,368	93,921
56,802	605	3	3,402	. . .	267	515,265	42,893
460,406	2,761	35	48,661	2,115	2,246	5,046,041	452,829

XI. Definitive Land Distribution

YEAR	Restitution			Donation			
	Number of Villages	Area in Hectares	Number of People Receiving Land	Number of Villages	Area in Hectares	Number of People Receiving Land	Number of Villages
1915....	0	...	...	..	.....	.....	..
1916....	1	605	403	..	.....	.....	..
1917....	2	509	454	5	4,981	2,229	..
1918....	6	19,322	1,244	53	49,923	14,629	..
1919....	1	456	447	58	37,585	16,487	..
1920....	1	217	2,792	60	55,598	12,802	3
1921....	8	53,166	1,272	110	126,457	23,858	..
1922....	8	39,339	1,273	57	90,066	12,540	..
1923....	6	49,826	1,116	119	206,803	28,815	..
1924....	13	78,586	2,058	297	521,734	62,037	..
1925....	9	41,349	1,572	395	696,195	78,217	7
1926....	11	177,886	2,527	383	538,801	74,389	6
Totals..	66	461,261	15,158	1,537	2,328,143	326,003	16

*Comisión Nacional Agraria (Manuscript copy).

1915–1926, by Type of Grant*

Confirmation		Amplification			Totals		
Area in Hectares	Number of People Receiving Land	Number of Villages	Area in Hectares	Number of People Receiving Land	Number of Villages	Area in Hectares	Number of People Receiving Land
. . . . .	. . .	. .	. . . . .	. .	. . .	. . . . .	. . . .
. . . . .	. . .	. .	. . . . .	. .	1	605	403
. . . . .	. . .	. .	. . . . .	. .	7	5,490	2,683
5,435	. . .	. . .	. . . .	. .	59	74,680	15,873
4,230	. . .	. .	. . . . .	. .	59	42,271	16,934
9,217	789	. .	. . . . .	. .	64	65,032	16,383
2,879	. . .	3	3,198	. .	121	185,700	25,130
7,207	. . .	4	5,567	. .	69	142,179	13,813
14,940	. . .	2	1,418	. .	127	272,987	29,931
32,240	. . .	1	1,000	. .	311	633,560	64,095
81,458	1,287	7	5,061	. .	418	824,063	81,076
120,730	783	14	15,064	. .	414	852,481	77,699
278,336	2,859	31	31,308	. .	1,650	3,099,048	344,020

XII. Ownership, Area, and Value of Rural Holdings

STATE	Estimated Number of Rural Families a	Number of Owners of Rural Land	Ownership		
			Owners of Land Valued at 5,000 Pesos or Over		
			Number	As Percentage of Number of Rural Families	As Percentage of All Rural Land Owners
Aguascalientes...	12,124	2,941	118	*1.0*	*4.0*
Baja California..	9,732	1,761	223	*2.3*	*12.7*
Campeche......	9,585	897	230	*2.4*	*25.6*
Chihuahua......	61,220	6,028	561	*0.9*	*9.3*
Chiapas........	70,560	13,026	1,199	*1.7*	*9.2*
Coahuila........	43,865	4,000	805	*1.8*	*20.1*
Colima.........	12,685	809	183	*1.4*	*22.6*
Durango........	53,137	7,389	744	*1.4*	*10.1*
Guanajuato.....	120,183	12,455	1,614	*1.3*	*13.0*
Guerrero........	103,144	4,012	384	*0.4*	*9.6*
Hidalgo.........	110,552	44,614	513	*0.5*	*1.1*
Jalisco..........	168,733	60,580	1,744	*1.0*	*2.9*
México........ .	156,505	31,640	684	*0.4*	*2.2*
Michoacán......	151,337	42,334	1,645	*1.1*	*3.9*
Morelos.........	18,372	4,519	64	*0.4*	*1.4*
Nayarit.........	20,363	1,492	128	*0.6*	*8.6*
Nuevo León.....	45,317	6,780	329	*0.7*	*4.8*
Oaxaca.........	169,877	43,289	523	*0.3*	*1.2*
Puebla.........	170,874	27,026	593	*0.4*	*2.2*
Querétaro.......	36,920	10,080	194	*0.5*	*1.9*
San Luis Potosí..	68,257	4,144	741	*1.1*	*17.9*
Sinaloa.........	56,025	5,761	374	*0.7*	*6.5*
Sonora.........	41,590	3,255	708	*1.7*	*21.8*
Tabasco........	38,106	8,959	489	*1.3*	*5.5*
Tamaulipas.....	32,021	4,116	552	*1.7*	*13.4*
Tlaxcala........	30,399	1,470	375	*1.2*	*25.5*
Veracruz........	168,014	41,298	383	*0.2*	*0.9*
Yucatán........	42,290	9,640	1,251	*3.0*	*13.0*
Zacatecas.......	65,021	26,996	316	*0.5*	*1.2*
29 States b..	2,086,808	431,311	17,667	*0.8*	*4.1*

* Data from tax records, except number of rural families which is based on census data.
a The rural families were estimated by dividing the rural population by five.
b Distrito Federal and Quintana Roo not included.

VALUED AT 5,000 *Pesos* OR OVER AND OF ALL RURAL HOLDINGS, 1923*

Area			Value		
	Holdings Valued at 5,000 *Pesos* or Over			Holdings Valued at 5,000 *Pesos* or Over	
All Rural Holdings (In thousands of hectares)	In Thousands of Hectares	As Percentage of All Rural Holdings	All Rural Holdings (In Thousands of pesos)	In thousands of *Pesos*	As Percentage of All Rural Holdings
647	462	71.4	8,351	6,993	83.7
6,738	5,789	85.9	56,871	39,287	69.1
3,635	3,363	92.5	15,193	13,230	87.1
19,809	16,529	83.4	. . . .	49,409	. . . .
6,899	2,856	41.4	43,995	33,054	75.1
13,977	13,014	93.1	64,450	50,951	79.1
521	519	99.8	6,052	5,375	88.8
11,276	9,191	81.5	39,061	33,394	85.5
3,057	2,147	70.2	112,166	93,830	83.7
5,488	1,313	23.9	14,290	10,510	73.5
2,088	715	34.2	46,331	40,603	87.6
7,959	3,369	42.3	102,560	68,870	67.2
2,140	1,483	69.3	54,547	46,575	85.4
6,008	2,027	33.7	134,609	106,128	78.8
496	. . . .	. . . .	4,408	2,391	54.2
1,486	1,300	87.5	11,407	9,654	84.6
6,510	3,156	48.5	12,649	7,770	61.4
9,421	1,989	21.1	27,960	18,382	65.7
3,400	683	20.1	49,184	41,009	83.4
1,148	634	55.2	24,982	22,675	90.8
6,231	5,768	92.6	45,050	42,642	94.7
5,371	2,627	48.9	18,622	13,715	73.6
7,274	4,190	57.6	49,069	43,470	88.6
1,777	756	42.5	18,820	12,262	65.2
7,570	3,839	50.7	20,946	17,052	81.4
403	301	74.9	26,004	24,428	93.9
7,137	4,218	59.1	189,455	155,705	82.2
3,460	2,495	72.1	124,899	115,770	92.7
7,180	6,379	88.8	18,697	13,322	71.3
159,106	101,112	63.6	1,340,628	1,138,456	84.9

XIII. Ownership, Area, and Value of Private Rural Holdings of 5,000 Hectares or Over, and of All Rural Holdings, 1923

STATE	All Privately Owned Rural Lands		Privately Owned Rural Lands of 5,000 Hectares or Over				
	Area in Thousands of Hectares	Value in Thousands of Pesos	Area		Value		Number of Owners
			In Thousands of Hectares	As Percentage of All Privately Owned Lands	In Thousands of Pesos	As Percentage of All Privately Owned Lands	
Aguascalientes	647	8,351	291	44.9	3,967	47.5	26
Baja California	6,738	56,871	5,237	77.7	29,091	51.2	69
Campeche	3,635	15,193	2,971	81.7	9,095	59.9	73
Chihuahua	19,809	a	17,128	86.5	15,438	...	256
Chiapas	6,899	43,995	1,376	19.9	8,303	18.9	72
Coahuila	13,977	64,450	12,311	88.1	36,835	57.2	282
Colima	521	6,052	359	69.0	2,483	41.0	26
Durango	11,276	39,061	8,406	74.5	27,967	71.6	277
Guanajuato	3,057	112,166	767	25.1	20,297	18.1	78
Guerrero	5,488	14,290	587	10.7	2,363	16.5	38
Hidalgo	2,088	46,331	227	10.8	9,058	19.6	26
Jalisco	7,959	102,560	1,346	16.9	17,735	17.3	126
México	2,140	54,547	438	20.5	12,160	22.3	36
Michoacán	6,008	134,609	953	15.9	37,411	27.8	76
Morelos a	496	4,408					
Nayarit	1,486	11,407	1,127	75.8	6,891	60.4	40
Nuevo León	6,510	12,649	1,919	29.5	4,248	33.6	123

XIII. OWNERSHIP, AREA, AND VALUE OF PRIVATE RURAL HOLDINGS OF 5,000 HECTARES OR OVER, AND OF ALL RURAL HOLDINGS, 1923—(Concluded)

STATE	All Privately Owned Rural Lands		Privately Owned Rural Lands of 5,000 Hectares or Over				
	Area in Thousands of Hectares	Value in Thousands of Pesos	Area		Value		Number of Owners
			In Thousands of Hectares	As Percentage of All Privately Owned Lands	In Thousands of Pesos	As Percentage of All Privately Owned Lands	
Oaxaca	9,421	27,960	1,008	10.7	9,361	33.5	66
Puebla	3,400	49,184	118	3.5	6,035	12.3	12
Querétaro	1,148	24,982	367	32.0	9,290	37.2	24
San Luis Potosí	6,231	45,050	4,433	71.2	28,404	63.0	139
Sinaloa	5,371	18,622	1,662	30.9	6,454	34.7	133
Sonora	7,274	49,069	3,035	41.7	18,592	37.9	149
Tabasco	1,777	18,820	342	19.2	1,995	10.6	21
Tamaulipas	7,569	20,946	3,543	46.8	11,765	56.2	161
Tlaxcala	403	26,004	39	9.8	2,201	8.5	5
Vera Cruz	7,137	189,455	2,029	28.4	42,989	22.7	116
Yucatán	3,460	124,899	1,037	30.0	27,692	22.2	72
Zacatecas	7,181	18,697	6,706	93.4	12,804	68.5	160
29 States b	159,106	1,340,628	79,762	50.1	420,924	31.4	2,682

a Data incomplete.
b Quintana Roo and Distrito Federal not included.

XIV. Ownership, Area, and Value of Rural Holdings of

STATE	Holdings of 5,000 to 10,000 Hectares					Holdings of 10,000 to 20,000 Hectares				
	Area		Number of Owners	Value		Area		Number of Owners	Value	
	In Thousands of Hectares	As Percentage of Total Area		In Thousands of Pesos	As Percentage of Total Value	In Hectares	As Percentage of Total Area		In Thousands of Pesos	As Percentage of Total Value
Aguascalientes......	108,082	16.7	16	1,950	23.4	147,462	22.8	9	1,636	19.6
Baja California......	259,958	8.1	39	1,227	..	276,431	8.6	19	864	..
Campeche.........	253,773	7.0	36	1,517	10.0	263,624	7.3	18	1,513	10.0
Chihuahua.........	623,847	3.1	90	1,160	3.1	478,874	2.4	32	779	2.1
Chiapas...........	302,539	4.4	46	2,898	6.6	167,337	2.4	13	1,462	3.3
Coahuila..........	686,234	5.1	97	5,484	8.5	993,723	7.3	71	2,918	4.5
Colima............	72,769	14.0	11	578	9.5	146,479	28.1	10	1,210	20.0
Durango...........	664,223	5.9	99	2,928	7.5	1,168,959	10.4	81	3,690	9.4
Guanajuato........	368,774	12.1	55	12,591	11.2	237,159	7.8	19	6,214	5.5
Guerrero..........	122,529	2.2	20	805	5.6	164,797	3.0	13	694	4.9
Hidalgo...........	105,306	5.0	16	5,010	10.2	121,264	5.8	10	4,048	8.2
Jalisco............	577,228	7.3	85	9,903	9.7	407,689	5.1	31	4,445	4.3
México............	129,618	6.1	18	3,460	6.3	158,722	7.4	12	4,582	8.4
Michoacán.........	290,712	4.8	42	10,083	7.5	301,382	5.0	23	13,577	10.1
Nayarit...........	93,880	8.1	12	703	8.2	210,565	18.3	14	1,070	9.4
Nuevo León........	419,924	6.5	62	914	7.2	560,326	8.6	41	1,705	13.5
Oaxaca............	272,004	2.9	38	2,967	10.6	272,667	2.9	20	2,587	9.3
Puebla............	32,728	1.0	6	575	1.2	84,779	2.5	6	5,460	11.5
Querétaro..........	75,333	6.6	11	2,520	10.1	79,936	7.0	6	2,175	8.7
San Luis Potosí.....	355,688	5.7	53	3,837	8.5	489,299	7.9	34	5,615	12.5
Sinaloa............	485,631	9.0	70	1,479	7.9	634,615	11.8	47	2,763	14.8
Sonora............	523,264	7.2	75	4,335	9.2	562,447	7.7	42	4,851	10.3
Tabasco...........	66,255	3.7	10	426	2.3	101,474	5.7	8	449	2.4
Tamaulipas	630,636	8.3	88	2,264	10.8	591,553	7.8	42	1,762	8.4
Tlaxcala...........	29,289	7.3	4	2,051	7.9	10,107	2.5	1	150	0.6
Veracruz...........	425,611	6.0	61	13,810	7.2	441,089	6.2	32	7,589	3.9
Yucatán...........	391,346	11.3	49	13,057	10.4	172,453	5.0	12	5,447	4.3
Zacatecas..........	394,314	5.5	59	1,129	6.0	586,051	8.2	40	1,619	8.7
28 states [a]........	8,761,495	5.5	1,268	109661	8.2	9,831,263	6.2	706	90,874	6.8

[a] Distrito Federal, Morelos, and Quintana Roo omitted.

5,000 Hectares or Over, by State and Size of Holding, 1923

| Holdings of 20,000 to 30,000 Hectares | | | | | Holdings of 30,000 to 40,000 Hectares | | | | |
| Area | | Number of Owners | Value | | Area | | Number of Owners | Value | |
In Hectares	As Percentage of Total Area		In Thousands of Pesos	As Percentage of Total Value	In Hectares	As Percentage of Total Area		In Thousands of Pesos	As Percentage of Total Value
....	....	....	....	....	35,112	5.4	1	380	4.6
95,269	4.0	4	783	....	39,711	1.2	1	80	....
25,427	0.7	1	118	0.8	67,750	1.9	2	334	2.2
1,111,620	5.6	53	2,589	7.0	976,124	4.9	28	1,606	4.3
51,733	0.7	2	691	1.6	135,616	2.0	4	667	1.5
621,397	4.6	24	1,664	2.6	729,000	5.4	21	3,032	4.7
69,801	13.4	3	305	5.0	70,267	13.5	2	390	6.4
534,976	4.7	21	1,924	4.9	579,403	5.1	17	1,463	3.7
69,176	2.3	3	1,063	0.9	....	....	....	....	....
70,310	1.3	3	50	0.4	35,325	0.6	1	610	4.3
....	....	....	....	....	....	....	....	....	....
74,514	0.9	3	1,401	1.4	140,144	1.8	4	1,010	1.0
85,278	4.0	4	2,619	4.8	64,844	3.0	2	1,500	2.7
151,423	2.5	6	9,526	7.1	111,053	1.8	3	1,745	1.3
128,581	11.1	5	1,213	10.6	39,694	3.4	1	505	4.4
249,224	3.8	10	678	5.4	32,015	0.5	1	50	0.4
48,840	0.5	2	220	0.8	66,566	0.7	2	368	1.3
....	....	....	....	....	....	....	....	....	....
76,645	6.7	3	2,133	8.5	134,905	11.8	4	2,462	9.9
516,504	8.3	21	4,419	9.8	319,658	5.1	9	2,759	6.1
258,912	4.8	10	629	3.4	66,222	1.2	2	602	3.2
262,176	3.6	11	2,088	4.4	177,130	2.4	5	1,162	2.5
47,079	2.6	2	120	0.6	....	....	....	....	....
265,922	3.5	11	1,473	7.0	229,465	3.0	7	945	4.5
197,676	2.8	9	5,896	3.1	97,333	1.4	3	1,601	0.8
113,343	3.3	5	3,767	3.0	102,642	3.0	3	1,479	1.2
416,090	5.8	17	899	4.8	178,521	2.5	5	405	2.2
5,541,916	3.5	233	46,268	3.5	4,428,500	2.8	128	25,155	1.9

XIV. OWNERSHIP, AREA, AND VALUE OF RURAL HOLDINGS OF

STATE	Holdings of 40,000 to 50,000 Hectares					Holdings of 50,000 to 75,000 Hectares				
	Area		Number of Owners	Value		Area		Number of Owners	Value	
	In Hectares	As Percentage of Total Area		In Thousands of Pesos	As Percentage of Total Value	In Hectares	As Percentage of Total Area		In Thousands of Pesos	As Percentage of Total Value
Aguascalientes	.....	..	..	..	..	.....	..	..	..	..
Baja California	.....	..	..	..	..	.....	..	..	..	..
Campeche	47,370	1.3	1	55	0.4	303,354	8.3	4	1,171	7.7
Chihuahua	558,045	2.8	12	1,273	3.4	1,082,055	5.5	14	1,714	4.6
Chiapas	45,358	0.7	1	369	0.8	180,978	2.6	3	1,268	2.9
Coahuila	549,690	4.0	12	1,003	1.6	1,767,274	13.0	29	5,153	8.0
Colima	.....	..	..	..	..	.....	..	..	..	..
Durango	770,159	6.8	17	7,922	20.3	807,568	7.2	13	2,168	5.6
Guanajuato	.....	..	..	..	..	.....	..	..	..	..
Guerrero	.....	..	..	..	..	.....	..	..	..	..
Hidalgo	.....	..	..	..	..	.....	..	..	..	..
Jalisco	83,953	1.1	2	49	0.1	62,739	0.8	1	928	0.9
México	.....	..	..	..	..	.....	..	..	..	..
Michoacán	40,115	0.7	1	2,100	1.6	58,487	1.0	1	380	0.3
Nayarit	45,304	3.9	1	60	0.5	203,173	17.6	3	1,881	16.5
Nuevo León	134,656	2.1	3	296	2.3	187,795	2.9	3	228	1.8
Oaxaca	.....	..	..	..	..	122,008	1.3	2	1,128	4.0
Puebla	.....	..	..	..	..	.....	..	..	..	..
Querétaro	.....	..	..	..	..	.....	..	..	..	..
San Luis Potosí	223,641	3.6	5	1,954	4.3	515,259	8.3	9	4,338	9.6
Sinaloa	145,178	2.7	3	677	2.6	71,380	1.3	1	304	1.6
Sonora	129,216	1.8	3	972	2.1	369,910	5.1	6	2,507	5.3
Tabasco	.....	..	..	..	..	.....	..	..	..	..
Tamaulipas	132,825	1.8	3	339	1.6	338,942	4.5	5	1,071	5.1
Tlaxcala	.....	..	..	..	..	.....	..	..	..	..
Veracruz	140,049	2.0	3	2,650	1.4	114,566	1.6	2	1,107	0.6
Yucatán	.....	..	..	..	..	61,592	1.8	1	1,135	0.9
Zacatecas	186,488	2.6	4	737	4.0	1,052,017	14.7	17	2,363	12.6
	3,232,056	2.0	71	20,456	1.5	7,299,097	4.6	114	28,844	2.1

5,000 Hectares or Over, by State and Size of Holding—(*Concluded*)

Holdings of 75,000 to 100,000 Hectares					Holdings of 100,000 Hectares or Over				
Area		Number of Owners	Value		Area		Number of Owners	Value	
In Hectares	As Percentage of Total Area		In Thousands of Pesos	As Percentage of Total Value	In Hectares	As Percentage of Total Area		In Thousands of Pesos	As Percentage of Total Value
....	....	....	....	....	4,565,360	67.8	6	26,137	....
180,359	5.0	2	889	5.9	1,829,564	50.3	9	3,498	23.0
261,885	1.3	3	755	2.0	12,035,225	60.8	24	5,561	14.9
....	....	....	....	....	492,309	7.1	3	948	2.2
635,077	4.7	7	2,235	3.5	6,328,224	46.6	21	15,348	23.8
1,128,095	10.0	13	2,953	7.6	2,752,306	24.4	16	4,918	12.6
91,562	3.0	1	429	0.4	....	....	....	....	....
....	....	....	....	....	194,477	3.5	1	204	1.4
....	....	....	....	....	....	....	....	....	......
....	....	....	....	....	....	....	....	....	......
....	....	....	....	....	....	....	....	....	......
281,085	24.4	3	676	5.9	124,427	10.8	1	782	6.9
....	....	....	....	....	334,800	5.1	3	379	3.0
89,689	1.0	1	829	3.0	136,474	1.4	1	1,261	4.5
....	....	....	....	....	....	....	....	....	....
174,097	2.8	2	726	1.6	1,838,973	29.5	6	4,755	10.6
....	....	....	....	....	....	....	....	....	....
174,055	2.4	2	1,166	2.5	837,058	11.5	5	1,509	3.2
....	....	....	....	....	127,000	7.1	1	1,000	5.3
....	....	....	....	....	1,354,157	17.9	5	3,910	18.7
406,625	6.0	5	8,131	4.2	206,000	2.9	1	2,206	1.1
195,782	5.7	2	2,808	2.2	....	....	....	....	....
605,954	8.4	7	1,149	6.1	3,287,098	45.8	11	4,504	24.1
4,224,265	2.6	48	22,746	1.7	36,443,452	22.9	114	76,920	5.7

XV. AREA OF FOREIGN OWNED RURAL HOLDINGS VALUED AT 5,000

STATE	Total In Hectares	United States		Spanish	
		In Hectares	As Percentage of Total	In Hectares	As Percentage of Total
Aguascalientes....	6,426	534	8.3	5,892	91.7
Baja California...					
del Sur........	1,454,447	636,885	43.8	....	....
del Norte......	496,475	481,217	96.9	....	....
Campeche.......	1,398,704	1,388,708	99.3	5,903	0.4
Chihuahua.......	8,464,040	4,026,473	47.6	93,937	1.1
Chiapas.........	1,200,846	611,026	50.9	304,925	25.4
Coahuila........	3,172,501	1,192,486	37.6	679,279	21.4
Colima.........	60,901	41,811	68.7	....	....
Durango........	2,166,702	1,082,604	50.0	496,848	22.9
Guanajuato......	258,591	16,331	6.3	205,950	79.6
Guerrero........	308,744	263,551	85.4	28,039	9.1
Hidalgo........	96,152	13,853	14.4	45,309	47.1
Jalisco..........	293,423	141,647	48.3	37,579	12.9
México..........	344,362	4,011	1.2	216,190	62.8
Michoacán.......	324,241	25,915	8.0	168,104	51.8
Nayarit.........	622,210	264,878	42.6	296,473	47.7
Nuevo León......	236,614	52,676	22.3	113,421	47.9
Oaxaca..........	786,696	323,129	41.1	370,554	47.1
Puebla..........	200,658	24,154	12.0	124,470	62.0
Querétaro........	160,372	4,693	2.9	116,912	72.9
San Luis Potosí...	1,713,478	824,227	48.1	723,434	42.2
Sinaloa..........	1,146,373	985,336	86.0	77,773	6.8
Sonora..........	1,968,825	1,682,667	85.5	14,131	0.7
Tabasco.........	199,651	7,876	4.0	62,305	31.2
Tamaulipas......	1,663,371	929,524	55.9	670,942	40.3
Tlaxcala.........	31,947	....	....	30,823	96.5
Veracruz.........	1,277,849	744,250	58.2	241,770	18.9
Yucatán.........	15,423	5,966	38.7	....	....
Zacatecas........	1,934,024	781,214	40.4	1,102,279	57.0
28 States [a]...	32,004,046	16,557,642	51.7	6,233,242	19.5

a Distrito Federal, Morelos, and Quintana Roo not included.

English		German		French		All Others	
In Hectares	As Percentage of Total	In Hectares	As Percentage of Total	In Hectares	As Percentage of Total	In Hectares	As Percentage of Total
. . . .	. . . .	. . . .	. . . .	. . . .	. . .	. . . .	. . .
210,800	14.5	3,584	0.2	603,178	41.5	. . . .	. . .
5,120	1.1	. . . .	. . . .	1,141	0.2	8,997	1.8
. . . .	. . . .	2,293	0.2	. . . .	. . .	1,800	0.1
3,689,464	43.6	189,816	2.2	45,022	0.5	419,328	5.0
9,010	0.8	97,774	8.1	145,202	12.1	32,909	2.7
668,233	21.1	217,781	6.9	58,257	1.8	356,465	11.2
. . . .	. . . .	9,190	15.1	9,900	16.2	. . . .	. . .
88,676	4.1	311,111	14.3	47,463	2.2	140,000	6.5
135	0.1	767	0.3	34,838	13.5	570	0.2
217	0.1	2,200	0.7	10,912	3.5	3,825	1.2
26,559	27.6	1,500	1.6	546	0.6	8,385	8.7
63,217	21.5	26,788	9.1	22,716	7.7	1,476	0.5
7,683	2.2	6,936	2.0	92,458	26.8	17,084	5.0
58,232	18.0	6,650	2.1	33,152	10.2	32,188	9.9
2,676	0.4	56,861	9.1	1,322	0.2	. . . .	. . .
919	0.4	11,049	4.7	3,180	1.3	55,369	23.4
40,678	5.2	45,626	5.8	3,162	0.4	3,547	0.4
5,626	2.8	538	0.3	42,247	21.1	3,623	1.8
. . . .	. . . .	29,766	18.6	5	. . .	8,996	5.6
26,856	1.6	18,994	1.1	119,758	6.9	209	0.1
13,650	1.2	56,445	4.9	4,911	0.4	8,258	0.7
160,650	8.2	30,889	1.5	36,131	1.8	44,357	2.3
. . . .	. . . .	1,815	0.9	127,000	63.6	655	0.3
42,688	2.6	9,519	0.6	5,703	0.4	4,995	0.2
. . . .	. . . .	853	2.7	271	0.8	. . . .	. . .
187,682	14.7	15,937	1.2	36,642	2.9	51,568	4.1
5,939	38.5	3,518	22.8	. . . .	. . .	. . . .	. . .
. . . .	. . . .	13,313	0.7	37,218	1.9	. . . .	. . .
5,314,710	16.6	1,171,513	3.7	1,522,335	4.7	1,204,604	3.8

XVI. Assessed Value of Foreign Owned Rural Lands Valued at

STATE	Total in *Pesos*	United States		Spanish	
		In Pesos	As Percentage of Total	In Pesos	As Percentage of Total
Aguascalientes........	83,501	22,533	*27.0*	60,968	*73.0*
Baja Cali- ⌠ del Sur	3,409,297	1,284,635	*37.7*	....	...
fornia ⌡ del Norte	24,670,388	24,002,603	*97.3*	....	....
Campeche...........	3,199,704	3,114,500	*97.3*	42,500	*1.3*
Chihuahua...........	13,926,131	8,140,663	*58.5*	222,000	*1.5*
Chiapas.............	12,847,369	4,319,933	*33.6*	2,614,689	*20.3*
Coahuila.............	15,120,663	3,068,609	*20.3*	3,278,839	*21.7*
Colima..............	665,460	305,460	*45.9*	....	....
Durango.............	11,436,441	2,150,039	*18.8*	3,524,876	*30.8*
Guanajuato..........	14,029,387	769,138	*5.5*	10,538,602	*75.1*
Guerrero.............	1,312,099	751,796	*57.3*	421,403	*32.1*
Hidalgo.............	5,484,172	228,727	*4.2*	3,142,516	*57.3*
Jalisco..............	4,753,390	1,311,125	*27.6*	588,176	*12.4*
México..............	11,418,181	413,260	*3.6*	9,129,105	*79.9*
Michoacán..........	22,758,654	1,370,830	*6.0*	12,926,434	*56.8*
Nayarit.............	3,325,728	1,250,540	*37.6*	1,746,238	*52.5*
Nuevo León.........	1,122,220	323,555	*28.8*	286,670	*25.5*
Oaxaca..............	11,257,256	4,241,032	*37.7*	6,022,757	*53.5*
Puebla..............	10,396,678	698,659	*6.7*	7,253,229	*69.7*
Querétaro...........	5,332,583	174,900	*3.3*	3,902,683	*73.2*
San Luis Potosí.......	10,455,788	3,185,409	*30.5*	5,003,939	*47.9*
Sinaloa.............	5,458,021	4,750,224	*87.0*	323,086	*5.9*
Sonora.............	21,019,961	17,871,496	*85.0*	637,208	*3.0*
Tabasco.............	2,210,100	356,700	*16.1*	770,400	*34.9*
Tamaulipas..........	5,081,294	2,627,838	....	2,128,644	....
Tlaxcala............	3,116,022	....	....	3,005,022	*96.5*
Veracruz............	43,728,396	24,877,211	*56.9*	9,423,547	*21.6*
Yucatán............	430,900	46,000	*10.7*	....	....
Zacatecas...........	1,799,262	769,643	*42.8*	797,619	*44.3*
28 States a	269,849,046	112,427,063	*41.7*	87,791,150	*32.5*

a Distrito Federal, Morelos, and Quintana Roo not included.

5,000 Pesos or Over, by State, and by Nationality of Owner, 1923

English		German		French		All Others	
In Pesos	As Percentage of Total	In Pesos	As Percentage of Total	In Pesos	As Percentage of Total	In Pesos	As Percentage of Total
. . . .	. . .	. . . .	. . .	1,217,236	35.7	. . . .	. . .
900,000	26.4	7,426	0.2	151,087	0.6	. . . .	. . .
41,022	0.2	. . . . . .	. . .	. . . .	. . .	475,676	1.9
. . . .	. . .	32,704	1.1	. . . .	. . .	10,000	0.3
4,471,616	32.1	323,852	2.3	77,000	0.6	691,000	5.0
941,014	7.3	3,515,083	27.4	961,226	7.5	495,424	3.9
4,501,657	29.8	2,365,500	15.6	1,031,500	6.8	874,558	5.8
. . . .	. . .	242,000	36.4	118,000	17.7	. . . .	. . .
4,523,498	39.6	860,348	7.5	97,680	0.8	280,000	2.5
6,343	0.1	45,897	0.3	2,470,921	17.6	198,486	1.4
7,500	0.6	13,400	1.0	88,000	6.7	30,000	2.3
1,520,514	27.7	153,745	2.8	30,270	0.6	408,400	7.4
843,221	17.7	823,543	17.3	1,069,500	22.5	117,825	2.5
258,521	2.3	510,050	4.5	557,260	4.9	549,985	4.8
1,618,650	7.1	3,725,150	16.4	1,467,350	6.5	1,650,240	7.2
6,500	0.2	312,050	9.4	10,400	0.3	. . . .	. . .
139,700	12.4	89,500	8.0	25,000	2.3	257,795	23.0
367,470	3.3	489,815	4.4	36,910	0.3	99,272	0.8
370,693	3.6	32,228	0.3	1,871,879	18.0	169,990	1.7
. . . .	. . .	1,065,000	19.9	10,000	0.2	180,000	3.4
871,772	8.3	486,638	4.7	892,179	8.5	15,851	0.1
58,954	1.1	228,302	4.2	49,220	0.9	48,230	0.9
1,244,880	5.9	512,070	2.5	281,377	1.3	472,930	2.3
. . . .	. . .	50,000	2.3	1,000,000	45.2	33,000	1.5
178,741	. . .	38,776	. . .	28,515	. . .	78,780	. . .
. . . .	. . .	81,000	2.6	30,000	0.9	. . . .	. . .
4,526,834	10.4	639,646	1.4	1,622,387	3.7	2,638,771	6.0
356,400	82.7	28,500	6.6	. . . .	. . .	. . . .	. . .
. . . .	. . .	70,000	3.9	162,000	9.0	. . . .	. . .
27,755,500	10.3	16,742,223	6.2	15,356,897	5.7	9,776,213	3.6

XVII. Area and Value of Foreign Owned Rural Lands Valued at 5,000 Pesos or Over

STATE	Assessed Value		Area	
	In Thousands of Pesos	As Percentage of All Privately Owned Rural Lands	In Hectares	As Percentage of All Privately Owned Rural Lands
Aguascalientes.	83,501	1.0	6,427	1.0
Baja California.	28,079,685	49.4	1,950,922	29.0
Campeche.....	3,199,704	21.1	1,398,704	38.5
Chihuahua....	13,926,131	....	8,464,040	42.7
Chiapas.......	12,847,369	29.2	1,200,846	17.4
Coahuila......	15,120,663	23.5	3,172,501	22.7
Colima........	665,460	11.0	60,901	11.7
Durango......	11,436,441	29.3	2,166,702	19.2
Guanajuato...	14,029,387	1.3	258,591	8.5
Guerrero......	1,312,099	9.2	308,744	5.6
Hidalgo.......	5,484,172	11.8	96,152	4.6
Jalisco........	4,753,390	4.6	293,423	3.7
México.......	11,418,181	20.9	344,362	16.1
Michoacán....	22,758,654	16.9	324,241	5.4
Nayarit.......	3,325,728	29.2	622,210	41.9
Nuevo León...	1,122,220	8.9	236,614	3.6
Oaxaca.......	11,257,256	40.3	786,696	8.4
Puebla........	10,396,678	21.1	200,658	5.9
Querétaro.....	5,332,583	21.3	160,372	14.0
San Luis Potosí	10,455,788	23.2	1,713,478	27.5
Sinaloa.......	5,458,021	29.3	1,146,373	21.3
Sonora........	21,019,961	42.8	1,968,825	27.1
Tabasco.......	2,210,100	11.7	199,651	11.2
Tamaulipas....	5,081,294	24.3	1,663,371	22.0
Tlaxcala......	3,116,022	12.0	31,947	7.9
Veracruz......	43,728,396	23.1	1,277,849	17.9
Yucatán......	430,900	0.3	15,423	0.4
Zacatecas.....	1,799,262	9.6	1,934,024	26.9
28 States [a]...	269,849,046	20.1	32,004,047	20.1

[a] Distrito Federal, Quintana Roo, and Morelos not included.

XVIII. FOREIGN OWNED RURAL LANDS EXPROPRIATED FOR
EJIDOS 1915-1926 INCLUSIVE, BY STATE*

STATE	Provisional Expropriation.		Definite Expropriation.	
	In Hectares	As Percentage of Total Foreign Rural Lands	In Hectares	As Percentage of Total Foreign Rural Lands
Aguascalientes......	0	0.00	0	0.00
Baja California......	724	0.04	1,755	0.08
Campeche..........	0	0.00	0	0.00
Coahuila...........	554	0.02	38,677	1.22
Colima.............	0	0.00	441	0.72
Chiapas............	10,313	0.86	8,100	0.67
Chihuahua.........	52,117	0.61	28,768	0.34
Durango...........	2,745	0.13	10,978	0.50
Guanajuato........	9,226	3.57	5,287	2.04
Guerrero..........	21,681	7.02	16,449	5.32
Hidalgo...........	4,852	5.05	32,678	33.98
Jalisco............	10,573	3.60	14,403	4.90
México............	5,809	1.69	24,259	7.04
Michoacán.........	12,291	3.79	17,747	5.47
Nayarit...........	6,519	1.05	9,614	1.54
Nuevo León........	0	0.00	4,078	1.72
Oaxaca............	3,544	0.45	2,807	0.36
Puebla............	32,399	16.15	42,017	20.93
Querétaro.........	1,227	0.76	2,792	1.74
San Luis Potosí....	79,264	4.62	69,440	4.05
Sinaloa............	790	0.06	15,986	1.39
Sonora............	136	0.01	136	0.01
Tabasco...........	11,344	5.68	542	0.27
Tamaulipas........	14,528	0.87	4,452	0.26
Tlaxcala..........	165	0.51	8,101	25.35
Veracruz..........	12,338	0.96	22,510	1.76
Yucatán...........	8,760	56.79	4,688	30.39
Zacatecas.........	0	0.00	2,665	0.14
28 States [a]........	301,899	0.98	389,370	1.24

* Compiled from information supplied by the *Comisión Nacional Agraria*.
[a] Data not available for Quintana Roo, Distrito Federal, and Morelos.

APPENDIX D

ARTICLE 27 OF
THE MEXICAN CONSTITUTION OF 1917 [1]

Art. 27. The ownership of lands and waters comprised within the limits of the national territory is vested originally in the Nation, which has had, and has, the right to transmit title thereof to private persons, thereby constituting private property.

Private property shall not be *expropriated* except for reasons of public utility and *by means of* indemnification.

The Nation shall have at all times the right to impose on private property such limitations as the public interest may demand as well as the right to regulate the development of natural resources, which are susceptible of appropriation, in order to conserve them and equitably to distribute the public wealth. For this purpose necessary measures shall be taken to divide large landed estates; to develop small landed holdings; to establish new centers of rural population with such lands and waters as may be indispensable to them; to encourage agriculture and to prevent the destruction of natural resources, and

[1] *The Annals* of the American Academy of Political and Social Science, May, 1917, pp. 15-25.

to protect property from damage detrimental to society. Settlements, hamlets situated on private property and communes which lack lands or water or do not possess them in sufficient quantities for their needs shall have the right to be provided with them from the adjoining properties, always having due regard for small landed holdings. Wherefore, all grants of lands made up to the present time under the decree of January 6, 1915, are confirmed. Private property acquired for the said purposes shall be considered as taken for public utility.

In the Nation is vested direct ownership of all minerals or substances which in veins, layers, masses, or beds constitute deposits whose nature is different from the components of the land, such as minerals from which metals and metaloids used for industrial purposes are extracted; beds of precious stones, rock salt and salt lakes formed directly by marine waters, products derived from the decomposition of rocks, when their exploitation requires underground work; phosphates which may be used for fertilizers; solid mineral fuels; petroleum and all hydro-carbons— solid, liquid or gaseous.

In the Nation is likewise vested the ownership of the waters of territorial seas to the extent and in the terms fixed by the law of nations; those of lakes and inlets of bays; those of interior lakes of natural formation which are directly connected with flowing waters; those of principal rivers or tributaries from the points at which there is a permanent current of water in their beds to their mouths, whether they flow to the sea or cross two or more States; those of intermittent streams which traverse two or more States in their main body; the waters of rivers, streams, or ravines, when they bound the national territory or that of the States; waters extracted from mines; and the beds and banks of the lakes and streams hereinbefore mentioned, to the extent fixed by law. Any other stream of water not comprised within the foregoing enumeration shall be considered as an integral part of the private property through which it flows; but the development of the waters when they pass from one landed property to another shall be considered of public utility and shall be subject to the provisions prescribed by the States.

In the cases to which the two foregoing paragraphs refer, the ownership of the Nation is inalienable and may not be lost by prescription; concessions shall be granted by the Federal Government to private parties or civil or commercial corporations organized under the laws of Mexico, only on condition that said resources be regularly developed, and on the further condition that the legal provisions be observed.

Legal capacity to acquire ownership of lands and waters of the nation shall be governed by the following provisions:

I. Only Mexicans by birth or naturalization and Mexican companies have the right to acquire ownership in lands, waters and their appurtenances, or to obtain concessions to develop mines, waters or mineral fuels in the Republic of Mexico. The Nation may grant the same right to foreigners, provided they agree before the Department of Foreign Affairs to be considered Mexicans in respect to such property, and accordingly not to invoke the protection of their Governments in respect to the same, under penalty, in case of breach, of forfeiture to the Nation of property so acquired. Within a zone of 100 kilometers from the frontiers, and of 50 kilometers from the sea coast, no foreigner shall under any conditions acquire direct ownership of lands and waters.

II. The religious institutions known as churches, irrespective of creed, shall in no case have legal capacity to acquire, hold or administer real property or loans made on such real property; all such real property or loans as may be at present held by the said religious institutions, either on their own behalf or through third parties, shall vest in the Nation, and any one shall have the right to denounce property so held. Presumptive proof shall be sufficient to declare the denunciation well-founded. Places of public worship are the property of the Nation, as represented by the Federal Government, which shall determine which of them may continue to be devoted to their present purposes. Episcopal residences, rectories, seminaries, orphan asylums or collegiate establishment of religious institutions, convents or any other buildings built or designed for the administration, propaganda, or teaching of the tenets of any religious creed shall forthwith vest, as of full right, directly in the Nation, to be used exclusively for the public services of the Federation or of the States, within their respective jurisdictions. All places of public worship which shall later be erected shall be the property of the Nation.

III. Public and private charitable institutions for the sick and needy, for scientific research, or for the diffusion of knowledge, mutual aid societies or organizations formed for any other lawful purpose shall in no case acquire, hold or administer loans made on real property, unless the mortgage terms do not exceed ten years. In no case shall institutions of this character be under the patronage, direction, administration, charge or supervision of religious corporations or institutions, nor of ministers of any religious creed or of their dependents, even though either the former or the latter shall not be in active service.

IV. Commercial stock companies shall not require, hold, or administer rural properties. Companies of this nature which may be organized to develop any manufacturing, mining, petroleum or other industry, excepting only agricultural industries, may acquire, hold or administer lands only in an area absolutely necessary for their establishments or adequate to serve the purposes indicated, which the Executive of the Union or of the respective State in each case shall determine.

V. Banks duly organized under the laws governing institutions of credit may make mortgage loans on rural and urban property in accordance with the provisions of the said laws, but they may not own nor administer more real property than that absolutely necessary for their direct purposes; and they may furthermore hold temporarily for the brief term fixed by law such real property as may be judicially adjudicated to them in execution proceedings.

VI. Properties held in common by co-owners, hamlets situated on private property, pueblos, tribal congregations and other settlements which, as a matter of fact or law, conserve their communal character, shall have legal capacity to enjoy in common the waters, woods and lands belonging to them, or which may have been or shall be restored to them according to the law of January 6, 1915, until such time as the manner of making the division of the lands shall be determined by law.

VII. Excepting the corporations to which Clauses III, IV, V and VI hereof refer, no other civil corporation may hold or administer on its own behalf real estate or mortgage loans derived therefrom, with the single exception of buildings designed directly and immediately for the purposes of the institution. The States, the Federal District and the Territories, as well as the municipalities throughout the Republic, shall enjoy full legal capacity to acquire and hold all real estate necessary for public services.

The Federal and State laws shall determine within their respective jurisdictions those cases in which the occupation of private property shall be considered of public utility; and in accordance with the said laws the administrative authorities shall make the corresponding declaration. The amount fixed as compensation for the expropriated property shall be based on the sum at which the said property shall be valued for fiscal purposes in the catastral or revenue offices, whether this value be that manifested by the owner or merely impliedly accepted by reason of the payment of his taxes on such a basis, to which there shall be added ten per cent. The increased value which the property in question may have acquired through improvements made subsequent to the date of the fixing of the fiscal value shall be the only matter subject to expert opinion and to judicial determination. The same procedure shall be observed in respect to objects whose value is not recorded in the revenue offices.

All proceedings, findings, decisions and all operations of demarcation, concession, composition, judgment, compromise, alienation, or auction which may have deprived properties held in common by co-owners, hamlets situated on private property, settlements, congregations, tribes and other settlement organizations still existing since the law of June 25, 1856, of the whole or a part of their lands, woods and waters, are declared null and void; all findings, resolutions and operations which may subsequently take place and produce the same effects shall likewise be null and void. Consequently all lands, forests and waters of which the above-mentioned settlements may have been deprived shall be restored to them according to the decree of January 6, 1915, which shall remain in force as a constitutional law. In case the adjudication of lands, by way of restitution, be not legal in the terms of the said decree, which adjudication has been requested by any of the above entities, those lands shall nevertheless be given to them by way of grant, and they shall in no event fail to receive such as they may need. Only such lands, title to which may have been acquired in the divisions made by virtue of the said law of June 25, 1856, or such as may be held in undisputed ownership for more than ten years are excepted from the provision of nullity, provided their area does not exceed fifty hectares. Any excess over this area shall be returned to the commune and the owner shall be indemnified. All laws of restitution enacted by virtue of this provision shall be immediately carried into effect by the administrative authorities. Only members of the commune shall have the right to the lands destined to be divided, and the rights to these lands shall be inalienable so long as they remain undivided; the same provision shall govern the right of ownership after the division has been made. The exercise of the rights pertaining to the Nation by virtue of this article shall follow judicial process; but as a part of this process and by order of the proper tribunals, which order shall be issued within the maximum period of one month, the administrative authorities shall proceed without delay to the occupation, administration, auction, or sale of the lands and waters in question, together with all their appurtenances, and in no case may the acts of the said authorities be set aside until final sentence is handed down.

During the next constitutional term, the Congress and the State Legislatures shall enact laws, within their respective jurisdictions, for the purpose of carrying out the division of large landed estates, subject to the following conditions:

(a) In each State and Territory there shall be fixed the maximum area of land which any one individual or legally organized corporation may own.

(b) The excess of the area thus fixed shall be subdivided by the owner within the period set by the laws of the respective locality; and these subdivisions shall be offered for sale on such conditions as the respective governments shall approve, in accordance with the said laws.

(c) If the owner shall refuse to make the subdivision, this shall be carried out by the local government, by means of expropriation proceedings.

(d) The value of the subdivisions shall be paid in annual amounts sufficient to amortize the principal and interest within a period of not less than twenty years, during which the person acquiring them may not alienate them. The rate of interest shall not exceed five per cent per annum.

(e) The owner shall be bound to receive bonds of a special issue to guarantee the payment of the property expropriated. With this end in view, the Congress shall issue a law authorizing the States to issue bonds to meet their agrarian obligations.

(f) The local laws shall govern the extent of the family patrimony, and determine what property shall constitute the same on the basis of its inalienability; it shall not be subject to attachment nor to any charge whatever.

All contracts and concessions made by former governments from and after the year 1876 which shall have resulted in the monopoly of lands, waters and natural resources of the Nation by a single individual or corporation, are declared subject to revision, and the Executive is authorized to declare those null and void which seriously prejudice the public interest.

APPENDIX E

ARTICLE 123 OF
THE MEXICAN CONSTITUTION OF 1917 [1]

TITLE VI.—OF LABOR AND SOCIAL WELFARE

Art. 123. The Congress and the State Legislatures shall make laws relative to labor with due regard for the needs of each region of the Republic, and in conformity with the following principles, and these principles and laws shall govern the labor of skilled and unskilled workmen, employees, domestic servants and artisans, and in general every contract of labor.

I. Eight hours shall be the maximum limit of a day's work.

II. The maximum limit of night work shall be seven hours. Unhealthy and dangerous occupations are forbidden to all women and to children under sixteen years of age. Night work in factories is likewise forbidden to women and to children under sixteen years of age; nor shall they be employed in commercial establishments after ten o'clock at night.

III. The maximum limit of a day's work for children over twelve and under sixteen years of age shall be six hours. The work of children under twelve

[1] *The Annals* of the American Academy of Political and Social Science, May, 1917, pp. 94-102.

528

years of age shall not be made the subject of a contract.

IV. Every workman shall enjoy at least one day's rest for every six days' work.

V. Women shall not perform any physical work requiring considerable physical effort during the three months immediately preceding parturition; during the month following parturition they shall necessarily enjoy a period of rest and shall receive their salaries or wages in full and retain their employment and the rights they may have acquired under their contracts. During the period of lactation they shall enjoy two extraordinary daily periods of rest of one-half hour each, in order to nurse their children.

VI. The minimum wage to be received by a workman shall be that considered sufficient, according to the conditions prevailing in the respective region of the country, to satisfy the normal needs of the life of the workman, his education and his lawful pleasures, considering him as the head of a family. In all agricultural, commercial, manufacturing or mining enterprises the workmen shall have the right to participate in the profits in the manner fixed in Clause IX of this article.

VII. The same compensation shall be paid for the same work, without regard to sex or nationality.

VIII. The minimum wage shall be exempt from attachment, setoff or discount.

IX. The determination of the minimum wage and

of the rate of profit-sharing described in Clause VI shall be made by special commissions to be appointed in each municipality and to be subordinated to the Central Board of Conciliation to be established in each State.

X. All wages shall be paid in legal currency and shall not be paid in merchandise, orders, counters or any other representative token with which it is sought to substitute money.

XI. When owing to special circumstances it becomes necessary to increase the working hours, there shall be paid as wages for the overtime one hundred per cent more than those fixed for regular time. In no case shall the overtime exceed three hours nor continue for more than three consecutive days; and no women of whatever age nor boys under sixteen years of age may engage in overtime work.

XII. In every agricultural, industrial, mining or other class of work employers are bound to furnish their workmen comfortable and sanitary dwelling-places, for which they may charge rents not exceeding one-half of one per cent per month of the assessed value of the properties. They shall likewise establish schools, dispensaries and other services necessary to the community. If the factories are located within inhabited places and more than one hundred persons are employed therein, the first of the above-mentioned conditions shall be complied with.

XIII. Furthermore, there shall be set aside in these labor centers, whenever their population exceeds two hundred inhabitants, a space of land not less than five thousand square meters for the establishment of public markets, and the construction of buildings designed for municipal services and places of amusement. No saloons nor gambling houses shall be permitted in such labor centers.

XIV. Employers shall be liable for labor accidents and occupational diseases arising from work; therefore, employers shall pay the proper indemnity, according to whether death or merely temporary or permanent disability has ensued, in accordance with the provisions of law. This liability shall remain in force even though the employer contract for the work through an agent.

XV. Employers shall be bound to observe in the installation of their establishments all the provisions of law regarding hygiene and sanitation and to adopt adequate measures to prevent accidents due to the use of machinery, tools and working materials, as well as to organize work in such a manner as to assure the greatest guarantees possible for the health and lives of workmen compatible with the nature of the work, under penalties which the law shall determine.

XVI. Workmen and employers shall have the right to unite for the defense of their respective interests, by forming syndicates, unions, etc.

·XVII. The law shall recognize the right of workmen and employers to strike and to lockout.

XVIII. Strikes shall be lawful when by the employment of peaceful means they shall aim to bring about a balance between the various factors of production, and to harmonize the rights of capital and labor. In the case of public services, the workmen shall be obliged to give notice ten days in advance to the Board of Conciliation and Arbitration of the date set for the suspension of work. Strikes shall only be considered unlawful when the majority of the strikers shall resort to acts of violence against persons or property, or in case of war when the strikers belong to establishments and services dependent on the government. Employees of military manufacturing establishments of the Federal Government shall not be included in the provisions of this clause, inasmuch as they are a dependency of the national army.

XIX. Lockouts shall only be lawful when the excess of production shall render it necessary to shut down in order to maintain prices reasonably above the cost of production, subject to the approval of the Board of Conciliation and Arbitration.

XX. Differences or disputes between capital and labor shall be submitted for settlement to a board of conciliation and arbitration to consist of an equal number of representatives of the workmen and of the employers and of one representative of the Government.

XXI. If the employer shall refuse to submit his differences to arbitration or to accept the award rendered by the Board, the labor contract shall be considered as terminated, and the employer shall be bound to indemnify the workman by the payment to him of three months' wages, in addition to the liability which he may have incurred by reason of the dispute. If the workman reject the award, the contract will be held to have terminated.

XXII. An employer who discharges a workman without proper cause or for having joined a union or syndicate or for having taken part in a lawful strike shall be bound, at the option of the workman, either to perform the contract or to indemnify him by the payment of three months' wages. He shall incur the same liability if the workman shall leave his service on account of the lack of good faith on the part of the employer or of maltreatment either as to his own person or that of his wife, parents, children or brothers or sisters. The employer cannot evade this liability when the maltreatment is inflicted by subordinates or agents acting with his consent or knowledge.

XXIII. Claims of workmen for salaries or wages accrued during the past year and other indemnity claims shall be preferred over any other claims, in cases of bankruptcy or composition.

XXIV. Debts contracted by workmen in favor of their employers or their employers' associates, subordinates or agents, may only be charged against the workmen themselves and in no case and for no reason collected from the members of his family. Nor shall such debts be paid by the taking of more than the entire wages of the workman for any one month.

XXV. No fee shall be charged for finding work for workmen by municipal offices, employment bureaus or other public or private agencies.

XXVI. Every contract of labor between a Mexican citizen and a foreign principal shall be legalized before the competent municipal authority and viséed by the consul of the nation to which the workman is undertaking to go, on the understanding that, in addition to the usual clauses, special and clear provisions shall be inserted for the payment by the foreign principal making the contract of the cost to the laborer of repatriation.

XXVII. The following stipulation shall be null and void and shall not bind the contracting parties, even though embodied in the contract:

(a) Stipulations providing for inhuman day's work on account of its notorious excessiveness, in view of the nature of the work.

(b) Stipulations providing for a wage rate which in the judgment of the Board of Conciliation and Arbitration is not remunerative.

(c) Stipulations providing for a term of more than one week before the payment of wages.

(d) Stipulations providing for the assigning of places of amusement, eating places, cafés, taverns, saloons or shops for the payment of wages, when employees of such establishments are not involved.

(e) Stipulations involving a direct or indirect obligation to purchase articles of consumption in specified shops or places.

(f) Stipulations permitting the retention of wages by way of fines.

(g) Stipulations constituting a waiver on the part of the workman of the indemnities to which he may become entitled by reason of labor accidents or occupational diseases, damages for breach of contract, or for discharge from work.

(h) All other stipulations implying the waiver of any right vested in the workman by labor laws.

XXVIII. The law shall decide what property constitutes the family patrimony. These goods shall be inalienable and shall not be mortgaged, nor attached, and may be bequeathed with simplified formalities in the succession proceedings.

XXIX. Institutions of popular insurance established for old age, sickness, life, unemployment, accident and others of a similar character, are considered of social utility; the Federal and State Governments shall therefore encourage the organization of institutions of this character in order to instill and inculcate popular habits of thrift.

XXX. Coöperative associations for the construction of cheap and sanitary dwelling houses for workmen shall likewise be considered of social utility whenever these properties are designed to be acquired in ownership by the workmen within specified periods.

APPENDIX F

BIBLIOGRAPHIC NOTE

In view of the fact that a considerable portion of this book is based upon material not available in published form, it has seemed best not to include an elaborate bibliography. Good bibliographies on Mexico may be found in George McCutchen McBride, *The Land Systems of Mexico,* American Geographical Society Research Series No. 12; Vicente Lombardo Toledano, *La Libertad Sindical en Mexico;* Herbert Ingram Priestly, *The Mexican Nation;* Ernest Gruening, *Mexico and Its Heritage.* For a bibliography of the revolution up to 1916, see *Bibliografía de la Revolución Mexicana de 1910-1916,* Ignacio B. del Castilo, and *Bibliografía de la Imprenta de la Cámara de Diputados,* Ignacio B. del Castillo, in *Concurso de Bibliografía y Biblioteconomia, Convocado por la Biblioteca Nacional,* Mexico, 1918. For the population and landholding statistics in this book, Appendices B and C give in detail the source and the character of the data used.

Part of the material used in this book is derived from official but unpublished reports on file in the

Mexican Departments of Education and Agriculture. The reports in the Department of Education which have been used consist mainly of questionnaires filled in by rural teachers, *maestros misionarios,* and school inspectors between 1923 and 1926. These reports are in the *Archivo General* of the Department of Education and classified under 12-1-1 to 12-12-12. The material from the Department of Agriculture was taken from the reports of the *agronomos regionales,* who since 1923 have sent in monthly reports describing the agricultural conditions in their districts. These reports consist of answers to an elaborate questionnaire which the agronomist in each region has to fill in for the *municipios* in his particular locality. With a few recent exceptions, these questionnaires have remained unpublished. They contain a great deal of material on contemporary Mexican agricultural and agrarian problems.

In addition to the reports of the regional agronomists, there were made available to the author the replies to letters sent out by the *Oficina Investigadora Agricola* covering problems of landholdings in villages, irrigation area, rural organization, and so forth. All of this material is on file in the office of the Mexican Department of Agriculture, located in San Jacinto, D. F.

In addition to the above, use was made of a fairly complete collection of the federal and state agrarian laws, state labor laws, tax laws, reports of governors for 1925, 1926, and 1927, and between 500 and 600 pamphlets dealing with contemporary Mexico. This is in addition to the more generally-known books on Mexico. A large portion of the material described above is on file in the library of the Institute of Economics.

INDEX

Publications of the Brookings Institution

THE INSTITUTE OF ECONOMICS

(Titles starred are publications of the McGraw-Hill Company; all others are published by The Macmillan Company.)

*GERMANY'S CAPACITY TO PAY.
    By Harold G. Moulton and Constantine E. McGuire.
        1923. $2.50. 384 pp.

*RUSSIAN DEBTS AND RUSSIAN RECONSTRUCTION.
    By Leo Pasvolsky and Harold G. Moulton. 1924.
        $2.50. 247 pp.

*THE REPARATAION PLAN.
    By Harold G. Moulton. 1924. $2.50. 325 pp.

THE FRENCH DEBT PROBLEM.
    By Harold G. Moulton and Cleona Lewis. 1925.
        $2.00. 459 pp.

THE RUHR-LORRAINE INDUSTRIAL PROBLEM.
    By Guy Greer. 1925. $2.50. 328 pp.

WORLD WAR DEBT SETTLEMENTS.
    By Harold G. Moulton and Leo Pasvolsky. 1926.
        $2.00. 448 pp.

ITALY'S INTERNATIONAL ECONOMIC POSITION.
    By Constantine E. McGuire. 1926. $3.00. 588 pp.

THE INTERNATIONAL ACCOUNTS.
    By Cleona Lewis. 1927. $2.00. 170 pp.

AMERICAN LOANS TO GERMANY.
    By Robert R. Kuczynski. 1927. $3.00. 378 pp.

ECONOMIC NATIONALISM OF THE DANUBIAN STATES.
    By Leo Pasvolsky. 1928. $3.00. 609 pp.

WORKERS' HEALTH AND SAFETY: A STATISTICAL PROGRAM.
By Robert Morse Woodbury. 1927. $2.50. 207 pp.

THE BRITISH COAL DILEMMA.
By Isador Lubin and Helen Everett. 1927. $2.50.
370 pp.

A WAY OF ORDER FOR BITUMINOUS COAL.
By Walton H. Hamilton and Helen R. Wright. 1928.
$2.50. 365 pp.

LABOR AND INTERNATIONALISM.
By Lewis L. Lorwin. 1929. $3.00. 682 pp.

INTEREST RATES AND STOCK SPECULATION.
By Richard N. Owens and Charles O. Hardy. 1925.
$2.00. 197 pp.

TAX-EXEMPT SECURITIES AND THE SURTAX.
By Charles O. Hardy. 1926. $2.00. 216 pp.

THE BALANCE OF BIRTHS AND DEATHS.
By Robert R. Kuczynski. 1928. $2.00. 140 pp.

INSTITUTE FOR GOVERNMENT RESEARCH

(Published by the Johns Hopkins Press.)

Studies in Administration

THE SYSTEM OF FINANCIAL ADMINISTRATION OF GREAT
BRITAIN.
By W. F. Willoughby, W. W. Willoughby, and S. M.
Lindsay. 378 pp. $3.00. 1917.

THE BUDGET: A TRANSLATION.
By Rene Stourm. 648 pp. $4.00. 1917.

THE CANADIAN BUDGETARY SYSTEM.
By H. C. Villard and W. W. Willoughby. 390 pp.
$3.00. 1918.

THE PROBLEM OF A NATIONAL BUDGET.
By W. F. Willoughby. 234 pp. $3.00. 1918.

THE NATIONAL BUDGET SYSTEM, WITH SUGGESTIONS FOR ITS IMPROVEMENT.
By W. F. Willoughby. 359 pp. $3.00. 1927.

THE MOVEMENT FOR BUDGETARY REFORM IN THE STATES.
By W. F. Willoughby. 266 pp. $3.00. 1918.

THE LEGAL STATUS AND FUNCTIONS OF THE GENERAL ACCOUNTING OFFICE.
By W. F. Willoughby. 204 pp. $3.00. 1927.

MANUAL OF ACCOUNTING AND REPORTING FOR THE OPERATING SERVICES OF THE NATIONAL GOVERNMENT.
By Henry P. Seidemann. 421 pp. $5.00. 1926.

MANUAL OF ACCOUNTING, REPORTING, AND BUSINESS PROCEDURE FOR THE TERRITORIAL GOVERNMENT OF HAWAII.
By Henry P. Seidemann. 598 pp. $5.00. 1928.

THE DEVELOPMENT OF NATIONAL ADMINISTRATIVE ORGANIZATION IN THE UNITED STATES.
By Lloyd M. Short. 531 pp. $5.00. 1923.

THE REORGANIZATION OF THE ADMINISTRATIVE BRANCH OF THE NATIONAL GOVERNMENT.
By W. F. Willoughby. 314 pp. $3.00. 1922.

THE FEDERAL SERVICE: A STUDY OF THE SYSTEM OF PERSONNEL ADMINISTRATION OF THE UNITED STATES GOVERNMENT.
By Lewis Mayers. 624 pp. $5.00. 1922.

THE STATISTICAL WORK OF THE NATIONAL GOVERNMENT.
By Laurence F. Schmeckebier. 590 pp. $5.00. 1925.

THE NATIONAL GOVERNMENT AND PUBLIC HEALTH.
By James A. Tobey. 441 pp. $3.00. 1926.

THE DEPARTMENT OF JUSTICE OF THE UNITED STATES.
By Albert Langeluttig. 334 pp. $3.00. 1927.

THE PROBLEM OF INDIAN ADMINISTRATION.
By Lewis Meriam and Associates. 894 pp. $5.00. 1928.

THE DEVELOPMENT OF GOVERNMENTAL FOREST CONTROL IN THE UNITED STATES.
By Jenks Cameron. 480 pp. $3.00. 1928.

ORGANIZED EFFORTS FOR THE IMPROVEMENT OF METHODS OF ADMINISTRATION IN THE UNITED STATES.
By Gustavus A. Weber. 408 pp. $3.00. 1919.

TEACHERS' PENSION SYSTEMS IN THE UNITED STATES.
By Paul Studensky. 474 pp. $3.00. 1921.

THE DISTRICT OF COLUMBIA; ITS GOVERNMENT AND ADMINISTRATION.
By Laurence F. Schmeckebier. 963 pp. $5.00. 1928.

THE GOVERNMENT AND ADMINISTRATION OF GERMANY.
By Frederick F. Blachly and Miriam F. Oatman. 784 pp. $5.00. 1928.

GROUP REPRESENTATION BEFORE CONGRESS.
By E. Pendleton Herring. (In Press.)

Principles of Administration

PRINCIPLES OF PUBLIC ADMINISTRATION.
By W. F. Willoughby. 742 pp. $5.00. 1927.

PRINCIPLES OF GOVERNMENT ACCOUNTING AND REPORTING.
By Francis Oakey. 582 pp. $5.00. 1921.

PRINCIPLES OF GOVERNMENT PURCHASING.
By Arthur G. Thomas. 290 pp. $3.00. 1919.

PRINCIPLES OF PUBLIC PERSONNEL ADMINISTRATION.
By Arthur W. Procter. 256 pp. $3.00. 1921.

PRINCIPLES GOVERNING THE RETIREMENT OF PUBLIC EMPLOYEES.
By Lewis Meriam. 508 pp. $3.00. 1918.

1. Geological Survey. 174 pp. Out of print. 1918.
2. Reclamation Service. 190 pp. Out of print. 1919.
3. Bureau of Mines. 174 pp. $1.00. 1922.
4. Alaskan Engineering Commission. 134 pp. $1.00. 1922.
5. Tariff Commission. 84 pp. $1.00. 1922.
6. Federal Board for Vocational Education. 86 pp. $1.00. 1922.
7. Federal Trade Commission. 92 pp. $1.00. 1922.
8. Steam-boat Inspection Service. 142 pp. $1.00. 1922.
9. Weather Bureau. 100 pp. $1.00. 1922.
10. Public Health Service. 312 pp. $2.00. 1923.
11. National Park Service. 184 pp. $1.00. 1922.
12. Employees' Compensation Commission. 98 pp. $1.00. 1922.
13. General Land Office. 236 pp. $1.50. 1923.
14. Bureau of Education. 172 pp. $1.00. 1923.
15. Bureau of Navigation. 136 pp. $1.00. 1923.
16. Coast and Geodetic Survey. 120 pp. $1.00. 1923.
17. Federal Power Commission. 138 pp. $1.00. 1923.
18. Interstate Commerce Commission. 182 pp. $1.00. 1923.
19. Railroad Labor Board. 96 pp. $1.00. 1923.
20. Division of Conciliation. 48 pp. $1.00. 1923.
21. Children's Bureau. 95 pp. $1.00. 1925.
22. Women's Bureau. 44 pp. $1.00. 1923.
23. Office of the Supervising Architect. 150 pp. $1.00. 1923.
24. Bureau of Pensions. 150 pp. $1.00. 1923.
25. Bureau of Internal Revenue. 283 pp. $1.50. 1923.
26. Bureau of Public Roads. 134 pp. $1.00. 1923.
27. Office of the Chief of Engineers. 178 pp. $1.00. 1923.
28. United States Employment Service. 142 pp. $1.00. 1923.